I'm a Man *Sex, Gods and Rock 'n'*

by the same author

poetry
SUMMER SNOW
ANGEL
FUSEWIRE
REMBRANDT WOULD HAVE LOVED YOU

non-fiction
IN AND OUT OF THE MIND
WHOM GODS DESTROY

I'm a Man *Sex, Gods and Rock 'n' Roll*

RUTH PADEL

ff
faber and faber

First published in Great Britain in 2000
by Faber and Faber Limited
3 Queen Square London WC1N 3AU

Phototypeset by Intype London Ltd
Printed in England by Clays Ltd, St Ives Plc

All rights reserved

© Ruth Padel, 2000

Ruth Padel is hereby identified as author
of this book in accordance with Section 77
of the Copyright, Designs and Patents Act 1988

A CIP record for this book is available
from the British Library

ISBN 0-571-17599-6

for John

Contents

Acknowledgements xi

INTRODUCTION Rock Music and *What?*
Fucking Grape Leaves, Wrapped Round Rice 1; What's Natural? 3; '4 REAL': Angst, Masculinity and 'Beat' 9; How Did We Land up Here? 12; My Generation? 16

PART I Origins: Myth, Sex and Electricity

1 Orpheus and the Myths of You and Me
   Music, Myth, Hero 23; Music and Violence 25; Sung Myth 26; Survival 29; The Power of Love: Eros, Orpheus, Narcissus 30

2 Inventing the Teenager: Repression, Freedom, Electricity
   Black, White, Electric 33; Electric Guitar 40; Repression and Getting Free 42; From Zero to Hero: Sound of the Male Teenage Body 45; Rock God: 'A Hurricane Called Elvis Presley' 48

3 Power, War and Creativity: The Male Gods Round Desire
   The Oldest Youngest God 52; Father: Castrated King 52; Husband: Crippled Creator, Armour-maker, Fire 54; Sex Pistol, Heavy Metal: the War-God Lover 58; Son: Naked Omnipotent Baby 61; Rock God Package: The Maleness All Round Sex 64

4 The Holy Axe
   The Mississippi Delta, Shining Like a National Guitar 66; Erection, Impotence and Rage 70; A Man Mattering to Other People 73; Guitar Hero to Rock Divinity 78

CONTENTS

5 Voices in the Sea of Desire
In the Hero's Way: Monsters, Father-figures, the Underworld, and Women 83; Birthplace of Venus: Men Master It, Women Are Carried Away on It 87; Abandoned Women, Empowering Male Music 90; The Faraway Voice 93; The Voice Men Leave Behind Them? 98

6 Marine Magic: Saving, Veiling, Faking
White Samite Syndrome: Women's Magical Element 99; Made Up? Women's Doubleness 104; Blindfold and Underwear: The Doubleness of Desire 106; Faking and Illusion: the Femaleness of Rock Display 110

7 The Hero's Journey: Song of Myself
Epic: Alone and With Your Mates 112; Solo Riff plus Companionable Chords 116; Teenage Bedroom, Open Road 118; Sound of Male Freedom: Could You Ever Take Cock out of Rock? 122; American Romanticism and the Freedom of Narcissus 124; Why Blues? 129

PART 2 Impersonation:
The Black Empowering of Rock and of Its Violence

8 The Black Hero: Call of the Wild
Sex and Envy: Orientalism, Exoticism, Otherism 133; Primitivism: Africa in New York 139; The Lure of Black Rhythm: Community and Dance 143; Drum and Soul 149

9 'I'm Damn Guilty': The Song of Someone Else
Theft 153; Black Fire, White Gold: Soul, Funk, Reggae, Hip-Hop, Rap 160; The Mix: Graceland and Guilt 170

10 The Dark Self:
Sex, Knowledge and a Century of Blacking Up
Cock Rock and the Black Sex Stereotype 174; Laughing Inside the Mask: Making Black 'Black', Making Black White 179; Why Dark? 184; 'Primitive' Dionysus 185; Learning from the Dark: Inner, Ancient, Dangerous, Knowing, Mad 187; All This Darkness Once Was Mine 190

CONTENTS

11 'Black': The Voice of Male Need
Suffering is Power 192; Boy or Man? Oppression, Sex and Politics 198; Teenage Protest and the Slave-to-Freedom Story 203; Fighting Back 205

12 When the Guitar Became a Gun: Empowering Violence
Black is Bad, Bad is Cool: Leadbelly to Gangsta Rap 207; Impersonating Violence 212; The Gun Guitar: Weight, Goths, and Heavy Metal 215; Precipitating Violence? From Altamont to Colorado 219; Hendrix and Vietnam 223

13 Heroes Are Violent, Dark, Against –
Especially in the Theatre
Where Did Rock Violence Come From? 227; Why Does Sex Choose Violence for Her Lover? 228; Why is the God of Theatre Violent? Why Does Orpheus Provoke Violence? 229; Uses of 'Blackness' 232; Epic Heroes: Power-Packed Bodies 233; Tragic Heroes: Self-Destruction Centre Stage 234; Falling: Alone in the Dark 238; Sacrifice 241

14 America: The White Romance with Violence
Impersonating America 245; Gun Law: Outviolencing Nature 246; Getting in Touch with Evil: 'Charlie' Manson and Black Flag 251; The Black Excuse: An Echo, Mirror, Shadow of Yourself 257

PART 3 Relationship and Artifice:
Misogyny, Cross-dressing and the Fans

15 'Counter' and Contradiction
Counter-Culture: Dylan and the Problems of Protest 261; Being Against What You Depend On 267; Over that Counter: Selling or Sell-Out? 271

CONTENTS

16 The Comforts of Misogyny
Misogyny? Really? 274; Baby – and Resenting Male Need 275; Trapped in an Alien World: That Magical Female Element 280; Penetrating the Alien World: Secrets of Venus 283; Heavy Metal: Parody – or Theatre of Misogyny? 284; Being Against What You Desire: Not Just Teenage, Male 289; The Harmony of Misogyny 290

17 Dylan: Creativity, Misogyny and Echo
Staging Maleness, for Echo 292; 'Man' – and Sixties Illiberalism 296; It's Not Me, Babe: Dylan's First Girlfriend 300; When Creativity Came 301; Rap Misogyny, White Theatre 304

18 Misogyny on the Hoof
Groupies: Is Misogyny Sexy? 306; Exclusion: Women DJs, Journalists, Managers 312; 'Breasts Are a Big Problem': Guitars Again 316; Women's Bands: Punk – and Lynn Breedlove's Black Cock 318

19 Cross-dressing, Castrati, Camp
Impersonation, Again 324; Quest – and Made-up Women 328; I Am a Cliché: Impersonating Women's Voice 330; The Truest Poetry is the Most Feigning 334; Electricity and the Truth of Artifice 335

20 A Love Affair With Love
We Were Pointing at Each Other: Fan, Fantasy and Star 339; Ever Get the Feeling You've Been Cheated? 343; Sex and Soul: Looking and Being Looked At 347

21 A Dream of Being Male   354

Notes   359

Bibliography   376

Index   382

Acknowledgements

I owe a lot of people a lot of thanks for help. I had a great time interviewing the professionals: many warm thanks to Tom Adès, opera composer; Gaye Advert, guitarist, and TV Smith, singer-songwriter, who formed the punk band The Adverts; Dame Josephine Barstow, opera singer; Betty Compden, singer and librettist for *On the Town*; Marianne Faithfull, singer and songwriter; Shirley Manson, singer and writer with Garbage; Louis Philippe, singer-songwriter; Patsy Rodenburg, Voice Coach at the National Theatre and Teacher of Voice at the Guildhall; Mat Snow, former editor of *Mojo*; Paul Trynka, current editor of *Mojo*; Graham Vick, opera director; Yoko Ono, singer and songwriter.

Many other people inspired and guided things. Warm thanks to: Nicholas Pearson who commissioned *a* book (though not this one), told me to go where it led and kept badgering me to interview people; my editor Julian Loose for much patience and sending of useful books, for accepting a radical change of subject with equanimity and an inscrutable smile, and for his watchful eye on structure; Derek Johns, who kindly read drafts way beyond calls of duty and friendship; Luke Vinten, Charles Boyle; and Lee Brackstone, who read a whole draft in detail and gave me the benefit of his rock expertise. Sarah Hulbert, tactful, eagle-eyed efficient and expert, is the only person I've ever met with whom copy-editing is fun as well as illuminating. Thanks also to institutions: the Society of Authors for a bursary; the Tyrone Guthrie Centre at Annamaghkerrig, where large chunks got written; Glyndebourne Opera for making me write and lecture about operas I didn't know; Exeter College and Oxford

ACKNOWLEDGEMENTS

Anthropology Department for putting up with talks on rock music rather than Greek myth; the English Department, Liverpool University, for inviting me to give the Kenneth Allott Memorial Lecture where I could explore issues in poetry and rock music; the *London Review of Books*, the *Independent Magazine* and *Glyndebourne Festival Programme*, where some of this material first appeared. Many thanks and much love to Alexander Nehamas, Dimitri Gondikas and the Modern Greek Department in Princeton, for letting me teach opera in a discipline that doesn't have any. And I can't thank enough the rock experts Robert Sandall, Mat Snow and Paul Trynka. After I interviewed them, Mat and Paul went on answering questions generously and interestingly. Even on Press Day at *Mojo*, Mat would always ring back: information and balanced judgement would pour down the line in seamless paragraphs without a pause. Paul answered intricate questions of guitar scholarship by fax and phone in generous detail. Many thanks also to Paula Johnson, for flooding me helpfully with rock biographies to review for the *Mail on Sunday*.

Marina Warner generously responded to answerphone queries about paintings; many other friends showered me with books and CDs, answered ignorant questions or just let me ring when they were working and try things out on them. They include Tom Adès, Jenny Diski, Michael Donaghy, Anne Enright, Anthony Farrell, Arnold and Elaine Feinstein, Lavinia Greenlaw, Vivian Guinness, Hannah Griffith, Tim Hilton, Steve Martinez of the rock group Satellite, Gerry McNamara, Grainne Millar, Don Paterson of the folk-jazz group Lammas, John Price, Christopher Reid, Jo Shapcott and Colm Tóibín. John Ryle and Mark Kidel read just-researched drafts and were immensely kind, critical and illuminating. Thanks also for a sunlit train from Glasgow to Oban on Andrew O' Hagan's thirtieth birthday: we downed a bottle of Oban whisky and sang, and while Katriona Crow, Janice Galloway and Colm Tóibín read and discussed a crucial run of chapters, Andrew and I watched the glittering landscape. It was fantastically helpful as well as a great journey.

ACKNOWLEDGEMENTS

Many thanks and much love to Gwen, who always has brilliant ideas about design, and on titles ranging from *Male Chauvinist Piglets* to *Punk, Funk and Spunk*. I'm very grateful for her perspective on the worldview of today's thirteen-year old male. I know, as she says, I don't know the half of it, and I hope her friends won't think I'm a transvestite for ever. Many warm thanks to Myles Burnyeat for unfailingly generous encouragement, criticism and suggestions, keeping arguments straight; also for finding much-needed books, both in libraries and on my own chaotic shelves. Also to my mother Hilda, for reading chapters about music she will never *ever* like. And to my father John, who died before the book was published, for his comments on Greek myth and psychoanalysis, and handing me a wonderful book on blues by his godson, Giles Oakley. To Andrew O'Hagan, who advised on approach at key moments, was revelatory about punk and generously commented on a messy manuscript at a time of peak pressure in his own working life. Finally, special thanks to John Walsh, who showed me what I was writing about, criticized, inspired and expostulated (especially re misogyny and the concept of 'Guyville'); who read and savaged endless drafts, came up with the right music at the right time, made vital connections, laughed when I got things wrong and explained again. I couldn't have written it without him.

Introduction Rock Music and *What*?

Fucking Grape Leaves, Wrapped Round Rice

Rock music and ancient Greece? What has Greek myth to do with rock 'n' roll, or with any boy's ideas about himself and his maleness today? 'Look, Socrates was fucking Greek, man,' Dave Pirner, singer with rock group Soul Asylum, observed recently to a *Rolling Stone* reporter, sitting on a hotel sofa with his drummer Sterling Campbell leaning on his shoulder. 'I mean, what influence has that culture had on us as a people now,' he went on as his publicist fumbled for the stop button, 'those wrapped-up leaves with rice in them? Those motherfuckers they ate this shit and made a bunch of motherfuckers drag fucking rocks up a hill to build some big old colossal thing. And they tried to create this whole society. And what was the food left over from that? These fucking grape leaves wrapped round rice.'[1]

Every society, even ours, thinks itself the pinnacle of naturalness. That its own ways of dressing, eating, showing off and making music are the most natural and right ones there ever were. We take Dave in all his glory, and everyone like him, for granted. The rock star, and the ideals of maleness he embodies, feels like a natural part of our world. A friend of mine recently had a drink with a mate on his birthday. The pair of them, one forty-five, the other thirty-seven that night, ended up at three in the morning with an empty bottle of whisky, swaying around, lips and pelvises stuck out, playing air guitar manically with eyes half-closed, singing the words to 'All the Way to Memphis' by Mott the Hoople, a not very good rock group from the early seventies. They had a wonderful time. But why was their wonderful time, their celebratory male moment, exactly like that? How come we do not realize how extremely strange rock culture and its conventions are? Why the enormous stadia? Why the groupies, the screaming, hysteria, crowd surfing and larger-than-life theatricality? Why are rock stars' faces reproduced absolutely everywhere, their divorces, pacemakers and one-night stands taking precedence in the tabloids over wars, massacres and peace treaties? Why the aggression, the postures, the mad alphabet of leg and pelvis? Why do rock stars sing the songs they do – and why do millions pay so much to listen to them? Why is the guitar the fetishized instrument? How did this music start black and end up white?

A lot of talk about rock breathes a feeling that rock culture has no past except a purely musical, technical one, plus a mass of anecdote about the misbehaviour of its stars. Rock's passion for the moment, the here and now, the new and the young ('I don't care about historee' sing the Ramones), makes people feel it is depthless. But it has a huge past, which is our past too and can only be explained in much wider terms than music. Rock is part of all that has happened, everywhere, in the last fifty years – revolutions in race relations, sexual relations, relations between parent and child, America and Britain. Its history is tied up with the discovery of electricity, the invention of the telephone and the teenager; with American gun laws, Hollywood Westerns, Vietnam, and male fantasies about female underwear. And also with major shifts, over several centuries and in several countries, in aesthetic values and a good few ethical ones too, like an increasing premium on aggression. Rock culture, product of Western culture, is indebted to that culture's entire packet of myths, symbols and changes.

All these things are the immediate context in which rock evolved, so they had to be part of the framework of this book. But its deeper framework comes from patterns of feeling about what a man is, or feels like, when he faces a woman and reckons up his own desire. What is he – naked lover, armed warrior, world-ruler, creator, beloved omnipotent child? Or the inadequate shadow of all these? Specific ways of feeling about this – the clichés, the stereotypes – have long been part of the Western grammar of hoping and dreaming. You find them everywhere – in songs, novels, films, television commercials. But they got their first story shapes, and models of relationship, in Greek myth.

What's Natural?

Popular culture today takes all the baroque manifestations of rock display, the behaviour of rock fans as well as stars for granted. This is all 'natural': the word gestures to a shared belief in some deep, inner, true, universal, animal-but-spiritual, instinctual part of humanity. Rock taps in to the desire to be 'authentic' – the most magical set of syllables in the rock lexicon;[2] a word that shot to fame in the early seventies, when rock went moody and intellectual, reacting against the large-scale *richesse* of big sixties bands. Doing the music because you believed in it, rather than making records just for money, was 'progressive'. Many punters found progressive rock, available on LPs, difficult to listen to and pretentious. 'Commercial' rock appeared on singles, was accessible and jolly. The progressive lobby said it was utter crap. Or, worse, inauthentic.

'Authentic' hives rock off from 'inauthentic' pop. 'Authentic' groups come together naturally. They write and direct their own music, are not 'put together'. There is nothing passive, no being 'put' anywhere, by anyone else, about authentic rock.[3]

I have now met hundreds of distinctions between rock and pop. Many seem ambitious but imprecise. Pop is acquiescent, compliant, artificial, producer-led, 'commercial' and essentially feminine (whatever *that* means). Rock is transgressive, masculine, artist-led. Rock has to have edge, attitude, or 'guitars in it'. Pop is European harmony: the Beatles' Schubertian legacy. Rock is all Africa and rhythm. (Hendrix, the Stones.) Many people brought up in the eighties think rock is boring, macho and takes itself too seriously, whereas pop is the market-place: cool,

INTRODUCTION

millennial, innovative, going places. My thirteen-year-old daughter thinks rock happened in the Middle Ages when mum was young, and there isn't any now. What there is, is either garage – MC-ing, mixing 'n' scratching, drum 'n' bass – or else (horror of horrors) *chart pop*. Rock is what there was Before Us. (Itself a rockist belief, if ever I heard one.)

After taking all this on board, I spent a fascinating winter evening in the offices of *Mojo* magazine. The features editor, now editor, Paul Trynka, told me 'rock' first appeared between 1965 and 1966, when 'and roll' fell away, songs changed their subject matter, and Beatles stopped singing 'she loves you'. Paul put the beginning of rock in the Beatles' song 'Day Tripper' when, inspired by Dylan, they began to address new lyrical concerns and music got 'heavier' (a word I'll explore in Chapter 12). Suddenly we weren't in 'popular music' or family entertainment any more. Among other things, this rock wanted to be much more intellectual.

After Paul, Mat Snow, then the editor, took me in hand. Did rock music really 'have to have guitars in it'? I asked. No way, according to Mat. *Any* music, even purely electronic, can be rock when played to a rock audience. Rock is a subset of pop. Mat uses 'pop' to prick the pomposity associated with 'rock', and remind it that it is still part of showbiz. But the terms have changed over the years; 'rock' really did mean something rebellious in the sixties. Something harder, teenage, anti-parental. Romantic rebel stuff.

What Mat was saying there is what my book is about. I can feel the myth of ferocity at the heart of rock. The biographer of the Charlatans describes how their wild boy, the keyboard player Rob Collins, died in a car crash in 1996. The group was asked if they wanted to pull out of their next gig. They sent back a ferocious telegram: 'THERE WILL BE NO CHANGE. WE ARE FUCKING ROCK.' 'We are fucking pop' would have made no sense. That is where the myth of difference kicks in.

But I can see most rock–pop distinctions are now collapsing. I'm going to take 'rock', as Mat told me, as a sub-group of pop.

But even if no expert can give me a hard and fast rule, I think I react differently to pop and rock and I think this is mostly a musical reaction. (Though it may be due to my generation, too.) There is music I respect, find original, breath-taking, exciting; and music I don't.

A lot of it is how singers use their voice. Voices I respect sound *themselves*. In women's voices, P. J. Harvey, Sinead O'Connor, Tori Amos, k. d. lang, Shirley Manson, Kristin Hersh and Liz Phair sound fine, strong, themselves. But an awful lot of pop girl voices at the moment (I can't bring myself to name names) sound like marzipan. They are using only the Tinkerbell part of their range. Sonic Barbie: aural Kate Greenaway. A voice with deliberate little-girl breath in it, fine-edged with glitter. A tinsel cloud.

Thanks to my rock tutors, I can now recognize, say, Sting, Paul Simon or Bruce Springsteen instantly, even when I don't know the song. I know what they do with their voices (I probably also recognize, without knowing it, how their producers use synthesizers to get the texture they want for their voices), and I'm interested in it. How one ends his consonants just before the beat so you get the feel of hurrying the beat on. How the other comes up under the note. How their voices treat sung words with respect as well as fun – as if each note is expecting something dangerous, surprising or illuminating round the next corner. But the sanitary, sincerely yours voices of Boyzone sound factitious to me, as if someone computer-decided this is how boy-voices are dressing this year. As if a sung word is a handshake whose point is its effect and not itself. This is what feels inauthentic. But you might tell me the whole point is its inauthenticity.

The Charlatans' biographer uses 'authentic' to show you how good Rob Collins's playing was:

> Its sheer classiness gave them an authenticity crucial in crushing detractors who said the band was lightweight. The

slash and burn riff Rob employed for 'Weirdo' was one of the greatest moments of their recording career.[4]

He is talking musical technique: but why 'authenticity' and not, say, 'excellence'? Because 'authentic' is the highest kneejerk praise.

But it is a very odd one. What does rock think it is authentic of? Every culture is man-made; an artificial, evolved, constructed thing, the opposite of nature. Rock music is the first music that created a whole culture. Pop music created pop culture — which is our culture, today — and rock is pop's yearning for the authentic. Yet rock culture is the product of complex twists and turns of technology and history: not just in the twentieth century but much further back. And music is as artificial as culture. Music is a brilliant agent of ideology. It has unique power to make something else seem natural, seem 'just the way things are'. It can twine itself into everything in a society, or a mind. 'It is one of music's special characteristics', says a professor of music, 'that it appears to be a product of nature — that it appears to be a universal language. But this is an illusion.' Music everywhere involves the body and the soul. But though harmony, voice and body as we know them in pop music today seem 'natural' — especially to teenagers, pop music's target audience, who are seeing the world anew from their own newly changed bodies — all this is really the complex historical product of a process: how music has been in particular times and places, how it has changed, what baggage it still carries with it.[5] Rock music is anything but 'natural'. It just sums up, to some people, a current ideal of naturalness.

Authenticity (in anything) is a wildly artificial ideal, the product of a society that has found new meaning in the word 'virtual'. Authenticity is the Great Good Thing in everything we have, wear, listen to and eat, from Nike trainers to yoghurt. The appearance of authenticity in, say, music gets manufactured like a laser sculpture, according to myths currently running round our own heads today. But myths have a history like anybody else. The ones we are conscious of are always standing on the shoulders of older, more shadowy ones.

Rock authenticity comes partly from class, partly from pain. Working-class is authentic. Punk was authentic; punk rockers felt that the glitzy stuff of the early seventies had nothing to do with their own lives and created something that was. Bruce Springsteen's early songs pulse with anger and sympathy for the socio-economically trapped maleness of his own 'home town', for his blue-collar father's striving for a male life that *means* something. Fans clung to the authenticity of country and folk with sentimental intensity. That was why, when Dylan went electric, he upset the faded-cotton folk apple-cart so badly that revered music moguls like the folklorist Alan Lomax got into punch-ups and the folk-singer Pete Seeger took an axe to the electric cable. Dylan was folk's golden boy, mascot of a movement which was itself part of something bigger and included the civil rights movement. Country music ran in his arteries. His extraordinary creativity and in-tune-ness with folk and country tradition meant his sixties songs seemed authentic almost before they hit the ground. One evening, Donovan was among the hangers-on in the great man's hotel suite. He had been billed as 'The English Dylan', and everyone wanted to see what Dylan would make of him. Poor Donovan began singing *his own words* (about a girl with 'tangerine eyes') to the tune of 'Mr Tambourine Man'. After letting him go on a bit, Dylan stopped him. 'You know,' he drawled, 'I haven't always been accused of writing my own songs. But that's one I *did* write.' Donovan nearly expired. 'I didn't know, man. I didn't know! Thought maybe it was an old folk-song.' 'No', said Dylan. 'It's not an old folk-song *yet*.'[6]

At that point, just after *Bringing It All Back Home*, Dylan and his road manager Bobby Neuwirth, a pop courtier and master of the feline put-down, were into country music, not folk. 'Country is the last authentic goddamned shit left', said Neuwirth that same evening, 'for us to rip off.' That appearance of authenticity was part of Dylan's creative process. His songs had been sung at Martin Luther King's 'I have a dream' rally: he had been there himself, had shared the brotherhood vision. When he popped up in 1965 with an electric guitar and black leather jacket, he seemed to betray everything: as if he had never stood for peace and purity, 'had never truly been where he appeared to be a year before – and if he had never been there, those who had felt themselves there with him had not. If *his* heart was not pure, one had to doubt one's own. As if it had all been a trick – a trick that he played on them and that they had played on themselves.' That black leather, said a bitter fan, 'was a sellout jacket'.[7]

The rock dream of authenticity begins with black. Not just black jackets: black of every kind, musical, cultural, personal, spiritual, symbolic. What black means to white is at the heart of rock.

Blues became an ideal of musical authenticity in America in the thirties, when the black singer Leadbelly began to sell massively to a white audience, creating the 'folk' market which later bought Woody Guthrie, and later still, Dylan. Leadbelly's songs were then called 'folk'. Music or politics, in any language, that word 'folk' always has a headstart in the 'authenticity' stakes. Blues became a touchstone of authenticity again, in Britain too now, in the sixties. For white audiences, that idealization of blues rested on ideas (about the noble savage, among other things) that went back to Rousseau. But the bluesmen themselves did not care a damn where their songs came from. Leadbelly told the folk-song collector John Lomax, Alan's father, that he learned 'Goodnight Irene' from his uncle. In fact, it was probably early Tin Pan Alley and composed by an Irish immigrant. Songs passed on easily – all you needed was a record. Juke-boxes spread like fire through the South after the 1933 repeal of prohibition. Muddy Waters had one in his Mississippi shack. Even twenties bluesmen knew thousands of songs, many very different from blues; thirties and forties bluesmen also sang Bing Crosby and jazz hits. When Lonnie Johnson sang in the sixties at a very purist New York folk concert, his manager (identifying blues, as one did then, with folk) said, 'This is a folk audience, Lonnie: give them blues.' The audience was panting for the Real Thing. The early Delta blues were now glamorized and collected. Lonnie, a survivor of real, early blues, was living history: he would connect them to their own authentic past. Lonnie nodded, and launched into a welter of slushy, croony white songs: 'Red Sails in the Sunset' (written in 1935 by another Irishman, Jimmy Kennedy from Omagh), and Frank Sinatra's very own 'This Love of Mine'. His manager nearly burst with rage and shame. 'I thought you said, give them my best', said Lonnie. The manager never knew if he'd been taking the piss.[8]

Yet what could 'authentic' or 'natural' possibly *be*, in music? A particular sound, instrument or style? In a way, Lonnie singing Sinatra was as authentic as anything. He liked the song; he sang it. So what if it wasn't blues? Him singing it was authentic *something*. Music is a made-up thing. Like myth; or like men's fantasies of women. It may be natural to *make* music, but music itself is not natural. (Is 'bird-song' music, or our metaphor for music? Do we turn it into song when we listen?) You hear a song, like it, and pass it on re-stuffed with your own fantasies, myths and words. The whole lot is a product of history, like any artefact. But music is brilliant at making things *feel* 'natural'. The idea that there was a 'natural' relationship between sound and sensuality rose from a swamp of twentieth-century musicological, psychological and even racist assumptions – confused ones, riding on nineteenth-century romanticism – about what was 'natural'. Assumptions about rhythm and body, about adolescence, desire and the primitive. 'Authentic' often means 'sanctified by a job-lot of second-hand myths'.

'4 REAL': Angst, Masculinity and 'Beat'

Rock is fun. But for boys, especially, it involves a load of pain and anger too. Fans who kill themselves listening to heavy metal, who killed themselves when Kurt Cobain did, are male. The angst which Tupac Shakur and Cobain 'summed up for their generations' (as *Rolling Stone* put it, in both memorial issues) was male. It is boys, far more than girls, who have that edge of religious desperation in their loyalty to rock. ('Clapton is God' used to be chalked up all over London.) One middle-aged friend of mine longed for a large silver demon-headed skull-ring exactly like Keith Richards's. Why? 'To keep the faith', he said – as if rock 'n' roll were some persecuted sect, hanging out in the hill-caves of Asia and hunted by the emperor's guard, instead of one of the largest-scale money-spinners on the planet. What faith was he talking about, precisely?

Faiths spawn martyrs. In 1991 Richey Edwards, guitarist and lyricist with The Manic Street Preachers, was burning with frustration that they were not taken as seriously as he thought they should be. He wanted the band to be 'so intelligent they'd never get beaten'. After a gig in Norwich he was interviewed by the DJ Steve Lamacq for *New Musical Express*. During the interview he slashed '4 REAL' with a razor into his own left arm. Lamacq was so mesmerized by what Richey was saying it didn't occur to him to stop him, and Richey got photographed in a lavender shirt with SUICIDE on it, looking blankly at his arm, scarlet from the elbow down, the jagged two-inch inscription gaping black in all the red. Four years later, his Vauxhall Cavalier was found abandoned by the Severn Bridge. His body was never found. In retrospect, the Preachers' *This is My Truth Tell Me Yours*, which won Best British Album in the 1997 Brit Awards, has a desolate ring: even though it was lyrically a more upbeat album than the last, which expressed Richey's darkness, nihilism and pain, as in the song about his anorexia, '4st. 1lb'. For some men, rock authenticity, chimera or no, really is a matter of life and death.

Why? Does it reflect an increasing desperation in the young male soul? In Britain, the rate of suicide in men under thirty-five *doubled* in the twenty years from 1978 to 1998. Accidents are the biggest killer of young men, but suicide is now the second. A quarter of these come from mental illness; the rest, apparently, from anxiety about unemployment, money, and 'inadequacy'. Is this why it is men who get so upset about rock authenticity? In those twenty years, boys have grown up into a world of increasing anxiety about adequately being male. Of course there are objective political issues here, of education and employment, but also pressures created by increasing emotional, social and commercial girl power. Music is a refuge from this. Thirteen-year-old boys come home from school, shut themselves in a room and turn garage up to its highest volume.

They also curl not-yet-bristly lips at chart pop because (so one told me) it doesn't have 'beat'. It may sound old-fashioned, but 'beat' is the word my thirteen-year-old friend used. He may not want to actually *dance* to it (God forbid), but '*good*' music must have *beat*. The rest is 'crap'. Rock has a powerful rhetoric of community, an old ideal of 'dancing in the street'. But a lot of it, especially in male attitudes, turns on exclusivity. 'Crap' is the instant, ubiquitous condemnation. Where precisely does that scorn, standard in thirteen-year-olds but pretty odd when you meet it in the thirty-something, forty-something male rock buff, come from?

Rhythm and beat are the centre of rock. Rock has often been pictured as African rhythm roaring through European harmony, energizing white harmony till it did not know itself. Rock is 'spirit and rhythm, message and beat'.[9] The generation that made rock was 'the beat generation'. But 'beat' is also the essence of male sexuality. 'Male ecstasy in performance starts here,' said Patti Smith in 1978, jerking an imaginary cock at her groin. 'Building and building till the big spurt at the end.'[10] How do we tie this up with thirteen-year-olds clutching at 'beat' with precarious scorn? Rock sometimes seems to women a steel-panelled men's club: furious armour, defending male self-fantasy. Is this because, for boys, rock music is painfully, clingfilmily, *about* maleness – with hundreds of factors, social, emotional and philosophical, working together to identify this fantasy with a specific musical style?

The people who absolutely hate me saying this, the people who are preparing to pounce on mistakes of rock fact and

INTRODUCTION

judgement, and who despise others for their record collections like Nick Hornby's hero in *High Fidelity*, are nearly all male.

How Did We Land up Here?

How did Dave Pirner (for example) happen? How did the authenticity dream embodied by blues and Dylan evolve into that of The Prodigy? How did the heavy metal band AC/DC come to represent a global ideal of masculinity – for boys, if not for girls? How did rock get so far into the parody of masculinity that it produced a camp, spoof maleness, which is at the same time a bulgingly enduring ideal, so cool it keeps its socks in the fridge, renewed by every generation of teenage boys? You only appreciate how new it is when you try really hard to imagine Frank Sinatra singing naked in a red satin G-string, or mounted on a motorbike in studded leather with silver in his nose and cobra tattoos writhing up his arm. How did we get here? How, in the century when women finally, in every Western country, got to vote, did this display of male artificiality, aggression, swagger and meanness – in which violence and misogyny play a central, if very stagy, role – become so sexy?

Whatever Dave Pirner says, all our myths of maleness, of which he is a part, ultimately go back – in a pyramid of dreams and anxieties about sex and heroism – to the Greeks. Our own imagination still operates along myth-lines stamped 'Ancient: Made in Greece'. Whenever you want to give something a really classy pedigree, sure-fire authenticity, that's where you start.

The Greeks did not (in fact) invent the *dolmades* eaten by Dave Pirner. They did not know about rice. But they did invent three words, plus some immensely potent, longlasting concepts to go with them: the words and concepts *music*, *myth* and *hero*, which power-drive rock culture. It may seem odd, but without these words, and what they have meant through Western history, which dictates what they mean to us today, no one would give a toss what Pirner said to anyone; rock music might have lingered on as a musicological curio in Memphis, Tennessee. As Pirner himself continued, to that delighted *Rolling Stone* reporter, 'I mean, what the fuck could possibly be interesting about us? What's *Rolling Stone*'s angle here? Do they think we're rock stars and suck, or what?' The point is, being rock stars is enough. Their maleness may seem natural, but is actually extremely carefully (if unconsciously) staged. Why does it move us, or matter?

Call me a bigot, but to explain the phenomenon of rock fully, and the new image of maleness it saddled the world with, I think you've got to start by going back – to a whole range of different things. Opera, with its theatrical maleness, its castrati, its men singing as women, its glaring staginess. Greek drama, which opera thought it was reinventing and whose plots it stole. And the even older myths Greek dramatists used, which became the West's basic blueprint of sexual adventure: of relationships between men and women, between yourself and any different, maybe hostile and dangerous, other person.

I am not a rock buff; and not a man, either. In no way is this book definitive. Not a history of rock, nor a map of its maleness. It wants to raise new questions. I was trained in classics, poetry, classical music and a bit of anthropology. I came to rock fresh, so its strangeness strikes me, maybe, that much harder. I was writing a book about women, opera and desire. From 500 BC till roughly 1970 (give or take a few trailblazing women), whenever women or female characters sang on stage about desire, the music and words they sang were mostly written by men. This process began with Greek drama, and was still going strong in nineteenth-century opera, and twentieth-century torch music. Bessie Smith, Billie Holiday, Edith Piaf wrote some of their own songs, but most were written by men (like Andy Razaf, who wrote 'Kitchen Man' for Bessie). How could women know what their own desire might sound, when the ways men said women felt, the feelings men paid women to express in song, were continually buzzing round their heads? Women have always lived their lives, and sung songs, within horizons of feeling laid out by men. As the nineties singer Liz Phair put it, women's life in a man-made world is 'Exile in Guyville'.

INTRODUCTION

I interviewed people, male opera composers and directors, women opera singers, rock singers, Broadway singers. But the younger women, singer-songwriters who came up in the eighties and nineties, like P. J. Harvey and Tori Amos, seemed to be handling things differently. Listening to them, reading about them, I began to see they all had one enormous problem, which they tackled in different ways – the medium itself. Rock music was made by men and is fundamentally about being a man. The authenticity it so aggressively clings to is authentic maleness. Rock is a vast wishing well of masculinity: a masculinity it wants, coercively, to see as 'natural'. It is lots of other things as well. It is about injustice, about being manhandled. But it traditionally treats most of the other things it is about (including women) as something trying to stop you being a man. Being a man is the centre – for cast-iron historical reasons.

I began to see rock as something created as a mouthpiece for male joy, defiance and need; a mix of emotions which drew, via the weird way tradition works in rock, on mythic connections between male sexuality, aggression, anxiety and violence. Connections which, as it happens, are basically Greek.

Is this, I wondered, at the bottom of the problems women musicians face – in male audiences, the rock establishment, rock codes for how men think about women? Is this why one Californian punk group of women singers (see, in all the gory details, chapter 18) features a large black rubber penis which men in the audience kneel and suck and which then gets cut off by a sharp knife at the climax? Does everything in rock, even women's rock, come back, at the end, to maleness?

Rock's maleness was, and is, a very fertile problem for women musicians, for rock is strongest when it challenges something. Women's rock has a fantastic history of its own; so do women's blues, jazz and country music. But what I wanted to explain was what the women rock singers I admired were doing with the wall of maleness they encountered. Like women poets, they have to make their starting-point their own reaction to the maleness of the genre and its traditional ways of seeing women. To do that, I had to find the genesis and ingredients of all that maleness. How it worked, how it got going. So a book about opera and women poured itself into the question, 'Where does this maelstrom of male aggression and self-image come from?' The further I got, the more I felt the ultra-maleness of rock was part of many larger-scale changes in the twentieth century. This was the century when white popular culture, especially the teenage end, remodelled itself on black; when white masculinity re-made itself by copying black. Black music led the way, but it interacted with a whole load of associations, symbols and connections made in nineteenth-century white romanticism and early twentieth-century primitivism and modernism – but ultimately, again, in ancient Greece. A whole package of ancient fantasies are buried in white stereotypes of blackness.

Now, in the new century, teenage take-over of black culture means a blonde eleven-year-old in rural Hertfordshire, who has never heard of Harlem, or Compton, in Los Angeles, tossing her head when daddy rumples it to snap 'Don't diss the do!' But black cool matters far more to boys than girls. Black music changed white ideals of male, not female, sexuality. Black athletes rule the world of male bodies; a little prince, future heir to the English throne, gets snapped by the media in rap pose, baseball cap on backwards.

Once I'd begun to put my questions together, I saw they were a book in themselves: the book that had to come before the book I started out writing. The original book was hijacked by the complex archaeology of rock maleness: by the way that the white masculinity in charge of the world – Clinton with his saxophone and blow-jobs; Blair, who donated his Stratocaster guitar to the Museum of Scotland; every man currently between thirty-five and fifty-five who struts round his living-room playing air guitar to records of his youth – re-made itself through music, by impersonating black.

What does it say about rock music that it spearheaded this process? Rock music's power is mythic. Like myth, it is amazingly transformative. It alchemizes and changes its originals. Not just the blues, but images of maleness handed down to us by both blues and Greek myth.

How deeply do Greek images of heroism underlie rock? Men's need for a male group, for instance, plus their need to go it alone? Or their need for a female Echo: to get response from, yet also to silence, any voice different from their own? What does Greek myth say about men's fears of their own power, and their fear that it will never be enough, they are going lose it any second? What about a son's relation to his father, and the violence with which he has to take on the world, including dad, to become a man? What about men's need for women – and terrible need to escape them? Their dreams of women's magic, and their fear of drowning in it? Their need to think women's attraction is due to illusion and their desire for men is fake? All this basic mythic coin which funds rock aggression and misogyny was first formulated (for Western minds) and given story-shapes by ancient Greece. These are the themes which rock music, as it got busy turning black to white, plundered and transformed.

My Generation?

In a lovely book called *My Generation*, Irish writers, songwriters and film-makers wrote about the rock 'n' roll that meant a lot to them as teenagers.[11] It is a gorgeous book: funny, touching, revealing. But I felt, as I read it, so sad. I wished I'd heard this music when *I* was a teenager. A few tracks come rushing in, bringing back a thrill at a new voice and texture like Roy Orbison's 'Running Scared', the only single I ever bought. Songs bringing back people and parties – 'Hey Jude', 'Mr Tambourine Man' – or pure dance gorgeousness like 'Satisfaction'. And that's it. At a Little Richard and Chuck Berry gig I went to at Wembley in 1998, the hall was full of leather-jacketed fifty-five-year-olds jiving in the aisles with women straight from the dance-hall scene in *West Side Story*. The ones beside us had come, they said, *from all over Norway* to hear rock 'n' roll's founders and re-play their teenage selves.

I wish I could do that; but I missed it. I was learning other things. I could sing you the whole Greek hit parade from the seventies. But back-street Heraklion, where I was mostly living, had no time for David Bowie. I was brought up in a Central European tradition of playing chamber music at home. All the family played, my cousins, brothers, sister. The name is supposed to be Wendish. In family myth, the Wends were nomadic, gypsy-like Slavs on the East banks of the Danube, and mostly musicians or scientists. (Can this be true? Are gypsies ever scientists?) One great-grandfather was a concert pianist in Leipzig. After emigrating here, my grandad taught the whole of Carlisle Grammar School, masters and boys, to play instruments sold off by an orchestra at auction, which he bought when he was supposed to be looking for new desks. Many of my family are classical musicians. My parents met playing chamber music. When I was little and stayed up late, it was to hear my dad, a cellist, play string quartets. One of his favourite violinists was a Jewish refugee from Iraq. My dad was teaching in Preston when they first played together; his friend was doing British National Service nearby, sleeping in the barracks with his fiddle strapped to his leg because other soldiers peed in it. We all learned string instruments and played together: the last time we played with my dad, he was eighty-three and we did a Brahms sextet. The first money I ever earned was five pounds playing the viola in Westminster Abbey.

So music was a big thing. I love playing quartets (I wasn't brilliant and I get lost in Brahms), but my real heart was always in singing. I had a piano teacher for a while, a wonderful Jamaican woman called Miss Lewin, who bribed me to practise by accompanying me, after each lesson, in songs from the *Penguin Song Book*. For a time, that was the highlight of my week. Then she went back to Jamaica, started a Jamaican folk-singing group and sent us the records they made. I still have the songbook, filthy and floppy-edged, much Sellotaped. I learned from it all the old English and Scottish songs, every verse. I also learned that singing with other people is one of the greatest pleasures there is. I've sung in choirs from the Schola Cantorum at Oxford to the choir of St Eustache in Paris, in which Rubens once sang, and the Heraklion Town Choir which gave Crete its first performance of Handel's *Messiah* in Greek. Carols, madrigals, sixteenth-century, twentieth-century – anything, you name it, the less accompanied the better. I've sung 'Early One Morning' solo on Belgian radio, Verdi in an Istanbul night-club, Greek songs on Wadham high table at Oxford, troubadour songs in the echoey car park under the Place de la Concorde in Paris. The ex-mayor of one southern Cretan town has me on tape in a Greek duo with a pot-mender from Peiraus. 'Greensleeves' goes down well in Crete, too. When I discovered Ireland, it was heaven – a whole country that spends the whole night singing. You listen to Christy Moore and you just know, there's a man who loves every way a voice can be a word or a note. When I was drafted to Knossos as a classics student to help British archaeologists, I fell in love with Cretan songs. The trench I worked in uncovered a new branch of the Royal Road, the road that led away to the mountains from the palace of Minos. I was supposed to record its dimensions, but the archaeologists found *mantinadas* (improvised rapping couplets, whose melody and language go back to Venetian Crete and right through the Cretan epic romance *Erotokritos*, which the Knossian workmen knew by heart and could sing for hours on end) scribbled all over their measurements. Singing has been my own royal road to everything I love.

And dancing. As a little girl, a doctor's daughter on the island of Bute, Morag my granny danced the sword-dance in front of Queen Victoria. (So family tradition says.) Crete or England, I always loved dancing. I loved throwing myself about to 'Satisfaction'. *But I didn't know who played it and I didn't care.* Blues? Never heard of them.

I didn't know how peculiar all that was. Now I wish – but it's too late, and I'm glad I had to write this book. It gave me a chance to catch up. It may concentrate on mythic connections rampaging unconsciously through the sexuality of singers, audiences and the sounds that bond them in crazed excitement. But it's been driven by the delighted discovery of music I hadn't known till now.

PART I Origins: Myth, Sex and Electricity

1 Orpheus and the Myths of You and Me

Music, Myth, Hero

Like the lives of pop stars, Greek myths spotlit lovers, families, mistakes, death, shame, grief, jealousy, regret, fame, conflicting desires and overreaching yourself. They dealt with characters – more famous, rich, clever, glamorous and generally bigger in every way than you and me – coming up against the limits of humanity. JIM MORRISON FOUND DEAD IN BATH IN PARIS? Wife Clytemnestra and lover murder Troy veteran husband in bath. MARVIN GAYE SHOT BY DAD IN BEDROOM? Oedipus kills father at crossroads. HENDRIX CHOKES TO DEATH IN HOTEL? Ajax stabs himself on beach. MANAGER ROMANCES BABY SPICE IN HOLIDAY HIDEAWAY? Zeus rapes Europa in Crete. MICHAEL HUTCHENCE HANGS HIMSELF IN SEX-GAME BEDROOM? Oedipus blinds himself in bedroom with brooch from wife-cum-mother's corpse. BRIAN JONES FOUND FLOATING DEAD IN POOL? Narcissus found floating dead in pool.

Greek myths were about heroes – a word as male as Greek culture, which means extra-competitively male. Both rock and Greek mythology are the architecture of a highly aggressive male self-image crystallized in that word 'hero'. Greek heroes fought, and killed, and slept with loads of women. The vast scale on which they did so made them heroes. The women were crucial, for in Greek (as in rock) mythology, maleness depends on images of women and their desire for you. But the values that breathed through these stories, replayed endlessly in male Greek music, were as male as the competitions on which Greek society ran.

Men competed for prizes everywhere, in drama competitions, Olympic games, public speaking, music contests.

Music and myth were the double core of Greek culture. *Mousike*, 'the musical art', *meant* culture, as well as simply music. It also meant poetry. 'Music' meant *music and lyrics*, as it does in pop. 'Music' also included dance as salads include lettuce (i.e. there were a few kinds that didn't, but most did). Most of this music was sung myth. Myth, *muthos*, meant 'story' – especially a sacred story, one you might hear in ritual as well as tinkling round your ears at dinner.

Like popsong and its singers today, myth operated in popular Greek culture like a communications web: a network of storylines with relationships, personalities and feelings attached. These stories were salacious, grisly, funny, awesome, sad; a source of interest and a point of reference. You and your friends pondered your family, lovers, and what ordinary people did to each other, through the grammar of behaviour these thousands of stories provided. Everyone thought with them.

Greece also infected Western culture with some very potent ideas about what music can do to you. It was supposed to have creative, spellbinding, communal, unifying power. Music could draw everyone together; it created the city. When Apollo sang, the walls of Troy rose stone by stone into towers. Orpheus was a man, not a god, but his voice pulled everyone together to listen – not just people but rocks, trees, animals. A typical Orpheus landscape in London's National Gallery, by the seventeenth-century Dutch painter Roelandt Savery, has elephants, unicorns, lions, ducklings, horses, parrots – a whole safari park of fans around him, with skeins of geese and a bird of paradise winging in, latecomers from the blue.

Greek society was communal to the core. Music and dance symbolized community. In music, all individual parts were meant to move together to make the whole. *Mousike* meant culture, so a 'musical' education was education itself, making you part of the community. Ideally, music was the basis of community as well as its image. The magically unifying pulling-power of

Orpheus slots into a deep Greek belief about 'harmony' which runs through Greek philosophy and medicine like a fertilizing river. Harmony is an image of society and of health. It means the right balance, or equilibrium, of all elements in the body politic, and in your own body and soul. *Harmonia* (from *harmottein*, 'to join'), was also the way you pegged and strung and tuned your lyre, the 'mode' to which you tuned it. Other people judged you by the way you did it. These days, *Cosmopolitan* expects a girl to check out what bands you like before she goes to bed with you. In ancient Athens too, music was a way of summing people up. People judged you morally by how you placed your fingers on the strings.

The Sirens sang entrancingly but they were female. They knew a lot, but lured men to their death. It was man-made music which brought society together and created – as Dave Pirner puts it – 'big colossal things'. City walls rise. Lambs and lions creep down together and listen. The first power of Orpheus is spellbinding; magic creating a community based on loving music.

Music and Violence

Music's second power, dancing out at you from the myth of Orpheus, is the way it tangles with death and violence, and survives. Orpheus is almost the only Greek hero who is not a killer, but he dies by violence: torn to pieces by maenads, followers of the god Dionysus. They flung his head in the River Hebrus but, as it floated out to sea, it kept on singing.

Elsewhere in myth, music is constantly coming up against violence. Marsyas challenged Apollo to a musical contest, and Apollo flayed his skin off. One of Hitler's generals said in his memoirs that when his men sacked a place, they always smashed the musical instruments first. 'Mars', he concluded, 'is the enemy of Apollo.' But though the enemies of music dismember Orpheus, they cannot silence his art. Music triumphs over violence and death. One of the moments in the *Odyssey* I find most poignant is when the singer–player, who has had to entertain the loutish suitors in Odysseus' palace, sees Odysseus shooting them. He cowers in the chaos, protecting his beautiful lyre: then runs out and begs Odysseus to spare him – and he does. Music, such a fragile thing, made with such smashable instruments, always, somehow, survives. Despite a trail of burnt guitars and a tragically burnt-out life, Hendrix's music lives on. Whatever the violence around, music means immortality, even after the musician's death.

Recording put an extra spin on that idea. How amazing, to hear the voices of Morrison, Hendrix and Joplin from the CD player by your bed, as if they were living, breathing and singing, now, to you.

Sung Myth

In most myths I talk about in this book, I am gunning for patterns of feeling, not particular stories. The stories are hooks to hang the feelings and themes on. Some still have a currency in popular culture, and get resurrected in films like Disney's *Hercules*. People like feeling they are connected to origins, in their own culture and, farthest back, in ancient Greece. Origins plug you in; they give what you are up to a bigger stake in the world. 'Mothers' Day', a DJ on Magic 105.4 has just informed me, 'dates back to spring celebrations in ancient Greece when they honoured Rhea, mother of the gods.' (Well, maybe.) 'It started again in England in the seventeenth century.' True or false, that idea connects us all to an important-sounding past. It gives our feelings about mothers a pedigree.

Specific ancient stories and symbols do sometimes surface in rock. See Prince's hieroglyph of ancient male and female symbols, the head of Nefertiti tattooed on the right pectoral of Tupac Shakur, the cabbalistic symbols of Led Zeppelin's fourth LP (variously called *Led Zeppelin IV*, *Untitled*, or *Four Symbols*), inspired by the mysticism of Aleister Crowley. In lyrics, you get Pete Frampton's Orphic hit or Jim Morrison's Oedipus in

'The End'. A lot of women's rock uses and challenges specific ancient myths.

But most of these are isolated pop-ups. I am talking about something different: the unconscious circulation of mythical connections, running through ways we think about ourselves. The Orpheus connection, for instance, an image-package of craft, loss, poetry, violence and immortality, created the background of feelings from which we react to the death of young musicians like Hendrix. Many Greek image-clusters like that are knotted into rock mythology: the Ulysses resonances of the 'open road' and roving male (chapter 7), or the composite of male aggression, anxiety, and vulnerability (simultaneously combative, infantile and creative; see chapter 3) around the goddess who embodied sex.

In all this, rock draws on a shared reservoir of relationships and self-images which these myths somehow bricked down at the very bottom of our consciousness. The names and story-lines have fallen away in popular culture; but the connections are still there. Greece gave European languages and stories a basic mythic grammar which is different from others. It is not Chinese, Indian or African (despite the influence of African rhythm on rock music). Greek connections have been overlaid in modern Western imagination by borrowings from other cultures, but how we think is still basically organized on Greek lines.

Like Greek myth, pop song is about relationships, staged in the teenage mind rather than the theatre of Dionysus. The rock industry is driven by the young end of its market, the just-teenagers who want to dance and meet the opposite sex. Even if you're dancing or dreaming by yourself in the bedroom, you're still thinking about boys, girls, yourself. It is sung and performed mainly by early twenty-somethings, produced by mainly male thirty-somethings, and criticism of it is led most magisterially, at present, by male forty-somethings. But the whole project is focused on an intensely teenage search for identity through music. And the currency of its lyrics is relationship.

Pop song is sung myth. Mostly self-myth, starring Narcissus. But also, almost as important, myths of relationship, of you and me. Like Orpheus' last song, most pop is the song of a 'me' hooked on 'you'. You do something to me. You went away. I'm so in love with you. What can I do to make you love me? You don't have to say you love me. Pop song depends on myths of mutuality. Our own culture's basic image of intimate, two-way talk is a telephone, the archetypal instrument of modern listening and talk (especially teenage). It creates an inter-subjectivity, my body in my voice, your body in my ear, a wonderful mythic mutuality. This is the image of the intimate you-plus-me cell, on which popsong soars to world dominance. Pop-singers' lives give everyone myths to think with about themselves, but the lyrics themselves work like that too, creating an ever-expanding, globally sharable network of feeling and reference.

Like myth, these lyrics work through images and symbolic connections. The logic comes from the unspoken connections you get by juxtaposing images in melody. Robert Johnson, one of the most demonic voices in all blues and a big inspiration for sixties rock, was a master of it. In his 'Love in Vain Blues',

> The train it left the station with two lights on behind.
> The blue light was my blues, and the red light was my mind.

In Paul Simon's 'I Know What I Know',

> She said, Didn't I see you at the cinematographer's party?
> I said, Who am I to blow against the wind?

Both times, it is the music that carries you, making that jump from one image to another heartbreaking, memorable, significant. Or take a daft line in Fleetwood Mac's 'Rumours', 'Thunder only happens when it's raining.' It is portentous meteorological bollocks. But because harmony is a powerful metaphor (making something seem true when it is not) as well as a musical device, you remember the line. It seems important. Melody and harmony reinforce images. They dress the idiotic, the trivial, the banal, up into significance. In its downward-melting way, even that thunder song is emotionally persuasive. 'Strange, the potency of cheap music,' someone says in Noel Coward's *Private Lives*. But it is not strange at all. It works by the open-ended relation of music and symbol. Anyone can connect to an image when harmony and melody tie it up in satin ribbon.

Popsong works through fantasy, through images which millions of listeners fill with their own personal script. 'Great singers use lyrics as a shell into which they put their own emotions,' said Simon Napier-Bell, talking about Dusty Springfield singing a song he co-wrote. But listeners do the same thing. Popsong sings the myths by which most people live the most important part of their lives. Everywhere, all over the country, all over the world, every night, national and local radio shows play phone-in romantic requests. Some songs have been turning-points in past erotic lives, some are love-messages to current partners. Popsong gives shape to feelings that could be yours and mine. A recognizable shape, comfortingly shared by the rest of the world.

Survival

The way music keeps going after death has made Orpheus one of the supreme myths for poets. *Mousike* meant poetry as well as music: poetry began in song. From Homer on, poets have felt that what music is, poetry is too. For poets, as for the Greeks, 'song' means 'poetry'. As the German poet Rilke said, 'It's Orpheus when there's song.' The Romantics saw Orpheus as the poet who dies violently and young, whose works wield creative, spellbinding, truth-telling power beyond death. In Tennessee Williams's *Orpheus Descending*, the hero, a gentle but glowingly attractive guitar-slinging blues-player (a poet, in the first version), is torn to pieces by jealous townsmen and their dogs. The survival power of music developed tragic political dimensions in our century. Repression, censorship, exile, work-camps, death. The young Lorca, killed by Franco's forces. What if Dylan had written 'Blowing in the Wind' in Moscow, not Minnesota?

Russian poets like Mandelstam, murdered by the Soviet régime, suffered for poetry's truth-telling will, its power to brave the system. Their poetry shook that system far more deeply than Western guns, and became the talismanic international witness in our time for humanity and art.

But Orpheus is just as potent when the violent death is connected solely to the artist and the demands art makes on his soul. Baudelaire, *âme damnée, poète maudit.* Or the quite extraordinarily long list of rock singers who died young because of rock and what it meant to them. As the Irish poet Paul Durcan says in 'The Death by Heroin of Sid Vicious',

> Jesus, break his fall.
> There – but for the clutch of luck – go we all.

The Power of Love: Eros, Orpheus, Narcissus

Music's third power is erotic. Music is the food of love. Desire is rock music's big theme, and in Greek myth the great musician was a lover too. It was as lover, as well as a torn-off head, that Orpheus challenged death. His beloved died from snake-bite. Singing and playing, Orpheus went down to Hades to get her back. The guardians of Hell were so bewitched, they let him guide Eurydice back to the living world, as long as he did not look behind him. At the last minute, he *had* to check she was there, and so got his very last glimpse of her as she was wafted back to the underworld for ever. He sang of his loss ever after. That was what he was doing when the maenads got him: singing some variation on 'I've lost my Eurydice' (as Gluck has it, in his most famous aria, 'Che farò senza Eurydice?'). One reason for the maenads' murderous fury was that Orpheus would never look at other women.

Like rock tracks, myths get recycled all the time. Western music, literature and art has recycled Orpheus to stand for an amazing number of things. The myth has as many facets as a rose diamond. That descent to the underworld in the name of love, that lover who harrows hell to get his girl back and loses her again for ever, has been comic and tragic, been the image of the shaman, of Christ. It inspired the rock song 'From the Underworld' (1967) by Pete Frampton. Salman Rushdie's rock-music-'n'-Greek-myth novel, *The Ground Beneath Her Feet*, is a love story which shows how fully the elements of Orpheus' story, the sex plus the crowd-pulling power of music, fit rock 'n' roll. Music and poetry throw a gauntlet down to death, yes – but so does love. Plus love makes you go down into yourself and come up different.

All these faces of Orpheus, the poet, the lover, the harrower of hell, sum up different aspects of the package of ferocity enshrined in sixties rock. The longing for freedom *and* community, to confront the far edges of desire, of experience; to battle against oppression; to liberate the self. It all created some wonderful music but also, as in the Orpheus myth, violence and fragmentation. Hendrix, Morrison, Joplin, Lennon: the music, lives and deaths of those legendary figures (and hundreds more) sum up Greek insight into ancient connections between music and danger, violence, longing, sex, madness, death – and love.

As a love duo, Orpheus and Eurydice have something in common with two other mythic pairs in which one look spoils everything. Orpheus lives by the ear but is destroyed by the eye. Narcissus is a gorgeous golden boy, adored by everyone but most of all by a nymph called Echo. He never looks at her. Instead he looks in a pool, falls narcotically in love with his beautiful self, tumbles into the water and drowns in his own reflection. Echo too is ear and voice. She cannot be silent when someone else speaks, but she cannot speak at all unless the other has spoken first. She is condemned for ever to utter the tail-end of other people's words, never her own. She can never tell her love unless he tells it first – and he never will. Another myth re-played endlessly in stories and paintings. And in theories, like Freud's work on narcissism.

Then there is Eros and Psyche. Psyche is forbidden to see her bridegroom. She does not know he is Eros, god of love. But she checks him out asleep one night, with a lamp. Whaaat? This winged, young, softly breathing, sleeping, beautiful – *my husband*? Then a drop of oil from the lamp wakes him. Eros looks at Psyche looking at him – and vanishes. Eventually after much tribulation (well, hers) they are reunited and live happily ever after. Looking shatters but does not break the bond. But Orpheus's look cuts the lovers apart for ever.

Some of these characters will come up again. Narcissus a fair bit. (This book is about maleness, after all.) Echo too. We are talking music, and *echos* means 'sound'. Eros gets everywhere, and Psyche will reappear at the end. But Eurydice has not got much of a story. Her role is to be the lost beloved. She loves Orpheus, she'd like to come back, but the rules do not allow a second chance. Her job is to love Orpheus and be the theme of his song. 'I've lost my Eurydice.' Eurydice stands for the subject of male song. She is the woman you are looking for, rescuing, mourning; the woman you will never find. Usefully so, if you want to go on singing.

She makes a great song. One theme of this book is how both in rock music and Greek myth men depend on women for their own identity, self-image and hero status. Not on real women; on a set of inherited images of them. You can't explain men without going into their fantasies of women. What matters to Orpheus' song is not Eurydice at the breakfast table with unbrushed hair but Eurydice as you dream of her. Above all, as you dream of her desiring you. Women wanting you makes you a man. Like Bruce Springsteen says in 'Real Man',

> All I need is your sweet kiss
> To get me feeling like a real man.

A kiss in a song, male myths about women's desire: this is what makes a hero. In male music, anyway.

2 Inventing the Teenager: Repression, Freedom, Electricity

Black, White, Electric

Where's this from? Who's talking?

> If a man comes for initiation into a mystic recess of overwhelming beauty and size, sees many mystic sights and hears many sounds in darkness with suddenly changing lights and many other things happening, and sits down, and people dance around him, how could he experience nothing in his soul?[1]

No, not a rock concert rather distantly described, but an ancient initiate of the first century BC, on what happens when you walk in to a mystery cult. Initiation was awesome, overwhelming, transforming. It involved music, a sacred myth or two, a communal, larger-than-life meeting of darkness, fantastic lights and dance which swept everyone up in exultation and joy: a wildly intense bodily experience that changed your soul. Like Pink Floyd at Earls Court, 1996. Like any swirlingly lit rock gig. Rock 'n' roll's first initiates also talk in terms of belief and transformation:

> We had never heard anything like it but we reacted instantaneously. We were believers before we knew what it was that had ripped the dull familiar fabric of our lives. It was so much more vital and alive than any music we had heard before. Rock 'n' roll was much more than new music for us. It was an obsession and a way of life.[2]

Like ancient mysteries, rock music overwhelms and transforms.

What it mainly transforms is the teenager. It is music for teenagers, and it began with electricity. Electricity makes things louder. 'Why is the rock sound so loud?' Yoko Ono said to me, pouring tea, kneeling on the fluffy brown carpet of the Knightsbridge hotel where she used to stay with John Lennon: 'Because you want to annoy your parents *and* communicate with them. "Can you hear me, I'm shouting so loud, can you *hear* me?" A teenage thing. That's the strength of rock 'n' roll – the energy of – of a baby, almost. "We're trying to communicate!" That's its deep power, really.'

But electricity had more up its sleeve than volume. Rock 'n' roll came out of profound cultural and technological changes in America which electricity made possible through recording and radio. It was electricity that created the first pre-condition for rock 'n' roll: bringing black music into white homes.

The blues were first recorded in the South in the twenties and thirties, on 'race' (or 'sepia') records. Black listeners heard them on juke-boxes and on local radio stations which sprang up in the late thirties. In 1941, the bluesman Sonny Boy Williamson hosted one of the first black radio shows, *King Biscuit Time* on white-owned KFFA in Helena, Arkansas. These stations had a strong public-service ethos, giving local agricultural news as well as music, and stringent broadcasting limits. But there were ways of flouting these. You could water the earth round the transmitter, for instance, so it reached further. Their audiences, farm workers travelling huge distances to follow seasonal work, talked about these shows all over the South. *Biscuit Hour* had listeners from Baton Rouge to Indianapolis.

White parents told their kids not to listen to black stations; they listened, of course, like mad. Elvis in the forties 'dug the real low-down Mississipi singers, mostly Big Bill Broonzy and Big Boy Crudup, though they'd scold me at home for listening. "Sinful music", the townsfolk in Memphis said it was. Which never bothered me, I guess.'[3] His own first records sold to white kids turned in to forbidden black shows. For kids, radio and records created a new invisible freedom. Parents no longer controlled how you heard the world. They could forbid you to tune the thing but couldn't check all the time. Electricity meant freedom even in your parents' home to range outside it, hear things parents didn't like. Black faces were not seen regularly on TV until 1965, but black voices got into white homes more than twenty years before.

Rock 'n' roll is part of American race relations. Jazz had already made black music central to white popular music, but many white interests were desperate to keep black and white music apart. By 1942, Duke Ellington was fusing elements of classical music with jazz. His Carnegie Hall début, *Black Brown and Beige*, now seen as a landmark in jazz composition, was hated by music pundits afraid of that fusion. 'The whole attempt to fuse jazz with art music should be discouraged,' said *The New York Herald Tribune*. But fusion was unstoppable. Unlike critics, classical composers increasingly admired Ellington. 'We stopped using the word jazz in 1943,' said Duke. 'That was the point when we didn't believe in categories.'[4] But pop charts believed deeply in categories. Black and white were segregated. Peggy Lee and Billie Holiday both began their careers in the thirties, but white Peggy outstripped Billie in sales and public profile in their first two decades.[5]

From the audience point of view, rock 'n' roll began when white kids, having heard black music on radio, started buying black records in the early fifties. Leo Mintz, owner of a record shop in Cleveland, Ohio, watched them at it. In 1952 he invited the DJ Alan Freed, with a quality-music radio programme, to see.[6] Freed was staggered. 'I wondered,' he said. 'I wondered for a week. Then I went to the station manager and talked him into permitting me to follow my classical programme with a rock 'n' roll party.'[7] Playing black music to white audiences was a wild success. The pop music magazine *Billboard* reported it with wonder. In 1954 Freed joined a New York station, WINS, and established it as New York's leading pop music station. He sat there, the 'Pied Piper of rock 'n' roll' with twenty-seven hours of prime-time a week, playing songs sung by original black performers and promoting black performers. This made him powerful enemies among record companies promoting white artists.[8] In 1958 his TV show was cancelled when the camera caught a black singer, Frankie Lymon, dancing with a white girl; a Boston concert he promoted broke into violence, he was charged with incitement to riot and the court case bankrupted him; then he was made a scapegoat in payola scandals. Everyone practiced 'pay for play'. One DJ, Dick Clark, built a whole empire on *his* financial interests. But his profits came from the white teen-idols he promoted on *American Bandstand*; he survived the payola scandal unscathed. Freed was held up to Congress as the villain of the whole thing. In 1959 he was sacked from WABC and sobbed 'goodbye' during a song called 'Shimmy Shimmy Ko-Ko-Bop'.

But while they resented Freed, record companies and managers running white singers wanted part of the black gold themselves. Blacks couldn't appear on television or tour with white bands (Ellington had a separate coach for black and white members of his entourage), and black charts were compiled separately, so copying black hits was money for easy rope. 'It was accepted practice,' singer-songwriter and pop historian Louis Philippe told me. 'White singers had literally hundreds of hits with black songs.'

Classical singers sing other people's songs all the time, but in pop you call it singing 'covers'. Someone else's song is your 'cover'. In the fifties it was indeed (as the word suggests) a camouflage or disguise, exploiting segregation for commercial ends. In 1954, for instance, a black group called the Chords had a hit with 'Sh'boom!'. Harvey Fuqua, a key figure in fifties black music who later became a producer at Motown, did an affectionate parody of it; the brilliant fifties satirist Stan Freberg did a more venomous parody. But a month after the black hit, a version by the white Canadian group the Crew Cuts became a million-selling No. 1. There are over fifty contenders for the title of first rock 'n' roll record, and several for its first hit;[9] among them the Crew Cuts' 'Sh'Boom'.

Some black performers made it big too; at first. Another contender for title of first hit is Chuck Berry's 'Maybelline'. Chuck, a St Louis hairdresser, began writing his own lyrics to blues tunes and developed a unique performance style. Standing in a roaring, packed, beer-wet Wembley in 1998, I saw him still doing it forty-five years later, at seventy. There it was, just for a moment – the famous 'duck walk'. Some bluesmen (like T-Bone Walker) threw themselves about and did fancy tricks like playing guitar behind their heads or with their teeth, but most had a very understated style. Vocally and physically, Chuck was brilliantly showy. In 1955, he set off for Chicago with a song he'd written his own words for, given a boogie-woogie beat, and set to a country tune. 'Maybelline' came out that year – and changed everything. The film *Back to the Future I* gives a nice twist to history's knife when a *white* boy goes back in time to the fifties and hears a black band playing bland, boring music. He starts to riff to it, inspires the musicians and switches them on to rock. In real life, things went the other way, and Chuck was one of the main forces behind it.

But the spearhead was a white, nervous, soft-faced lorry driver. Everyone knows the myth. It is the founding myth of rock 'n' roll. How thirty-one year old producer Sam Phillips, putting out blues and black artists on his fledgeling Sun label, muttered one day, 'I'd make a million if I found a white boy who could sing like a nigger'. Then he opened the door and found Elvis on the step.

It wasn't quite like that. The Sun Studio doubled as home of the Memphis Recording Studio whose motto was 'We Record Anything-Anywhere-Anytime'. People walked in and paid four dollars to make an acetate dub of themselves singing. One Saturday in 1953, an eighteen-year-old just out of high school came in with a battered child's guitar. He fidgeted nervily in the tiny outer office, crowded with other walk-ins. Marion Keisker, office manager and a Memphis radio personality, struck by his mix of boldness and crippling self-effacement, was sorry for him and chatted as he waited his turn. 'What kind of singer are you?' she asked. 'I sing all kinds.' 'Who do you sound like?' 'I don't sound like nobody.' Afterwards she typed out his label. He hung round for a while, hoping something might happen, and left. She made a little note, misspelling his name. 'Good ballad singer. Hold'.

Much later, he used to say he went in to make a record for his mum, but over the next few months it was obvious he was longing to make a commercial record. He would call in on truck-journeys, asking if Marion knew any band that wanted a singer. A year later, on 26 June 1954, Phillips was keen on recording a yearning, slightly amateurish lament called 'Without You'. He suddenly thought of trying out 'the kid with the sideburns'. Marion rang him and asked 'Can you be here by three?' 'I was there', Elvis would say long after, 'by the time she hung up.' But it didn't click, the song wasn't right. Still, a young guitarist Scotty Moore heard about him, and rang a week later. They went to the studio just for a try-out on 5 July. Again, nothing went right. They took a break for a Coke. It was very hot. Elvis felt his chances slipping away; he started fooling around, singing Arthur Crudup's 'That's Alright.' Scotty and the other guitarist joined in. Sam Phillips stuck his head round the door. 'What are you doing?' he asked. 'We said, we don't know,' remembered Scotty. 'Well, find a place to start,' said Sam, 'and DO IT AGAIN.'[10]

Rock historians have built many theories on this myth. Elvis reconciled two strands of Romantic primitivism in the South; rock 'n' roll was created by the ideological needs of liberal America, desperate to heal the racial divide, and his voice was the golden catalyst. (Then, goes the argument, rock de-radicalized itself and evolved its own conservativism, restricting women, restricting blacks.)[11] But for teenagers at the time, rock 'n' roll simply began when the electrodes of black and white touched; Elvis was where they met.

Musically, rock 'n' roll came from a mix of blues, jazz, country, Texas swing and pop. The licks of country music, the more soulful bends and chord progressions of the blues. Both black and white musicians were experimenting with new technology for playing and for reaching audiences; they were listening, blending, borrowing.¹² Creative musicians (as opposed to, say, the manager of the Crew Cuts ripping off last month's black hit) hardly thought in terms of stealing. Like all artists, they wanted to do it better, and new. Artists are carnivores. To do something new, they take ideas from all over. But to many white adult listeners, rock 'n' roll sounded like white country music contaminated with black. And to many black musicians, especially in retrospect, it was exploitation and theft.

1954, when Phillips recorded Elvis, was when Alan Freed went to New York, both versions of 'Sh'Boom' came out, and the Supreme Court made segregation unconstitutional in public schools. Black and white were meeting in the schools (to a lot of people's fury) and in the charts. After 1956, at least a quarter of best-selling records were (for a while) by black singers.¹³ The Top Forty broke racial barriers every week. Southern whites hated it. Don't let your children listen to niggers' music, they roared. The North Alabama White Citizens Council declared rock 'n' roll 'a racial plot' against the white community.¹⁴

In schools or in record stores, children were the ones for whom this fusion happened. For them it was not, then, a political issue. That came in the sixties. But the ambiguous morality (so clear retrospectively) of 'covering' black songs for white financial gain was there from the start. Elvis, 'the boy who stole the blues' was an icon of black impersonation. He didn't see it this way himself. He had, said Sam Phillips, 'the most intuitive ability to *hear* songs without ever having to classify them, or himself.' But the estranging politics were alive underneath. White kids have dreamed black ever since. Between 1955 and 1963 they bought increasing numbers of black records. Sounding black was the big dream. Buddy Holly's group The Crickets were delighted when promoters who had heard and not seen them assumed they were black. In the sixties, 'black was authentic.' Richards and Clapton pinched early riffs from Chuck Berry. Jagger was a black impersonator.¹⁵ Twenty-five years later, The Beastie Boys would hijack the black rhythms and attitudes of hip-hop in their album *Paul's Boutique*.

Like jazz, rock 'n' roll drew on black sexuality and got the same backlash, especially in the South. But you cannot segregate an airwave, or bat it away. With the transistor, kids could move music round the house, away from grown-up ears. Through airwaves, the soul of the Mississippi Delta swept into white consciousness via the teenage nervous system. Record companies have competed for teenage attention, through electricity, ever since.

Electric Guitar

Radio was a revolution in hearing. People were reacting to sound in a new way; more people listened to the same thing at the same time. Technology was also racing to make instruments themselves louder. Everyone wanted loud. T-Bone Walker tried playing banjo to get loud, till he went electric. The first electric guitar came in 1931. At the Rickenbacker company, Paul Barth and George Beauchamp made two kinds, solid-body and hollow-body. The solid-body looked outlandish: few people used it apart from Hawaiian-style guitarists. The hollow-body was more popular. Gibson brought out a fat hour-glass thing with elaborate S-holes in 1936, which Charlie Christian played in jazz, T-Bone Walker and Robert Lockwood Jr played in blues. By 1945, hollow-bodies were popular in North and South. but solid-body still hung in there. Two early solid-body players from Lousiana were the country player Jimmy Bryant and the bluesman Clarence 'Gatemouth' Brown. Also Guitar Slim, who pioneered distortion. To get more volume, some players distorted the sound by removing valves from amplifiers or adding a lily-headed phonograph bell. Electric guitar was first heard on radio and live round Arkansas and West Memphis in 1942 and 1943, but it was first recorded in mid-forties Chicago. By 1950, Leo Fender had perfected rock's talismanic, solid-body electric. It conquered the market and spread like forest fire. By 1954, nearly all Chicago players had one. And the man who played it first on disc, making the final public link in the chain from blues and rock, was Muddy Waters. He was first recorded in the Delta in 1941 with acoustic guitar. He listened, liked it, decided to go professional, and in 1943 lit out for Chicago where he loaded trucks, played in bars at night, and made the moves which led to rock: he took up electric guitar ('Nobody couldn't hear you with an acoustic') and started a band.

When you pluck a string on an acoustic guitar, the note dies in three seconds. Electricity lets you sustain it. The instrument becomes another singing voice; its relation to the body changes. Acoustic guitars are all curves and chambers. 'A man playing an acoustic thinks of being with a woman,' my friend Don Paterson, of the folk–jazz group Lammas, told me. 'You feel the vibrations through your rib-cage. It's like having another heart.' A solid-body electric is quite different. 'You hold it in your hands. What you're aware of is the long neck, not the body. You identify with it. It's like jacking off.' Playing a riff on electric guitar is 'spanking the plank'. This guitar became part of the male body in a new, openly sexual way. Muddy began recording with it in 1948. The day his 'I Can't Be Satisfied' (a big influence on the Stones' 'Satisfaction') came out, Muddy was on his lorry. When he tried buying his own record that night, its price had doubled; shops were limiting everyone to one. Muddy's wife had to buy him a second copy. The record made his name and put electric guitar on the map for ever. His later recordings sold brilliantly, especially 'Rollin' Stone' (1950). In the early fifties, he had national hits.[16]

And the band format? That classic group of rhythm, lead and bass, a few men with electric guitars and a drum kit, had evolved in the South. Sonny Boy Williamson got a group together for his Arkansas radio show in 1943. But Helena and Chicago were closely connected by migration. 'Musicians who made it in Chicago had been hanging around Helena playing for radio,' Paul Trynka told me. 'Electric music was played in Helena and West Memphis but not recorded. People listened to it on radio

– then they wanted the records. The musicians went to Chicago around 1948 to 1950 and the record companies latched on.'

After Muddy, the band format never looked back. He became a bandleader with a strong sense of ensemble and no hang-ups about sharing the spotlight. He got Chuck Berry his first recording contract, let Jimmy Rogers cut a side of his own in his recording time; he taught others to lead. 'I took 'em into my band and made good blues stars out of 'em.' When sixties white boys knocked reverentially on his door, he adopted them too.[17] Male blues was a one-or-two-man show; rhythm and blues was a party.[18]

Sex was the key to performance and sound. With his snakey slide solos, Burgundy voice and wild imagery, Muddy told an ever-widening market that electricity spelt sex. Howlin' Wolf, his protégé (at first) in Chicago, writhed orgasmically on the floor as he sang. He was no virtuoso player. He depended on guitarists and made his impact on disc by the curdling sexuality of his voice: one of the great rock precursors precisely because what counted was that lust to perform, to make pure musical performance spell sex.[19]

Repression and Getting Free

Other changes in late-forties America prepared the ground for rock 'n' roll in a more sinister way, summed up in 1950 when the black singer Paul Robeson had his passport taken away. Warm, charismatic, internationally adored, the first black actor to play Othello at Stratford in a white cast, Robeson had been the nation's darling since *Showboat* (1928). White America hugged him to its showbiz-proud bosom. 'They felt he was doing their thing,' said a black friend of Paul's on a 1998 TV documentary. But he was also an increasingly committed political activist. In the forties he joined picket lines and went on marches, showing sympathy with workers' rights in America and abroad. He visited Russia; he said he believed in Communist ideals. 'It is', he pointed out, 'a legal party'. He was an actor, and southern theatres were segregated. He campaigned against segregation and personally asked the President to end the lynchings.

Meanwhile the two deepest American fears, of Communism and black resentment, were producing a string of FBI file-notes on Duke Ellington. In 1941, while writing *Black Brown and Beige*, Duke called the Negro 'the creative voice of America... Our voice sang when America grew too lazy and confident to sing.' Not what your average FBI man wants to hear. Marrying jazz and classical harmonies, exploring black contributions to American music, that piece outraged the critics and proceeds went – shock, horror – to the Russian War Relief Fund. In 1944, Duke played in a 'Tribute to Fats Waller' Carnegie Hall concert, sponsored by American Youth for Democracy, which was 'cited by the Attorney General of the USA' says the FBI file-note, 'as Communist within the purview of Executive Order 10450'. This concert, adds the file darkly, became 'a tremendous spontaneous demonstration of inter-racial unity'. The same year, Duke volunteered for a concert sponsored by the Joint Anti-Fascist Refugee Committee, which the FBI thought was also Communist. In 1948 he joined the Hollywood Democratic Committee, which the California Committee on Un-American Activities said was a Communist front.[20] To the FBI, black musicians were inevitably subversive.

Publicly, Ellington kept a low profile on black rights (the black press criticized him for it until 1959), and the double paranoia, Communism and blackness, converged far more cruelly on Robeson. From 1950 Robeson was banned from radio, TV, concerts, recordings, film and theatre. The FBI and media isolated and vilified him, spied on him, made him a moral and political pariah. Even in the sixties his name was so dangerous that Martin Luther King and Malcolm X, following up the civil rights Robeson promoted in the forties, could not afford to associate with him.

Bad politics make good art – see the Italian Renaissance city-states and Stalin's Russia – and rock 'n' roll appeared in America's most repressive decade. McCarthy was sniffing out reds in the

Senate, but successful blacks were under special scrutiny because injustice was at last being challenged – often on a modest, gentle scale but maybe the more threatening for that. On 2 March 1955, fifteen-year-old Claudette Colvin refused to give up her bus seat to white high-school students in Montgomery, Alabama. In the same city on 21 October, Mary Louise Smith, closing her eyes on the bus after a long day, was roused by a white passenger who wanted her seat. She too refused to get up. On 1 December, Rosa Parks refused to move from the front to the back of a bus. All were arrested for violating Montgomery's transport segregation laws; the Rosa Parks case sparked off historic civil rights protests.[21]

It was an age of homogenization, hastened by television; of wanting to sweep all difference and inequality – colour, sex or generation – under the newly fitted, wall-to-wall post-war carpet. Throughout lynchings in the south and witch-hunts in the Senate, white middle-class America beetled to its golf-links and listened on radio to adult crooners like Perry Como. In 1958 Alan Freed's downfall began. He had been doing what everyone in radio did: accepting money for playing certain records. He was brought down, basically, for promoting black music on white airwaves: for giving teenagers rock 'n' roll.

No one had spoken for or to teenagers. Freed did it at national level, and gave them a new sound: country musicians integrating blues forms into their music, blues musicians using country rhythms in theirs, the energy and crackle of Chuck Berry and Little Richard, the soaring sexuality of Elvis, all made and played in the teeth of repression (and at the cost of Freed's career) especially for them. Rock 'n' roll got its energy from the repression gripping the country when it began. Like a guitar in a noisy bar, it had to be aggressive to get heard. Malcolm McLaren, future manager of the Sex Pistols and architect of British punk, said early rock 'n' roll was 'anarchy'.[22] But not political anarchy, except in the broadest sense. It stood for freedom; its energy was defiance; but the politics, then, were to do with generation. Teenagers were shaking free from parents by modelling themselves on another myth of getting free, carried – subliminally, for most of them – in the voice of black music.

I Was Born A Slave, a two-volume anthology from the Library of Black America re-edited in 1999, contains thousands of eighteenth and nineteenth-century accounts of insane hardship, resistance, escape and hard-hitting humour from black authors whose tone ranges from indignant to defiant, grotesque to inspirational. It represents the birth of African-American writing. The slave narrative, a story of suffering-and-getting-free, is the foundation of black American literature – and also of the blues. Its Orpheus-like voice of defiant survival continues in the monologues of nineties hip hop. It is still the power behind ghetto voices in the new millennium.[23] This, at a very deep level, was what fuelled the music which set the first white teenagers on fire.

You could say kids have always defied mom and dad, and the freedom-voice of rock 'n' roll trivialized an appalling, inhuman narrative by plundering it to glamorize teenage bolshiness. Too bad. The process was inexorable. That black voice was both metaphor and inspiration for teenage rebellion. By taking it over, rock 'n' roll used music as a weapon against grown-up white society. Teenage music; made specifically, battlingly, for the young.

From Zero to Hero: Sound of the Male Teenage Body

Fifties teenagers were beneficiaries of forties black experimenting with electric guitar, electricity's third input to rock. Record, radio, guitar: electrifying made music louder than music had ever been before. But electricity also spelt community, innovation, communication. It plugged you in. Its metaphorical implications were limitless, and belonged to the future, the young. Electricity was newly running the world: light, heat, the dangerous toy, shocking, flowing through the home, reaching out to connect you to the world. Electricity was teenager power, a bright unarguable force in the adult world, a wonderful emblem for the teenage sexuality it disseminated through American homes. 'You shall take this electrical power out of the wall,' said Norman Mailer, 'and send it through the guitar and you bend it and shape it and make it into something like songs for people and that power is a wonderful thing.'[24] Electricity invented the teenager, both through the US defence industry (developing electronics in the Second World War) and through music.

Rock 'n' roll was the world's first commercial music to create and define an age-group. Plenty of music has sustained revolutionary group-consciousness; many national anthems began as revolution songs. Irish exiles from the Famine sang songs in Chicago about the 1798 rising against the British. A Cretan friend of mine, a sailor becalmed on a cement boat in an African harbour for seven months, swam through a shark-heavy bay to the one ship where he heard the Cretan anthem, which bloodily rehearses Cretan risings against the Turks. But rock did this for an *age*; and does it again as each generation comes along. Ever since Elvis, each generation (politicians, builders, hairdressers, accountants) defines itself by the soundtrack to which it grew up.

Electricity, the power behind it, amplified and recorded that music, brought it into the home, gave teenagers a community even when they were alone. As a fifties sociologist remarked, 'When the teenager listens to music, even if no one else is around, he listens in a context of imaginary "others". Indeed his listening is often an effort to establish communication with them'.[25] Electricity gave teenagers its own global power and metaphors – flash, danger, voltage, energy, input, output, juice; galvanizing, destroying, fusing, flowing, amplifying. From *Wired* magazine to 'I sing the body electric' – sung, for instance, by showbiz graduates in Alan Parker's film *Fame* – electricity is youth culture's defining metaphor: ubiquitous, sexual, instant. 'Rock seemed to come from nowhere', said Paul Trynka, 'but it was so phenomemal, so quick, because it was driven by radio. With new radio formats and transmitters, this was music for the electric age.'

When 'Maybelline' came out in 1955, American teenagers became, almost overnight, 'a cult with its own life-style and set of rules'.[26] In January 1956 came Elvis Presley's 'Heartbreak Hotel', playing non-stop for two months, everywhere. Elvis appeared on the Dorsey Brothers' television show; the record went to the top of the charts in April. There it stayed, like a new planet, for eight weeks. Elvis 'walked the nation's air-waves like a laughing god'.[27] In 1957, Chuck Berry's 'School Day' ('Hail hail, rock 'n' roll/Deliver me from days of old') showed everyone, especially record companies, how far America had come in two years towards youth culture. One television network set up *American Bandstand* for these first Americans who suddenly found they were an age-group in touch with each other. Not adults condemned to an eternal diet of Perry Como, not children chivvied on the road to adulthood, but teenagers having a great time being themselves, now.

'Don't know much about historee', sang the slubbed-silk voice of the black tenor Sam Cooke, one of the great precursors of soul, in his own song, the million-seller hit 'What A Wonderful World' (1960). Two decades on, the Ramones would sing 'I don't care about historee' ('Rock 'n' Roll High School', 1980). 'That's not where I wanna be. I just wanna have some kicks.' Rock 'n' roll is against history – teenagers know the world and sex began with them – and all about now. It is based purely on feeling. 'If you feel it 'n' like it, then reel it 'n' rock it', sings Chuck Berry. 'Hope I die before I get old', sing The Who in 'My Generation' (1965): the song Sid Vicious (for one) put into tragic practice. 'I just wanna be with you/I just wanna have something to do/ Tonight tonight tonight tonight tonight', sing the Ramones ('Road to Ruin', 1978). As rock 'n' roll went on, negative feelings came in: rage, frustration, despair. But the now of sex, and feeling, was channel for it all.

These songs laid down the rock 'n' roll ideal. If you heard them as a teenager, you have them in your head for ever. The hero of Hornby's *High Fidelity* says, 'People worry about teenagers watching violent videos. Nobody worries about kids listening to thousands – literally thousands – of songs about broken hearts and rejection and pain and misery and loss.' When a successful-looking guy walks into his failing record shop, Hornby's hero worries. Does he himself like pop because he's unhappy, or is he unhappy because he likes pop? 'It would help me to know if *this* guy has ever taken it seriously, has ever sat surrounded by thousands and thousands of songs about... about... (say it, man, say it)... well, about love.'[28]

Rock 'n' roll feeling is everything a teenager can feel about love and sex: fury, despair, hope, frustration, triumph, but also about the immortality of the moment, of sex, of rock ('When we shake the earth moves/We're gonna live for ever', sings Kristin Hersh in 'Shake' [1998], ironizing that); and about infinite self-invention, trying things out. The guitarist Robbie Robertson, who played in Dylan's famous 'Basement Tape' sessions, said 'It was all a goof. We weren't doing anything we thought anybody would ever hear.'[29] In 1998 the Beatles tried to stop the release of a tape made of them illicitly in 1965. 'It was just a lot of kids messing about,' said George Harrison. But kids messing about *was* rock 'n' roll. That was the spirit in which Elvis began 'That's Alright', the song that made his name. You fooled about, tried yourself out, because you were going to live for ever. As the Meat Puppets sing in 'Oh Me' (1983):

> I don't have to think
> I only have to do it.
> The results are always perfect...
> I formulate infinity.

Rock God: 'A Hurricane Called Elvis Presley'

Teenage girls were central to rock 'n' roll – as the boys' audience. When Little Richard sang, they threw their panties at the stage. The big story for British journalists reporting Elvis was his effect on girls. 'I have just escaped from a hurricane called Elvis Presley,' wrote a *Daily Mail* journalist in 1956. 'I saw him send five thousand girls into a mass of screaming hysterics.' The rock 'n' roll industry is driven by teen sexuality. Boy meets girl in its music: music to dance to, 'the sound of the teenage body', whose beat is the 4/4 of the heart, of sex.[30]

White popular music of the twenties to forties projected a long-vistaed adult perspective on romance and sexuality: the voice Sinatra was so good at. As for blues – hear Muddy Waters singing 'I'm ready for you, I hope you ready for me'. No adolescent inexperience there: this is adult, all the way down. A blues picnic held one day just below Memphis in 1978, filmed by the blues archivist Alan Lomax, began with the dancers' pelvic salute to the drum that inspired them. The male dancers simulated sex with the drum, the earth, each other. Then his hosts asked Lomax to turn off the camera. He realized 'normal American audiences might mistake this sexually hyperactive, virtually all-male dance for a homosexual orgy, which it certainly was not. The women's movements were as openly sexual as the men's. They too showed off – showed what they could do with a man inside them'. Blues sexuality was openly experienced, mature. Its dance was music, its music was dance, and 'both were powerfully genital'.[31]

But rock 'n' roll sex was not adult. The white adult world was egg-box bras, deodorization, glistening fridges, McCarthyist repression, Cold War. Rock sexuality was hotly teenage: a boy playing a man. This was the first generation self-defined by sex, claiming sexuality, identity, rebellion and freedom, through (for the first time) its own music. It focused on new, angry, edgy desire, felt by the newly sexual teenage body and psyche, and was bought by newly potent teenage money. In one jump the teenage mass market, that new golden goose, became the largest slice of the record-buying public.

Five decades on, what began as a rebel yell is ruling the world commercially and emotionally. US figures show that rock music sold three times as much as country music between (for example) 1979 to 1983, and seventeen times as much as classical. It occupies half the American airwaves:[32] it occupies the world. Lebanon's top-selling album in 1997 was The Prodigy's *Fat of the Land*. Those five thousand girls who screamed at Elvis are now pushing sixty. Their boyfriends are almost past running the country (though not past running its money). 'The music industry' now basically means rock music, the sound they were the first to dance to, which made everyone define sexuality in terms of teenagers to a degree which those girls (and Elvis) could not have dreamed of. Rock 'n' roll spotlit the teenager as the desiring, desired self; made sex a teenage monopoly, on loan to everyone else.

Teenage – teen models, teen feeling – has become society's touchstone as in no culture ever before. 'Most men my age (and I'm thirty-nine)', Mat Snow told me, 'have long-term partnerships and children, but one foot firmly anchored in the idea that they're part of quasi-rebellious rock culture.' The teen self, the self in making, the formation of new-minted sexuality, became the self with which the whole culture identifies. Grown-up means finished. To be beautiful, be desired, be rock, you have to be young. Maybe in the West you can stretch a point or two, but in Japan, the West's rock 'n' roll mirror, the doctrine is ruthlessly applied. James Young, keyboard player on Nico's tour of Japan in the late Eighties, was in Tokyo when a Japanese star killed herself because her record company dropped her on her birthday. She was suddenly too old – at seventeen.[33]

Rock music helped form the credo of our age, that sexuality defines individuality. How you boogie is who you are. This idea would have sounded barmy in the civilized world anywhere from the sixteenth to nineteenth centuries AD. In fifth-century Athens, Imperial Rome, Renaissance Florence. Maybe you couldn't even have thought it before Freud. It makes us historical freaks.

Male teenagers have had huge, charismatic power before. Edward the Black Prince was sixteen when he helped the English win at Crécy in 1346. But rock was the first time teenagers ruled the world imaginatively, and became millionaires, through music; the first time music made sex the channel by which teenagers challenged everything, parents to politics. And its first model was Elvis, walking the Fifties airwaves 'like a god'.

But what sort of a god? Look at the names. Little Richard, Chuck Berry, Billy Fury. Or Elvis's titles: Pelvis and King. Rock 'n' roll was the sound of the teenage body, but more specifically the male body. Sound – and sight: young male sexuality gathered in one voice, one body, and worshipped by five thousand girls at once. As venues and audiences got unimaginably bigger, it would be fifteen, twenty, a hundred thousand. Out of the electric foam of myth and cult that raged up round rock 'n' roll, the rock god was born.

He never looked back. In a Tokyo hotel in the nineties, a woman musician from one rock band happened to have the room next door to a male guitarist from the LA Guns. She heard him through the wall all night with groupies. Next morning his door was strewn with tiny, beautifully folded white notes, despairing snowflake confetti from unsuccessful candidates. She opened one. It read, 'I will wait for you. Room 361 on third floor. I cherish a dream The Rock God will come see me.'[34]

3 Power, War and Creativity: The Male Gods Round Desire

The Oldest Youngest God

The centre of my city is the Greek god of desire. In the eighteenth century, Piccadilly Circus was known for its prostitutes, and *eros* means 'desire'. Eros is the only infant god. His age varies – in some statues, paintings and stories, he is a teenager (as in Piccadilly) – but he is always young. Yet early Greek cosmogonies put him at the beginning of the world. First Chaos, then Earth and Heaven, then Eros. He has to be there, so other things get created; he brings things together to make new life, is part of the move from chaos to order. He is primevally young, and also ancient.[1] The oldest youngest god.

Greek gods incarnated the thing they represented. Just as the war-god was war and the fire-god was fire, Eros literally was desire. But Greeks also thought of gods in terms of divine society and parentage; they said the mother of Eros was Aphrodite, goddess of sex and love. She literally *was* sex. I shall use her Roman name, which we use most in our own culture: Venus.

Father: Castrated King

In rock 'n' roll you know roughly how a myth started, as with Sam Phillips's dream-come-true of a black voice in a white body. In Greek myth, this is unreachable. I cannot tell you Greek myth was man-made. Nobody knows. But the poets and painters who shaped and recycled it were male. As it comes to us, Greek culture, like rock culture, was a male creation – 'Guyville', as Liz Phair calls it in her album which sees women as exiles in a man's world (*Exile in Guyville*, 1993). Greek mythology basically addresses male psyches. When you look at relationships in it, you have to think what they were saying *for men* about Guyville's self-image.

Greek myth gave Europe its basic male self-image – and its image of sex. It could have picked any emblem for sex, from a dragon to an ocean wave. What it came up with was a woman. Unlike the Madonna, so often in the company of other women, Venus is related only to men. She has no mother, but a father, husband, lover, and son. So sex, in Greek myth, is purely male-related? What were these men like? The range of maleness round her tells us how Greek culture – and Western culture after it – basically saw its own maleness in relation to sex.

Venus, like Eros, arrives near the beginning of the world. Earth emerged from Chaos and made herself a consort, Heaven. The pair produced various children including world-forces like Ocean; and also three giants whom Heaven hated, and shut up inside his wife. Earth resented it and told her other kids to assault Heaven with a flint sickle, but they were all afraid except the youngest, Kronos. When Heaven approached Earth at night, 'longing for love', Kronos cut off his dad's erect genitals and took over world rule. Heaven's blood shot out over Earth (generating Furies where it landed) and Kronos tossed the genitals in the sea. Foam (*aphros*) fizzed round them. A girl grew in it, bobbing through the waves, getting washed up in Cyprus – where Botticelli painted her coming ashore, born more tastefully in a shell rather than bloody froth round a severed cock.[2] Aphrodite means 'Foamborn'. The goddess of sex begins life as foam round Heaven's penis, full of desire at the moment it is cut from its poor owner. Desire is foam, 'coming' to land, becoming something else. The origin of sex is the worst male fear. Venus, who could have had any origin, comes from castration. Sex begins when you do away with your dad's sexuality and impose your will on the world. It is tied up with father–son conflict, male–female antagonism; male resentment, power-struggle, vulnerability, damage. Like the male anger, conflicts and vulnerabilities which worked their way into rock 'n' roll.

One classic early British rock 'n' roll album, *The Sound of Fury* (1960), featured the toughly vulnerable, anguished voice of a young Liverpool docker called Ronnie Wycherley, who wrote the songs while working on Mersey tug-boats. Who renamed him Billy Fury? Who thought up the names 'Marty Wilde' and 'Tommy Steele' as well? Larry Parnes, fifties impresario of British rock 'n' roll. He knew what rock 'n' roll was all about and knew, too, exactly what teenage rebellion wanted. Rockers had to be hard. Their first name could be cute but their surname must be 'steel' or 'wild'. A flint sickle, taking over the world. The sound of fury. The rock god, like sex itself, begins with male rebellion – against dad.

Husband: Crippled Creator, Armour-maker, Fire

Venus is married to Vulcan, divine metalworker, god of flame. His Greek name Hephaestus means 'volcano' in modern Greek; ancient myth said volcanos were his workshop. Surrounded by bellows and melting-vats, he makes palaces, jewellery, moving tripods, self-automated statues, thunderbolts, armour. Fire is his medium. Like fire, he is fantastically strong. 'No god can fight him.' But he is also lame, and that is connected to the traumas of his story. He was once thrown out of heaven, either by his dad Jupiter because he took Juno's side in a marital quarrel, or by his mother Juno, ashamed of his lameness. (When he got back to heaven, Vulcan chained her to her chair in revenge.) 'I fell all day', he says, remembering, 'and landed at sunset.' (Christian myth thinks here of Satan, the fallen angel.) Vulcan landed in the sea. Sea-goddesses 'saved' and hid him. 'Round me flowed Ocean, murmuring with foam.'[3]

Marital conflict at the top? Something male flung out of heaven, damaged? Recuperating creatively, surrounded by foam? Something female appearing, savingly, in the sea? Vulcan's fall matches the tale of his wife's birth. The couple have other things in common too. He makes chains – think of the 'chains of love'. He works with heat underground – Greek began the thousands of European images for women (and their insides) as the underworld, earth, an oven. A women is 'an oven crying for heat' in 'I Must Have that Man', sung most famously by Billie Holiday.[4]

Flames of love power-drive Western love poetry and lovesong from the start. 'My heart burns with desire' sings Sappho in the seventh century BC. 'Thin fire runs under my skin'.[5] In the fourth-century BC dialogue *Charmides*, by Plato, Socrates 'bursts into flames' when he glimpses a boy's genitals under his tunic. In a third-century BC Greek epic, Eros 'burns' Medea with desire for Jason; in the first-century AD Roman poet Virgil, Dido is 'fired' with desire for Aeneas. Venus tells Eros to start a fire in Dido's breast where it burns until she dies and 'all heat leaves', as if love had burnt her to death. As if the heat begun by *eros* turned into her pyre. Virgil's story shifts from burning Troy, where Aeneas loses his wife, to Dido's burning desire which lands her in the flames.[6] In early seventeenth-century lovesong, 'More is desire/There where it wounds and pines,/As fire is far more fire/Where it burns than where it shines.' 'Lo here I burn' sings another poet-composer, 'in such desire/That all the tears that I can strain/Out of mine idle empty brain/ Cannot allay my scorching pain.'[7] Think of 'torchsong'; or Bruce Springsteen's 'I'm on Fire' (1984), voted 'top sexy song' in *Q Magazine*'s 1998 survey of sexy songs. The rock convention of holding up your lighter says it all. At the sexiest, slowest climax of a vast James Brown concert at The Point in Dublin, in 1998, we watched matches and cigarette lighters waving slowly, a sea of little flames in the dark. 'C'mon baby,' sings Jim Morrison. 'Light my fire.'

Venus is gorgeous, scented, soft; Vulcan subterranean, filthy, lame. But he is also the heat and movement of making, and specializes in metal, the hardest material, and in self-automated mobile statues. He is mobility but also immobility: he immobilizes his enemies, lashing his mother to a chair, forging chains that bind Prometheus to a rock or wires to trap his wife's lover.[8]

Tongues of fire make hard things soft and soft things hard. Metalwork is all softening and hardening. Vulcan's work is kinetic, a male dream of tools, friction, inflation, hammering, stiffness. Fire has to be laid. As Bjork said once, 'Creativity is an aphrodisiac. Sex is basically creating another person, innit?'[9] Vulcan and Venus are the marriage of fire and sex, creativity and making love. Each of their elements is an image for the other.

After sex, the creative act most important to early civilization was making pots out of clay, for which you also need fire;[10] to which softening and hardening are, again, crucial. Fire begins, and empowers, civilization. (If Vulcan had been around in the twentieth century, he might have been not fire but electricity.) The god of making pots was Prometheus, and he was often worshipped beside Vulcan. Here together, at the same altar, were the two gods of making-with-fire. But they were rivals too: Prometheus was the thief of fire.

Fire is creativity twice over. You have to make it, as well as make things with it. But in many mythologies fire starts as a secret, like creativity. You have to discover how to make it, steal the secret, find where it is 'hidden'. Physically, in wood, iron, metal, flint, or the firestone, iron pyrites. Alchemists said fire was hidden 'in the stone'.[11] In myth, you find it in heaven, where Prometheus got it from. (Plato imagines Prometheus burgling Vulcan's studio.) Or in the underworld: Samoan myth has an earthquake-god who keeps fire underground, as in Vulcan's subterranean workshops. Or amazingly, in several mythologies, in the sea.[12] Just as Prometheus takes fire down from heaven to earth, Vulcan is thrown down from heaven: fire travelling down to earth. But he also hides in the sea, cherished by sea-goddesses: fire as a female-guarded secret in that same element where Venus was born.

Fire belongs with sex as Vulcan belongs with Venus: many myths of discovering fire spell out that analogy between fire and sex. In one myth, fire begins when a man making love to his wife cannot extract himself from her; flames burst from the friction between them. Sometimes fire comes from the 'finger' of some demonic figure; or from other sorts of friction, stones pounded on flint, one stick drilling holes in another.[13] These stories are all about relationship. It takes two to make fire. Two materials, flint and steel; two different woods; two people, two sexes. You also get it from inside an animal, or inside women who have fire between their legs. You get fire from friction: rubbed sticks, sexual conflict.[14] You get it by singing fire-songs – singing flame out of wood and stone,[15] perfect analogy for a love song which sings desire out from inside another person. You serenade a girl under her bedroom window. In torchsong, you carry a torch for someone which will (you hope) kindle desire in them.

You cannot have civilization without fire, or desire. But you worry about losing both. The secret of fire is not just making it but keeping it, lighting it next time. Like male desire, fire is all-potent – no god can stand up to Vulcan – but also deeply vulnerable. It gets out of control, burns everything up and goes out. In many myths, you steal it, then cannot rekindle it. People withhold its secret. Fire stories are saturated in sex and jealousy, people trying to keep fire for themselves. But they are also full of people sacrificing themselves for others, suffering to steal fire for them, like Prometheus who stole it for men and was punished. Like stories of desire, fire stories radiate both selfishness and generosity.

In Greek myth, the fire-god helps punish the theft of fire twice over, directly and indirectly. Vulcan forges Prometheus' chains: technology punishing the person who stole its secret. But as part of the divine plan for avenging the theft of fire, he creates something else. He makes the First Woman, beautiful Pandora; the gods give her to Prometheus' brother, who is too obtuse to see past her gorgeous surface to the gods' dastardly plot. Pandora carries a lidded jar, full of plague, war and evils. She releases this lot into the world, leaving Hope behind inside; men will suffer for ever because this idiot accepted the woman Vulcan made.[16] Men stole fire whose god was married to sex. So get that god to make sex a curse: punish men through desire, make it bondage. Woman is man's punishment. As Prometheus languishes in chains, men are chained to women, by desire. The literary pedigree of Western misogyny, which rock culture reproduces as potently as any, begins here, with Pandora.

Vulcan has great power. Sex is his wife; his medium is the source of civilization. Yet both are stolen. Venus takes a lover. 'She scorns me because I am lame,' Vulcan complains, 'and loves destructive Mars because he is handsome'.[17] Vulcan is creative potency stolen, crippled, flung away. His story is full of making, but also full of losing power. Creativity, loss, rejection. Venus' father ruled the world and was castrated; her husband has the secret of creativity, but is lame; and the source of his power is stolen. Sex is yoked to male creativity and power, plus male vulnerability, damage, and loss.

Sex Pistol, Heavy Metal: the War-God Lover

The husband makes armour, the lover wears it. The husband is creative, the lover destructive. Sex is married to creativity, but her lover is Mars, god of war. Painters do not often show her with her husband – a few Renaissance painters show her waiting in his forge while Vulcan makes weapons for her son (usually Eros, but occasionally her other son, the human hero Aeneas) but most painters show her happy with her son or lover. Loud and clear, Greek myth said sex has physical and social ties with creativity and war, the two power-bases of Liz Phair's 'Guyville'. ('God, I hate that word Guyville,' said a male friend of mine.) But the active bond is the illicit one. Venus' birth says sex began with conflict, but her choice of lover says what she really gets off on is violence.

No one has to believe this is necessary or *true*. Not in the world, nor in the human psyche, if there is such a universal thing. It is only a perception, almost certainly male, which took shape in a particular culture and place. Just because it is Greek, ancient and male does not mean it is right. But it may *feel* right, to us who inherit the Greek tradition. The Greek poet–

philosopher Empedocles said the world was governed by two principles, Love and Conflict: sex and war operate together. The first European poem, Homer's *Iliad*, is a moment in a war fought for the sexiest woman in the world, begun when Venus took Helen from her husband and gave her to a lover. An actress – I don't know who – once described men as 'those people who start wars and I have to sleep with'. That link between personified Sex and personified Violence has become a fixture in Western imagination.

There are no worries about potency with Mars, but he is all armour. There is nothing to him but handsome destructiveness. This is masculinity as armour – and what does armour say? That men depend on what they hide behind. As Sting told Q *Magazine* in 1993, 'Being on stage is a fucking war. That's not confidence you see, that's armour. It's not real.'

Greek culture ran on war. Cities were always at war with each other. From 800 BC to AD 300, all men everywhere did active national service. When the Greeks rush out to battle in the *Iliad*, what you see is a glittering mosaic of armour:

> Thick and fast as snowflakes through freezing wind
> The gleaming helmets, embossed shields, ash spears
> And corslets with massive plates came streaming
> From the ships. The gleam of it went up to heaven
> And earth laughed with the flashing bronze.[18]

Armour comes in many pieces – there's a lot of a man to protect. When Achilles has no armour, he cannot fight. Armour is the admission of male vulnerability, the difference between surface hardness and the vulnerable being inside.

In film, the chief icon of that difference is the gun. Under the Hays Code of censorship, film-makers suggested sex in many images like corks popping or trains plunging into tunnels, but guns going off were top of the list. These days, film-makers tease this code. In Pedro Almodovar's film *Live Flesh*, the gun is no longer a cliché of male dominance: it is about failure in sexual confidence. When the pizza delivery boy looks up the woman who took his virginity, she pulls a gun on him. According to sixty years of film symbolism, she is questioning his virility. He struggles – and the gun goes off at the wrong moment, which was what made the sex disappointing in the first place. The weapon stands for male anxiety; men driven to extreme behaviour by sexual inadequacy (a common theme in Almodovar's work). The gun is male sexuality in jeopardy.

When Vulcan makes Achilles a new suit of armour in the *Iliad*, the shield has the whole universe on it – earth, sky, sea, sun, moon, stars – plus two cities. One is full of lawsuits and parties. A bride comes to her wedding; young men dance, women admire them. (Remind you of something?) The other city is besieged by warriors whom the citizens are planning to ambush. Each side 'hauls away the bodies of the enemy'. All around is ploughland, reapers, vines, cattle, an open-air dancing floor. The armed hero is a cosmos in himself. His shield reflects the world: civilization, agriculture, law, conflict, dance, sex, life and death, war and peace. Everything, from heavenly bodies to men's bodies meeting women's in the dance; or women admiring men.

When Achilles puts this armour on, he shimmers: corselet on chest, greaves and silver anklets on legs, silver-studded sword hung from shoulder, huge helmet crested with horsehair and gold. The huge, heavy spear is his father's. 'No one else could wield it.' The description reeks of male love of technology: all those different bits, how they are made, what they are made of; all the aggressive–defensive accoutrements which define a hero, plus a unique weapon you inherit from dad. A hero is his armour, what he knows, what he carries on his outside. Computers, motorbikes, guitars, mixing-decks, route-finders, he flashes the lot at the world. Armour 'is wings to him, it lifts him up'[19]; it is bravado, display of surface which covers vulnerability or need. Men hide behind shiny desks, shiny cars, Armani suits, swaggery rhetoric, technical know-how, displays of knowledge, intimations of enormous salaries, myths of being hard. Iggy Pop liked music that was 'exciting', 'unpredictable', 'hard'. He wanted his band, The Stooges, 'to make a big noise: monolithic, metallic, like a big machine – like the drill presses at the Ford plant, stamping out fenders'.[20] Like armour. Or the biggest erection in heaven.

Son: Naked Omnipotent Baby

Vulcan makes armour, Mars *is* armour; Eros is naked. In Latin, Eros is Amor or Cupid. All those name mean 'desire' or 'love'. Desire and sexual love are the same word, in Greek. Eros is Venus' son – though some Greek writers had fun inventing alternative parents, calling him Venus' servant, child of earth and heaven or of Iris and Zephyr, Rainbow and West Wind.[21] Whatever his relationship to Venus, he is always male youth personified: naked, blind, but 'conquering' everyone, even gods. *Amor vincit omnia*. Infant maleness, winning every battle. Though naked, he is armed. Mars and Eros, the male gods closest to Venus, both have weapons. Eros is 'pain-giver'. He 'goes out to war':

> Eros, you carry sweet joy to the soul
> of your victims, but don't come to me
> with evil and fire, weapons more deadly
> than shafts from the stars.[22]

In more recent popular song, this little gold boy with bow and arrow fills us with joy or chills us to the marrow.

This arrow business was not inevitable. The Greeks did not have to represent desire as a childish, blind, all-conquering archer, but the West has milked the image ever since. The Renaissance adored painting him stringing his bow, whittling the arrows. The arrows say a lot about how we see desire. They are its pain and irrevocability: when you fall in love, you are pierced and inflamed with 'sweet poison' in the wound. They tell you about distance and violence. A spear needs in-your-face contact. Bows and arrow (says Greek poetry) are a coward's weapon – because you can hide and be safe while you shoot. Don't expose yourself, don't get close. Eros makes links that can be desperately unfair and remote. In all versions of *Death In Venice*, the hauntingly beautiful boy is fatal from a distance – a cricketball on glass, a destructive glance that kills one person and is supremely unimportant to the other. In the 'Habanera' from Bizet's *Carmen*, *amor* is 'a rebel bird no one can catch', unpredictable as a bullfight. 'If you don't love me, I love you', sings Carmen. 'And if I love you – watch out!' (*'Prends garde à toi'* – as in the bullring.)

Many operas have gorgeous duets of mutual desire, like the long-drawn-out duo of Tristan and Isolde in Wagner's *Tristan*. Eros can be 'harmony', image of perfect communication, voices mingling like bodies. 'Look at them', says Hornby's hero jealously in *High Fidelity*. 'Entwining the naked melody lines, mingling their saliva, almost!' But even there, what are the two voices singing? 'Love Hurts'. Opera and popsong both come down on the side of love's pain, inequality; separation that can be both physical – love across a crowded room, ships passing in the night – and spiritual. 'I can feel the distance as you breathe', sings Tori Amos in 'China':

> Sometimes, I think you want me to touch you
> But how can I, when you build the Great Wall around
>   you?

The arrows of Eros fly through space, connecting two beings who may be unconnectable. His weapons are absence, silence, gaps.

Eros is a master of communication.[23] (If he had been born in the nineteen thirties, he too would have been an electrician.) But Greek gods are negative as well as positive: they help you in their special sphere of influence, whatever it is, but that is where they get at you, too. Vulcan makes statues mobile and immobilizes his enemies, Mars helps you win wars and makes you lose, and Eros joins lovers but also mucks up the join. He is communication and its opposite. 'How can you be so far away, lying by my side?' sings Beverley Craven ('Promise Me', 1990). Eros is being wounded by someone you have no connection with; the danger, or impossibility, of communication between lovers. Military aggression is often not reciprocal or equal, and nor is desire. You can desire someone desperately, but they may not desire you back. Or there may be an unbridgeable distance between you. 'Sexuality seems to offer a common space to join two souls, but is more likely to be what separates them,' writes a psychoanalyst whose gloomy starting-point is 'the loneliness of each sex'.[24] Some poets said Eros had two arrows, joy and despair. Joy for communication, despair for when it goes wrong.

Some of this pain lies behind Plato's teasing denial that Eros is 'tender or beautiful'. Love, he says in one story, is the accidental offspring of 'Resource' and 'Poverty'. This story begins with a divine birthday party for Venus. Resource ('son of Cunning') gets drunk and goes outside to sleep it off. Poverty, an unsuccessful gatecrasher, is hanging round outside, begging. She has no resources herself, but wants Resource's child: so she lies down by him, gets to work, and conceives Eros:

> So Eros is poor, parched, barefoot, homeless. He sleeps on bare ground with no covers, on doorsteps, or at the roadside in the open air. Like his mother, he is always in want. Like his father, he schemes for everything beautiful and good. He is brave, strenuous, a great hunter, always planning, a master of juggling, witchcraft and words. He is always after wisdom and truth. But the resources he gets hold of always ebb away.[25]

Plato is getting at Eros's vulnerability. Eros is need personified. He may be omnipotent, combining the strengths of his mother's husband and lover (armed and destructive like Mars, creative like Vulcan, burning you with the fires of love), but is also naked, blind, needy as a baby, always losing the gains he makes. Painters often show Venus punishing Eros, taking away his bow and arrow. Or he comes to her crying and hurt. He needs her, needs Sex, as men need women's desire, to 'feel like a real man'.

Rock God Package: The Maleness All Round Sex

World-supremacy, creativity, war, desire. There is male power all round sex; but also male vulnerability and disrepair – castrated father, lame husband, blind baby son – all crippled, disabled, needy, losing power. Mars's armour, that shiny cover-up, is the biggest statement of vulnerability of all. These kinds of male power reappear over and over in rock music and myth: creator, armed warrior, the father whose power must be defied. The rock star sums up the lot. He is all that male power, in relation to sex, combined: the young male, desire incarnate, with the closest, blood-related bond of all, yelling that sex belongs to the young. He also encapsulates the fears these figures sum up. Part of the appeal of Hornby's *High Fidelity* is the way the hero voices exactly this mix. Fantasies about omnipotence, sexual conquest, technological power, defensive armour and creativity blend with crippling fears about losing power, of being a child beside the woman you desire.

Women know very well what comes from this mix of vulnerability, pride and dependence in relation to sex. Not surprising that rock erupted, in places, into violence and misogyny. But that only became clear in the sixties. What you got first was that divine being whom Tokyo groupies hope to meet in bed on the third floor: the rock god, created out of teenage girls' desire. This god, born in the fifties, still rules the airwaves today. Royal power, Elvis the King, Sting the 'king of the jungle'.[26] Power lost: Elvis the lumpen, a fat man dying on a grotesque parody of a throne; Brian Jones, founder of the Stones, face down in his pool. The creator, working at fire and fever pitch: Bob Dylan, John and Paul, Mick and Keith in the studio, 1967 to 1969. The young armed god, Eros as Mars: Elvis in *GI Blues*, hyper-macho Jon Bon Jovi, leader of the eighties American hard rock band which headlined the first ever heavy-metal concert in Moscow's Lenin Stadium in 1989;

Led Zeppelin or Aerosmith, 'Godfather of American Hard Rock', in the armour of the rampant male, summing up the challenge facing women musicians: that rock was, from the start, about male rule.[27]

4 The Holy Axe

The Mississippi Delta, Shining Like a National Guitar

'The blues had a baby and they called it rock 'n' roll,' sang Muddy Waters.[1] Just as Eros, the baby god, has weapons as omnipotent as those of the war-god, rock 'n' roll gods have a weapon too, and got it from the blues. The ultimate pared-down persona of sixties Bob Dylan, the visionary singer-traveller, a world unto himself, a one-man-band with guitar and harmonica, came from the early male blues musicians. It was they who made the guitar the great totem instrument of rock music: the 'easy rider', the instrument that symbolizes male power, musically, technically, emotionally, sexually.

Before all this, the guitar had a humble profile in the West. Only Spain appreciated it as its cousin the lute was appreciated in sixteenth-century Europe: as the one instrument which, held close to a man's body, can become a whole world of subtlety and power. The instrument which uses harmony and rhythm, (which express a shared, social world) to support a personal single thing: that single melody. Outside Spain, piano, drums, violin or woodwind divided this power between them.[2]

The guitar came up in the world from blues to rock music, zero to hero, as a male image: rising up from the ground, saying for people with no power or money, 'I can go down every road with just this. Music and sex, laughter and tears, everything that matters to other people. I carry with me the power to make a world.' The self-romance of a man alone, with nothing but his capacity to play, sing and make love, plus his 'mojo hand', a little bag slung round the neck. The mojo was a magic charm, a legacy from African magic, worn only by men. It brought luck. It could help in games of chance but it was mainly for sexual conquest: an erotic charm, bringing you luck with women. Muddy Waters has 'got his mojo working': it just (damnably) isn't working on the woman he's trying for that night. The lyrics of early bluesmen are full of mojo power. In this scenario, again, your male self-image depends on female desire, on your capacity to arouse it. The maleness of early blues is an existential swagger empowered by the guitar, a virility empowered by magic. All histories of blues carry photos of bluesmen with their empowering instrument on their lap. The other empowering instrument is hidden. Male equipment, the family jewels, quintessence of masculinity: the one thing you know is yours.

The guitar was also a move from country to city. Early players covered small dances and drinking-houses in rural areas in the Mississippi Delta. The twenties bluesman Blind Lemon Jefferson led the archetypal life and sang the archetypal songs: fluid images of violence, death, wandering, fleeting relationships, social wretchedness, delivered in an amused, ironic, resilient voice.[3] The blues guitar was first recorded on plantations in that decade: as the vehicle for describing a rubbish world with tenderness, fury, loneliness, laughter, detachment, sympathy and wit.

Thirties bluesmen began to base themselves in cities, with burgeoning night-spots, but went on travelling, playing the country gigs that first paid them. Lonnie Johnson, born 1894, whose career began when he won a blues contest in a St Louis vaudeville theatre in 1925, called himself one of the first to sing urban blues. Cities were now the place where people and their problems, sex with its laughs and sorrows, were really at:

> My blues is built on human beings, how they live, their heartaches and shifts they go through with love affairs, things like that. That's what I write about. It's understanding others.[4]

But the all-time 'King of Delta blues' was Robert Johnson. He grew up in Robinsonville, a music-struck boy with eye trouble in a north Mississippi cotton community, forty miles south of Memphis. He went south to Hazelhurst and became a professional musician, playing at country suppers, and came back in 1930. He based himself in Helena, Arkansas, a river settlement and big musical centre, but went on travelling, playing all over – the Mississippi and Arkansas Delta, South Mississippi, Eastern Tennessee. Son House, Willie Brown, Charlie Patten and Ike Zinnerman had all acted as musical mentors; now they found he outstripped them all. He influenced everyone who came through: Sonny Boy Williamson II, Howlin' Wolf, Robert Nighthawk, Elmore James.

There are a thousand legends about his playing. His guitar played anything a piano could, 'talked with him like no one in the world could do'. He'd chat and drink as the radio played a new song, then play that song exactly, note for note. He tried out unusual tunings; he had bought his astonishing skill by selling his soul to Satan; Satan himself tuned that guitar. Johnson guarded that skill jealously. He might play with his back turned, to stop you copying his fingering. If you asked how he played something, he shut you up by saying 'Just like you'. If you eyed his fingers too close he would get up and go and not be seen for months. He was a musicianly Lone Ranger.[5]

The twenty-nine songs he recorded inspired musicians at two key stages in the move from blues to rock. Muddy Waters heard the recordings and took their impact with him to Chicago in the forties.[6] In 1963, the records, with Johnson's marriage of demented emotion and dazzling technical possibility, were a revelation to Eric Clapton, Brian Jones, Keith Richards. 'It came as a shock', said Clapton, 'that there could be something that powerful.' Keith Richards heard Johnson when he first visited Brian Jones's bed-sit:

> All he had was a chair, a record-player and a few records. When I first heard it I said, 'Who's that?' 'Robert Johnson.' I said, 'Yeah, but who's the guy playing with him?' Because I was hearing two guitars. It took me a long time

to realize he was doing it all by himself. It was like listening to Bach.'

Pure technique, pure passion, pure control. These boys formed their own style in measuring themselves against him, trying to get *that*, use *that*, imitate *that*. 'I realized I couldn't play his music,' said Clapton. 'It was too deep for me to deal with.' But they tried – because artists are carnivores. 'It became a question of finding something that had a riff, a form that could be interpreted simply in a band format,' said Clapton. Keith worked out with Mick how they could use 'Love in Vain Blues':

> I sat around playing it all kinds of styles. A little bit more country, a little bit more formalized, and Mick felt comfortable with that. In a way it was, 'We've got to do this song, one way or another.' Because it was just so beautiful, the titles, the lyrics, the ideas, the rhymes, just everything about it.

The songs brought them formidably up against their own limits, emotional as much as musical. 'Certain songs I wouldn't touch,' says Clapton: 'They were just too fragile, too beautiful, to be arranged. I was trying to draw out the spirit of what was being said as much as the form or technique, to extract as much emotional content while respecting the form.' The lyrics, the themes, were as inspiring as his guitar. 'A song like "Hellhound on My Trail" ', said Clapton, 'is hardly there':

> It's in the air – what he doesn't say, what he doesn't play. It's so light and menacing at the same time. His music is the most powerful cry I think you can find in the human voice. When I first heard it, it called to me in my confusion, it seemed to echo something I always felt.

'He came out with such compelling themes,' said Keith. 'Subject-matter, apart from music and performance. I've never heard anybody before or since use the form and bend it quite so much to make it work for himself.'[7]

This was a musical and emotional response, for the power of Johnson's lyrics and the legends of his life matched to a T the extra-musical values which sixties rock music assembled round guitar-technique. Driven ferocity, menace, metaphysical *angst*, sexual rage, violent themes and violent death, a Faustian bargain and Faustian self, became part of the sixties image-package of male technical virtuosity. Something dark, wild and bitter, in music, words, and life: the ultimate blend of music and virility.

Erection, Impotence and Rage

Johnson's lyrics have a schizoid surprise in them, a flawless mix of silence and metaphor which seems nearly out of control; but the song-form, irony and playing contain the lot. Theme-wise, it is a high-wire balancing act. You never know what's coming next:

> From Memphis to Norfolk is a thirty-six hours' ride.
> A man is like a prisoner and he's never satisfied.
> A woman is like a dresser, some man always ramblin' its
> drawers.
> It cause so many men wear an apron overall.[8]

Stunning playing, plus the lyric revelation of throwaway menace; love, travel, 'evil thoughts', and a demonic being-out-of-kilter with everything around you. He waits at the crossroads; no one sees. He walks 'side by side' with devils: he opens the door to them. ('I said "Hello Satan", I believe it's time to go'.) And he does it all with exemplary irony. 'You may bury my body, down by the highway side,/So my old evil spirit can get a Greyhound bus and ride.' That Greyhound bus is a flick of self-laughter from the bottom of an unspeakable well, a human nod to everyday living just at the moment he's giving the whole human thing right up.

Above all, you get sex. The way bluesmen used guitar to howl out male sexual need – the whole rainbow, musical, emotional and lyrical, despairing longing to swaggery arrogance, jealous rage to violent frustration, cold indifference to feverish crawling – was a key factor in the development of rock. 'Uum, better find my mama soon', sings Jefferson in 'Black Snake Moan' (1926). 'Woke up this morning, black snake was makin' such a ruckus in my room.' They did it with wonderful wit, amusement, irony, and sharp everyday images; from the farm, from domestic technology. 'Now I feel like milkin' and my cow won't come', sings Johnson. 'I feel like churnin' it and my milk won't turn. I'm cryin' pleeease don't do me wrong.' His woman can 'squeeze my lemon till the juice runs down my leg'. (Led Zeppelin got the image here.) 'I wanna wind your little phonograph, Just to hear your little motor moan,' he tells 'Beatrice' in 'Phonograph Blues'.

Playing guitar displayed what you could do when you'd got your mojo working up to form. Some bluesmen handled their instruments, as the folklorist Alan Lomax devotedly reported, 'with guitar butting against the hips, neck pointing straight ahead, in a masturbatory way.'[9] Erections are a big blues theme. Take Jefferson's 'Black Snake Moan':

> Black snake is evil, black snake is all I see,
> I woke up this morning, he was moved in on me.
> Um-um, black snake crawling in my room,
> Yes, some pretty mama better get this black snake soon.

The eighties heavy-metal band Whitesnake made its own version of this (1983), snarling 'Slide it in, baby'. But blues was made by grown-ups who ironized erections as they ironized everything else. 'Well, wonder where that black snake's gone', ponders Jefferson. 'Lord, that black snake, mama, done run my darlin' home.' White rock was made by younger men, and for its first three decades took its own erections very seriously indeed.

What white boys did not pick up on in blues sex – until punk ironized and debunked cock rock – was the other side of the erection theme. Impotence is also a major theme in male blues. Bluesmen sing about it with savageness, pathetic collapse and feathery wit, all at once. 'What makes me love my woman, she can really do the Georgia crawl', sings Blind Willie McTell (the subject, himself, of one of Dylan's songs) – but alas, he's not up to his woman. 'Feel like a broke-down engine, ain't got no drivin' wheel.' Johnson's Beatrice has 'broke my windin' chain':

> My needles have got rusty baby
> And they won't play at all
> Mmm Beatrice I love my phonograph
> And I'm 'bout to lose my mind
> Why'n't you bring your clothes back home
> Baby, and try me one more time.

These themes, erection and impotence, belong with the misogyny, violence and rage that runs through male blues, especially Johnson. 'I'm gonna beat my woman until I get satisfied', he sings. 'She's making whoopee in Hell tonight'.[10]

Blues guitar began simply as a powering accompaniment to the voice, as the mojo charm swinging under the shirt accompanied and empowered the player's sexual adventures. But like the guitar, the mojo rose in importance after early blues. By forties rhythm and blues (copied by sixties rock), it was associated with the instrument that accompanied that male voice. The guitar acquired the same resonance of magical potency. The magazine *Mojo*, which stresses the history as well as current trends in rock music, was launched in 1993, and chose its title to appeal to readers in their thirties and forties who knew the word from Muddy Waters and the Rolling Stones. (See 'the mojo filter' in the Beatles' 'Come Together' on *Abbey Road*.) Male blues gave the guitar its sexual magic. It is the instrument that brings you women. Potency is *the* extra-musical value of the rock guitar.

Cock rock began here. Straight or gay, very few men aged between thirty-eight and forty-eight now, in 2000, have not 'looked at themselves in a mirror as teenagers and imagined themselves with a guitar', said a friend of mine. Amazing numbers of middle-aged males – writers and journalists seem particularly prone – played guitar in groups, or dreaming alone, when young.

How male this attachment is to the guitar, you can see from 'air guitar' – when a guitarless man closes his eyes, pushes his lips into a Mick Jagger pout, goes 'der-dummm', and fiddles about with his right hand at crotch-level. Strumming is the same motion as a man wanking: forefinger and thumb together, a loop of space, a fillable O, in the middle, fingers down in a line behind. (Male writers of the same generation, Martin Amis and Nicholson Baker, used 'strumming' to mean masturbating.) The rock guitar let you put on stage, quite literally, how you feel yourself.

Playing guitar is a million times harder than masturbating but it does also symbolize that act so crucial to male teenagers. And there is something even more important. 'The bluesmen's skill with guitar gave them power among their music-and-dance-mad brothers,' says Lomax. 'One man and guitar could turn on a whole dance hall.'[11] Back to Dylan, his guitar-and-harmonica act. The guitar makes how you feel yourself (in every sense) important to other people; makes something taboo and private enormously public; makes how you feel matter to thousands of people, the whole world. A guitar riff is aural erection, rising up saying, 'This is Me'.

A Man Mattering to Other People

This is the core of the problem for women guitarists. 'There is no reason for rock to be male,' I once read in a book on women bands. But historically, there is a monumental reason. Equating the guitar with maleness was part of rock's pre-history in male blues. The irony is that though rock 'n' roll came from male blues, the first people to record blues, and sell blues records, were women.

The first blues recording was Mamie Smith's 'Crazy Blues' in 1920, the year American women got the vote. In 1923 came Bessie Smith's 'Down Hearted Blues' and Ma Rainey's 'Bo

Weevil Blues'. The Paramount Catalogue for 1924 had no male blues but a load of women: like Ida Cox, Lucille Hegamin, Rose Henderson, Ma Rainey.[12] Vocally, these singers had deep links to the church, whereas male blues came from field songs. As entertainers, the women came from vaudeville: they were showy, stage-oriented, showbiz to the last sequin. With a supporting team of musicians they 'travelled all over the world', as Memphis Minnie sang in 1940, memorializing Ma Rainey. Rainey sometimes appeared on stage bursting out from a huge, cardboard cut-out Victrola, embodying that great new mystery, recorded sound. Their power, apart from the musicianship, was in voice, glamour, self-presentation, *entourage*. They became legends in their time, made fantastic recordings and a lot of money – for a while. What they did *not* do was play guitar.

In the mid-twenties, male records began appearing: bluesmen accompanying themselves on acoustic guitar. The great recording years were from 1927 until the Depression brought the record industry to a near-standstill in 1933. When recording restarted, vaudeville's day was over, blueswomen were less in demand, men were turning to urban and finally electric blues. In jazz, women instrumentalists played piano, trumpet, saxophone, ukulele, accordion, reeds, vibes – anything but guitar. Not till the forties were there woman guitarists in jazz, and their numbers were tiny compared to women on other instruments.[13]

Some women did sing country blues and play guitar like bluesmen; a few (Mattie Delaney, Ethel McCoy, Rose Lee Hill, for instance) were recorded. But they were rare. (They didn't have a mojo working for them, either.) Women on electric guitar were even rarer. Sister Rosetta Tharpe took up electric guitar soon after T-Bone Walker. On some records she sounds like Chuck Berry nearly a decade earlier. She sang mainly gospel music, though the gospel community rejected her for joining gospel to those sinful blues. She was also a respected band leader. Memphis Minnie was as much a feature of the Chicago era as Muddy Waters. Her voice had a hard authority – she won blues contests against Big Bill Broonzy and Muddy. But she was the exception that proved the rule that the guitar was a male thing. She played 'like a man'. She also 'gambled like a dog', chewed tobacco and sang with a spit-bowl beside her ('even when she was singing, she kept that tobacco in her mouth'), and once broke a guitar on the head of a puppy who chewed her wig. Even in a woman's hands, 'guitar' said 'male'. As Alan Lomax said about bluesmen he recorded, 'holding and manipulating such a sex-symbol in public seems an act appropriate only to men'.[14]

Maleness was paramount also in the other main guitar source of rock 'n' roll. When rock 'n' roll is particularly conservative in its harmonies, textures or emotions, it is drawing on its country music legacy. The standard story is that blues married country music and made rock 'n' roll; which means black music marrying white. But country music was never only white. From its commercial beginnings, 'country' was a hybrid, mingling many popular and religious Southern styles, black and white. 'If Chuck Berry had been white he'd have been a country singer,' said Buck Owens, an influential country singer who, like many others – A. P. Carter, Bill Monroe, Bob Wills, Hank Williams, Johnny Cash – had had a black mentor.[15]

Yet the specific male edge which country music handed on to rock 'n' roll did come more from white communities than black. Blues gave the male guitar sexiness, violence, energy; but country gave it a grim, paternalistic authority. Like the blues, country music was first recorded in the early twenties. Jimmie Rodgers, 'Father of country music', sold during the Depression to rural people moving from workless, very poor country areas into southern cities, finding things just as tough there.[16] Early country is the voice of a community facing a life of harshness, collecting all its bodies and dreams round a man with a guitar – as in Steinbeck's vignette from *The Grapes of Wrath*:

> A man brought out his guitar to the front of his tent. And he sat on a box to play, and everyone in the camp moved slowly in toward him, drawn in toward him.

Country music saw life as a struggle: this is how it is, how it's always been; nothing we can do, folks, but share it. Steinbeck's singer voices the misery, memories and dreams of migrants fleeing starvation for worse misery in the treacherous El Dorado of California. 'The country musician', said Hank Williams, most famous of all, 'sings more sincere than most 'cause he was raised rougher than most.' His music 'has to be played with feeling'.[17] The man played, says Steinbeck,

> and the people moved slowly in on him until the circle was closed and tight, and then he sang, 'Ten-Cent Cotton and Forty-Cent Meat'. And the circle sang softly with him. And he sang, 'Why Do You Cut Your Hair Girls?' And the circle sang.

The message is desperate economic entrapment for a whole community: one man playing, that lone-man-bare-resonance sound, voicing common suffering, gathering all his listeners, like Orpheus, into the song, in sadness that is 'like rest, like sleep':

> And now the group was welded to one thing, one unit, so that in the dark the eyes of the people were inward . . . And after a while the man with the guitar stood up and yawned. Good night, folks, he said.
> And they murmured, Good night to you.
> And each wished he could pick a guitar, because it is a gracious thing.

Feeling, and the technique to get it across, was everything. 'Many men can chord a guitar, but perhaps this man was a picker', says Steinbeck. 'There you have something – the deep chords beating, beating, while the melody runs on the strings like little footsteps. Heavy hard fingers marching on the frets.'

Heavy hard fingers? Male ones. The tenderness of something rough, despairing, violent. Williams, *âme damnée* of country music, drank himself to death at twenty-nine. The bass-baritone of Johnny Cash, with its dark, close-to-tears thrill of pain, is also 'flat and grim, the way the white poverty-stricken South was flat and grim'. Another singer, George Jones, was often violent – 'the man cares too much', said one interviewer – and his phrasing of the bare words comes over with an open razor pain.[18]

All this feeling in early country music is not just any old feeling; it is male. Women are betrayers. Love means male pain. When the first few women started singing country and occasionally playing guitar, they were not loners like Hank Williams; they sang in family groups. Country music laments the *status quo* but supports it to the hilt. Family values reign: female playing, like female life, is ruled by men. Maybelle Carter, 'one of America's most influential guitarists', invented the 'Carter lick', which combines melody with brushing the strings for rhythm. Along with Jimmie Rodgers, she showed what the guitar could do on country music records. But she did it through The Carter Family. Her sister Sara's husband A. P. ran the show. The three made a record in 1927. 'Aw', said Sara, 'ain't nobody gonna pay that much money to hear us sing.' But they did, thousands of them. A. P. went off hunting for more songs in the Virginia mountains with a black musician called Riddle, who 'played mean blues guitar' and helped Maybelle with technique.[19] But the famous thirties players went on being men. 'Country music was a man's world,' said a country woman singer who grew up in those years. 'You didn't hear women on the radio when I was growing up. I never thought anything about it. Men came first, men dominated,' said another.[20] The big theme, 'crying over you', was a male-voice lament over a treacherous, hard-hearted female flirt.

The female riposte, when it came, was also male-orchestrated, from another family group. In 1952 Hank Thompson had a big country hit called 'The Wild Side of Life'. It put the standard complaint about a no-good woman in a sneerily catchy way. 'I didn't know God made honky-tonk angels/I might have known you wouldn't make a wife'. Johnny Wright, a male singer whose wife had a lovely, resonant, bruised voice, got hold of a reply song, also written by a man: 'It Wasn't God Who Made Honky-

Tonk Angels'. This song cheekily, uniquely, blamed men for women's pain. He gave it to his wife, Kitty Wells; she sang and played with Wright and his brother-in-law, Jack Anglin. The record was a wild success. They did many more. Kitty Wells gave country music a female perspective, became fantastically popular singing songs (written by men) which complained that women stayed home with kids while men ran around. She had a fine and tranquil life herself, none of the grief her songs went on about. She sang with her husband, and for him.[21]

These women appeared with their family under the man's name (until the woman's voice became the group's star attraction, which sometimes caused problems). The photos say it all. A guitar held on the woman's lap, close to her body, domestic as a pet. The guitar as hearth, womb, a babe in arms, flanked by the family-group which is guarded, like a bison herd, by males. In the nineties, male control of country music loosened up a bit. Women's songs began tackling issues like wife abuse, yet they were still careful not to alienate middle America. 'None of them call themselves feminist,' said Joanna Bailey, Director of the 1998 TV documentary *Naked Nashville*. Country music stood for male control, even when women's voices mourn the pain men cause or women's fingers shiver the strings. Family values, written into country harmonies, embedded in the acoustic's hollow body, are the resonant safety net for country music's pain. When this lot meshed with blues in the fifties to make rock 'n' roll, it brought a resentful paternalism, a grown-up 'that's how it's always been' authority, to the way a man with guitar matters to other people. And ungrown-up male rock music liked all that just fine.

Guitar Hero to Rock Divinity

When Alan Lomax recorded Muddy Waters in 1941 with acoustic guitar, he was looking for Robert Johnson, who was dead. Lomax found Muddy instead, working in the fields. By recording him, he set him on the path to Chicago, to give the stamp of publicity to that electric guitar – which broadcast to the whole world the urgency of male blues. In its journey from the blues, the guitar spotlit the male supremacism vital to rock. From the moment the electric guitar got going in the forties, great performers kept adding new things, technically or personally, to the drive towards male display. Musically, you got showier fingerings, vocal melisma, longer solos.[22] Mythically, you got a whole poetics of swagger, developing a way of using a power tool responsive to the slightest touch. The guitar hero was born.

Technical changes kept propelling the player's persona towards heroic status. The guitar began as accompanying instrument; the thirties made it a soloist. Players like Django Reinhardt, strong candidate for the title of first guitar hero (he had also lost two of his left-hand fingers), gave it daring, inventiveness, playfulness, passion. Chet Atkins used it 'to banter like a butcher or brag like a senator'. This virtuosity was heroically sexy. 'As a young man Chet Atkins was diffident: as a player, he figured how to flirt with dazzling subtlety.'[23] Musical dexterity was coded sexual – and forties technique, increasingly virtuoso, was also increasingly aggressive. 'Don't You be Messin' with the Man', sings Muddy with threatening urgency. 'Grab your telephone', snarls Howlin' Wolf. 'Evil is goin' on. I'm warning you brother, better watch your happy home.'[24]

When Duane Eddy played the whole melody line in 'Moovin' 'n' Groovin'' (1958), he became the first pop 'guitar star'. Pop guitar had been mainly backup rhythm with occasional solo. Now it took centre stage. 'Boys place a high value on being good with your hands,'[25] and sixties guitarists – Clapton, Richards, Peter Green – listened, tried out and increasingly invested in new technique. Keith Richards spent hours trying to figure out how Scotty Moore fingered his solos on Elvis recordings. Over in the States, Lou Reed was doing the same:

> I liked 'Ooby Dooby' and 'Down the Line' and was interested in the guitar playing. Roy Orbison was doing it himself!

I liked watching Ricky Nelson because James Burton was in the back playing guitar. You'd always get to hear one of these amazing guitar solos: I'd wonder how the hell he did it. That's one of the reasons I learnt guitar, to be able to play like that. I'd try over and over to play the solo from 'Hello Mary Lou'.[26]

Boys everywhere dreamed of forming bands. By 1967 most British blues-based groups were dominated by the sound of their guitarists – who were tearing into new ways of making sound, searching for new sound through distortion, volume, new tunings and possibilities on this now perfected electric instrument. As Robert Palmer says,

> Once a certain volume threshold has been passed, an electric guitar becomes another instrument. Its tuning flexibility can now set up sympathetic resonances between the strings, so that techniques such as open tunings and bare chords can get the entire instrument humming sonorously, sustained by amplification until it becomes a representation in sound of the wonder of creation ... It doesn't just 'ring'. It produces overtones, sum and difference tones, interference patterns, and other acoustical phenomena.

The licks or riffs were often more important than the songs; so were the enharmonic effects, the resonances set up by new tunings, the interaction of tones, the vibrations from notes pitched beyond any ordinary volume level.[27]

All this made the electric guitar a sacred instrument for players and fans. Like any shrine, the 'Church of the Sonic Guitar' had priests, worshippers and gods. Hendrix, 'the guitarist's guitarist', 'the Robert Johnson of the Sixties', 'really the first cat to totally play *electric* guitar', reinvented the rock guitar's vocabulary and symbolism. At the 1967 Monterey festival, Brian Jones announced 'The Hendrix Experience'. After some inspired playing, Hendrix said 'I'm gonna sacrifice something I really love', and set his guitar on fire. He humped it, bowed to it, threw the smouldering splinters into the audience and left the stage – leaving the amp on. The audience heard the strings snap and curl. It was now official – rock guitar meant dazzling musicianly innovation plus passion for turning all experience, all sound, into art. Hendrix was 'primitive and classical, further out than anyone else', 'the finest rock appreciation of blues you'll ever hear', soul, blues, jazz and rock fused in one personality; a hero.[28]

In Greek terms, a hero is a man with a bit of god in him, divinity that flares in heroic daring and the way women keel over before him. Hendrix was also a world-wide sex symbol, a guitar ejaculating over the world: far-out innovation plus daring technique went with legendary sexuality. A guitar hero, brandishing the magic weapon that turned him into a god.

It was particularly the solo, the riff, which made the guitar hero a rock god. A riff is an exploit: the killing spree of a Homeric hero on the battlefield, Sir Lancelot galloping alone into the forest like Jimmy Page of Led Zeppelin doing 'Black Dog'. You hold your breath, caught up in the daring, the far-outness, the risk. Dreaming a riff is dreaming sexual heroics. Hornby's hero sees his friend come into the shop humming a Clash riff: 'Actually, "humming" is the wrong word: he's making that guitar noise all little boys make, the one where you stick your lips out, clench your teeth and go DA-DA! Barry is thirty-three years old.'[29]

The urgency, volume and power of electricity doubled the blues equation of musical and sexual power. It amplified everything: sexuality, self-image and sound. With guitar and amp, says one guitar book, you can 'unchain emotion' while 'testing the limits of your dexterity'.[30] Rock 'n' roll was the sound of the male teenage body, and the symbolism of its music – swollen volume plus 'dexterity' – is deeply male. Electricity gave boys control of their volume. 'Energy can be directed', sing the Kings ('Switchin' to Glide', 1980). 'I'm turning it up, I'm turning it down'. Electric equipment is a fast track to sex. In rock shop windows the display of different-sized amps, the 'Enhancer',

'Equalizer', 'Turbo Overdrive', is a pornography of male parts. The neck of the guitar lengthened; so did the strap, to hold it at crotch level. You plug it in with snaky cables, dark writhing magic wielded by male technicians from the mixing desk at a gig – the power area in concert venues which men hang on to, and keep women out of, long after they have accepted them on stage. 'PA crews are sort of macho,' said one woman guitarist to a researcher. 'You're not taken seriously,' said another:

> PA crews ask men what sound they want. They don't ask *you* what sound you want. Many times I've said, 'We want a sharper sound – take more off the bass', and they turn round and look at you and think, 'What does she know?'

'You convince them you can do the mixing', said another. 'You're sitting there and he's right behind you, waiting for you to make a mistake.'[31]

So an instrument originally in woman's shape became the supreme phallic symbol whose male mystique extends to all technology around it, accompanying a male voice. But, increasingly, as weapon, not vehicle. The hero's spear, not his charger. Your guitar is your 'axe', but only, so jazz musicians tell me, *if it belongs to a man*. Men, I was told, never say 'axe' of a woman's instrument. Playing guitar is laying about you with your chopper.

5 Voices in the Sea of Desire

In the Hero's Way:
Monsters, Father-figures, the Underworld, and Women

Knights ride into forests full of sorcerers and dragons and most Greek heroes have a journey and enemies to their name. Theseus makes his way to Athens across the Isthmus of Corinth teeming with brigands like Procrustes, who lays travellers on a wrong-sized bed, chopping or stretching them to death to make them fit. Theseus deals with the brigands, cleans up the Isthmus, gets to Athens and then on to Crete where he kills the bull-man Minotaur. Hercules, 'saviour of Greece', travels everywhere doing his Labours which rid Greece of dangerous boars and lions, the hundred-headed Hydra, and hosts who feed their guests to flesh-eating mares. Bellerophon kills the flame-breathing goat-lion-snake Chimaera; Perseus lights out for the Gorgons' land to kill Medusa.

Many of these journeys are quests, set by wicked father-figures blocking the hero from his rightful throne; they hope he'll perish on the way. A son's-eye-view of the struggle against father and the parent-run world. Kronos castrates his father, Heaven, and takes over world-rule, and human heroes tend to journey and struggle against dangers imposed by another older man, whom they eventually defeat to get their throne. Hercules' Labours are set by the man who usurped a throne intended for Hercules. Theseus journeys towards his father, king of Athens, then goes on to Crete to rescue Athenians from the Cretan king who feeds Athenians to the Minotaur. Perseus is barred from his throne by a king who asks for the head of the Gorgon, whose eyes turn to stone whoever meets her gaze. When Perseus brings it and holds it up, the king gets what he asked for but is also turned to stone. The usurper of Jason's throne asks for the Golden Fleece, from the other side of the Aegean Sea. Jason gathers other heroes on his ship, the *Argo*, calls them Argonauts, and brings back the Fleece after escaping the Clashing Rocks (which pulverize ships), harpies, storms, battles and a dragon.

Heroes also travel to Hades. Hercules goes there on one Labour to kidnap its three-headed guard-dog. Theseus goes for bravura, to kidnap the Queen of the Dead. He fails, gets stuck there, and has to be rescued by Hercules. Orpheus goes to get Eurydice, and fails. The god Dionysus goes to recover his dead mother. Going down there doesn't work if you go to carry off women, but does if you go to learn. Aeneas gets shown the future of Rome, the city he will found. Ulysses goes to ask a dead seer how to get home. *Katabasis*, 'descent' to the underworld, now features in psychological reveries about shamans visiting other worlds; or the 'inner journey' undergone by spiritual heroes like poets and psychoanalytic patients; and in a lot of pop psychology. 'Search for the hero inside yourself, search for the secrets you hide,' M People are singing (lyrics by M. Pickering and P. Heard) on my radio. 'Until you find the key to your life'. Which is also what Aeneas and Ulysses go to find.

Above all, the hero encounters women. He captures, fights, gets helped by, fallen in love with and endangered by them; and gets rid of them. Part of being a hero is being a lover. Bruce Springsteen sings 'Lovin' you is a man's job'; Sheryl Crow asks if you're strong enough to be her man? But the hero is a mobile lover, gathering negligible moss, moving on to the next patch of grass. Hercules and Theseus have a series of women. Hercules dies because of them while chasing a younger woman. His wife gives him clothes soaked in what she thinks is love potion, and turns out to be corrosive poison.

The free-wheeling hero on the road, a high theme of male sixties rock, harks back to these myths as well as to the roving bluesman. Father-like kings stop young men getting their throne? See anti-parent rebellion. Monsters? Jim Morrison faces darkness and huge snakes in the desert; heavy metal has grotesque gothic battles. But the main point of rock's male journey is leaving girls behind. 'If I'm free it's 'cos I'm always running,' Hendrix said once. 'I'll love them and I'll leave them, break their heart and deceive them, everywhere I go', sings Paul Young with unforgettable smugness (see Chapter 7), in Marvin Gaye's 'Wherever I Lay my Hat, that's my Home'.

Why are women the greatest danger as well as greatest help? Why do you have to escape them? Look back at the greatest hero journey of all. The Church Fathers took pagan Odysseus as an image of the Christian soul surmounting every obstacle and temptation in its journey to God. Ulysses, Odysseus's Roman name, is the great Western image of the human journey through life – and also an utterly male one. The *Odyssey* is the archetypal male voyage of world-discovery and self-discovery. Male writers from James Joyce to Cavafy have taken it as pattern of a man's journey to self-understanding. The sea is the main enemy, what Ulysses must get through. Its male god Neptune shipwrecks him, makes him lose ships, rafts, companions. He also faces giant cannibals and the lotus (which makes you forget your home and identity). But most of the *Odyssey*'s dangers are female. In the sea, Scylla the multi-dog-headed underwater predator and Charybdis the whirlpool who swallows ships and sailors. On shore, Sirens sit in a meadow littered with skin rotting on the bones of men drawn on to rocks by their song. The places where Ulysses wastes most time are the kinder islands, where he sleeps with goddesses. Circe turns his men to pigs and tries to turn him into one too. He stops all that, but stays there a year not as pig but as man, having sex with her. Calypso saves him after shipwreck and offers him immortality, hoping to keep him in her bed for ever. The gods make her give him up, but she feels he is choosing his wife instead of her. 'I know she's not beautiful like you,' he says. 'But I still want to go home.'[1]

Why escape female things? Because they swamp you, cover

you, pull you in and down. Every danger Ulysses meets, male or female, tries to drown or swallow him. Scylla, Charybdis and the Cyclops swallow his men, the lotus douses their memory of who they are. But it is typically a female thing to do: see Bruce Springsteen's 'Cover Me' (*Born in the USA*, 1984), or Yeats's poem 'On Women', where woman 'covers' what the man brings, 'As with her flesh and bone'. Calypso means 'Coverer'. She and Circe keep Ulysses in bed. Women suck you down. 'When he comes my way, I'll do my best to make him stay', sings Billie Holiday in Gershwin's 'The Man I Love'. Poignantly, from her side. Women hold you back from where you belong: your island, where you are king. For Ulysses to get his life back, he has to get away from her. Men must keep moving. From their fixed places, bedrooms, caves, islands, women detain men in dark hollows. That's the male fantasy laid down in myth. Kat Bjelland mocks it in her song 'Swamp Pussy', where her voice is exactly that dark femaleness, threatening male identity from that caricature of female biology: the swamp, the abyss.[2]

Song is women's strategy for enticing men down, covering them up. Like Sirens, or mermaids. Ulysses' men hear Circe before they see her. 'A goddess or woman is walking up and down in there beside a loom, singing sweetly so all the floor echoes. Let's call her.' Woman's voice is her temptation, bait for the physical entrapment to come. 'The Sirens sent out their lovely voices and my heart longed to listen'. Women singing – say, Carmen in Bizet's 'Habanera' – are an ancient emblem of seduction. In *King Lear*, the king considers hiring a new servant and asks him how old he is. 'Not so young', replies the servant, 'as to love a woman for singing.'[3] 'Calypso' is now the generic name for a lotus-like island song about forgetting care.

Ulysses gets away. He shakes off all coverings the sea throws at him, sweet voices, deep-tapestried beds, deep-wooded islands full of shadows and song. His companions yield to appetite and drown. He is the self-controlled hero inherited by Hollywood and Western romance, making his way steadily to his true identity, true home, leaving behind on her island any yearning Billie Holiday who tries to make him stay.

Birthplace of Venus:
Men Master It, Women Are Carried Away on It

The sea is a hoary pop image of ungovernable love. 'Am I the moth or flame? I'm all at sea', says Gershwin's 'But Not For Me'. 'I'm a ship without a sail', urges Lorenz Hart. 'Love took over my heart like an ocean breeze,' sing the Carpenters. 'I knew I was losing,' sings Karen's voice with its freight of pain. 'Love was washed away with the drifting tide.' On the sea of love, of sexuality, you get blown off course and drown. 'I know the deep blue sea will soon be calling me,' mourns Billie Holiday.[4]

That sea, where Heaven's genitals fell, where Sex was born, is the great place of danger and adventure in Western myth and song because these myths were invented by a nation of sailors. If rainforest-dwellers or desert tribes had laid down the roots of our mythology, our imagination would run on very different symbols. From the Bronze Age on, the Greeks knew sea dangers all too well. A hero could master the sea with technology (well, rudder and sail) plus gods and luck on his side. But you needed a boat; which women, of course, never had. Men carry women across the sea. Throughout Greek myth and deep into all Western art, women are constantly waiting on the shore – think of Meryl Streep, on the poster for *The French Lieutenant's Woman* – for a lover's sail to show on the horizon.

When Theseus faces the Minotaur in Crete, the Cretan princess Ariadne helps. She falls for him, gives him a string to tie to a fixed point (women are good at fixing points) outside the labyrinth where the Minotaur lurks. Then he takes her off in his boat. When Jason has to tackle a dragon guarding the Golden Fleece, the princess Medea falls for him, deals with the dragon; he takes her (plus Fleece) off in his boat. When Paris of Troy falls for Helen, wife of a Greek king, what does he do? Takes her off in his boat. Women fall in love; the hero sweeps them away on his vehicle. In the sea where sex is born, women are passengers, depending on man's mobile power. 'Let me ride, just let me ride, let me ride on your grace for a while,' sings P. J. Harvey in 'Teclo'. As Bessie Smith puts it (in the words of L. and W. Wilson), 'You take me for a buggy ride.'

The prototype is Europa, the Syrian princess whom Jupiter in bull-disguise carries off into the sea on his back. He swims her to Crete and makes love to her there.[5] 'Rape' means 'snatching away', from Latin *rapio*, 'I plunder' (as in 'The Rape of the Sabine Women', who were 'carried off', or Alexander Pope's satire *The Rape of the Lock*). When a woman is raped, she is first swept away from her father, her home: and often, in Greek myth, over the sea. That sea-journey is a shorthand symbol for the rape itself. The rape of Europa produced Minos, king of Europe's first great civilization. 'Europe' begins with a girl carried off into the sea; with woman carried away.

These rape stories all explain international relations in the Greeks' breathtakingly competitive contact with their Eastern neighbours, like Troy. Europa and Medea came from what are now Syria and Turkey. History was invented by Herodotus, the 'Father of History' who wrote up the story of the Greek wars with Persia (490 to 480 BC) in the late fifth century BC. He begins the whole thing with a tit-for-tat sequence of women carried away. Europa, Helen, Medea and others become images for commercial relations between Greek and non-Greek. All these women: 'robbery on both sides'. Helen, carried off, sparked the Trojan War. Sex doesn't happen in a vacuum. It involves politics, relations between one race and another, people separated by an estranging sea and everything that 'sea' stands for. History and wars are made by men. But they begin with women carried away.[6]

You can interpret Europa a thousand different ways.[7] From the Italian Renaissance to Russian Symbolists, painters love her. She's in every gallery. The story talks up male sexuality and female helplessness. The male seducer, disguised as the most dangerous domestic animal, but really the most powerful god, sweeping a sexually unwoken girl off her feet into the untried sea of sex. Animal, mobile male; helpless, passive girl swept off her (usually bare) feet. They make a fantastically self-glamorizing male hieroglyph of seduction. Man takes charge: of her body, the sea and sex. As she faces the frothy swelling waves, all she can do is hold on (as Ovid has her do) to his glistening horn. But the animal is also an external image for passion, by which women are also swept away.

For both sexes, 'can't help it' is a potent pop theme. 'Can't Help Falling in Love with You', 'Can't Keep it In', 'Can't Stay Away from You', 'Can't Stop the Love', 'Can't Fight this Feeling'. But it comes over particularly persuasively about women. 'Can't Help Lovin' Dat Man' (Kern and Hammerstein, 1927). 'The Girl Can't Help It', sings Little Richard. When Marlene Dietrich sings 'Falling in Love Again' ('Never wanted to, What am I to do? I can't help it'), that smoky passivity seems wished on her, beyond her control in the lyricist Sammy Lerner's three-beat phrase, 'Can't help it'. Like Europa, she is desire's helpless victim. From opera to torchsong, suffering – being a victim of a man or your feelings for him – is a key feature of songs men write for women to sing. In real life, there have been a lot of things for women to be victims of; but it was men who gave them that victim voice.

They started two thousand years ago. After all Medea has done for Jason (getting him that Fleece, etc.), after she has borne him two children, he decides to marry someone else. In his play *Medea*, Euripides makes her complain, and say that men's pain is nothing to women's. 'I'd rather stand three times behind a shield', she says (her complimentary way of describing male battle), 'than bear a child once.' From there on, in folk-song, opera, torch and pop, the injured victim has been *the* great legacy of the female voice. 'Where have all the loving moments gone?' sings the desolate Countess, wife of a relentless womanizer, in Mozart's *Marriage of Figaro*. Listening women identify with her, but who wrote the script? Male composers, male librettists, male lyricists – who also laid down the pattern: women are carried away by their own feeling. Euripides' Medea says her 'passion' (for revenge, in this instance) is stronger than anything else.[8]

Real women follow this track too in their own songs. 'There's nothing I can do, to keep from loving you: I'm helpless in your arms. Can't keep from lovin' you', sings Gloria Estefan in her own song 'Here We Are'. 'I feel the earth move under my feet whenever you're around,' sings Carole King ('I feel the earth move', 1971) on the album *Tapestry*. 'I know my emotions are something I just can't tame.' But from Ovid writing about Europa to Sammy Lerner writing for Dietrich, it is male myth, male art, male directors who have formulated the lot. For two millennia, men have got women to sing of being a victim not only of heroes (or gods, or bulls) but of their own uncontrollable passion. They are swept off their feet by both.

Women in Greek myth don't cross the sea by themselves. One princess, Danae, does – but only because her father set her adrift with her baby in a floating box. The sea is on men's side. It helps them leave women on islands to face, alone, the un-recrossable waves of passion they were swept off into. Sailing back from Crete, Theseus abandons Ariadne on the island of Naxos. She wakes to see his sail sinking over the horizon. Dido, Queen of Carthage, burns herself to death as her lover Aeneas sails away to found Rome. Women don't sail. The sea where sex is born, where a man carries a woman off her feet, is the sea that lets him leave her high and dry on the island. One of the most powerful forces in all male art is the song of an abandoned woman.

Abandoned Women, Empowering Male Music

The abandoned woman longing for her lover sings the most flattering song there could be, for men. Not morally flattering, perhaps, but who cares about that? Sexually, it is the best personal reference you could get. You've been there, she wants you back. For two thousand years, male composers and lyricists made abandoned women sing how desperately they want their man. The hero goes off on his free-wheelin' way, empowered by being wanted back at the ranch.

On Naxos, Ariadne is abandoned several ways at once. She abandoned her home (she had to – she betrayed her father's palace to her lover as Medea betrayed *her* father's home to Jason). She abandoned herself, to the hero. She became an 'abandoned woman', abandoning decent behaviour, for a lover. Now she is abandoned by him. What does she do? Abandon herself again: to grief, in song. She is a hieroglyph of abandonment. This energy of abandonment, loneliness and need empowered the great male musical art whose titles echo *abbandonnata* over and over again.

From the beginning, women's sexual grief has been opera's strongest suit. One of Monteverdi's most famous operas was *Ariadne Abandoned*, and its high spot was her lament when Theseus sails away. In the 1640s, there were few literate Italian families who did not have a copy. It is a woman's tears made melody, and began the whole male opera tradition of exploring emotionally, musically and technically the power of woman's voice in sexual grief. Three centuries of flinging notes into the air in Jackson Pollock splashes of free-sliding chromatic tonality (as in, for instance, the 'mad' aria of Lucia di Lammermoor), to express uncontrollable passion edging into madness.[9] Male art shows off the soprano voice best, apparently – shining florid *coloratura*, wild melody, harmony, pitch and tone high up out of reach of the rest of us, the purest expression of high-flying far-out passion – if what the woman is singing is sexual lament. As Richard Carpenter wrote, and Karen sang, 'The best lovesongs are written with a broken heart'. Or rather, to *express* a broken heart: especially a female heart.

Opera began as Florentine scholars were discovering the Greek legacy of tragedy with emulative delight. The contemporary buzz-word was *pathos*. Monteverdi (who was a brilliant hand at *pathos*) felt he was reinventing Greek tragedy. Ariadne's 'Lament' picked up on Greek tragic 'monody': when a character abandoned tragedy's normal metre for wild lyric song full of –

well, *pathos*, which was the Greek word too. When a female character did that, it was often sexual lament even then: especially (see Medea) in Euripides.

Euripides wrote many parts for women suffering from far-on-the-edge desire. He was mocked for 'Cretan monodies', a sneer based on one of two plays (we do not know which) set in Crete. Both are lost, but we know that in one, a queen lusts incestuously after her brother-in-law. In the other, a queen has sex with her husband's bull. Euripides coupled this with stylistic experiment. While sexualizing women's stage-image, he showcased solo musical expressiveness, bringing in slurs (two or three notes to a vowel) and sensuous repetition. It must have sounded wonderful to late-fifth-century ears dying for something new, and provoked the conservative complaint hurled at fifties rock 'n' roll: this new music was repellent in itself and also had too much sex. Euripides 'dragged *gamous* [fucking] into tragedy'. His monodies reeked of women's desire. The comic playwright Aristophanes parodied them with a kitchen maid lamenting a lost rooster: a song full of *double entendres*. 'Glyce's gone, she's snatched away my cock! He flew away to the sky and left me laments, laments laments.'[10] It cracked them up in 404 BC, one man parodying another's ventriloquy of female grief. But though moralists scolded, all that emotion, musical abandonment and hurt female eroticism went down great with the punters. Euripides won very few prizes but was fantastically popular. Athenian infantry, prisoners of war in Sicily in 412 BC, bought their freedom from their Sicilian captors by singing new Euripides numbers, a story which shows not just that Sicilians liked the songs but that Athenian soldiers knew them by heart. Innovating musically and morally, Euripides gave tragedy the sexiness of female grief which has driven opera, Greek tragedy's reincarnation, ever since.

Euripides also wrote antiquity's most famous love scene, when Perseus, coming back from killing Medusa, catches sight of Andromeda, a very fixed abandoned woman indeed: her father has chained her to a rock in the sea to be eaten by a monster. The scene is lost but bits of the prelude survive. From her rock, Andromeda sings a monody of abandonment, answered by an invisible voice: the first time I know of when Echo operatically accompanies another abandoned woman. Echo is the archetypal marker of female solitude. Her own story is desertion: Narcissus rejects her for his own reflection. From Euripides to Kat Bjelland's 'Swamp Pussy', the hollow places of woman's isolation resound with echoes. When Ulysses' men hear Circe, she is making the cave-floor echo with song.

Strauss's opera *Ariadne on Naxos* is a brilliant fantasy on operatic form, which stages the staging of an Ariadne opera. One character, the nail-bitingly anxious Composer of that opera-within-an-opera, insists Ariadne should have 'nothing round her but sea, rocks, forest and Echo'. Echo is a voice in that opera too. She is the voice who shows you how alone the heroine is. 'No company but Echo.' Whatever a woman does on stage, she is also an echo-chamber for male imagination, male ideas of solitude and loss. Island or cave, a woman alone is the dead end, the cul-de-sac of sexuality. But dead ends and hollow places resonate. Enclosed, surrounded by reflecting surfaces, women are a grand place for an echo.

The Faraway Voice

After Narcissus drowns, Echo gets murdered in the same way as Orpheus and for the same reason: mourning her lost love exclusively. The goat-god Pan is after her; she refuses him; he makes the shepherds tear her to pieces, just as maenads tear Orpheus. The shepherds scatter her body over the hills, but her voice, like Orpheus' head, goes on singing. Both express the power voice has to sustain itself, even after its original source has died. This is voice without a body.

For us, this idea lies behind two of the twentieth century's most potent voices. When Ma Rainey burst out of her cardboard victrola she turned into sequined female flesh that amazing new thing, recorded voice. 'Telephone' means a voice 'far off'. *Phone*, voice, is feminine in Greek, and the voice on the phone is, like Echo, archetypally feminine. As the country boy sings in Rodgers and Hart's 'Kansas City',

> I put my ear to a Bell Telephone
> And a strange woman started in to talk!

But who invented the phone? A man with a very odd take on female voice. The day after Alexander Bell patented the telephone, he married a deaf woman who could lipread but not talk. She begged for sign-language lessons. In a lecture Bell gave to the Social Science Association, Boston, December 1871, he explained why he refused. Sign language is 'pernicious'. You should communicate thought only by words. You mustn't 'translate' it into 'any other language'; even fingers.[11] So she never talked. The man who created the twentieth century's emblematic disembodied voice married a body without a voice.

Opera plays with other bodiless voices, like voices offstage. From Euripides on, the voice of a letter has had a crucial power in tragedy and opera. In *Hippolytus*, Phaedra is burningly in love with her stepson. When he repulses her, she hangs herself but leaves behind a tablet accusing him of attempted rape, which causes his death. The 'letter scene' is the heart of Tchaikovsky's *Eugene Onegin*. Tatiana, a lonely girl on fire with love, writes a love-letter to Onegin, the cynical man of the world who will freeze her off. She sings it as she writes: the song of an isolated woman anticipating her abandonment. Some women's stage and fiction letters (like the valentine Bathsheba sends Farmer Boldwood in Hardy's *Far from the Madding Crowd*), are pretend confessions of love. In *Twelfth Night*, a servant writes a letter in her mistress's handwriting, which gets her boss believing his employer loves him. In Mozart's *Marriage of Figaro*, the Countess and her maid write and sing a note to the philandering Count, to get him to meet (as he thinks) the maid he's after. These letters are one form of the great vocal invention of Greek tragedy which led to the pop single: the soliloquy, the aria. A voice alone and not alone, revealing (truly or falsely) its deepest feelings intimately to an audience of thousands.

These days, the sound-waves of the heart are measured by a machine called an echo-cardiogram. Most of Euripides' great soliloquies were female. Ever since, male drama and song has found a fictional female heart the best echo for successful sound-waves. Side Two of *A Woman's Heart*, the bestselling nineties album of Irish woman singers, opens with a song by Paul Brady. Dolores Keane's voice invites her lover to woman's archetypal place: 'Let me take you to the island'. In opera, the aria or soliloquy is often a voice in a bedroom or courtyard, the classic enclosed female space where women's voices get overheard.

Opera and tragedy specialize in bringing the inner feelings of characters locked in complex, wounding human situations out to an enormous public. The audience, privileged eavesdroppers, super-overhearers, adore scenes that reflect what they themselves are doing: 'overhearing' scenes, when a woman alone says what those letters say (that she fancies a man) and the guy overhears. The balcony scene, repeated in *West Side Story*, begins when Juliet whispers to the night sky how she loves Romeo, and Romeo hears. In Verdi's *Rigoletto*, Gilda, another protected girl irrevocably in love, sings one of the most brilliantly vulnerable arias of all, about a man who is really a heartless seducer. He hears, having slipped into the secret courtyard as she reaches top A on 'ecstasy' ('My heart in *ec*stasy murmurs, "I love you" '), and repeats the 'I love you'. In Walt Disney's *Sleeping Beauty*, the princess in the forest sings (to bright-eyed, bushy-tailed woodland animals rather than Echo) her love for a prince she's met in a dream. The animals find his clothes on a tree (don't ask why), dress up, and dance with her to Tchaikovsky's *pas de deux*. The real prince overhears, and takes over from the animals. 'Did I startle you? I'm sorry. But we've met before. You said it yourself: "Once upon a dream." ' The female voice, confessing love, invisible, designed to be overheard: the archetypal voice on the balcony, the radio, the CD.

Apart from a few women singer-songwriters who took control

of their recordings, a woman singing a pop song has nearly always, at least until the mid-eighties, been produced, directed, signed up and recorded by men. That female disclosure of feeling, supposedly private as a body, enormously overheard. 'I'm left all alone' sings Billie Holiday ('Mean to Me', lyrics by Turk-Ahlert); but she's not: there's Lester Young and the boys, and the tenor sax as Echo. Like backing vocals, a male band, supports and points up her lonely longing.

The female pop single, that recorded, apparently lonely voice overheard accidentally-on-purpose, is part of a long tradition by which men use the abandoned but overheard woman to represent the whole human condition of loneliness and longing: as the *vox humana* (also the name of the most plangent organ stop). Poulenc's entire opera *La Voix Humaine*, with script by Cocteau, is one woman on the phone to the lover who dumped her. We gradually realize he is lying, is not where he says. She ends up strangling herself on the phone-line that carries his voice. *That* is 'the human voice' which opera inherits. A woman abandoned and stranded: not necessarily in the sea, but in what the heroine of Verdi's *La Traviata* wearily calls 'this desert called Paris'. A city-sea of alienation cuts Poulenc's heroine off from her lying, faithless lover. In Strauss's *Ariadne on Naxos*, the Composer says no one else must be on stage with Ariadne. 'She is the symbol of *human* solitude.'

Why should male opera use a woman's voice for the human voice? Partly because opera is such a big show. Above a big orchestra, in a huge hall, you hear a soprano best. But also because Greek tragedy and the whole tragic tradition, from Racine and Shakespeare on, used female characters as a profound image of the inner life. Greek poetry imagines the mind as female, an enterable vessel. From Euripides through Verdi and Mozart to Eddie Holland (sixties lyricist for the Supremes), male writers often put their deepest emotions into female voices. 'I noticed women were more interesting to write for,' said Eddie. 'We men are taught we can't say we hurt. We deal with that through writing for women.'[12]

Of course there are poignant songs written for a male voice in every tradition. Neil Young's song 'When A Man Needs A Maid' has male vulnerability at its heart. But the Western tradition has used woman *more* as image of hurt innerness. For the woman speakers of his monologues, Tennyson recreated the soliloquy tradition begun by Euripides, searching out Shakespearean, Arthurian and Greek abandoned women: Oenone (abandoned by Paris when he went after Helen); Mariana in her 'moated grange' (rather than moated island), the deserted mistress in Shakespeare's *Measure for Measure*; the 'Lady of Shalott' pining for Sir Lancelot. Making women sing of their abandonment by men is one of the things men have done best. Male listeners can identify with the longing: say, with Billie Holiday's voice, resonant with loneliness. 'I've been told nobody sings the word "hunger" like I do,' she said. 'Or the word "love". Maybe I remember what these words are all about.' Everyone listening can thrill to the pain of her own lyrics in 'I cover the waterfront, I'm watching the sea, Will the one I love be coming back to me?' But what they are identifying with is first of all a man's version of a woman's longing.

In song, suffering is power. As sorrow empowered the blues, so (the composer Tom Adès told me) 'A woman's power in opera is her fragility. The more she breaks, the more power she gets.' Women singer-songwriters have used this power to enormous advantage, especially in our culture of confession whose greatest model of disclosure is *The Oprah Winfrey Show*. As a recent book on gender in rock puts it, women singers from Janis Joplin to Courtney Love 'lift up their skirt and speak'. Woman 'opening the heart' brings catharsis. Baring a soul, like baring a body on stage, 'turns suffering into affirmation'.[13]

But that was a by-product of male tradition, which empowered itself by using the image of the abandoned woman. Since Euripides discovered its secret, the song of woman's sexual grief has been big box-office. Such a turn-on, the private feelings of a woman hurt by a man. Men could identify both with the longed-for man and the hurt woman. As Carly Simon sang in

'You're So Vain' to (probably) Warren Beatty: 'You think this song is about you, don't you?' For two thousand years, from Euripides on, men have written songs of abandonment for female voices to sing – about men.

The Voice Men Leave Behind Them?

Before a boy becomes a man, he has a woman's voice. His mother's voice was his. He breaks with mother, when *it* 'breaks', – and goes off with other women. You leave a woman's voice to be a man. Every hero has left both a woman who loves him, and her voice that tells him so. The voice of Ariadne is what a hero wants to hear: its hurt empowers him on his way. Gilda, Violetta, Billie Holiday, Tatiana: *la voix humaine*, wanting him. 'Man is born to go a lovin',' sings the gauzy, acceptingly hurt voice of Peggy Lee singing 'Black Coffee' (1953) to music and lyrics by two men:

> Woman's born to weep and fret,
> To stay at home and tend her oven
> And drown her past regrets
> In coffee and cigarettes.

These songs say women need the hero. They abandon themselves to him, abandon decency, home, family for him. He abandons them; and they wait for him for ever:

> It's drivin' me crazy
> This waitin' for ma baby
> To maybe come around.[14]

Abandoned woman was *the* great empowering voice of man-made song – until rock 'n' roll came along.

6 Marine Magic: Saving, Veiling, Faking

White Samite Syndrome: Women's Magical Element

If a Greek hero gets into trouble at sea, femaleness of another sort is on hand with magic power to help him. Abandoned women are only one side of the sex–sea coin, the side that underwrites how great and desirable the hero is. The other side is his vulnerability – like the power-losing, dysfunctional side of male gods around Venus. If men are vulnerable at sea, if they get into difficulties, they are sorted out not by helpless, stranded mortal women, but by women who are powerful when men need them to be. Goddesses.

Goddesses are women who are magic for men. Circe and Calypso give Ulysses provisions and instructions to get home; sea-goddesses look after Vulcan when he falls from heaven. When Odysseus is in the sea clinging to a broken spar, the sea-goddess Ino gives him a magic veil to wrap round him and save him. When he reaches land after three days in the sea, flesh swollen, water gushing from his nose, he tosses it into a river which sweeps it out to sea, where Ino 'receives it into her hands'.[1] In Tennyson's *Idylls of The King*, the Lady of the Lake gives King Arthur a sword. When he is dying, a hand catches the sword thrown back in the lake:

> So flash'd and fell the brand Excalibur,
> But ere he dip't the surface, rose an arm
> Clothed in white samite, mystic, wonderful,
> And caught him by the hilt.

This is woman as goddess, helping men 'at sea', in need.

Hans Anderson's version is the Little Mermaid who saves the drowning prince. Mortal women cannot deal with sea. That is where goddesses and mermaids belong. They are in their element when men are out of their depth. Resenting women's power in a place where men are helpless is another factor in misogyny.

Even mortal women save men at key moments. Theseus and Jason would get nowhere without princesses: Ariadne helps Theseus kill the Minotaur, Medea deals with Jason's dragon. But the male writers telling the story emphasize goddesses behind the scenes. Goddesses made the princess fall for the hero. Venus gets Eros to shoot Medea, so she'll help Jason. The Cretan king (another wicked father-figure) asks Theseus to prove he is the son of Neptune, throws a ring into the sea and tells him to retrieve it. Theseus dives and dolphins zoom him off to Neptune's submarine palace. There he gets not only the ring but new clothes and a wedding-crown which prepare him to be seen and fallen in love with by Ariadne:

> He saw with awe the lovely daughters of Nereus.
> Brightness fell from their bodies like fire
> And gold ribbons writhed in their hair. Their dancing feet
> Stunned his heart. In that steep-roofed house he saw
> His father's wide-eyed wife, Amphitrite, who gave him
> A purple cloak. On his thick hair she pressed
> A coronet, the wedding gift of rose-crowned Venus.
> Theseus came up dry from the deep, dressed
> In the gifts of gods.

He comes up glamorous; Ariadne falls instantly in love and decides to help.[2] Bonnie Tyler's 1984 version of 'Holding Out for a Hero' ('I wanna hero; he's gotta be strong, he's gotta be fast, and he's gotta be fresh from the fight') was used to advertise Gillette razors, which says something about 'the hero's' pulling-power. The idea of helping a hero, however humbly, is often as seductive in real life as in myth. 'I only remember a city by its chicks,' said Hendrix once. 'They wash your socks and try to make you feel nice when you're in town.' White samite syndrome, I call it: woman as helper, from sock-washing to Jung's *anima*, the hero's salvation and guide, which works best through water. In Leonard Cohen, 'Suzanne' is 'our lady of the harbour'. She 'takes you down to her place near the river', 'holds the mirror', shows you your self:

> She gets you on her wave-length
> and she lets the river answer
> that you've always been her lover.

Giving you herself as a stage in your journey is giving you yourself.

In the twenties, the poet Hugo von Hofmannsthal and composer Richard Strauss wrote the daft opera *Helen in Egypt*. Keen on using Greek myths for contemporary relationships, they turned female sea-magic into marriage guidance for the couple most counsellors would run a mile to avoid: Helen of Troy, back with her husband after the war. The sea goddess Aithra has a talking Sea-shell (image for the newly invented radio), meant to sound 'amusing and mysterious' but impossible to stage. Audiences find omniscient shellfish hard to take: the opera has never been a hit. But it is a brilliant synthesis of Greek ideas of female magic, sex and sea. Helen prays to Moon and Sea ('allies of ever-deceitful womanhood', says Strauss in a letter to Hofmannsthal); Aithra uses drugs, illusion and lies to help Helen when her husband tries to murder her. Husband and wife are re-united 'under the sea's protection': he drowns in her contentedly. 'I lose myself in you.'[3]

In seventies rock music, sea and water became increasingly and mystically female. Gavin Sutherland's 'Sailing', as sung by Rod Stewart (1965), became not only a hit but a soaring anthem roared out by football crowds: 'I am sailing, stormy weather, to be with you, to be free.' Dry is despair. The male German band Can sang a blues about being parched of woman's love ('Soul Desert', from *Soundtracks*, 1970). Woman 'brings the rain': she saves, moisturizes, makes the male soul blossom. The same year, Hendrix sang 'Drifting' (on his posthumous *The Cry of Love*), about sailing a sea of 'forgotten teardrops' to the harbour of a woman's love. Robert Wyatt (of Soft Machine) broke his back when he fell from a window drunk, and was condemned to a wheelchair for ever. The cover of *Rock Bottom* (1974), his next album, shows him in the ocean with tentacles and weed instead of legs. 'Sea Song' serenades a mermaid lover. In 'A Last Straw', the ocean floor is 'home from home'. 'Alfibib' and 'Alife' are plays on his wife's name, Alfie. He's at rock bottom, cringingly submerged, dependent on Alfie. The music is ripplingly woozy; synthesizers and bubbling horns get across the drowning disablement plus the floaty secret sense of an underwater home where you depend, like crippled Vulcan, on women.

Women's songs were claiming sea as a female principle: staking a monopoly on turbulence and disorientation, on sea as primeval bosom and womb. In Yoko Ono's 'Don't Count the Waves', the sea dissolves any male efforts to measure and master nature. In 'The Sea' (1970), the folk-rock singer Sandy Denny identifies with sea because it moves wherever it wants, never mind male horizons. The 'coming of sea' will be a flood, washing under everybody's door, breaking down defences. In 'Donkey Ride' (1977), oceans of love sing in her veins.[4]

It was not just sexual, all this; it was oppositional. Patti Smith said most male performance built up to the single climax, 'the big spurt', while her band played 'feminine' music. 'We'll go so far and peak and then start again and peak, over and over': a sequence of crescendos and diminuendos, not a single release of tension. 'It's like ocean,' she explained. Her song 'Land' (a paradoxical title, given this oceanic context) repeats its phrases in a flowing torrent of sound. The female 'we' in the title song of Kristin Hersh's *Hips and Makers* (1996) is fecundity incarnate, rocking and sucking on the sea. Liz Phair's *Exile from Guyville* had a visual sea-pattern around the CD. It is a convention both of pop psychology (one chapter in the bestselling *Men Are From Mars Women Are From Venus*, an image suggested by the author's wife, is 'Women Are Like Waves') and of women's rock, that women's waves frustrate men's mastery.[5] But men got to that image first. Male myth and male art first linked women with the sea. For women, claiming sea as symbol of female sexuality plays into the hands of male myth. Men are still going to see the sea of sexuality as a flood of dangers they are proud of mastering, women among them. The women are sea-dangers you negotiate and flee.

Men and women do different things with the image, but male myth has burnt into everyone's pyches the idea that women have two sorts of relation to 'sea' (and to what sea may stand for). Magic marine power on one hand, which gulps men down like Charybdis or saves them like Ino. And no-go Ariadne helplessness on the other. Men's self-image depends on this doubleness. You can sweep her off into the sea of sex, but she may 'take you down' like Suzanne (though Leonard Cohen likes it at the time), 'cover' you like Calypso, devour you like Scylla, shipwreck you like Sirens. However much you like being there with her, in her, you have to get away, leave her on the island. You can remember her fondly afterwards, as Christy Moore does with his 'Creole Girl on the shores of Ponchitrane'. But you're still going to leave her far away.

Sexuality – the sea – helps you do it. Hans Andersen's Little Mermaid tries to cross the divide. She helps the prince in the sea, then at great cost joins him on land, where he does not need or remember her. Man needs woman when he's in her territory: in passion, in her. Then he leaves. That's the report from the mythic male frontline. Men attribute power to women in the very sphere, sexuality, where men get power from abandoning them. Men want to enter their magic element. 'Within her', says the writer John McGahern in *The Pornographer*, 'was this instant of rest, the glory and the awe, that one was as close as ever man could be to the presence of the mystery, and live.'

Then they see it as danger and have to escape. And because women are also helpless at sea, and stay where they are put, men can.

Made Up? Women's Doubleness

'She fakes, just like a woman,' grinds Bob Dylan ('Just Like A Woman'). 'But she breaks like a little girl.' Male myth divides female nature in the sea of desire. Femaleness knows and saves but also needs to be saved. But if this place women cannot cross without male help is really their place of power, then the helplessness must be fake. 'Ever-deceitful womanhood', says Richard Strauss, is in league with the sea. Behind those paintings of Europa is the male suspicion that she is faking the girlish innocence. Inside the girl on the brink, Gilda or Tatiana ('I am sixteen going on seventeen' as the eldest daughter sings invitingly in *The Sound of Music*), is the goddess. This virgin on the ballroom's edge knows all about 'sea'; she knows what you know, that sex is her element. Maybe she knows more than you know. Women pretend not to know about sex, but sex is their true magic. Women's surface, like the sea, hides something different inside.

In Greek myth, it is women who know spells and drugs. Medea is an innocent virgin but also a sorceress who magics the dragon to sleep, for Jason. In Egypt, Helen learns *nepenthe*, the drug that makes you forget trouble.[6] Any sudden enslaving desire you feel for a woman must be due to her magic. Women get you to desire them by illusion: their appearance is 'made-up'. 'Mascara' means 'mask'; male Roman poets (and eighteenth-century British ones) sneered at women for painting their faces to attract them.

This suspicion of illusion, magic and pretence goes into the doubleness of male fantasy about women. Women use wiles to get what they want from men; they fake and cheat. They make Eros, male desire for women, blind to what they really are. Hence the male resentment, expressed in elegantly made-up verse, against women who make themselves up into elegance, to please a man. This Mobius strip of cross-sex suspicion made these made-up creatures a male byword for artificiality. Men have as double an attitude to women's efforts to please them as they do to women at sea. They love the veil and make-up because it is beautiful, a sheen, shimmer, dazzle; and attack it because it is pretence.

All this wishes on real women a masquerade: masking is part of the whole male fantasy of female covering. The soft-hung bed in Calypso's cave, the murmuring foam round wounded Vulcan, delight and save you. 'I'm looking for a lover who'll come on and cover me' sings Bruce Springsteen ('Cover Me'). Softness and covering are part of the package men want: the way women save you, give you power. Ino's veil holds Ulysses up in the waves; the Lady of the Lake's arm, brandishing the sword that gives King Arthur his power, is draped in white samite. Both women's strength and their allure belong with that softness and covering. (The voice of Nancy Storace, Mozart's friend, Susanna in the first *Marriage of Figaro*, had 'the sheen of dark satin'.) But like the sea, women's soft coverings have a double power. As women are helpless and powerful at sea, their coverings save and endanger you. You might go under and never come up again. Women are a harbour, a haven, both emotionally and sexually. (For eighteenth-century gentlemen rakes, *limen*, Latin for 'harbour', was a pornographic code-word for 'cunt'.) But haven can suddenly turn into trap. They seem to be the same shape in male minds.

If masquerade is thrust upon women, all they can do is use it. Hence the cosmetics industry; hence singers who play into the double role, helpless and powerful, knowing and innocent, that male myth hangs upon them. Marlene Dietrich encouraged the image of herself as Trilby to the Svengali of Josef von Sternberg, the director who called her 'his bird of paradise'. They seemed a double act: male power, male direction, exotic female pet. But biographers tend to think she created her own persona, factoring designer-helplessness into her allure. Her husky soft rasp, singing 'Falling in Love Again', says she is a helpless victim of passion but also seeks it out: it is her medium.

ORIGINS: MYTH, SEX AND ELECTRICITY

Blindfold and Underwear: The Doubleness of Desire

Power, danger and pretence are all packaged into the Greek mythic source of desire, a mysterious garment worn by Venus under her breasts. At one point in Homer's *Iliad*, Juno asks to borrow it. Juno is on the Greek side in the Trojan war and wants Jupiter to have sex and then sleep while the Greeks batter the Trojans into the ground. She asks Venus for 'love and desire, with which you tame everyone, mortals and gods'. Venus takes it off, this all-powerful undergarment:

> Venus undid the embroidered strap under her breasts.
> It has all charm in the world woven into it, love and desire
> and flirting which undoes every man's mind. 'Put this close
> to your breasts,' she said, 'and you won't come back
> without achieving whatever you want.' Juno smiled
> and slipped the strap close to her breasts.[7]

The Greeks wore different clothes from us, and translating words for vanished underwear is dicey. What is this garment: a strap, girdle, veil, liberty bodice? It seems to me a vestigial sort of bra. I don't think Greeks wore knickers. Men did not see Knickerbox on every high street. Whatever this bra-girdle exactly was, sartorially, it was also the most intimate female underwear that male myth could dream up.

But European painters turned it into a veil, with which Venus' son Eros has a close and ambiguous relationship. In *Venus and Amor*, the Italian painter Lucas Cranach (1472–1553) shows Venus with Eros as a wizened blindfolded toddler. He leans towards her, arm behind his head, and his blindfold is made of the same gauzy fabric as the strip of veil across his mother's naked body.[8] The filmy flimsy fabric hides nothing, on her or him. You hardly see it, except for the folds. It is a feathery mock of a veil, a diaphanous joke about concealment and revelation. Cranach paints the same joke in *Venus in a Landscape* (1529, in London's National Gallery) where she stands in the open, naked but for a red velvet hat, a choker, and that veil. She holds it over her belly-button and crotch, spelling out her nakedness: so see-through, you only see its faint edge where it's coming away, like the last edge of frost melting off fallen leaves.

In *Venus and Amor* the blindfold on Eros (Amor) is also a joke, not about concealment and revelation but blindness and seeing-through. Is he really blind? The scrap of gauze looks like faint spectacles, held by ribbon tied behind his head. What covers his eyes, the same stuff that covers and reveals his mother's target area, resembles something that makes you see better. And does something see-through stop you seeing? Venus' veil, source of desire, is the same stuff that makes Love 'blind'. It conceals and reveals; his blind eyes have see-through wrapping round them.

Venus and Eros have an infinitely complicated relationship, bound up with concealment, forbiddenness and display. In European paintings they play with each other's accessories. She teases him about his weapons, he lifts up her fabrics. In Watteau's painting *Cupid Disarmed by Venus* (1715), Venus holds his bow out of reach. He is a naked toddler scrabbling up her naked body to snatch it. Is she reproving, forbidding, teasing, or just enjoying him clambering up? Their classical names, Venus and Cupid, make a basically erotic painting OK. A prostitute dressed and displayed by a maid is a common erotic theme in the sixteenth and seventeeth centuries, but their poses were completely interchangeable with Venus and Cupid scenes. In the mid-seventeenth century, Knupfer painted a prostitute waiting naked on a bed with Cupid on her open thigh, his heel in her crotch. He was copying Italian Renaissance paintings of Venus and Cupid, especially Venus waiting for her lover Mars with Eros on her thigh symbolizing her desire. In Watteau's *Judgement of Paris* (1720), the three goddesses show off their charms to Paris. Cupid lifts up Venus' gauzy chemise to display her, just as maids hold up a prostitute's chemise to attract a client in contemporary engravings of brothels.[9]

What are veils for? In most cultures, they are variations on the difference between the surface and what's under it; on purity, invitation, and danger. A nun's or bride's veil advertises purity, but also challenges you to lift, look and *wonder* about what is beneath. For men, so a male friend kindly told me, female underwear is about 'almostness, something hidden and half-displayed. To get at it you've got to put yourself in danger. Is this the right moment, are you going to get repulsed?' Underwear is 'about deferred display, stockings rather than tights, that vulnerable dangerous area shockingly revealed', just as Eros, Desire, displays his mother's 'vulnerable dangerous area' to the world by lifting her chemise. This garment of danger and desire, putting men at risk, is the target of one of Hercules' Labours. The strongest man in the world puts himself in danger by trying to get it off a dangerously armed, famously chaste queen. Veils are women's answer to male armour.

For, to spell it out, veils are also ideal emblems for the foldedness men see in female genitals: as in the 'veil of the hymen'. 'Is not every veiled apparition considered feminine?' asks the philosopher Gaston Bachelard. 'All that is hidden, is feminine.'[10] Women are sexual folds, both transparent and opaque. If armour reminds you how vulnerable men are underneath, veils suggest the power women get from permeability. The power of covering and revealing, of taboo (think of the 'veil of the temple' in Catholic mythology) and invitation both at once. In Islam, women are increasingly going back to the veil, not all because they are made to. One Western journalist first met some wives of Lebanon's Hizbollah movement when they were wearing the veil, the *chador*. When she met them again at a private women's tea-party, she hardly recognized the woman with waist-length blonde hair in a plunging décolleté nightie or the one in a filmy scarlet négligé. 'This is how we are at home', said one. 'Islam encourages us to be beautiful for our husbands.'[11]

Seventeenth-century scientists spoke of 'Nature' as a woman 'unveiled' by philosophers who 'penetrate her secrets'.[12] Venus' secret of allure, her veil, bra, girdle or under-strap, sums up the invitation men see in female hiddenness. What is the real source of desire, Venus' underwear or what it covers? Or the liftable possibility of display, the coveredness itself? The veil is about surface and interior at once: it encapsulates the doubleness of desire, the way it has two gods.

Greek myth handed on different ways of understanding maleness, and you can interpret what the Venus–Eros duo says about it a thousand different ways. Many Greek men were homosexual at some stage, and you can take the young male standing next to mum, who also operates freely on his own, as homosexual desire. Or you call infant Eros the beginning of desire, the sudden choice – expressed in that well-aimed arrow – of a particular person; while gorgeous grown-up Venus is desire's fulfilment, sex. And, in our society, desire's mature fulfilment (with luck), love – which is what Venus mainly stands for in post-Greek European imagination. Or try Venus as prior feeling, and Eros as her attendant coming after; something she gave life to, the consequence of sex.

Astronomy offers another image. As planet, Venus has a nomadic little satellite, a lumpy, potato-shaped asteroid twenty-two kilometres across. When astronomers spotted it a hundred years ago, they gave it her son's name, Eros. It is useful to astronomers because it operates close to Earth. Its movements help them measure the geometry of the inner solar system, apparently; plus the distance between earth, sun, and the combined earth–moon mass. But this Eros is also a potential world disaster. Every few years he wanders into Earth's orbit. Science correspondents say there is no *immediate* likelihood of collision, but there is something mythically exact about Eros as misshapen dwarf, an uncontrollable asteroid roving the sky, sometimes close to his mother, sometimes dangerously close to Earth.

Eros is the oldest and youngest god, around at the beginning of the world but still a baby. Even without his mother, he is a tangle of doubleness. He sometimes carries two arrows, one of happiness, one of despair. When desire is reciprocated, there are two of you: two arrows aimed at each other or, in a famous poem of Baudelaire's, two candles in a mirror, rays reflecting each other.[13] In song terms, we are talking duets. Soprano arias of grief and pain are some of the most popular moments in opera, but so are the love duets; yet they are not always kind, or truthful. In Monteverdi's opera *The Coronation of Poppea*, Nero cuts murderous swathes through everybody to get the woman he wants. Its musical highlights include two heartlessly enchanting duets. First, two completely irrelevant servants, a foil to the imperial lovers; then Nero with his bloodily won bride. The graceful 'now me, now you' twining of the voices in these songs breathes a spring-meadow innocence but is utterly amoral. So is Mozart's 'Là ci darem la mano', Don Giovanni's seduction song, where the peasant girl Zerlina joyfully joins her voice to that of a coldhearted rake. This is the song the faithless Molly Bloom sings with her lover in James Joyce's *Ulysses*. Eros has no morals. Love duets, the sonic image of making love, express his doubleness, that potential for destructive deceit in the midst of mutuality.

Greeks argued over where Eros came from, who exactly were his parents, how he began. Any love story has *the* moment when desire begins. Eros arrives – but is Venus always behind him? Can you have Eros without Venus?[14] Their partnership is a fertile muddle, a way of having it all ways (maybe made possible by a flourishing homosexual culture and the bisexuality of Greek men): mother and son stand for different aspects of how a man thinks of his own desire. Gay, straight or bi, the Venus and Eros duo made a complicated hieroglyph of sex, desire and love. Together they summed up what each sex was expected to desire. Straight men desire a beautiful woman, women and gay men desire a man, a teenager, a child. Hence woman with Eros, male child.

Faking and Illusion: The Femaleness of Rock Display

Men's complaints about women's hiddenness and artifice resound through Western art. Faking 'like a woman', as Dylan calls it, is a male idea. Men cannot fake desire. (Or not before Viagra – and even that, though chemically caused, is still desire.) Men's desire is upfront and obvious. But women can fake it –

and have sex without it. So maybe their desire for you is as false as their make-up. So the secret source of desire, the lifted veil or unstrapped bra, has got to be the first hint of display which suggests desire may come back at you from behind the veil.

Rock music is all about the doubleness of desire. The general message to women from The Stones in their heyday ('Under My Thumb', 'Yesterday's Papers') is 'I want you, I'm leaving you, fuck off and die'. The rock god is the incarnation of desire: but is also the ultra-desired male, on display. Woman's song, the counterpart to any 'dance of seven veils', traditionally epitomized seduction. When men wrote songs for women to sing that expressed men's ideas of female desire, they gave voice to what they imagined going hiddenly on behind the veil. Male rock took over all the faking, illusion and theatricality associated with women. It let men display themselves as objects of desire. The archetypal unveiling of the rock mystery is Iggy Pop or Jim Morrison baring his cock, Red Hot Chilli Peppers in the late eighties, naked, with only socks covering their cocks. It borrows women's power to rouse desire by hiding and (however comically) revealing. At the machismo heart of the Rolling Stones was Mick Jagger, with a veil.

Simultaneously, though, rock clung like mad to traditional male themes: moving on, disengaging from cover-up, getting away from clinging veils to sing the song of the open road.

7 The Hero's Journey: Song of Myself

Epic: Alone and With Your Mates

The teamwork strand of the male psyche, its football and baseball DNA, is basic to ancient epic and myth. Think Knights of the Round Table, Crusaders, Three Musketeers, Robin Hood's Sherwood band; as well as *The Magnificent Seven* or *Reservoir Dogs*. But maleness always has a double texture in these myths. You also tackle the adventures that make you a hero alone. In Tennyson's poem, Ulysses says he 'drank delight of battle with my peers, Far on the ringing plains of windy Troy', and travelled 'Both with those that loved me and alone'. The great Trojan expedition and war was a team effort, but Theseus, Hercules, Bellerophon, Orpheus and Narcissus (in his own odd mode of heroism) tackle danger alone. Ulysses starts off, like Jason, with a boatload of companions, but finishes the voyage on his own.

Since the sixties, the sense of doing it with your mates has been hands-off-sacred in male rock ideology. When the Charlatans refused to pull out of a gig because their keyboardist had died in a car crash, the full press statement they sent read 'THERE WILL BE NO CHANGE. WE ARE FUCKING ROCK. WE'VE LOST OUR MATE'. Three weeks later they played to 125,000 people at Knebworth with Oasis, Prodigy and Manic Street Preachers (themselves shaken by the disturbance and disappearance of their own wild boy, Richey Edwards). Team sympathy was overwhelming. Afterwards, Noel Gallagher turned down an award and dedicated it to Rob Collins.[1] Rock 'n' roll doesn't get much more emotional than all that – and it turned on Homeric group pride. 'We are rock. We've lost our mate.'

Epic team spirit happens not only on the battlefield (sports field, rock stage) but on the journey, that great image of male bonding – Argonauts, Crusaders, Vikings, the quest for the Grail (about which Marianne Faithfull bizarrely quizzed both Keith Richards and Jagger before she slept with either).[2] Homer is both battle and journey. The *Iliad* is the foreign war, where Greeks work together and every hero has his backing of men from his homeland. (As, at Gettysburg, Southern boys died on the hill in their local regiments, township by township.) The plot turns on the bond between Achilles and Patroclus. The chieftains argue strategy together, eat together, fight together. The climactic male bonding is the Trojan king ransoming his son's body from the Greek who killed him. The two men cry together for the wastage of war. But the *Odyssey*, the journey home, is as ultra-male as the war. Its first word is *andra*, 'man'. ('Sing of *the man* who wandered . . .') Ulysses is singular, but has mates he feels responsible for, cheers up, tries to protect. When Scylla ate a few, it was 'the saddest sight', he says, 'in all my travels'. Men belong epicly together on the journey too. (Women tend to turn up alone, on islands.) But team relationships are always difficult. The *Iliad* is the story of a row between Achilles and the Greek leader. Ulysses is bright, self-controlled, a strategist; his men are envious short-termists. Immediate satisfaction interferes with the long haul. Ulysses has a closed bag of stormy winds; the breeze outside wafts them nearly home; the crew think it's treasure and open it, and everyone gets blown away again. The boys eat lotus and have to be carried on board, get turned into pigs, get drunk and roll off roofs, eat the Sun's cattle when warned not to. They die because they put appetite over the long-term goal. Their fractious relationships with Ulysses mirror endless stories of rock bands on the road. Sting and the Police, for instance, 'fought like ferrets'.[3]

Rock music has the same double skein; all lads together one moment, lone hero the next. But it was not there from the start. Rock 'n' roll's first 'rockabilly' phase spotlit the man alone. The backing was there – Elvis owed his first real break to his guitarists, Little Richard had the Upsetters, Bill Haley the Comets, Buddy Holly the Crickets, Cliff Richard the Shadows, just as Dylan had The Band. But emotionally, for fans, they were background, 'backing vocals'; players in – literally – the shadows. This phase got a bit frozen at the end of the fifties. Elvis went into the army in 1958, Buddy Holly died, rock 'n' roll went on having hits, filling the teenage need for loud danceable music, but sugary vocalists like Pat Boone and Bobby Vee sang on. Rock 'n' roll seemed tamed or absorbed, as if it had simply ridden on the back of the soupy solo artist: Frankie Avalon, Paul Anka, Mitch Miller (an avowed enemy of rock 'n' roll) ruled the airwaves. Conservative observers decided decency and order had at last returned to the popular mainstream.[4]

Then the whole thing was re-charged by inspiration from the other strand of blues. American rock was still looking South, to Delta blues. In the sixties, British rock turned to that master of musical teamwork, Muddy Waters. The boys who transformed rock in 1964, the 'British invasion', the original models for the rock group, had sat worlds away from Chicago, electric guitar on the floor of the bed-sit, listening hungrily to Muddy Waters and Howlin' Wolf. Keith Richards, Eric Clapton, Brian Jones.[5] At their first American press conference in 1964, someone asked The Beatles what they wanted to see in America. 'Muddy Waters,' they said instantly. 'Where's that?' asked a reporter. The Beatles fell about. 'You Americans don't know your most famous citizens,' they said. The Rolling Stones, named after a Muddy Waters song, insisted on Howlin' Wolf appearing on their American TV début. Eric Clapton of Cream did a recording with Howlin' Wolf.[6]

Sixties boy-bands gave rock what always sustained male identity in heroic adventure: the team. The two first phases of rock 'n' roll drew on the two phases of blues. The different textures – acoustic Delta blues, electric Chicago blues – corresponded to two different sides of that adventure of being a man. The lone bluesman on the road, and boys together having that cardinal rock virtue, fun. Different group-members could develop different roles: you didn't have to be everything yourself. Eric Clapton became the pure musician in Cream while Jack Bruce the bass guitarist took on more of the sexual magnetism. Like soldiers on the march, you can bask in the community of what you sing. As in Bowie's 'Boys Keep Swinging', 'boys always work it out.' You face together, in your songs, all those problems involved in being a hero: the social or parental world (standing in for the monsters and underworld of Greek myth), and women. 'When you're a Jet, little boy, you're a man,' sing the Jets in Sondheim's lyrics in *West Side Story*. The gang is your strength. But rock also gives you the other side, the lonely *High Noon* of the stage: a hero facing the barrage of stadium spotlight alone, a cowboy crashing into the saloon through swing doors, a knight galloping into the enchanted forest, Perseus facing Medusa's snake-locks, Hercules facing the Hydra of the audience.

The music, sound and production, has consistently followed this alone-versus-together pattern. Voices, vocal and instrumental, answer and harmonize each other. The lonely riff spelling individual risk is one end of the spectrum; the cradling chords, harmonies spelling encouraging community, are the other. Much of the pleasure in sixties blues rock is guitar-lines answering each other: music as society, as relationship, individuals relating to each other, held together by a shared beat. Music you dance to, whose voices incarnate the meeting of bodies. In performance, you have the glittery isolation – lead guitar, solo riff, lead singer: Jagger, a Dionysian Jack Flash, fluid over the stage while the other Stones are flickeringly still – and group security, group fun.[7] There is enough individuality in each member that boys can choose who to identify with, and girls choose who to adore. You get the single magnetic voice, instrument and body, *and* the corporate thing. Summed up visually in clothes and bodies performing together as a team.

Solo Riff plus Companionable Chords

When the male group emerged as the key rock unit, the way the rest of the world saw rock began to change. At the same time that the group was giving rock its mythic and musical shape, rock was becoming, in the sixties, 'a genuine force of cultural and political consequence'.[8] One adult criticism of rock and pop songs was that they were ephemeral. In 1963, the phrase 'a rock classic' would have seemed a contradiction in terms. It is now a cliché. It was The Beatles and Stones, under Chicago influence, who made that happen. In Britain, The Beatles broadened rock's appeal to the middle class. Until 1963, rock 'n' roll was mainly working-class. Middle-class kids liked Elvis, but among older teenagers trad jazz was as popular as rock 'n' roll. The Beatles changed all that overnight. Their lyrics, craftedness and new angles on song – social comment and compassion as well as surreal cheek – found intellectual and emotional response from a world which did not normally listen to pop music. Their European-style dress and hair, their record-sleeves and French-movie look, spawned a more chic and knowing image for rock music. Photography became vital. The mix of faces, the togetherness, was the visual core.

No one realized how big the group thing would be, especially not the Fab Four. In 1964, a year into their career when they'd had four No. 1 hits, Paul McCartney said 'When all this' (he meant the screaming kids) 'is over, John and I want to concentrate on songwriting.' Assuming the group would stop having hits and break up, he wanted to write hits for the next generation. There was no game plan for being so big so long. It had never happened before.

They also began doing their own lyrics. That's what a rock group does now; it writes its own songs. But rock was not always this way. Elvis, for instance, mostly sang other people's songs. Rock songwriting essentially began with The Beatles and Stones (watching Dylan's unstoppable creativity coming in left of field from the folk market) under the inspiration of bluesmen like Robert Johnson. It was usually only one or two who originally came up with the songs, but recordings emerged from the teamwork and came over as a group effort.

This was when rock began to appeal to boys. Here were heroes to identify with, to belong with. All that creativity, male bonding, shared adventure. As David Bowie sang ten years later, 'When you're a boy/ You can wear a uniform.' Join the club: The Beatles in their boys-together yellow submarine or Lonely Hearts Club Band; The Stones, making Muddy Water's proclamation 'I'm a man, I'm a rolling stone' gloriously plural. One legend says Jagger and Richards played together as kids, and re-met by happy accident aged twenty on the London Underground. Both were carrying records by Muddy Waters and instantly recognized a kindred spirit. The two heroes, comrades well-met below the earth in a tunnel, go off together on a glorious quest, gathering about them a band of comrades who weather all dangers – though one drops tragically by the wayside. It happened; but the way it slid into legend was shaped by a thousand ancient stories, from Homer to King Arthur.

You have to fit this in to another aspect of rock experience: its two-sidedness. On one side, you have what comes over from the stars: the concerts, publicity, lyrical images and themes, the musical cockiness and energy, the legendary bad behaviour. On the other side, the fans. Girls worshipped, boys identified. Boys started going to gigs, especially to see the dangerous-looking Stones or The Who. Boys loved the show-off, gang aura of bad boys together. Gangs reinforce codes; they resist outside influences which dilute or destroy their unity. You identify, you want to do it too – whether 'it' means sixties and seventies air guitar, nineties MC-ing, mixing and scratching, or sex and drugs.

From the group era on, boys dreamed of playing guitar together, of being jointly the rock deity who gave a particular story-shape and persona (the young hero on the brink, being a boy being a man) to teenage dreams. The group provided different ways of doing that: individual proficiency – you could identify with what you felt you could do: when Hendrix knew he was going to England, the first thing he asked was 'Will I meet Eric Clapton?'[9] – but also the security of the gang.

Teenage Bedroom, Open Road

Rock music is music for teenagers. For listeners, even more than performers, rock is a journey, and its movement is outward, away from the parental home. The heroism dream begins in the teenage bedroom. Rock power begins in what goes on in the listening teenager's head. Here too, things swing between intensely public and intensely private. The public bit happens on the dance floor, or the garage where you play with your band. Boys experience rock as a collective culture far more than girls, and one point is the shared male world.[10] But the private headphones and bedroom, where you do your homework and listen, over and over, to that single you've just bought, is the target of the whole rock industry. Here you are in, say, the late sixties, listening to the Stones singing 'Let's Spend the Night Together'. Whaat?! You are alone in your room, dreaming of doing things exactly like that. This masturbatory solitude (see the Stones' album *Sticky Fingers*), the private making of a sexual persona that gets tried out in public, is rock's inner reality: a boy laying claim to his culture's glamorous images of maleness in a bedroom whose fixtures and economics are controlled by mum. (This, anyway, is the UK picture, drawn from sixties memoirs and the personal memories of my friends. Was it that different in Sweden or Japan, or in the US today?)

As a lone self in the bedroom, this boy is dying to get out of the house. Eric Burden of The Animals sings 'We've Gotta get Out of This Place'. On *Sticky Fingers* (1971), the Stones did a version of 'You Gotta Move' by Fred McDowell. 'We are the young', they sing, 'Breaking all the walls/ Breaking all the rules.' He wants out, this boy, but so far he is only at home here, his own private 'House of the Rising Sun' where he makes the music repetitively his own, reads *NME*, sends off for posters, puts rock-heroes so close on those otherwise unbreached walls that you can't see an inch of mum's wallpaper. He is alone, but also one of a tribe:

> It was obviously, inarguably, *our* music. If we had any initial doubt about that, our parents' horrified – or at best dismissive – reactions banished those doubts. Growing up in a world we were only beginning to understand, we had finally found something for us; for us together, for us alone.[11]

The teenage bedroom is the secret side of the rock stadium, your formative limbo, your lair where you assimilate what you hear, turn it into what you feel, use it as sounding-board for what happens in public. In crisis you collapse back on it, like Hornby's *High Fidelity* hero:

> I organize my record collection at times of emotional stress. What I like is the feeling of security... There's a whole world in here, a nicer, dirtier, more violent, more peaceful... more loving world than the world I live in.[12]

There are two big ironies about the teen bedroom (which now begins age eleven) as opposed to any bedroom conjured up by adult crooners of the forties. It is where you dream about sex, by yourself or with same-sex friends: not, at first, where it happens.

Second, this territory is yours but not yours. This is why rock has to be 'against'. You learn rock sexuality through a shared, hopefully subversive, electronic framework – radio, CDs, TV, spin-off magazines – while others are doing the same in similar bedrooms. Your territory, your sexuality; becoming more complex, more potent, more yours through music. But this territory is yours only on an increasingly uneasy lease. (See Randy Newman's 1969 song, 'Mama Told Me Not to Come'.) It is space carved out of your previous ways of being in this house. Carved out angrily (heavy metal can be a thorn-hedge keeping parents out, part of the point is that they cannot bear it), and critically, against parental values at a time of changing allegiance:

as rock itself became more potent, crashing its rebarbative way into power *via* money in the adult world. This is your generation, generating meanings your parents won't – thank God – share. 'Forget it, you wouldn't understand anyway,' says Flipper's misunderstood boy.[13]

So you have a paradox: you belong to a vast teenage club, a conspiracy, a group, from the place where you are most alone. As inspiration, the two main forms of blues met both needs, but for lone listeners in a bed-sit the big pull was the lone bluesman, solo voice on the open road. Richards and co. played electric blues but they thrilled to the single voice, the demonic solitude, of Robert Johnson. Roaming was a firmly male thing. Blueswomen went on the road with an entourage. Their blues are as rampant as the men's, the sex metaphors as funny, biting and surprising. But the metaphors are inner fixed things, doorbells, furniture, kitchens, not railways and the open road. And the self-image of rock was founded on male, not female blues. For a sixties boy confined to A levels and home, the great fantasy was being alone on the move. The bluesmen who sang the songs from which blues came had to travel to find work. Farm work was seasonal, labour short-term. Women stayed home to keep families together. In white legend, the blues were first heard in a context of travel, at a railway station, the great mythic place of blues' despair, hope, and journeys. W. C. Handy heard a man in 1905 playing slide guitar, singing a blues about going to the meeting-point of two great railroads. Going 'Where the Southern crosses the Dog'. Male twenties and thirties musicians were lone itinerants whom white tradition saw as wandering minstrels. 'I got ramblin' on my mind' sings Robert Johnson.

The male tool, the guitar, expressed male freedom to come and go. Rock translated Robert Johnson's 'ramblin'' into the power the guitar mysteriously bestows to move in, out and on through every part of the world, including women. No accident that Jack Kerouac's novel *On the Road* came out in the great year of Elvis Presley. 'Rambling', one of rock's talismanic words, echoed in the names of many groups and songs, is part of the macho 'Sorry babe, I'm on my way' stance. In a love and sex context, 'I'm a man, I'm a rolling stone' becomes 'I've got more important things to do than stay with you, babe.'[14] The guitar, the 'easy rider', fuels the heroic journey. As Dylan sang, in a song echoing a million male blues:

> How does it feel to be without a home?
> How does it feel to be on your own?
> Like a rolling stone.

In sixties rock, the hero's journey got mainly translated into sex. No more searching for work like the Delta bluesmen. Rambling defines a man, but its point is sexual: the questing penis. Kerouac's great hero, Neal Cassady, sees the right to move from one girl to the next as the modern definition of freedom. And the freedom is sexually defined, the flit from one bed to another. 'Are you crying over me, babe? I'm not worth it' is the message. Marvin Gaye's 'Wherever I Lay My Hat' sees it as a fact of nature:

> I'm the type of boy who is always on the road
> Wherever I lay my hat, that's my home.

As sung by Paul Young (one of the most expressive white soul singers of the eighties) in a putting-my-arms-round-you voice, the tune-shape and atmosphere are the quintessence of soothe. Aren't you lucky, babe, you're experiencing Nature as she really is, through me. 'What do I have to do, to make you understand/ I'm the type of guy who gives the girl the eye,/ Everybody knows./ Well, I'll love them and I'll leave them,/ Break their hearts and deceive them,/ Everywhere I go.' The self-gratulatory selfishness comes over in pseudo-comforting, seductively reasonable, sorry-to-break-your-heart mode: male roaming is as ancient and un-get-roundable as the hills. 'I can't help it, you see.'

ORIGINS: MYTH, SEX AND ELECTRICITY

Sound of Male Freedom:
Could You Ever Take Cock out of Rock?

On the cover of an excellent book on women's rock, advertised as 'taking the cock out of rock', a girl holds an electric guitar.[15] She's on the move, away from the power socket behind her, empowered on the road by guitar; and by the eternal availability of the next socket. The designer wanted to give her that archetypal rock detachability, sexual-cum-musical, of being free as long as you can plug in somewhere, for a while. The instrument is tool and rationale for the journey.

But this image is historically – and therefore archetypally, to eyes whose ways of seeing are formed by the iconography of the last fifty years – male. It is confirmed by the sexual symbolism of waiting socket, plus easy-come-easy-go instrument. The iconography, invoking the hero's movement away (from the last juke-house, last island, last woman) was constructed round the figure of a man and grew from a profoundly ancient male self-image. By the early sixties, the guitar had become the musical icon of all that on-your-bike, 'I can't help it you see' male narcissism. On the cover of his 1962 album *Have Guitar, Will Travel,* Bo Diddley (a great innovator in guitar distortion, feedback, echo, tremolo) straddles a red-and-white moped, colour-coded to his guitar. Guitar and bike belong together. One is emblem of the other. Guitar and bike power your journey. 'He's got a ticket to ride and he don't care' goes the song written by Lennon and McCartney, about the classic easy rider from the girl he has equally classically left behind (sung most poignantly by Karen Carpenter, in an arrangement made by the only man she really loved, her brother): 'He said that living with me was bringing him down, He would never be free when I was around.'[16]

What a man's gotta be is free. Traditionally, women's voices were good at accepting (and finding sexy) all this male rambling. 'He's a tramp', sang Peggy Lee in the song she wrote for Disney's *Lady and the Tramp.* 'He's a rover, and I wish that I could travel his way.' 'He's a rambler and a gambler, a sweet-talking ladies' man', sings Joni Mitchell. Mobility makes a real man. For boys, the guitar sound became the power dream to the sort of freedom – many women, no commitments, no walls – hymned by Kerouac's *On the Road*, the male Beat Bible.

So giving a girl that icon, with the little empty hole of the socket behind her, is not taking cock out of rock, but trying to add one, symbolically, to women. As some women rockers do quite literally with rubber cocks (Chapter 18), and others (so some people argue) do implicitly by impersonating an aggression our society construes as male. How can you take the cock out of rock, if maleness is what it is all about, and two thousand years of male imagination are at work behind its dreams and symbols?

Guitar technique reflects the old male dream of free-wheeling sexual mobility. A riff is male freedom in action: slide, leap, tremolo, risk, daring, adventure. As an object next to your body (on stage, in photos, on the road), the guitar can be your cock, your woman, or both. (Many guitarists, like Bo Diddley, gave their guitars a woman's name.) You take it with you, as the guitarist Chet Atkins said, 'for comfort'.[17] But whatever else it stands for, it is an emblem of male free-to-go sexuality. The rock cowboys of the sixties carried theirs through recording studios, airports and stadiums, not the open road. But beside them rambled the fantasy-shadow of the bluesman.

The black guitar-slinger, on the road between juke-houses and women, was elided in white imagination with the gunslinger, the rovin' white cowboy. 'Ramblin'' was not only a myth-driven justification of sexual infidelity; it also fed that other vital arena of the male self-image, violence. Here we go back from the epic journey to epic battlefield, from the *Odyssey* to the *Iliad*. In 1967 Peter Green's song made male detachedness cute and disarming: 'I'm a ramblin' pony, just roamin' from town to town'. But two years later, Jagger's 'Midnight Rambler' made it murderous. Nick Cave followed suit with 'Red Right Hand'.[18] Male rambling became sinister prowling, male mobility a lethal loose connection in the dark.

American Romanticism and the Freedom of Narcissus

The Greek god of movement was male. Hermes (Mercury, in Latin) was 'lord of roads': protector of the threshold, master of entry and exit, of male freedom to come and go. In every street of classical Athens, his bearded face and erect cock bristled outside every door.[19] His opposite number in the pantheon was Hestia, goddess of the hearth, fixed warm centre of the home. Inwardness (you'll be surprised to hear) was female, inner, still: male is in, out and away. The epic mobility of Ulysses, the journeys of Hercules, the sea-voyage of Theseus, predated blues by two thousand years. But these spatial symbolics infiltrated European imagination wholesale, including the imaginative reactions that went into white rock 'n' roll. The blues' rolling-stone image came from real-life need: twenties Delta farmworkers and thirties bluesmen had to travel to find work. But in white male rock, urban teenagers projected on to that image the whole European epic heritage of male mobility. The rock image of freedom was created by boys sitting still in a bed-sit or standing by a microphone, polishing the dream of a male self heading into the blue from within that 'roomful of mirrors' represented by the recording studio. Narcissus looking in the mirror, seeing himself as master of the open road.

Another force behind this use of the blues as a male rambling ideal was the male narcissism end of American romanticism. Created in America, rock 'n' roll spoke with an American voice, even when British boys got in on the act. Its great forerunner, hero of American romanticism, the man who wrote the words that became the archetypal teenage anthem, 'I Sing the Body Electric', was Walt Whitman. In the 1850s, a hundred years before the invention of the teenager, he put sex openly on the agenda of American literature. 'I believe in the flesh and the appetites,' he thundered. 'I am not a bit tamed ... I sound my barbaric yawp over the roofs of the world.' He gave sex an aggressive male voice:

> Sex contains all, bodies, souls...
> It is I, you women, I make my way,
> I am stern, acrid, large, undissuadable, but I love you,
> I do not hurt you any more than is necessary for you.[20]

Keeping quiet about being gay, he came out as poet of the male body, male crotch, turning it into baroque verbal display:

> The smoke of my own breath,
> Echoes, ripples, buzz'd whispers, love-root, silk thread, crotch and vine,
> My respiration and inspiration, the beating of my heart, the passing of blood and air through my lungs...

Song of the Open Road (1856) is the classic epic of the questing penis insisting on its freedom:

> Afoot and light-hearted I take to the open road,
> Healthy, free, the world before me,
> The long brown path before me leading wherever I choose.

As in Byron's *Don Juan*, travel is sexual and geographic at once. The naked male body is part of nature:

> I will go to the bank by the wood and become undisguised and naked, I am mad for it to be in contact with me

God exists, but the poet prefers to worship his own flesh:

> I hear and behold God in every object, yet understand God not in the least,
> Nor do I understand who there can be more wonderful than myself...
> If I worship one thing more than another it shall be the spread of my own body, or any part of it...
> Breast that presses against other breasts it shall be you!...

Winds whose soft-tickling genitals rub against me it shall be
you!...
I dote on myself, there is that lot of me and all so luscious.[21]

This is American Narcissus, glorying in his own physique. 'That lot of me, and all so luscious' – that line should float six miles high on the banner of male rock, ideal caption for a million photo-shots from Elvis to Jagger, Bowie to Prince. So should the first line of *Song of Myself*: 'I celebrate myself, and sing myself.' A whole sixties generation of American males found their own narcissism (or, to put it more gently, their wish to have their own sexuality noticed) mirrored in Whitman's. Bill Clinton gave Monica Lewinsky a copy of the *Collected Works*. American romanticism was a vital channel by which the narcissism of Greek male self-images came cascading out in the new voice of rock 'n' roll. When men finally stopped pouring sexual energy into writing songs for women to sing, and began singing their own young, strong, show-off 'song of myself'. Rock 'n' roll cashed the 'song of myself' cheque that Whitman wrote a century before. For the first time, a man could be the open object of desire while singing about his own.

Narcissism has a high profile anyway in all popsong. Popsong is a multiplicity of sonic images mainly used for thinking about yourself: for trying on roles in your mind, fitting your own self-image to a kaleidoscope of I-and-you relationships. Everything happens in that tiny echoing space between a you and a me. 'You' is a vital word in pop. The *Da Capo Companion to Popular Music* has a 145-page index of song titles: 285 begin with 'You'. The singer desires that magic 'you' ('You Make Me Feel Mighty Real', 'You've Got to Hold onto Me'), or complains ('You'se a Viper', 'You Keep Me Hanging On'). But 'You' is only the second largest entry. Pop is, above all, the 'song of the self'; and 785 songs (the largest category by miles) begin with 'I'.

Rock 'n' roll self-centredness can be sent up – like the first single of The Boomtown Rats, 'Looking After Number One' (1977), with its repeated hook line 'Don't wanna be like you';

or the group called Right Said Fred, with their song 'I'm too Sexy for My Shirt'. But it mostly takes itself extremely seriously. Women are not immune to narcissism. (Not at all.) But from Elvis on, rock 'n' roll was set up for the male sort. Echo is female. Traditionally, your audience of teenage girls, your fan-base without which no rock god can breathe, is a screaming cave of femininity, giving back the echo of your song. Rock 'n' roll let men claim the right to be both free and narcissistic. Mick Jagger was 'always starring in an endless movie' (said Marianne Faithfull). 'He has to look great all the time for the great director in the sky ... His damn image pervades everything.' She learned from him 'to disregard myself as a sexual object. *He* was the sex object! To everybody!' Narcissism was 'what made him Mick'.[22]

Celebrating male narcissism, rock 'n' roll created a new form of self-display out of the Greek scenario of male display and female echo. The screaming girls echo maleness celebrating itself. 'At my first appearance I was very nervous,' said Elvis once:

> They started howlin' out there and Ah didn't know why. Ah went off stage and mah manager told me Ah was – Ah was wigglin' mah legs. So Ah went out there and – did it some more.[23]

How you used your narcissism depended on you. Prince became a superstar by perfecting a brilliant brand of bawdy narcissism, of oral sex, incest, masturbation and 'Twenty-one Positions in a One-Night Stand'. But Elvis was the prototype, 'the first male white singer to propose that fucking was a desirable activity in itself ... He was master of the sexual simile, treating his guitar as both phallus and girl, punctuating his lyrics with the animal grunts and groans of the male approaching orgasm.'

You can see the Whitmanesque self-celebration in male rock critics as they gleefully identify with Elvis's sexiness:

> Earlier singers might carry great sex appeal, but they'd have to cloak it under the trappings of romanticism ... Elvis was blatant. When those axis hips got moving, there was no

more pretence about moonlight and hand-holding; it was hard physical fact.

Overt male sexuality was the new thing: 'hard' physical fact, celebrated in public as rampantly as Whitman went on about it in words. White male critics shared it by describing how it shocked their own culture:

> Elvis made it quite clear he felt he was doing any woman he accepted a favour. He dressed to emphasize both his masculinity and basic narcissism, and rumour had it that into his skin-tight jeans was sewn a lead bar to suggest a weapon of heroic proportions.[24]

Narcissism took its toll on singers, though. In every rock biography a point comes where it wrecks relationships with partners and colleagues. The life would foster narcissism even if it wasn't there to start with. After a year of superstardom, Hendrix wrote:

> I used to live in a roomful of mirrors
> All I could see was me...[25]

'Songs of self' can lead where Narcissus ended, crashing headlong into the image in the mirror. At his last concert in 1970, forced back on the road by management, Hendrix was bored out of his skull playing music he wanted to move on from:

> The guitar fought him, betrayed him; strings slipped from unaccountably numb fingers... He seemed exhausted, tormented, trapped. His death less than three weeks later seemed hideously appropriate. On the stage, he already seemed three parts dead.[26]

What Whitman couldn't foresee was how drugs got in on the rock 'n' roll act, how fame fed the narcissism, and how the two together put a stop to a whole lot of heroes' journeys.

Why Blues?

All right, then: music powered by an instrument which somehow became, visually and soundwise, the totem of male sexual freedom. A genre powered imaginatively, emotionally, sonically by different strands of the blues, the lone bluesman, the electric group. Symbolically as well as musically, blues were the foundation of rock. But why? What were the deeper reasons that the major new white music of the twentieth century came from copying black music, and impersonating the bluesmen who made it? What were the implications and knock-on effects of all this, on white music and on black?

PART 2 Impersonation: The Black Empowering
of Rock and of Its Violence

The negro is the creative voice of America. It was a happy day for America when the first unhappy slave landed on its shores.

DUKE ELLINGTON

8 The Black Hero: Call of the Wild

Sex and Envy: Orientalism, Exoticism, Otherism

What is imitation? Or impersonation? What do they do, to everyone – the impersonator, the imitated, the audience? If rock was a new male 'song of myself', how come it began as someone else's song? Where does imitation stop and being 'yourself' begin? Does the mask ever become the face inside? And why imitate at all?

There are different kinds of answer for what rock did with, and to, the blues. Not only musical but cultural, social, historical, emotional and mythic. They all raise questions about creativity itself. Does making something always involve theft? You identify with something not yours, steal something from outside yourself to make it new, and your own – is that it? Sculptors make stone and wood look like flesh. Poets look at landscape and turn it into words. A male composer imagines women's feelings, turns them into his, and writes 'Dove Sono' for women to sing about men.

Historical answers involve specific twentieth-century white fantasies of blacks, black sexuality and the idea that here was a community free to have the kind of fun which white society denied itself. Freud could only have made headlines by pointing out the centrality of sex, and the mechanisms of its repression, to a society that managed sex through symbols, codes and implication. Black culture did not need Freud any more than the Cretan village I lived in in the seventies, where everyone was so aware of phallic symbols that to an outsider like me older villagers politely said 'excuse me' before anything that could be the slightest bit phallic. Cucumbers, even donkeys. Conversation was peppered with 'excuse-me' ('I went to town on the excuse-me donkey, to sell my excuse-me cucumbers . . .'). Fifties white teenagers found in black music all that open awareness of sex so missing from fifties white life: what white America feared or was ashamed of, in people or society, was kept under wraps. Communism, black anger at inequality, and sex. Rock 'n' roll evoked the lot. Like funk and jazz, 'rock 'n' roll' *meant* sex. 'Good Rockin' Tonight' (a 1955 hit for Elvis) was written by the black singer Roy Brown in 1947. 'Good rockin' – you know what *that* means,' said Brown. 'I had my mind on this girl in the bedroom. Listen man, I wrote them kind of songs. I was a dirty cat.'[1] Impersonation has envy and lack at its core. You impersonate Roy Brown's dirtiness, you empower your own songs of self by borrowing someone else's joy in sexuality.

But all this had a history. Copying cultures you fear or laugh at, in order to buy yourself attributes you feel you lack (especially a more potent masculinity), had often happened before. One example was European orientalism. After the Crusades, Western Europe felt increasingly threatened by the Ottoman Empire. Between 1522 and 1664 the Turks captured Rhodes, Cyprus and Crete, shattered Vienna's walls, invaded Hungary twice and waged war with Austria and Venice. In the fashionable language of 'self and other' (two rhetorical soulmates who romp through psychoanalytic, literary, historical and anthropological writing today), 'the Turk' provided the ideal 'other' for any 'self' to fear or fantasize about. European operas and literature of the sixteenth and later centuries teem with fantasies of lust-driven Turkish potentates plus oriental luxury. Orientalizing swept into interior design, dress, painting, travel writing, fusing fantasies of wilder, deeper, spiritual and/or sexual power. Orientalizing meant dressing yourself physically or emotionally in everything 'of the East'; wisdom to turbans, bathroom tiles to harem pants.[2]

This sort of exoticism, orientalism or otherism involves imagining desires and pleasures you find unsatisfactory in your own self (or race, gender, society or country), projecting them on to someone else (often someone you envy, though you may disguise that with mockery), and imitating their outer trappings and symbols. You can get away with being 'baser' than your own society expects, by impersonating someone society stereotypes and laughs at, to cover up envy or fear. The glamour and luxury stand in for a set-up where masculine potency is more openly revered (think sultans, harems), where sex is freer.

Freer, that is, for the fantasizing male. This form of otherism tends to be a male speciality: the fantasy of going into 'other', summed up by the man in Tennyson's *Locksley Hall* who dreams of 'yonder shining Orient', where

> The passions, cramp'd no longer, shall have scope and
>   breathing space.
> I shall take some savage woman, she shall rear my dusky
>   race.

Nineteenth-century male fantasies were sexually as well as economically imperialist. From Alexander Pope, putting in an order to Lady Mary Wortley Montagu in 1718 for a Circassian slave, to Mozart's *Escape from the Seraglio* (1782), from James Silk Buckingham, a British journalist who had himself painted (in 1816) in Oriental costume with his wife like a Sultan sitting with a concubine, from Ingres' paintings of harems, of *La Grande Odalisque* (1814), *Odalisque and Slave* (1842), to Victorian pornography like *The Lustful Turk* (1828), an increasingly important force behind Europe's images of the orient was male sexual fantasy.[3]

But Western otherism goes much much further back: it is coded into the earliest Greek myths. Pre-classical Greeks were surrounded by *barbaroi*, 'non-Greek-speakers'. The great cultures across the sea, Persia, Egypt, Lydia, Babylon, Phoenicia, Crete, were older, richer, more powerful, more advanced. From the second millennium BC, Greeks traded with them; from the eighth century BC they learned from them not just styles and techniques (in dress, pottery, sculpture) but writing itself.

History begins with Greece carrying away not just women but other essential pieces of other people's cultural fabric: shapes and patterns, materials and tools, words, food, and technological or architectural ideas.

Yet Greeks were mercilessly racist, and despised non-Greek speakers, *barbaroi*. Their attitude ('We live in *our* land and language: any others are barbarians') provided the pejorative 'barbarian'; the first base of orientalism.[4] Yet their past was utterly implicated in these alien kingdoms. Those stories of 'women carried away' are fraught with international relations: the great European myths of desire belong with Greek relations with the South and the East. Myths of the Cretan royal family, riddled with bestiality and incest, turned on relations with Athens. Pasiphae, wife of King Minos, had sex with a bull and produced the Minotaur whom Athenian Theseus killed; her first daughter, Ariadne, eloped with Theseus and eventually married Dionysus, god of drink; her second daughter, Phaedra, married Theseus but lusted after his son and eventually got Theseus to destroy him. Democratic Athens had a great time portraying the destructive passion of exotic queens, stuffing its tragedies full of politically incorrect foreigners.[5]

Classical Greece effectively began when Persians invaded Greece in 490 BC and the Greek cities got together and threw them out. Persia remained the big enemy, yet was also a byword for effeminacy, luxury and glamour. Upper-class Athenians imitated Eastern fashions, slippers, jewellery, luxury fabrics, cuisine. So there was a double attitude: *barbaroi* were a package of ancient danger, luxury, superiority, envy and contempt, all muddled up with the issue of slavery. The slave market depended on war (enslaving captured populations) and trade with the East. Aristotle defends slavery politically by saying *barbaroi* were used to slavery because they lived under monarchies, not (like us) democracy. These richer, more elegant peoples, objects of envious fantasy, were exactly the ones Greeks thought appropriate to enslave. Non-Greek-speaking slaves are also stereotypically stupid. Athenian policemen were Scythian archers, slaves of the state. In one Aristophanes comedy, a Scythian policeman pathetically chats up a dancing-girl in pidgin Greek, while the Athenian hero escapes.[6] From way back, orientalism or otherism mingled slavery (with all its self-justifying rhetoric of inferiority) with stereotypes of people who cannot speak your language properly, and also with sexual fantasy.

In modern Europe, imperial rule over India and Africa expanded orientalizing from Turks to blacks. Sexual fantasy, the underside of imperialist imagination, poured into pre-existing stereotypes descending originally from Greek views – and a Greek poetics – of barbarians.[7] And was again used to justify slave trade.

Many ancient layers of white fantasy, therefore, underlay nineteenth-century white fear and envy of black sexuality. They all fed American racism, whose stereotyping became more vicious, determined and defensive after the Civil War.[8] In the eighteenth and nineteenth centuries, any virile young white man or male seducer was a 'buck'. By the early twentieth century a 'buck' was black, and the next word would be 'nigger'. One line on American racism and the rise of the American working-class is that poor white labourers felt blacks were sexually uninhibited in a way they themselves couldn't be after the industrial revolution got at them. A swashbuckling maleness that once belonged to every male (well, dream on) now belonged only to blacks. Whites saw in blacks 'a pornography of their former selves'; which fed white appetites for black-face shows like *The Black and White Minstrels Show*.[9] But these stereotypes of blacks were also a pornography of what whites longed to be. The other side of the black sexuality threat is wish fulfilment: the idea that blacks have bigger cocks.

The form your otherism takes, the way you steal or fantasize about bits and pieces of someone else's identity, depends on historical context; and on the other culture's relation to yours. Fifties white America stole from a looked-down-upon, ex-slave indigenous population; ancient Greece from mythicized trade rivals across the sea whom they enslaved whenever they could. But fear, suspicion and sexual envy fed both imaginative backgrounds; this is what drove the repression of the fifties and conservative reaction to rock 'n' roll as 'niggers' music'.

In the simmeringly de-segregating South, attack focused on blackness both of singers and sound. When schools were desegregated in Little Rock, Arkansas in September 1957, a thousand paratroopers went in to help. In music, the fundamental issue was fury at any black music mattering so much to white people. A man mattering to other people, a hero of music with the drawing-power of Orpheus: that image belonged patriarchally, in the South, to whites. In April 1956 even Nat King Cole, a jazz singer-pianist more popular with whites than blacks – not rock 'n' roll, little to do with black tradition, everything to do with Bing Crosby-type crooning – was dragged off his piano stool and concert platform in Birmingham, Alabama, in front of a white audience of three thousand. He was then beaten up – and one of the attackers was a Director of the 'White Citizens' Council' which supported audience segregation and wanted to boycott 'bop and negro music'. That month, white church groups asked for rock 'n' roll to be suppressed as a plot to corrupt white youth.[10]

Elsewhere, the main complaint was the anti-authoritarianness of rock 'n' roll, along with the cockily overt sex. Blackness exacerbated both. Moralists threw at rock 'n' roll the same mix of fantasy and envy sheened with revulsion that their dads threw at jazz and their grandpas at the Charleston. *Newsweek* in 1956 denounced rock as 'negroes' music' which encouraged 'animalism' and 'the base in man'. *Music Journal* in 1958 said it was 'a throwback to jungle rhythms', enticing teenagers into 'orgies of sex and violence, as its model did for savages'. 'Where do you go,' asked the TV critic John Crosby, 'from that unspeakably untalented vulgar young entertainer Elvis Presley; short of obscenity, which is against the law?'[11] Wealthy owners of private radio stations were barracked in their country clubs if their DJs played 'jungle music'. They pressurized DJs to take rock 'n' roll off the air. While smaller specialist R&B stations boomed, these DJs had the impossible task of keeping their audience while playing as few black-sounding records as possible.[12] Rockers, meanwhile, wanted to sound blacker than ever. Exoticism, primitivism, otherism worked in every segment of white society, firing responses to, above all, the sexiness of black music. Centuries of white fantasy went into creating those American psyches of 1956. Both the teenagers who loved it and the racist moralists who loathed and feared it felt blackness meant a dangerously bigger, wilder masculinity.

Primitivism: Africa in New York

In impersonating black music, rock harvested half a century of white revivification by black culture. Even in the 1900s, black dances like the foxtrot and Charleston usurped the waltz in upper-middle-class American society. Stravinsky's *Rite of Spring* came in 1913. Modernism had begun to marry the ultra-modern with ideas of the primitive, the ancient. Jazz summed this marriage up. Paris, where Picasso was inspired by tribal art, where America and Africa collided in a French accent, was a crucible of primitivism: 'In the wake of Woodrow Wilson's visit to Versailles in 1919, avant-garde Paris was Americanized. Black jazz swept the scene; Josephine Baker led the black company of the Revue des Nègres.'[13]

But primitivism and modernism's prime patch was New York, especially Harlem, because at their heart was the African origin of American blacks. In twenties Harlem the avant-garde and the atavistic stalked hand-in-hand in the concert hall, the art gallery, the sidewalk. European and American audiences of the twenties and thirties, responding to black music in night-clubs and cafés, increasingly felt these musicians they thought 'primitive' possessed energies and intuition they did not. 'I could hear new ideas being born,' said a London critic about Duke Ellington in 1933. 'I was amazed at the technical perfection of the instrumentation... Proof that the much-despised Negro is working out a culture all his own.' America suddenly found its underclass was a cultural asset: it not only learned from black imaginative and creative powers, but made them the symbol of modern America. When, long after, the culture which destroyed the American Indians co-opted them as its own ancestors by renaming them 'Native Americans', it was repeating the move that put New York at the forefront of modernism – when white America laid claim to indigenous Americanness, and finally sloughed off attempts to imitate tired old Europe by adopting black music as its own.[14]

Black music's dark laughter radically transformed the white profile of America. It merged ideas of far-off, savage, shadowy beginnings-of-things with the modern city. Jazz – modern but primitive, African but American, the USA's homegrown exotic – was the sound of 'the urban jungle'. And the hero of this jungle was black. In the Harlem Renaissance, negroes were the royalty of New York bohemia, the cutting edge of modernity. From 1927 to 1932, Duke Ellington played and broadcast from the Cotton Club and became a white household name. But except for black celebrities and performers' friends, the audience (seven or eight hundred a night) was white. Ellington came from the professional Washington middle-classes, but catered for primitivizing white taste by giving his pieces titles like 'Jungle Nights in Harlem' and 'Arabian Lover'. In his memoirs, Duke's bandleader Cab Calloway (whose 1930 recording début 'St Louis Blues' was backed by 'The Jungle Boys') described the scene:

> The bandstand was a replica of a southern mansion with large white columns and a backdrop painted with weeping willows and slave quarters. The band played on the veranda. The waiters wore red tuxedos like butlers in a southern mansion. The whole set was sleepy-time-South during slavery.[15]

This was race tourism, evoking times when white had complete control of black. For one evening, whites could surf black experience (as they imagined it), for a short below-stairs *frisson*.

It was voyeurism, based on clichés – as in the film *Titanic*, where the warm-hearted joys of lower-deck dancing are a stereotyped contrast to the self-satisfied control freaks in First Class. This voyeurism involves taking up the floorboards to see what's going on beneath – in your own home, history, society or psyche. Like Walt Whitman, 'the first white aboriginal poet' (as D. H. Lawrence called him), priding himself on his primitiveness, white audiences wanted to feel the jungle, as well as the cravat, belonged to them. Parading the savage sexuality of your civilized self, sending determinedly barbaric yawps through the world, nineteenth-century American romanticism paved the way for twenties primitivism.

Images of Africa were at the bottom of it all. Behind that vision of slave-time South was the primevalness that had driven the European fantasy of the dark continent. Duke's music seemed an African night-bloom, glimmering simultaneously through the smoke of a New York night-club and the gleaming clouds of American romanticism. But behind both smoke and gleam were imperial European associations of blackness with 'the animal in man', ancient ideas that 'primitive' people were closer to nature than us civilized folk.[16] Primitivism and racism were two sides of the same crystal. Turn it, you get the same fantasy. Primitivism idealized what racism feared. The concept did not change; 'primitive' simply became desirable.

All the arts, not only music, transformed themselves by images of 'primitive' energy. Intellectually and aesthetically, from Joseph Conrad's *Heart of Darkness* (1899) to Picasso's use of African sculpture, modernism made the West reappraise primitive forms.[17] It was a long falling-in-love. In psychology, Freud and Jung rewrote primitive myth into the Western unconscious. Anthropology like Frazer's *Golden Bough* helped Cambridge classicists Gilbert Murray and Jane Harrison turn inside-out that holy of European holies, Greek culture: to see its primitive side.

The value you put on 'primitive' depended on you. Few people really examined what it meant. In *Paleface* (1929), Wyndham Lewis presented primitivism as sentimental rubbish making civilized people feel inferior.[18] *Paleface* came at the end of the decade of first blues recordings, the year Bessie Smith recorded 'Nobody Knows You when You're Down and Out'. Her artistry, perfected as Lewis was satirizing the valuing of 'primitive' black culture, is now an essential part of white cultural history, which goes on inspiring other singers. Who (except for research) reads Lewis now? Sixty years on, what looks more 'primitive': his sulky clinging to the aesthetic he knew, or her flawless timing and phrasing, her generous, outflung vulnerability of voice?

The drive to be black which powered white rock 'n' roll came also from a hunger to find new forms to express depth of feeling. White society was suddenly claiming whole new swathes of wild feeling as its own. The whole business of *dancing by yourself* – like a dervish – seemed delightfully primitive. When rock historians stress the African origins of rock 'n' roll, they are responding not just to musical material but the legacy of modernism, so in love with 'primitive' roots of any art. Rock music identified with its own primitive origins. 'Let's bungle in the jungle,' sang Jethro Tull in 1974. (A Greek pop song I remember from that same year began 'Let's go to the jungle with Tarzan'.) Rock culture's heroes are masters of the primitive. Jackson Pollock, who learned primitivism from Picasso, appeared in the Museum of Modern Art's 1984 show on primitivism in twentieth-century art, but Patti Smith's 'Rock 'n' Roll Nigger' (1976) had outed him as rock hero long before. 'Hendrix was a nigger/ Jackson Pollock was a nigger':

> Baby was a black sheep, baby was a whore
> Baby got big and baby gets bigger . . .
> Baby baby baby was a rock 'n' roll nigger.[19]

Whatever his colour, the rock hero was black – and getting 'bigger'.

The Lure of Black Rhythm: Community and Dance

Musical imitation, impersonation and ventriloquism are different things in different contexts. White musicians borrowing black style and persona was utterly different from male composers writing songs for women which ventriloquized male fantasies of female passion. Opera composers did imagine feelings for black characters too (like lustful, vengeful Monostatos in Mozart's *Magic Flute*); they had fun with orientalizing motifs in the music. But blues was a whole musical vocabulary in itself, which expressed a whole, real, alien sensibility. You could copy vocal and instrumental techniques, a guitar-riff, words; or the whole spirit. 'White blues' took over the aura of community, sexuality and history which black styles brought with them, to express another persona; and transformed the original in the process.

Elvis 'was not exactly imitating blacks', says Greil Marcus. He said he 'didn't sing like nobody'. But like Jimmie Rodgers, 'Father of Country Music', he did absorb and transform black music.[20] White rock music went on building itself out of black music, assimilating its new stylistic and emotional themes. The worst stayed as flat copy, the best transcended the original and made something new. Out of the hybridizing eighties, thirty years after Elvis, the Beastie Boys got into hip-hop; they transcended it in the nineties with their seminal album, *Paul's Boutique*, pushing back boundaries, creating far more of a hybrid than the Stones made from blues in the sixties. But they were still imitating *something*: some essence of spirit or persona. From straight ventriloquy to Elvis copying black wiggles, and John Lennon copying Elvis's pelvic and splayed-leg language, it is all part of the same spectrum.

Musically, the vehicle of the sex and fun was rhythm. The 'Beat Generation' of fifties artists are supposed to have taken that name from white delight in black rhythm. Whites, feeling something missing from their own lives which blacks had 'naturally', used 'beat' to stand in for sex. (Though there are many other resonances in that title, from beatitude and heartbeat to beating the meat.) Twenty years later, Lou Reed's *Street Hassle* (Arista, 1978) encapsulated that idea: 'I wanna be black/Have natural rhythm/Don't wanna be a fucked-up middle-class college student.'

Western music always valued harmony over rhythm. That black music works through rhythm, and Western through harmony, is a cliché of music criticism. You can exaggerate the difference, but it is broadly true.[21] 'Harmony' comes from the Greek verb *harmottein*, 'fit together': as in fitting strings to a lyre. *Harmonia* first meant something like 'scale'. It was a 'mode of tuning' your lyre which came to define civilization as well as music. In Athens, 'musical' meant 'civilized', 'educated'; *harmonia* became a medical and political image for the way elements 'fit' in a healthy body or society. Health is a 'harmony', a balance of different humours or classes where every voice, body and note work together in an agreed system. In *The King and I*, the King of Siam proves he is not a barbarian by eating with a fork and dancing the polka. Look how he knows how to fit in, at the table, on the dance floor.

White pop uses the basics of Western harmony, developed over centuries, as an acoustic safety-net, image of an unchallengeable social and erotic system: what T. S. Eliot's *East Coker* calls 'The association of man and woman/In daunsinge, signifying matrimonie.' Before rock 'n' roll, white pop was not in the challenging business. You slotted formal rhythms and pretty tunes over amazingly basic harmonic structures. (Most pop harmonies still ignore developments that were revolutionary in Haydn's day.) Crude safe harmony, predictable rhythm, undemanding songs.

But no live art wants to be safe. Twentieth-century classical music developed several ways of challenging the safety-net of Western harmony: both from within the ultra-sophistication of Western harmonic tradition (dissonance, quarter-tones, the twelve-tone scale) and by plundering the alien sophistication of

Afro-American rhythm, as a source of brand-new energy. And in pop, rock 'n' roll came along.

From the twenties on, black musical styles changed white culture by rhythm, mainly because black music is so close to dance, and what the West wanted from dance was also changing. A lot of Western music evolved to support dance-patterns. From gavottes to 'The Dashing White Sergeant', you obeyed the rules and met your partner in them. The hero and heroine of *The Sound of Music* realize they are in love when they do a complicated folk-dance: an ideal 'fitting' of bodies and souls. The dances and harmonies of Western music confirmed society. *East Coker* sees them as 'A dignified and commodious sacrament'. Man meets woman: 'Two and two, necessarye coniunction,/ Holding eche other by the hand or the arm/ Which betokeneth concorde.' Precisely what fifties teenagers fled from – to where 'a lotta shakin'' was going on.

And then there's melody. Everyone has that, don't they? Well, yes and no. To Western ears, melody is a shape: of high and low, adventuring away from a key note and ending in some relation to that original home. Maybe a contented relation, maybe a poignantly unfulfilled one ending in the air, in the minor, unresolved. But there are other ways of hearing melody. Melody is time passing. How you articulate its passing depends on your musical *and* cultural background.

As white ears hear it, melody is not that big in black music. Instead of concentrating on line, you make melody complex by rhythmic decoration. Black music does not do the traditional Western thing and use harmony to chart the passing of time. Instead of what white ears listen for – melodic shape, statement, change, consequence, A to B to C – you get rhythmic elasticity and decoration. African dances start a rhythmic pattern (say, a repeated motif in 12/8 time) and get other rhythms coming in against it. With that polyrhythm behind it, a sung note in blues or jazz is a different thing: not a stage in a melodic journey, but a departure-point. The voice abandons the line for 'melisma', when you sing more than five notes to a single syllable, whose power (according to *Grove's Dictionary of Music and Musicians*) lies in 'the suspension of the syllabic relation of words to music', which means the particular syllabic relation which became the norm in Western music. In 1933, London music critics loved Duke Ellington's rhythms on his first visit to England but were baffled at where melody had gone. 'It shows you the advances made in jazz', said *The People*'s critic,

> that a Negro can come to the largest music-hall in the kingdom with a modern orchestra, cut out melody and excite a huge gathering, not with tune but with rhythm. When they play 'Some of These Days' it is almost impossible to hear any tune. Where there was a melody, you hear discordance. Where there was tenderness, there is now blare. Yet it is so exciting that some people compare it with hashish, others with falling off a train.[22]

Traditional white pop has very methodical harmony. 'It deals with melody through harmonic shifts and these dictate the rhythmic structure,' the composer Tom Adès said to me. White pop is standard eight-bar fare. 'Black pop', said Tom, 'moves and keeps going far more flexibly. It takes melody only as a starting-point.'

Of course black music uses harmony too. Vocal harmonies are essential to gospel, which was influenced by the harmonies of psalters used in churches when African-descended slaves began assimilating their own music to what they heard on the plantations: English, Scots and Irish folk-songs, drawing-room harmonies played on white pianos and, above all, hymns. But most black music is far more eclectic about harmony than white. 'Black pop only takes the harmony it wants,' said Tom Adès. Jazz challenged Western harmony by its eclecticism, by the 'blue note' that goes against the prevailing harmony, and by making rhythm and decoration its principles of movement.

The way black music handled the cardinal principle of Western music seemed to laugh the same challenge at white musical rules which black music's sexuality flung at white social horizons. For all music is sex, though white music has often been good at pretending it isn't. Musical rules, the ways notes relate to each other, reflect the social and erotic rules of relationship in the community it is played for. Western harmony controls sex with 'fittingness' and pattern; black rhythms make a different dance, where individual bodies show more freely who you are, how you belong to the community, the group. The freedom of the dancing bodies expresses the music's decorative freedom which comes from making rhythm the primary thing. This music, based on performance, implies community (rather than the lone, private pre-composition of Western music); but a community made by shared passion, not pre-worked pattern. This is the 'we' of gospel and soul, expecting the listeners to have the same background of oppression and poverty, the same hopes for sex and life, as the singer: the 'Hear me talkin' to ya' feel which Marvin Gaye got at the beginning of 'What's Going On?' by inviting the Detroit Lions into the studio to rap greetings like 'What's goin' on, man?'[23]

Rhythm and community go together. Black rhythms evoke black community just as eighteenth-century gavottes evoked the European *haute bourgeoisie*. Fifties white moralists heard black-based dance-forms defensively, as a menace to decent behaviour, and garrisoned themselves in behind beliefs that underlay the white supremacism developed after the Civil War. Thomas Dixon's *The Clansman*, published in 1905 (and filmed in 1915 as *The Birth of a Nation*), was set in 1867 South Carolina and radiates the racism which created the Ku Klux Klan. Blacks are satanic and 'jungle-eyed', full of 'onion-laden breath' and 'perspiring African odour'. Any whites keen on racial equality sink 'into the black abyss of animalism'. A white mother and daughter, raped by a black, decide to jump off a cliff in shame. They hesitate on the brink, then –

> Floating up from the river came the music of a banjo in a negro cabin, mingled with vulgar shout and song and dance.

A verse of the ribald senseless lay of the player echoed above the banjo's pert refrain:
'Chicken in de bread tray, pickin' up dough;
Granny will your dog bite? No, chile, no.'

It would be hard to imagine, now, a more innocent thing. If you took out the adjectives, what's going on in the cabin would be an Edenic vision of community. But the white women (or rather their narrator) hear it as 'senseless'. It tips the balance. They frog-leap into 'the opal gates of death'. Black song incarnates the black threat to a culture whose very death is opal-white. The sound sets off a paranoia driven by fear of that all-generations-together black community. But within fifty years, both sound and community would become a cinematic and musical cliché of joyous warmth, source not of white terror but facile envy.

In black dance, individual 'fits' differently into community. No ancient Athenian ideals of *harmonia*, like those behind a minuet. You fit not planned pattern but communal beat, which celebrates sex through shared rhythm.[24] Rock 'n' roll embraced all this with delight, wanting a sound, and a dance, whose rhythm gets melody into you, flooding your and everyone's body, coming out as energy that is both yours and shared. All this went into making teenagers a community whose tool and image was the key twentieth-century energy, electricity: the energy of communication, joining. Drugs, sex and rock 'n' roll all involve making something private (to a single body or consciousness) a shared thing. 'Soul is community,' says the trumpeter in Roddy Doyle's novel *The Commitments*. 'Soul solos fit into the thump-thump-thump. The solo is part of the song.'[25]

The solo that is part of the song, the beat that is a hotline between melody, individual and a whole community of bodies: this gift of black rhythm is at the heart of all white dreams of blackness, the modern dream of individuality within a group and on the street. White dances had rules and happened indoors, in ballrooms or barns. Rock saw itself as unruled, spontaneous togetherness: a musically engendered society of free bodies 'dancing in the street' which gives 'a chance for folks to meet'. 'Dancing in the Street': Marvin Gaye gave that title to Martha and the Vandellas' 1964 hit which became one of the most 'covered' rock songs of all time. See Little Richard (his 1971 album *King of Rock 'n' Roll*), The Who, Van Halen, David Bowie, Jagger (1985, for Live Aid). Robert Palmer took it as title for his history of rock 'n' roll.[26] It is rock music's ideal image of itself and what it does.

In that song, a 'call' comes from rhythm. ('Calling out around the world/Are you ready for a brand new beat?') Black dance-forms gave white teenagers sexual individuality within a group. Ever since, Western dance calls for free-fall physical originality, not pre-determined pattern: its ideal is being part of a group but individually free in your movements. 'Groupies' comes from 'pop groups' (before they were 'rock bands'), but the word sums up the kernel of the rock ideal: the 'group' in which everyone shows off their own sexual talent to the same beat. 'I wanna be where the bands are,' sings Bruce Springsteen. 'Tonight I wanna feel the beat of the crowd/And when I tell you that I love you/ I wanna have to shout it out loud.'

Drum and Soul

The chief instrument of 'beat' is that deeply un-white instrument, the drum. White music used drums in large orchestras, yes, but otherwise in military contexts. It was used as a signal for a flogging (the beat for a beating), the beat for a march – see those Orangemen's marches, or the huge drums carried by a massive piebald horse (currently named Spartacus) in the Queen's Household Cavalry; or the European figure of the little drummer boy. Other people's drums also spelt war, like the drums in the film *Zulu*. Imperialist adventure-tellers like Rider Haggard use drums as signals of barbaric attack. America did the same with its own image of barbarianness: 'Injuns' (named for another 'black' plundered continent), whom whites destroyed whilst portraying them as savages if they retaliated.[27] In white myth, the 'tom-

tom' called the tribe around it for barbaric dances: and for war on whites.

These are crude images compared to the rhythmic sophistication of black music. In Duke Ellington's 1956 fantasy on the history of jazz, *A Drum is A Lady* ('one of his most revealing works,' said Irving Townshend of Columbia Records), a drum becomes a woman. She travels from Africa to the Caribbean, New Orleans, New York, the moon, and everywhere she meets a man called Joe, whom she touches with magic before moving on to the next Joe.[28] The magic of African rhythm was bestowed on the world by the drum.

The first blues records with drums were city blues, recorded in forties Chicago. Drums put the 'rhythm' into rhythm and blues (joining the guitar to create the rock 'n' roll ensemble) and the 'rock', the communal energy, into rock 'n' roll. 'The Beat Generation' was Western appropriation of the drum. Most of Elvis's early Sun recordings did not have drums: Sam Phillips had to persuade him to add them for the 1955 hit 'I Forgot to Remember to Forget'. ('I thought we needed drums to show a little diversification,' said Sam).[29] Yet it was especially the drum which made fifties conservatives call rock 'n' roll 'jungle music'. In massive denial of black influence on country music, drums were forbidden on Nashville recordings of country music, or any broadcasts from WSM's 'Grand Ole Opry'.

The drum is not your mobile instrument like the easy-riding guitar. A drum-kit is a big deal to cart around and assemble. It is collective, earths everything and gives the basis of sound. This role can be expressed in surprising ways. Lennon and McCartney wrote most of the Beatles' songs but the drummer (Paul Trynka told me) gave the final yes: 'If they had a very experimental song it would always be Ringo who'd decide whether it was any good. At the end if Ringo said, "It's a load of bollocks", they wouldn't record it.'

The drum also often leads a style, or dance. In drum dances of the Mississippi Hills shot on film by Alan Lomax in 1978, the dancers began with a pelvic salute to the drum. Drummer and male dancers rubbed their cocks on it, shagged the earth to its beat.[30] James Brown 'sang like a drummer' (said his road manager), attracted great drummers and built new musical motifs around them.[31] Winston Rodney, a founder of reggae, called his vocal trio Burning Spear after Kenyan Independence leader Kenyatta. His 1974 Jamaican records, 'Marcus Garvey' and 'Slavery Days' (especially 'Marcus' with Rodney's mesmeric voice asking 'Do you remember the days of slavery?' over bass and drum), sold massively in Britain. The impact was from 'remember' and 'slavery' repeated over the drum. (The track is such a famous black icon, it is now used to sell Nationwide mortgages on television.) The drum made rock 'n' roll feel 'primitive' to enemies and devotees alike. 'My music', said Bo Diddley, 'has a bit of a spiritual side but it's also primitive. I play guitar as if I was playing drums.'[32] Drums represent the two basic attractions of black music for white teenagers: collectivity *and* sexual thrill.

The black way with harmony, weaving in and out of it, making it depend on rhythmic flexibility, reflects the way black cultures interwove categories which white culture, following the Greeks, tended to separate. This was part of black music's exponential appeal to white taste through the twentieth century: it melds together things which white culture traditionally keeps distinct – especially body, soul, and feeling. 'Soul' music could only have been black. Its voice *is* feeling, with the physicality as intense as possible: both interwoven with the sacredness endemic to black music and the community it reflects. 'Soul singers get down to the profoundness of their inner self and bring this up into the tune', said black DJ Enoch Gregory. As a boy in his father's church, Marvin Gaye 'began to see his voice as a gift from God that could sway people's emotions'. A church elder said he learned there 'how to put his very being into a song'. Soul is sacredness translated into sex. 'You make me *feel* like a natural woman', sings Aretha Franklin, 'queen of soul', in a song written specifically for her, with her 'gift for redefining the *feel* of a song'. 'Soul is feeling', announces 'Joey The Lips' to Roddy

Doyle's Dublin soul band. 'But it's corny,' complains one of the players, first time through. 'You're not singing it, Specky,' says the lead girl singer. In all black styles, the voice (or an instrument sounding like a voice) expresses the primacy of emotion along with the body's demands: demands so achingly urgent they become sacred. Increasingly through the twentieth century, white popular culture realized, overwhelmingly, that feeling ran the world and black music was its priest, its voice.[33]

Rhythm, feeling, collectivity, summing up body, soul and the shared excitement of both: the whole mix offered white teenagers exactly what white culture seemed to have spent centuries denying. How could they not try to make it for themselves? If white use of black music was a big steal, there was the urgency of ruthless need behind it.

9 'I'm Damn Guilty': The Song of Someone Else

Theft

So on to the mechanics of steal. Many mythologies say we got fire by stealing it, but the Greek one which underpins our own imagination goes further and implies that creativity belongs with fire, is the image of fire; and it, too, gets stolen. 'Covers' of black hits were just the iceberg tip of the rock 'n' roll steal. The whole thing, you could say, was theft: voice, gestures, style, the persona of display, identity, creativity and a thrillingly alien maleness whose core attribute was flaring sex. Black maleness licensed white boys to be sexy as they never had before except, maybe, in Greek myth – where Vulcan is married to Venus, where creativity belongs with sex and fire.

Musically, behind all this lay thirty years preparing the ground. The big story is blues, but the more detailed one includes ragtime and above all, at the back of everything, jazz. Some critics say rock 'n' roll was a dance extension of jazz. Lionel Hampton, for instance, grew up in Chicago with jazz, blues and boogie woogie. He formed his own band in 1940, switched from cool jazz after hearing a dervish-like revivalist band led by 'Whirling Willie', and coached his musicians to play equally wild: a rocking jazz to which you could dance. 'We started playing this real gutty jazz and people called it rhythm and blues.'[1] Elvis Costello's dad was a jazz band leader; Hendrix's was a jazz dancer. Jimi grew up listening to Duke Ellington. As a band player, he knew lounge-bar jazz standards like 'Harlem Nocturne' and was at ease with chords and scales far more sophisticated than blues-rock. His 'Third Stone from the Sun' (1967), with its innovatory rhythms, drew on Chuck Berry's double-stops but also on jazz beat, jazz tonalities, and the mock-orientalism of Coltrane.²

Behind the rock 'n' roll sunburst of the fifties were innumerable jazz musicians: innovative players of extraordinary sophistication, with individual ways of phrasing and improvising, who played together, listened, learned and moved on through American cities in the thirties and forties. Musically, rock 'n' roll was a confluence of many styles. Even 'rhythm and blues' covered a whole spread of different blues-based styles like dance blues, club blues, bar blues.³ But all the styles which went into rock 'n' roll were either black, or black-influenced. Country music contributed to rock its own brand of masculinity, plus melody, harmonies, chords and textures, yet it was never only white. All over the South, from the twenties on, country was influenced by black music and often called 'white man's blues'. Jimmie Rodgers, born 1897, became the Father of Country Music by absorbing black music more deeply than any white man, and then transforming it. He got called 'a white man gone black', a 'busboy in a roadside café singing nigger blues': and many other players (A. P. Carter, Bill Monroe, Hank Williams and Johnny Cash are a few of the most famous) had black teachers.⁴

What *is* 'black' music? Music played by blacks? But then any song is 'black' when blacks play it. Music blacks enjoy? But blacks have bought millions of white records, from Elvis's 'Hound Dog' to Kraftwerk, Elton John and Madonna. Songs composed by blacks? But what happens when whites sing them? Whether the white singing stays as simulacrum or transforms it into something new (like a metalworker making alloy from iron and gold), do they stay 'black' in white throats, white hearts?⁵

Rather than 'black music', you can talk about black styles: any style evolved and originally sung by blacks – rhythm and blues, soul, reggae, rap. I do *not* think it stays black when whites get their hands on it and take it further. Instead you get a crucial *awareness* of where a style came from, which stays with and marks the white musicians. This awareness may be guilty or gleeful, brash, cynical or self-deceivingly identificatory, depending on the person, but it empowers what white singers do with the music, and what they do with themselves as they put it across. Awareness of stolen fire, stolen persona, is a key ingredient in white rock 'n' roll, both its music and its masculinity. Its mask of maleness would never have developed without black style.

Music is never just music. Every style brings with it cultural codes and self-images. It was not his sultry chord progressions that made the maenads kill Orpheus. Music is self-presentation as well as notes. The crucial thing you hate or love in it is the self it puts across. The emotional and cultural self-messages in blues, the way singers gave themselves to an audience, were as potent as any melisma. Just as an innocent plucked instrument turned on the rock psyche with its symbolism as well as sound, so rock 'n' roll was empowered not just by black style and technique but by white *fantasies* of blackness, the values white culture placed on black gesture, feeling, sexiness. Rock 'n' roll began as white male imitating black, grabbing itself a weight, danger, anger and courage not its own.

These fantasies also dominated rock 'n' roll's reception. What the Council of Alabama hated, that this was 'niggers' music', was precisely what white teenagers loved. Ragtime and jazz transformed popular culture in the twenties and thirties. Throughout the century each new black sound and style injected into white culture a new network of values, symbols, resonance, associations. Rap is still doing it. White twelve-year-olds in suburban Hertfordshire copy gestures, vocabulary and music developed on the streets of Harlem – which, amazingly, according to newspaper reports, is currently the number-one location for tourists in New York. Rap is cool now because throughout the twentieth century black became increasingly cooler, and cooler. Rock 'n' roll set the seal on that process and made black style cool among the young. What black means to white created the teenager. Each time, a male 'song of myself' got sung in the voice of someone else. A roving bluesman for the sixties, an LA rapper for the nineties. When fifties rock forged white teenage identity by stealing a black voice, white teenage culture began a protean tradition of resting its own confidence on the voice of other people's defiance against oppression.

Hence rock's eternally murky moral heart, its frequent agonizing over that buzz-word, authenticity. In 1999, Billy Joel was inducted into the Rock 'n' Roll Hall of Fame along with Bruce Springsteen, Paul McCartney and, posthumously, Dusty Springfield. Joel was inducted by Ray Charles, one of the great figures of post-war black music. In his speech, Joel said he learned from three black masters: Charles himself, Otis Redding, Wilson Pickett. 'I've been called derivative', he said. 'I'm damn guilty. If everyone derivative was excluded from this institution, there wouldn't be any white people here.'[6]

His co-inductees and all his white predecessors are equally indebted. Elvis, 'the boy who stole the blues', shared many emotional and musical horizons with Delta blacks. He followed the black singer Roy Brown around, from his home town Tupelo to Hattiesburg, watching and learning. 'All that wiggling and stuff – man, the blacks had been doing that for years', said Brown. But Elvis still felt what he did came naturally from his background – unlike, say, the teenage Beatles, splaying their legs, working on Elvis body-language in Liverpool.[7] The Presleys were poor whites on the economic borderline. High-point of the week was hell-fire church on Sunday and, like many black rockers (Little Richard and Jerry Lee Lewis, driven by Southern fundamentalism, Marvin Gaye whose dad was a preacher), Elvis's first music came through religion. He was part of all the music of the South. His genius was for taking blues and country somewhere new. You can hear it on an early Sun recording. Eight bars into a hillbilly version of 'Milk Cow Blues', you hear him stop. It is a wonderfully direct rehearsal moment. 'Hold it fellas,' he drawls. (But so quickly: it is over in a second.) 'That don't *move*! Let's get gone, real gone'. Then, as Greil Marcus puts it, 'What follows is pure rock. No longer Elvis the country singer subduing every note to white taste, but Elvis the Pelvis.'[8]

Elvis grew up with blues. How could he think what he was doing was stealing? Like Chuck Berry, who *was* black, he developed a sound and style from what he knew. He listened, learned, watched black performers, and was exceptional for a white singer in the way he varied rhythm and emphasis.[9] The black writer Alice Walker gets this studying–stealing across in her short story 'Nineteen Fifty-Five'. A black singer is conned into selling her recordings dirt-cheap to a white producer for a young white singer. Then she hears him singing her songs:

> 'Well Lord have mercy,' I said, listening. If I'd a closed my eyes, it could have been me. He had followed every turning of my voice, side streets, avenues, red lights, train crossings and all.

You don't think of stealing when you sing. You just think, '*I could do it like that*'. Elvis drew on black culture, but said 'I don't sing like nobody'. One decade down the same road, when Keith, Mick and Brian listened to crackly recordings of Robert Johnson in a London bed-sit, something similar happened: they *had*, somehow, to make this thing they passionately identified with their own.

Homage, musical excitement, genuine artistic response, a creative use of someone else's work, a taking further – yes, all that; but it can be read differently. Walker's singer is modelled on Big Mama Thornton, the first to record 'Hound Dog' (written by the white songwriters Leiber and Stoller). She had an R&B No. 1 hit with it in 1953. Elvis had a million-selling pop hit with it in 1956. Walker's white boy explains, to the woman whose songs have made his fortune.

> They want what you got but they don't want you. They want what I got, but it ain't mine. That's what makes 'em so hungry for me when I sing. They getting the flavor of something but they ain't getting the thing itself. They like a pack of hound dogs trying to gobble up a scent.

It was not men who made the first blues recordings, but

women – like Ma Rainey and Bessie Smith, whom Mama Thornton modelled herself on. Alice Walker focuses on the deeper piracy, not men from women but white from black, and spotlights the musical dilemma of song-hungry (but racist) white America, the problem black musicians face. America loves black music but not black people. When The Animals toured America in 1965, Eric Burden met a white girl in Alabama who said she just adored the same black singers as he. He asked if she'd been lucky enough to hear Otis Redding there the night before. 'You gotta be joking,' she said. 'The place was full of niggers.'[10]

Elvis could be personally generous to the singers he learned from, yet blacks had every reason to accuse him of climbing to fame and riches on black backs.[11] 'That's All Right', the song that launched him, was written by the black singer Arthur 'Big Boy' Crudup, whose records (made in Chicago in the forties) Elvis had revered as a boy. Crudup recorded it in 1946, as a lament for lost love. Elvis turned it into a cocksure expression of independence: blues without *Angst*, a boy become a man, taking on the world. He may have lost one girl, but that is just the starting-point for a load of new adventures. Phillips put out the record in 1954 (alongside Muddy Waters), but Crudup never got any royalties.[12]

Sam Phillips' own genius lay not just in knowing black styles, spotting the voice and spirit behind it ('I had to be a psychologist in the studio,' he said), or knowing what sound he wanted to create plus the instruments to get it with, but also in understanding white taste.[13] Like Elvis, he grew up poor white. Like Alan Freed playing black music on his white programme, he saw white kids bored with white pop falling for black energy. At first he recorded blacks. After Elvis, he looked for white singers. They flocked to him with demonstration tapes – Carl Perkins from Memphis, Roy Orbison from West Texas, Johnny Cash and Conway Twitty from Arkansas, Jerry Lee Lewis from North Louisiana. Eventually Phillips was recording white singers almost exclusively. This was not his fault. Some black singers left for bigger outfits, fatter contracts.[14] But that switch was an omen

– of how white rock would rule the world by taking over black style.

Black classics were the favourite numbers for rock bands starting out. For The Yardbirds, it was Chicago blues like Gene McDaniels' 'I'm A Man'. For Lou Reed's Velvet Underground, it was Chuck Berry's 'Carol' and 'Little Queenie'. For The Animals, it was the blues–folk classic 'House of the Risin' Sun'. For Jim Morrison and The Doors, Willie Dixon's 'Backdoor Man'. Bill Haley said he 'got rock' from Jackie Brenston's 1951 hit 'Rocket 66' on the black Chess label. His rhythms – which seemed utterly new to white teenagers, though today's thirteen-year-olds roll their eyes in patronizing amusement at 'Rock Around the Clock' – came straight from black music. 'Nothing but an exhibition of primitive tom-tom thumping', said the classical conductor Malcolm Sargent when teenagers rioted at that song in the film *The Blackboard Jungle*. 'Rock 'n' roll has been played in the jungle for centuries.' 'Christians will not attend this show,' said a poster outside a 1956 Bill Haley concert in Birmingham Alabama. 'Ask your preacher about jungle music.'[15]

In the fifties it was suddenly cool to sound black when you weren't. Buddy Holly's big break came when he played in New York's Apollo Theatre. The all-black audience had heard him on radio and thought he was black: they went mad with excitement when they saw he wasn't.[16] In 1964, everyone was amazed again when the Righteous Brothers, singing 'You've Lost that Lovin' Feelin'', turned out to be white. It was official: white boys got unbelievably more fame and money than the blacks they learned from, for singing the same music. Marvin Gaye, a poor black kid with a fantastic voice, grew up in late-fifties Washington DC watching white boys get rich on black music. In the last quarter of 1958, four singers out of thirty-four in the American Top Twenty were black. With his smoochily watered-down rhythm and blues, Pat Boone got as many hits as three now-revered greats – Chuck Berry, Little Richard and Fats Domino – *put together*.[17] The Stones were the most successful appropriators of all. Failing to learn some dance steps from Tina Turner, Jagger once asked in mock desperation, 'Does this mean I won't be black in the next life?' 'Are you sure you want to be?' said Tina.[18] The Stones may have wished they were black when actually playing, but did a million times better by not being.

Muddy Waters and Howlin' Wolf, playing in little places in Chicago, were delighted when the Stones and Beatles hauled them into television studios, recording palaces, global limelight. Their music became popular again. 'But some black musicians', Paul Trynka told me, 'felt you shouldn't get ripped off, and resented it. There were The Stones, laughing all the way to the bank.' You may go from covers to writing your own music, like The Stones, but to many people it still feels as if something, some essence, spirit, and above all voice, has been stolen. There are harmonious collaborations (like AMC and Aerosmith, or Public Enemy and Anthrax); there are also genre-bending mixes of black and white styles. Yet it is still true that black songs mostly get more money when whites sing them. There was uproar when Simply Red frontman Mick Hucknall received a Lifetime Achievement Award at the second 'Music of Black Origin' prizegiving. The feeling was, 'It's him that should be thanking us'.[19]

Black Fire, White Gold: Soul, Funk, Reggae, Hip-Hop, Rap

Wholesale theft, then. In 1988, the black nationalist rap group Public Enemy put a song on their album *It Takes a Nation of Millions* called 'Black Steal in the House of Chaos'. What *could* black musicians do, faced with all that steal?

In Greek religious cult, Vulcan, god of fire and technology, was worshipped alongside Prometheus. Here was the master of creativity joining forces with the thief of its secret. That is one answer: to work *with* the robber, assimilate your own stuff to what white rock made of black style, and appeal to white expectations. It had a deep ancestry in black uses of white stereotyping. Slavery was abolished but the masks remained – and one way of using them was to play to them.[20]

Black singers could let white marketing do it for them. Through the pitifully few years of his success, Hendrix did not have a big black following. He was deeply sophisticated in, and experimented with, the whole spectrum of black styles. This is what he worked, and innovated, from. But because of his manner and clothes as well as his sound, he was marketed to white middle-class kids. 'The record companies didn't think blacks would relate to a nigger like him,' said Bobby Womack. 'I'd start seeing young black guys, fans, and they'd be dressin' just like him and I'd be thinking, "Damn, I never saw black hippies before." ' There *were* black sales, black fans: but little or no airplay on black radio stations. He didn't fit. He made his name in America through Monterey, a white festival, and was little-known in, for instance, Harlem. A 1969 gig there was not a success. After his death, his music did influence black groups popular among blacks, like War. But while he was alive, blacks criticized: especially for (as it were) joining Prometheus – for playing with white musicians. Though Hendrix invited more blacks into his band and gave donations to the Martin Luther King Foundation, these criticisms went on to the end of his life.[21]

Until 1956, people justified segregating the charts by saying black audiences only cared about black music.[22] White charts were where the money was. A hit on the rhythm and blues charts, compiled from black shops and radio stations, was all right, but a pop hit meant real money. 'R&B don't stand for nuthin' but rip-off an' bullshit,' says Bo Diddley in *Hail! Hail! Rock 'n' Roll*, a bio-documentary on Chuck Berry. He and Chuck were playing rock 'n' roll till the white boys moved in, he said: then suddenly '*they* was rock an' roll and we were R& B'. 'Pop meant selling whites,' said Marvin Gaye, 'R&B or soul meant selling the brothers and sisters back in the neighbourhood. Everyone wanted to sell whites 'cause whites got more money.'[23]

So even when the late fifties and sixties broke segregation

down, there was never anything like equality in the charts. The seventies put segregation right back with a new apartheid and new categories, created by black reaction against white imitation. If Vulcan does not co-operate with Prometheus, he leaves the thief to his spoils, goes back to the drawing-board, and invents new art-forms. Once rock 'n' roll took hold, many black musicians concentrated on another side of the black legacy, taking black music into places where whites might find it hard to follow. Yet ironically this move dictated the development of white rock and pop. For as black musicians mutated away from white imitation into new forms – funk, disco, electro, rap – white boys moved in on those, too: Prometheus, dipping in to Vulcan's workshop for the new designs.

The black idiom crucial to the new style was gospel, with its passionate vocal harmonies. Fifties 'Doo-wop', the most obviously gospel-influenced style of the early rock era, was soon stolen by white Prometheus. The most commercially successful black group was The Platters (who sold over fifty million records), but white imitators like Dion and The Belmonts did even better. Then came soul. In the late sixties, with white rock developing the guitar, black singers jettisoned guitar and developed 'soul'. Since 1952, the Four Tops had been a jazz quartet, crooners in sharp suits with no instruments and synchronized hand-gestures (*anything*, not to look or sound like whites). In 1964 they joined Motown, became the archetypal soul vocal group and had a string of hits. Most white kids found this stuff utterly uncool. No torn jeans, no guitars, hands clicking to match the changing harmonies – it all felt like something your parents (for heaven's sake) might like. It looked like Talk of the Town. Then soul hit bestseller status with songs like The Four Tops' 'Reach Out I'll Be There' (1966), and Percy Sledge's 'When a Man Loves a Woman', which topped the pop charts as well as R&B. But that same year the Righteous Brothers, with 'You've Lost that Lovin' Feeling' (produced by Phil Spector), were No. 1 in America and Britain. Two white boys, singing soul, sounding black, who were the start of 'blue-eyed soul'. Twenty years on, Hall and Oates, blue-eyed soul singers of the eighties, covered that song in homage to their predecessors.

Gospel voices in close proximity, moving lushly together as an aural image of bodies moving closely together, were sexy (subliminally or overtly) in themselves. Soul capitalized on that and made the sensuality secular. Soul found the central nerve in black culture's appeal to whites: a message of spiritual sex in which feeling, soul and body belong together and fuck any distinctions which Western thought draws between them. In Marvin Gaye's erotic songs, sexual fulfilment is spiritual salvation.[24] With seventies black musicians consciously increasing the gap between black and white, the white market fell for soul's intensity. Then it fell again for soul's even sexier, danceable, anarchic spin-off – funk, whose raunchily thrusting, complicated rhythms imitated sex even more nakedly.

As a word, 'funk' had been in black circulation for decades. It smacked of sex-smells and hot lifestyle. When New Orleans pianists played with the beat in their left hand, and bass players fancied up the timing between their own beat and the drummer's – that was funky. You get bored with the two-and-four off-beat, you mess it around. In Motown, the black session musicians who played on most hits (like bassist James Jamerson, guitarist Robert White, drummer Benny Benjamin, keyboard player Earl Van Dyke) had been known as the Funk Brothers.[25] In the mid-sixties, James Brown – 'Soul Brother Number One' – had a series of soul hits culminating in 'Say it Loud (I'm Black and I'm Proud)' in 1968. Then he became the pioneer of funk: soul with dance, with the sex all wildly explicit. How could white audiences – and white musicians – resist?

The other big sixties black style came from Jamaica. In the early sixties, ska was the dominant Jamaican form (synonymous in Britain with 'blue beat', for the records were released on the Blue Beat label). Ska developed for Jamaican sound-system operators like Lee 'Scratch' Perry and Coxsone Dodd, who produced records using local musicians to emulate New Orleans R&B, but emphasizing the after-beat in each bar and fusing it with the guitar-plus-syncopated-bass of Jamaican mento, a kind of calypso. Prince Buster in 1967 had a hit in the British charts with 'Al Capone'; Desmond Dekker and The Aces had an international hit with '007' in 1969. This was reggae's forerunner: mostly instrumental, with spoken voice-overs. In the West, the favourites were Al Capone and James Bond, archetypal macho (and white) heroes. Then came Jamaican songs celebrating 'the rude boys', tough street kids of Kingston: wildly popular to dance to, though their patois was famously incomprehensible and engendered wonderful wild mishearings. Everyone thought 'me Israelites', for instance, was 'me ears are alight'. If the words had been clearer, censors might have banned them for inciting violence. But it all came over as a hot, kaleidoscopic invitation to fun-loving co-existence.[26] Reggae – rhythmically new, lyrically ingenious, bursting with fun – became top dance genre in the UK. It was taken up enthusiastically too by the hippy white establishment in the US. But for a lot of US black taste it mostly seemed, like Hendrix, too hippy.[27]

Reggae also blended brilliantly with other styles. Jimmy Cliff fused it with soul: even Princess Anne was spotted buying one of his LPs. (In Harrods.) But most of Cliff's hits happened in Jamaica, whereas Bob Marley and Peter Tosh of The Wailers became known internationally. Throughout the seventies, Marley drew on soul, gospel, doo-wop, rock and, increasingly, African music. Tosh, who founded The Wailers with him, left in 1974 and recorded on his own. He joined The Rolling Stones' world tour: his *Bush Doctor* (1978) had contributions from Jagger and Richards. *Mama Africa* (1983) featured soul singer Betty Wright. Even punk, the only home-grown white rock form, made a weirdly effective fusion with reggae. Long before he joined the Sex Pistols, Johnny Rotten (then John Lydon) used to go to a reggae stall under Finsbury Park station:

> I had to go in for a year before I knew what to order. The black customers were so hostile and surprised I had to wait until the shop was empty.[28]

Sting co-opted reggae for Police singles in the early eighties. He got criticized for exploitation ('Someone should clip Sting round the head and tell him to stop singing in that ridiculous Jamaican accent,' Elvis Costello grumbled to *Melody Maker*) but there grew up a real bond of respect between Sting and Bob Marley. Chuck Berry, black king of rock 'n' roll, loved what he called the shit-kicking aspect of The Police. Yet many of the reggae musicians who inspired Sting were struggling and skint while he raked in the shekels.

Like Billy Joel, Sting agreed he was guilty but cited precedents. 'It's like The Stones in the sixties were just as valid as John Lee Hooker.' Hooker is a myth to himself: the man who, like Muddy Waters, brought country blues into an urban setting; and became a potent talisman of blues in the late eighties with his album *The Healer*. So what does 'just as valid' mean, exactly? 'There is a sense of guilt,' added Sting: 'that sense of duty to the black man. But,' he said, 'whenever we meet black musicians we're interested in what they think of us.' (Well, interested: yes, they would be.)

Sting's main defence, though, was innovation. 'Pop is dead. It's become reactionary and racist.'[29] Again, the artist's carnivore soul, seeing something new, thinking 'I could use that'. Like Elvis, the only white in black audiences all round Memphis, absorbing the language of black bodies, black voices.

The same thing happened when black musicians turned to another side of black creativity: verbal repartee, which began with hip-hop and spawned a Titan – rap. Hip-hop began with the 'sound system' and ways of reproducing the music while talking over it at dances. Bands in the Jamaican Brooklyn community jammed along to records and made rhythmic chat over them: they called it 'toasting'.[30] In the mid-seventies, disc-jockeys like Grandmaster Flash and Afrika Bambaataa began 'rapping' over tracks they played in New York clubs. They 'mixed' and 'scratched' records on several turntables at once; they became performers themselves. The great electro and go-go pioneers came in the late seventies. Afrika combined James Brown's soul-funk with the technological innovation of the electronic German group Kraftwerk in a version of Brown's 'Say it Loud (I'm Black and I'm Proud)'. In 1984, his 'Renegades of Funk' reached the British Top Thirty.

Afrika was a precursor of, not just rap and sampling in general, but black use of white material. In 1989, the rap group De La Soul sampled white artists such as Steely Dan for their album, *Three Feet High and Rising*. The mellow sound and general message meant they had nicknames like 'Daisy Age' and 'Hip-hop hippies' thrown at them. (Finally, their use of The Turtles' hit 'Happy Together' led to a lawsuit.) Their next album, *De La Soul is Dead* (1991) had a much harsher sound, though they went on sampling over a hundred other records. In 1988, Public Enemy's song 'Black Steal in the House of Chaos', on their album *It Takes a Nation of Millions*, reflected their musical affinity with the textures and distortion-sounds of heavy white rock.

Cutting-edge musicians of any colour have that carnivore edge. 'I think a similar sort of inter-trading was going on from 1900 to 1930 too,' Paul Trynka told me. 'Black soul guitarists lifted techniques from white country players, just as Tricky, now, has gone heavy metal completely.'

It is always the most innovative musicians who are keen to see where they can take the ideas they hear in other people's work. The influence can always go both ways. White Jay Kay, of Jamiroquai, said he 'used to be criticized for ripping off R&B and soul', particularly for sounding like Stevie Wonder. Before releasing his fourth album in 1999, Jay Kay said: 'It's gone full circle. I'm the white guy doing black music and all of a sudden we've got black guys sampling white guys. We've had five or six requests to use our tracks to sample over.' Full circle in his eyes, maybe. But at twenty-nine he is sitting in seventy-two acres of an eleven-bedroomed Georgian manor estate, bought by his multi-million-selling albums.[31] Are the 'five or six' blacks who sample his records going to get that?

Like its white contemporary, punk, black hip-hop was fiercely anti-élitist: DIY, almost anti-musical. You did not have to play an instrument. All you needed was a drum machine and your own voice – though in performance rappers were backed by DJs, who 'scratched' excerpts from any records they liked. What you got was an instant, free-form, aural collage. Some was irresistibly danceable. Some took on social issues like guns, drugs and crime. It was the most important new black style of the eighties: yet one of its most famous early bands was white. The Beastie Boys began as hardcore punk, but by 1983 were building hip-hop into it. They figured in a rap movie, *Krush Groove*; their 1987 album *Licensed to Ill* topped the US charts. They never abandoned punk, but there they were in 1987, three middle-class white boys, toting an inflatable penis onstage as mascot, making the eighties' biggest-selling rap album.[32]

Rap diversified. In America, the West Coast Niggaz With Attitude gave gangsta rap an international kickstart with their 1986 début, 'Boyz N the Hood'. Their 1989 album *Straight Outta Compton*, luridly evoking life on the streets of Compton, the South Central Los Angeles ghetto, outraged everyone with its track 'Fuck the Police'. Rap sold everywhere, spreading like flame to Hampshire, Hamburg, Kyoto – and Paris, where Senegalese rapper M. C. Solaar took off in 1990, entrancing France with fierce lyrics about homelessness, fashion victims and unrequited love. The Atlanta-based group Arrested Development began as gangsta rap in 1987, but jettisoned violence in the nineties for 'agrarian rap', combining African with rural Southern musical roots.

Yet the complex moral relations of Vulcan and Prometheus pervade even the world of gangsta rap. New York rappers Public Enemy became bestsellers with political albums focused round black nationalism. They had links to black nationalism groups, to Louis Farrakhan and the Nation of Islam. Yet their first album, *Yo! Bum Rush the Show* (1987), was produced by white record chief Rick Rubin (who produced the Beastie Boys' *Licensed to Ill* in the same year, and went on to specialize in rap and heavy metal). They toured America and England with the Beastie Boys; their second album, *It Takes a Nation of Millions to Hold us Back* (1988) shot into the UK Top Ten and US Top Fifty. They appeared with bodyguards: the SIWs (short for 'Security of the First World') who sometimes carried replica machine-guns. Black mainstream eighties music had been less resentful about racial inequality than in the sixties and seventies; Public Enemy redressed the balance with interest. They claimed whites were blue-eyed devils created by an evil scientist, or descended from cave-dwellers who fucked dogs. (White journalists interviewing them sometimes complained they'd never laid a finger on a dog, which must have raised a laugh.) They quoted the original deal for black slaves in emancipation, 'Forty acres and a mule, Jack'. And yet they recorded for a white-owned label and were co-managed by Ed Chalpin; the man who in 1965 had infamously advanced the unknown Jimi Hendrix one dollar for an exclusive recording deal, and then cashed in on his success in 1967, when he had to be bought off by a ludicrously unfair royalties deal, his dollar multiplied a millionfold.[33] Like male composers and opera-house managers enriched by imagining women's pain, white producers made a packet from records shouting black rage.

In the nineties, whites moved in on rap in a big way. Even the bubble-gum Spice Girls: the first word of their first hit 'Wannabe' (1997), was 'Yo!', straight from the rap lexicon. (Brilliant female rappers like Queen Latifah, innovative girl groups like Salt 'n' Pepa, never got the same global spotlight.) White male groups like The Prodigy, blond boys with a gift for rhyme like Vanilla Ice and Eminem, cash in on the big bestseller, gangsta rap. Eminem's début, *The Slim Shady LP*, sold 480,000 copies in its first two weeks in 1999. He has been booed on the mike and told by black hip-hoppers to get out and scuttle away to rock 'n' roll. 'It's very awkward shit', says Eminem's mentor, rap honcho Dr Dre, one of the founder members of Niggaz With Attitude, who put his credibility on the line when he signed Eminem. 'It's like seeing a black guy doing country and western, know what I'm saying?' People queried Dre's judgement, but Eminem (brought up in a mainly black lower middle-class

Detroit neighbourhood), is so quick, his rhymes and rhythms so violent, that he has the last laugh, at present. 'People who disrespected me are coming out of the woodwork to ask for collaboration,' he told *Rolling Stone* in 1999, 'But I like doing my own shit.' His lyrics are violent, weaned on sci-fi and slasher movies; they rage at dead-end jobs, poverty, frustration; they deal with sexual abuse, under-age sex. 'Yo, look at her bush/ Does it got hair?/ Fuck this bitch right here on the spot bare,/ Till she passes out and forgets how she got there.' His alias, Shady Slim, hangs himself with his own penis. The hip-hop underground adores it. 'I don't have a problem with white rappers,' said Nelson George, author of *Hip Hop America*. 'But there's no point if they copy what's come before.' Vanilla Ice was embarrassing, but black audiences feel Eminem is the real thing and has made the form genuinely his own.[34]

From guitar rock to soul, funk, reggae, hip-hop, rap, the copying–inspiration–stealing bowls merrily on. In the DJ arena too. The British middle-class white DJ Tim Westwood championed hip-hop through the nineties to become Europe's most influential figure in hip-hop. He is respected by American rappers like Sean 'Puff Daddy' Combs and Funkmaster Flex. When Westwood was shot in Stockwell in 1999, Puff Daddy called in on his London hospital twice to see how he was. But some people have ridiculed Westwood's faux-black accent. He talks of music 'with a raw uncut flava' as if he were hot from Jamaica. 'Some black people think he is exploiting every stereotype there ever was and making a career out of it,' said one rap commentator. 'But if he is going to be credible with his audience, he has to sound like them.'[35] Is he a latter-day Alan Freed? Or is it exploitation? Even among DJs, the 'blue-eyed devil' Prometheus is still piling up the gold by stealing black Vulcan's fire. Is it simply joining in? Exploitation? Or creativity?

The Mix: Graceland and Guilt

'There's not a problem that I can't fix,' sings Grandmaster Flash, one of the originators of hip-hop, "Cause I can do it in the mix.' After the seventies' re-segregation of the charts, the eighties broke down a few barriers. It became commoner for white and black to play together. They had played together for ever in jazz, though it was often hell for black musicians on tour. In the sixties, Jefferson Airplane played with black violinist Papa John Creech; in 1975, on the cover of *Born to Run*, Bruce Springsteen leaned against his black saxophonist Clarence Clemons whom he used to introduce as 'King of the World, Master of Disaster'.

But there was a terrible question-mark over white musicians asking black ones to play with them. Were they trying to improve the sound or prove authenticity? Were the gestures of debt genuine or manipulative? Homage, tokenism, or exploitation?[36]

In the sixties, Keith Richards and Clapton revered the black musicians they learned from. The Beatles loved Marvin Gaye's work (so did Jagger, who asked for an introduction to Gaye but was turned down by Dave Godin, founder of Britain's Motown Appreciation Society).[37] In 1985, after the break-up of his second marriage, Paul Simon became deeply interested in South African music. For his 1986 album *Graceland*, he broke the cultural boycott of South Africa, recorded with Soweto musicians (the Mbaqanga players Ray Phiri, the harmony group Ladysmith Black Mambazo) in Johannesburg, and toured South Africa with them: the first international musician to play there for over a decade. *Rolling Stone* put him on its cover in 1987 surrounded by nine smiling black men.

The controversial politics inflamed the basic issue of musical exploitation. In South Africa and abroad, Simon was accused of breaching United Nations sanctions. Before one Johannesburg concert, someone threw a grenade at the building where the instruments were stored. Simon sang to the audience of ten thousand under death threat. 'I was singing and closing my eyes, thinking I may never open them again,' he said six years later on the *South Bank Show*. Protests went on for years afterwards. *He* felt he was introducing the world to 'township jive': that his album helped break the isolation of black South African musicians. The musicians agreed. 'He gave us the chance to promote ourselves. *We* used *him*,' said the lead singer. It made Ladysmith's name internationally. Twenty years later, with the mass commercialization of black icons (Bob Marley's 'One Love' is now used to sell washing powder), they figure in baked-bean television commercials. But some critics saw Simon's actions otherwise. 'He waltzes into town, takes the catchiest thing he can find, marches back and has a great hit.'[38]

Graceland uses African music seriously, creatively – unlike, say, Malcolm McLaren's 1983 recording début, *Duck Rock*, which co-opted African sounds as a gimmick; he got accused of plagiarism. Simon set a precedent. In the nineties the white guitarist Ry Cooder, always fascinated by ethnic styles, spent three years in Cuba. In 1997 he resurrected the 'Buena Vista Social Club' with Cuban musicians playing on a fantastically successful album of that name. But *Graceland*'s concerns were very American and very personal. Simon defended it passionately, and the whole issue of white using black got the best and most bitterly argued airing, over the best possible music, it could. But it was not resolved. I do not think it can be. It is too central. The main image for the title-song's quest for personal salvation, is the pathetically regal home which the boy who stole the blues made with his wealth: where he died in 1977, a bloated forty-two-year-old slumped on a lavatory. With its indelible image of the Delta as a national guitar, this song also invokes the iconic instrument, foundation of 'The King's' wealth, played by blacks who had no wealth, except their music; who never owned anything but a guitar.

Springsteen and Simon are in a creative class of their own. Others use black musicians simply to revive their own credibility. The heavy metallist Gary Moore changed his image *circa* 1990 by playing with blacks. 'That sort of thing doesn't go unnoticed,' said Paul Trynka. 'Some black guys who'd been playing black music better for a long time really resented it. But there are probably guys who played with Gary and are grateful that he helped them reach a new audience.'

Mixed bands meant black musicians reached a wider market. But who likes forced gratitude, or a small handout from what you are in any case owed? And what about inferior musicians doing wildly better than black ones who cannot sell their music? At an eighties guitar conference, Vernon Reid of the black band Living Colour was booked to share a room with a white guy, whom he had not met, from a heavy metal band. When Reid arrived, the white boy was getting out of the shower and said dismissively, 'It's not time to clean the room yet'. White rock steals from black music, but thinks a black man is there to make the bed. 'Rather than being rejected by music companies or told my music can't be marketed,' said Reid, 'that incident told me more about what is happening racially than anything else.'[39]

Some white musicians are deeply uncomfortable with this debt. Charles Shaar Murray (to whom, talking of debts, I am profoundly indebted myself for his brilliant book on Hendrix and his context), interviewed Pete Townshend about the 1967 gig at Monterey. There was a pre-gig row with Hendrix over the playing order. Townshend afterwards tried to make it up with Hendrix, who got on well with Clapton but gave Townshend a devastating brush-off. 'I just *crawled* away,' said Townshend:

> Eric feels perfectly natural with his adoption of blues music. He feels it inside; I don't. I don't even really feel comfortable with black musicians. It's always been a problem with me and I think Jimi was so actutely sensitive in his blackness that he picked that up . . . I felt I deserved it somehow.

He felt Hendrix was rubbing in the guilt, saying,

> You've taken this, Mr Eric Clapton and Mr Townshend, you think you're a showman. This is how *we* do it. This is how we do it when we take back what you've stolen. I've

put it back together and *this* is what it's all about – and you can't live without it, can you?[40]

Guilty or grateful, sensitive to it like Townshend, Billy Joel and Springsteen, putting themselves into the political firing-line for the sake of an album like Paul Simon, or simply emanating 'what-can-*I*-do-about-it?' bafflement like the guy in the shower ('He was *terribly* embarrassed,' said Vernon Reid), none of these men can help being part of an incremental debt. 'The terrible truth', said Townshend, 'is we *couldn't* live without it.'

10 The Dark Self: Sex, Knowledge and a Century of Blacking Up

Cock Rock and the Black Sex Stereotype

'Stereotype' revolutionized printing in the last decade of the eighteenth century. *Stereos* is Greek for 'hard': 'type' comes from *tupto*, 'I strike'. If you set your letters separately, each copy can have different mistakes, but stereotype, a 'hard-struck' metal sheet with all the letters moulded in it, lets you cast the whole page the same every time: a great invention, for books. But as a metaphor for judging other people, an object that can be eternally repeated in which every individual is the same – something *you* can feel differently about (if you want) but which never changes in itself – is a rotten idea.

The black stereotype was moulded in white minds over many centuries. In the twentieth century, music helped to give it a positive rather than negative force and spearheaded a new appreciation of the body, especially the male body, in fashion, dance and sport, even though racism was and is increasingly vicious, in areas of both America and Britain. The stereotype does not seem to have changed much: only feelings about it, in some contexts.

Plumb in the middle of it was always the fantasy that black men have bigger cocks. 'That's alrigh' for the blackies, Jimmy,' says a Dublin band member in *The Commitments*, pondering the idea that soul music is actually about sex. 'They've got bigger gooters than us.' ('Speak for yourself, pal,' says his friend.) 'It is still true, alas,' wrote James Baldwin in the mid-eighties, 'that to be an American Negro male is also to be a kind of walking phallic symbol. One pays, in one's own personality, for the sexual insecurity of others.'

You can play into other people's fantasy knowingly or unwittingly. Hendrix's size was legendary. In 1968 the Los Angeles 'Whiskey a Go Go Bar' put 'Hendrix Super Sausage' on its menu. Hendrix was happy for this element of his legend to mirror white fantasy, but not everyone is. In 1998, the athlete Linford Christie sued a tabloid journalist for remarks about his 'lunch-box', saying no one would joke like that about female athletes' bodies. 'What *is* Linford's lunch-box?' asked the judge, Mr Popplewell. 'It is a reference to my genitals,' said Christie. He argued that the joke was a racist as well as sexist stereotype; he won his case.[1]

There is also the sexual appetite fantasy. 'Black girls just wanna be fucked all night,' sings Jagger in 'Some Girls'. In Nancy Friday's *Men in Love*, many white men's fantasies feature black men with tireless erections. Legends of Hendrix's prowess as well as dimensions mirrored musical awe at his playing. He went along with this part of the stereotype, too, with an innocently baroque gusto. On stage he shagged his guitar: backstage he had 'pussy for breakfast, dinner and supper'. One story said he 'balled seven chicks in three hours'. In 1999, as an editorial in the black magazine *Pride* pointed out, black models in British TV ads 'automatically mean sex'.[2]

Even when acted out, these fantasies are still also fantasies. They drive both racism and rock music. In 1971, the heavy metal band Aerosmith, busted by a Boston drugs squad, landed up at a police station where cops were laughing at a cartoon,

> of a black man tied to a post like a gallows with a string tied to his dick, the other end tied to the trigger of a pistol pointed at his head, so if he got an erection he would shoot himself. Standing in front of him was a buxom bimbo with everything hanging out. The caption was, HOW TO FIX THE BLACK PROBLEM.[3]

How to shock tough-looking white boys unaware of the depths

of racism in their own culture, whose music got its turn-on from black style. Thirty years later, New York cops were convicted of sodomizing a black suspect with a broom-handle, rupturing his intestines, and passing the handle round afterwards to smell. Chic and cool are one side of the coin; racism the other. Sexual envy drives both. By imitating black music, white rock 'n' roll took over the centre of white envy: black male sexuality.

In music, the sex came over through three things: rhythm, words and humour. Fifties white conservatives tried to keep control of what could be controlled, the words. Sexual explicitness and humour became pawns in the battle for the US airwaves. Large companies belonged to ASCAP, the establishment association of music publishers who had non-rock 'n' roll singers. Broadcast Music Incorporated represented smaller publishers handling the independent companies which pioneered rock 'n' roll. ASCAP tried to stop big radio networks playing BMI songs. Billy Rose, a senior ASCAP member, said in *Variety*, 'Most BMI songs are junk. In many cases pretty obscene junk on a level with dirty magazines.' ASCAP's big coup was in 1954, with Johnnie Ray's 'Such a Night'. The black tenor Clyde McPhatter (with The Drifters) had sung its banal lyrics with humorous intensity: everyone thought it hilarious. Johnnie Ray, 'Prince of Wails', the white 'Nabob of Sob', had none of The Drifters' wit and gave it his histrionic all. It was British No. 2 all summer but ASCAP got it banned in America, for suggestiveness.[4]

In black lyrics, humour was part of the sex. ' "Tutti Frutti" would crack the crowd up,' said Little Richard, rock 'n' roll's first bisexual icon. 'It had to be cleaned up for white rock. Not because it was obscene – because it was funny.' As he sang it to black clubs in the South, it originally went 'Tutti frutti, good booty: if you don't fit don't force it.' His sexuality made it all the funnier. His shows were a hothouse of sexual energy; hundreds of women beat on the doors afterwards. 'We'd make love to chicks all over,' said drummer Charles Connor. 'They'd be sitting on bar-stools waiting for us, almost naked. Sometimes

Little Richard would have boyfriends with him – or he'd sit on a table and watch us.'⁵ The humour enhanced the sex.

But what black audiences found funny, white radio found obscene, so white covers modified the lyrics. 'We steer completely clear of anything suggestive,' said Bill Haley. 'We don't want to offend anybody.' (Imagine a singer saying that today.)⁶ In Charlie Calhoun's 'Shake Rattle and Roll', the singer lies in bed watching sunlight 'shinin' through' his girlfriend's 'low dresses'. 'I can't believe my eyes that all this belongs to you.' Black audiences adored Big Joe Turner's 1954 recording. Bill Haley changed 'low dresses' to 'those dresses' and replaced see-through sunlight with 'hair done up so nice'. (He missed the penis-metaphor, though, in 'one-eyed jack peeping in a seafood store'.) But what censors balked at was exactly what fans wanted. 'Back when they wouldn't play my records on the white radio stations, they said "This is vulgar". But that was what people loved, that little sexy sound,' said Ray Charles.⁷

Elvis and his nickname established rock 'n' roll as crotch worship. 'They all think I'm a sex maniac,' he said. 'They're frustrated old types anyway. I'm just natural.' But 'natural' included years of watching black musicians. He is a mythic figure now, but he knew that singing black meant taking over the dream-power of the black cock. Rock 'n' roll made the male crotch its centrepiece of display. Andy Warhol's cover for *Velvet Underground and Nico* had a banana peeling back to flesh beneath; on his cover for the Stones's *Sticky Fingers* was a jeans crotch, bulge plus zip. Hendrix made his name at Monterey in velour trousers 'so tight they outlined his crotch to the thirtieth row'. Jim Morrison wore underpant-free black vinyl trousers.⁸

Like Elizabethan courtiers padding a codpiece, stars played up this tool of their trade. Marvin Gaye, a shy performer at first, was found with his hand down his trousers before an early gig. 'I've got to show a bit,' he explained. He was 'putting his penis in the best position and he wasn't wearing underpants.' David Lee Roth, original frontman for heavy metal act Van Halen, wore a bulging red G-string over black tights. Elvis's trousers supposedly had lead piping down the front: accusations of artifice have been crossly denied ever since. 'I do *not* wear a hose – my hose is my own,' said Freddie Mercury of Queen. The best form of denial was the naked display of Jim Morrison and Iggy Pop. (Morrison was arrested for it: in the film, he murmurs to the screaming audience, 'D'you want to see it?') Shooting a night-club scene for a rock 'n' roll gangster film (*Mojo*, which was never widely released), the actor Hans Matheson did it too. As an interviewer describes it.

> He stepped in front of the hormone-crazed extras and got in touch with his inner rock god. 'I went with it. The music started, I began unbuttoning my trousers, the girls were screaming – I've never felt a rush like it. The trousers came down, they were waiting for my pants to drop ... Yeah, I did it. But only their reaction was shot. Then I dived into the audience.'[9]

Rock history is full of penis-lore. The Plaster Casters of Chicago, those sixties teenagers who made casts of stars' erections, saw Hendrix as the jewel of their collection. On display at a cocktail party, it frightened off every white director in the record business. 'The president of one company bolted from the room.' On tour with American stars in the Midwest, Ian Whitcombe (an Irish boy whose 1965 'You Turn Me On' was a rock sensation) was studying Marx on the bus for exams when 'Suddenly, with a dull *thopp!!*, a human book marker hid the print. One of the rock stars had placed his dong, his *wedding tackle*, right on Marx.'[10]

As rock turned into penis-worship in the sixties (some Stones shows, later copied by the Beastie Boys, featured a giant inflatable phallus), verbal explicitness rushed into white songs, inspired by cock-imagery in the newly rediscovered blues. (Cotton-Eyed Joe, Ram Rod Daddy, Banana in your Fruit Basket, Warm my Wiener; Whitesnake took their name from 'Black Snake Moan'.) The white rock god took over blues virility: mojo magic, erection, urgency. Coining the phrase 'cock rock' in 1978, Simon Frith described the maleness which rock borrowed from the blues as rampant swagger. The seventies exaggerated it in group-names (Man-Sized Action, Throbbing Gristle) and comic boasting:

> Well I fucked a sheep and I fucked a goat
> I wagged my cock right down its throat.[11]

Easy to mock, all this. Take the mid-eighties US group Red Hot Chilli Peppers: the shot cover for their 'Abbey Road' EP was a pastiche of The Beatles; they appeared naked, with socks over their cocks. But it was incontrovertible: the rock god had cock at his centre as no white icon ever had before. Girls had swooned at earlier twentieth-century male singers, but open cock-worship was new. 'Only someone who has tried to imagine Frank Sinatra performing in a padded G-string', says one critic, 'can fully appreciate the chasm that separates rock from its pop predecessors.'[12] The rock god sings his own desire. ('I've got a hard-on for you, baby', sings Kevin Ayers.) With or without padding, he incarnates desire; but he is also its object. There are ten thousand girls out there, screaming with desire: for *him*. In Greek myth terms, this is Eros with the tackle of Ares. In race terms, white with the sexual pulling-power of black.

Laughing Inside the Mask:
Making Black 'Black', Making Black White

What can you do, imprisoned by fantasies sanctified by myth, history and sexual envy that are set hard in the minds of people who dominate the society where you sell your music? Black musicians have to use white stereotypes: to work *from* them, as women poets and singers in a male tradition have to start *from* their awareness of how men see them. 'Every Negro faces the problem', said Duke Ellington in 1941,

> of trying to give an American audience entertainment with-

out compromising the dignity of the negro people. He runs foul of offensive stereotypes instilled in the American mind by centuries of degradation. The American audience has been taught to expect a negro on stage to clown and 'Uncle Tom', to enact the role of a servile yet lovable inferior.

Playing *to* the white stereotype (either the unthreateningly servile one petted by white conservatives or the rampantly sexy one of rock) works commercially. Morris Wilson, a saxophonist and black activist talking in the eighties about Prince's successfully dirty lyrics, said 'That's the stereotype you have.'

> The record companies want to keep you there. In the black community, you almost can't get a contract unless you're writing that sort of thing. They kind of wanna keep you in the bag.

But it can alienate black audiences. Many blacks accused Hendrix of Uncle Tomming, hamming up the sexy stereotype. This reaction goes back to at least 1928, when black voices complained that artists in the Harlem Renaissance accentuated 'that licentiousness which conventional civilization holds white folk from enjoying'.[13]

There are two main options. One is to play to the stereotype but use it as a mask within which you develop what you want – new music, new lyrics exploring black issues. You make irony your starting-point, and parody white fantasies of black. Black audiences like the irony, white ones like the mask. Duke Ellington did this brilliantly in the twenties. The Cotton Club scenario parodied a white stereotype:

> It was not jungle music but creative irony, which masked commercial pandering to an upper-class white audience thrilled at the opportunity to witness what it thought was genuine black exotica.[14]

Within that armature, rather like Greek islanders living their own life beneath a tourist carapace, Duke wrote influential and original music for his band.

This option recalls nineteenth-century American 'blackface' entertainment. Even black performers were 'blacked up' to match the stereotype white audiences expected. In the thirties, Billie Holiday was thought 'too yellow to sing with the men in the band' in Detroit's Fox Theatre. She had to black up: she could not seem to be white singing with blacks. Blackface is the big shock thing. Prince, with his genius for the G-spot of shock, once outraged a black colleague by suggesting he blacked up on a pop video. At least they'd notice you, he said.[15]

Funk manifesto-bearers of the seventies like James Brown, George Clinton, Sly Stone, paved the way for Prince to sidestep racially defined roles in the eighties.[16] Clinton developed a *parodic* black consciousness, aimed politically at blacks. His group Parliament began as doo-wop, but after hearing Hendrix he changed style. In 1970 he formed Funkadelic. Using overamplified guitars and heavy rock drums, he developed a bizarre socio-political mythological form of satire, fusing a range of black styles: as in 'Chocolate City', his 1972 album *America Eats its Young*, or *Mothership Connection* (1975, in which aliens come to earth to take funk back to their planet).[17]

The seventies was a great decade both for exposing pop's fraudulence (like punk), and ironizing or exploiting its artificiality (like glam): for exploring a pop song's ambiguous terrain between fantasy and reality. In different ways, both glam and punk mocked, from within their own parish, what they themselves were doing.[18] Black music could do that too. Prince foresaw every twist of potential in parodying white fantasies of blackness. In the seventies he listened avidly to Sly Stone, one of the great black innovators, whose late-sixties records laid the foundations for funk and disco sounds of the seventies. He also listened to Clinton. But he was aiming at white as well as black audiences. He saw black records marketed as one-off dance hits while white marketing built up loyalty to particular artists. He was not going to stay in a pre-moulded black niche. 'To define himself as black would have restricted him.'[19] To break out of black definition and reach white markets which Clinton, with his embrace of blackness, could not reach, he combined parody with its opposite: crossover. Not making black black (as white sees it), but making black seem somehow white.

The crudest way of whitening down is surgery or de-melanization. In 1983, says Greil Marcus, 'An Afro-American with surgically-produced Caucasian features became the most intensely famous person in the world.' Michael Jackson 'seized the centre of white American life and attention' as no other black artist ever had.[20] That was half-way through Jackson's peculiar journey. It is terrifying now to compare pictures of him with his brothers in the sixties and the nineties. In 1967, the Jackson Five were a bunch of similar-looking kids. In his 1997 induction into the Rock 'n' Roll Hall of Fame, Michael has jumped age and race. Beside his brothers, dignified, heavy-shouldered black men, he is a witchy, pale, ringletted, old–young freak. Commercially, it worked; artistically, his whitening worked humourlessly against him.

But the really big, and deeply political, icon of racial identity has always, since the sixties, been hair-style. In the sixties, straightening your hair meant being ashamed of blackness. Peter Tosh of The Wailers, very hostile to black writers whose racial integrity he suspected, took any straightish hair as the first sign of weakness. He was outraged when the Afro gave way to sleeker fashions.[21] In the film *What's Love Got to Do with It?*, Ike Turner's increasingly flat hair marks his descent into violence, drugs, out of touchness with Tina.

Prince's hair changed dramatically. He began *For You* with an Afro cut, had a rippling page-boy on *Prince*, a lank punk lick for *Dirty Mind*, and a wave nearly over one eye for *Controversy*. For some videos he had long straight hair like Little Richard (the first black artist to brandish 'deviant' sexuality at the audience), or big hair like white fifties female stars. Hair-dos marked his move to a white market, but also the irony he brought to his crossover. Black hair parodying white hair-styles accompanied a black voice parodying – and also using, taking further – white musical style. In August 1979, 'I Wanna Be Your Lover' was top in the R&B (i.e. black) charts. After twenty-three weeks in the black Top 100 songs, it entered the National Top Forty. At that point, the marketing question was 'How un-black can whites be convinced Prince is?'[22] He whitened himself verbally in interviews, and (maybe) invented a half-Italian mother or Italian father. He was light-skinned anyway; by 1981 he was saying he was half-Italian. He treated interviewers mis-chievously, but was clearly aiming (cynically or ambitiously) at a whiter image. The message came over loud and clear to blacks. 'What I used to say, a kind of joke I did in the black community, was that Prince was the top *white* act,' said Morris Wilson. Many felt Prince had broken out of his culture and not given anything back: he was African America making good at the expense of its brothers. 'Prince doesn't want to be black', said his ex-colleague Rick James resentfully.[23]

Since he was short, he could play up a daintily unthreatening image, the opposite of buck nigger racist fantasy. He created an erotic personality that was submissive as well as assertive: an androgynous waif. Where Jackson seemed imprisoned by his girlishness, Prince seemed a male seducer, whose paradoxical femininity came from wit and style. He was a multi-faceted incarnation of 'crossing over'. The white press hailed him as the first black artist since Hendrix who might be a major superstar. They adored *Dirty Mind* (1980), which left behind the black pop image of earlier albums. 'Lewdness cleansed by art' pronounced *Rolling Stone*. 'Is Prince Leading Music To a True Bi-racism?' asked the *New York Times* in December 1981.[24]

But he also played along with the sexy stereotype. Musically he marked it by, for instance, 'stopped time': the beat that comes just behind the lyrics. In Muddy Water's famous 'Hoochie Coochie Man', it suggests a tough shock moment of pelvic thrust just after the key words. 'I Wanna be Your Lover' has a weaker version of that. He seemed to be laughing at 'the oppressive sexual neuroses of white power' but was also 'pimping the licentious stereotype which was a central instrument of that oppression'. Just as he was breaking out of black definition, blacks saw him playing into the stereotype.[25] In 1981 he also began inventing a lurid sexual past for interviews. He said he'd been taken to a shrink as a teenager for his terrible sexual obsessions. (No one from his childhood knew anything about it.)[26] These stories underscored his astoundingly sexy lyrics. As Reagan cheer-led a new Puritanism, Prince sang about having sex with your sister, getting drenched in her vaginal fluids. 'Head' was about oral sex with a virgin on her way to the altar: the singer comes on her wedding dress.

Sex is vital to 'crossover' success.[27] Black–white, male–female, straight–gay: in every culture the ambiguity of cross-dressing, of impersonating someone sexually different from yourself, the thrill of mistake, discovery, transgressing boundaries, has enormous erotic-dramatic energy. 'Am I black or white? Am I straight or gay?' teased Prince. Jackson abandoned the self-laughter of black culture along with the melanin; Prince parodied the carnality in white fantasies of black.

Why Dark?

Rock music blazed the path by which popular young white culture has now become, in some respects, black. In spite of racism, white culture through the twentieth century has developed a very close symbiotic relation with black art, black values. The quickness, cool, anti-élitism, and humour of 'street' is now everywhere in sitcoms, advertising, all-white classrooms. In fashion, black models mean 'young', 'exotic', 'urban'. When the future English king, baseball cap on backwards, adopts a gangsta rap pose for a photo shoot, a British tabloid captions it 'YO ROYAL HIGHNESS'.[28] It was music that led the blacking-up of white teenage culture.

Why? One reason was all that history: rock was part of mainstream white culture's assimilating of modernism, and what it did with so-called primitive forms. But behind that is something much deeper: the idea that darkness is central to white ideas of the self.

'Primitive' Dionysus

This goes back to another image of 'the primitive'. As modernism prepared the ground for rock 'n' roll, anthropologists and scholars were redefining Greece. Pioneering anthropological work, done in the twenties, stressed the savageness of ancient cult.[29] In the fifties, popular culture began to realize ancient Greece was 'primitive', even irrational. In 1952, two years after Leo Fender perfected the solid-body electric guitar, while the first rock records were hurtling into orbit in Tennessee and Alan Freed was eyeing white kids buying black records, lectures were heard up the road in Berkeley, California, which became a hugely influential book. E. R. Dodds's *The Greeks and the Irrational* laid down the ground-plan for Greek wildness. Combining modern anthropology and psychology with classical scholarship, Dodds made Greece central to any re-evaluating of 'primitive' psychology. By the sixties, ancient Greece no longer prowled modern society as the symmetrical cold tiger of rationality: it had become the source of our own darkness.

The rock historian Robert Palmer quotes Dodds to explain the sixties rock ideology he grew up with. For both him and Dodds, the key figure of irrationality is the 'mad god', Dionysus. Well, why? What range of meanings, resonance and connections did Dionysus donate to modern imagination? Each Greek god had a range of specialities. You met them, felt their presence, in human experience and in natural forces; their persona expressed a link between the experience and the natural force. You met Artemis, for instance, in the connection between women's blood, chastity, hunting and the moon. Dionysus was the link between new raw sappy growth (in vines or young men), crowd ecstasy, wild dance, wild nature (mountains, forests); drink, illusion and hallucination; madness, tragic theatre and violence. Greek culture handed on these connections to later societies – who therefore feel they are 'natural' and 'true'. Dionysus also incarnated the androgynous young male, catalyst of wild energy. He maddened his worshippers who tore up live animals and expressed their suddenly abnormal consciousness in hallucinating and crazy dance. And tragedy, the beginning of Western theatre, was written for his festival.[30]

Drink, drugs, ecstatic loss of self in illusion of every kind (especially drink and madness); violent dance, crowds, theatrical spectacle and violence: as a summary of sixties rock, Dionysus couldn't be bettered. There he was, mad, Greek and ancient. His academic stock rose in the fifties. In the sixties, popular culture made him the figure-head for male rock. He was Greek, therefore true. He lived on in rock till well into the seventies. 'The real energy, fire and restlessness of youth comes from the dole queue and is sung by a Dionysiac punk rocker,' wrote a male journalist, extolling Johnny Rotten in 1977.[31]

In the late fifties and sixties, psychologists too were working on responses to Dionysus. When Dodds called his Dionysus chapter 'The Blessings of Madness', he reflected several trends of his own day. If high art could learn from 'primitive', sanity could learn from madness. The psychologist R. D. Laing argued brilliantly that schizophrenia could teach so-called normal ways of seeing a thing or two. Similar re-evaluations of madness had happened before. In the fourth century BC, Plato suggested that madness gave us the 'blessings' of prophecy, orgiastic rites, poetry and love. This idea was a big hit in the Renaissance. Genius suddenly became linked to 'melancholy': madness became fashionable. That speech in *A Midsummer Night's Dream* about 'The lunatic, the lover and the poet', with the poet's eye rolling 'in fine frenzy', is full of Renaissance echoes of Plato. But the idea of 'good' madness would have shocked Plato's contemporaries, who were used to seeing madness as divine punishment, pollution, Furies, or *melancholia* (too much 'black bile'). Madness was frightening, violent and (whether you explained it demonically or medically) black.[32] If you learned from it, you were learning from the dark.

Learning from the Dark:
Inner, Ancient, Dangerous, Knowing, Mad

But Greek thought and language constantly suggested that darkness was indeed the place where you learned. Metaphors for knowledge and life were full of light, but the deepest learning came from the dark. In their *katabasis*, 'descent to the underworld', Greek heroes go into darkness to learn what they cannot learn in the light. Ulysses goes to ask how to get home: Aeneas learns the future of Rome. The philosopher Parmenides said he learned to know in the 'House of Night'. Early oracles were sacred to Earth or Night. To learn the future from one oracle, you trudged underground in a terrifying ghost-train sequence of tunnels. Temples that are now blazing skeletons of light were dark and enclosed, lit only by pierced roof-tiles and smoky torches. Mythical prophets were blind, and operated from caves. Darkness was where you met gods and found knowledge you could not find in light. Blackness symbolism pervaded all thinking and feeling, which happened (Greeks thought) in the entrails, not the head. These entrails were black (or dark; the same word, *melas*, covers both), and filled with black liquid. Prophets examined animal entrails because gods inscribed their wishes there; your own black entrails were a centre of divine interest, knowledge, violence, divinity, thought and passion.[33]

This inner blackness gets darker when we get passionate: when guts fill with black liquid and we behave violently, destructively. Blackness is also sinister and destructive: murderers have 'black hearts': death, Furies and Fates are black. So inner blackness is dangerous as well as illuminating. 'Black anger' bubbles in Agamemnon to cause his fatal quarrel with Achilles – and so the *Iliad*'s whole plot. The blackness of madness is something going wrong inside.[34]

Behind all this lay an idea of mental darkness as a sort of underworld. Everything inside human beings was the colour of Hades. Whatever overwhelms your mind, fainting, madness, grief, rage, is black. 'Black' Furies live both in Hades and the mind. The underworld is an image for the blackness in ourselves. Knowledge and passion come, like Furies, from your own inner dark.[35]

Another aspect of dangerous turbulent darkness within was, I'm afraid, its connection with women. Greeks thought women too were dark. The voices of most Greek poetry, and all prose – philosophy, history, science – are male and represent women as a different 'tribe' living darker, more enclosed lives: less civilized, less self-controlled, more in touch with nature and darkness. Ever since Medea, witchcraft, drugs, exorcism, poison, secret dark things belong with women.[36] Greece, that ultra-male culture, felt the inner darkness you learned from was female. So were Night and Earth, the earliest prophetic deities. A goddess in the 'House of Night' instructs the philosopher Parmenides, just as a mysterious priestess, Diotima, teaches Socrates about love,[37] a lesson that encapsulates the whole of metaphysics.

All this is connected to fantasies about the womb, which flows with 'dark' liquid just as Earth flows with underground rivers. (Think Styx, think Acheron.) Earth is a 'womb': going into a woman is going into earth, into the dark. (When Nick Cave sings 'I found God not His devils inside her', is he thinking of his own name, or mistily reflecting Greek fantasy?) Earth offered male imagination a basic model of innerness: dark, creative, where you come from, where you adventure.[38] You didn't touch a menstruating woman. Blood was 'black' and polluting at the best of times and menstrual blood was particularly polluting. You had to keep away from a woman's affinity for darkness, yet male Greek culture used women for rituals which got in touch with darkness: especially childbirth (blood, life coming from the dark), laying out dead bodies (blood, life going into the dark). At Delphi, Apollo spoke through the priestess; male priests interpreted. This dark source of knowing is useful but dangerous. Let women be the contact, via ritual insulation.

So, whether for Plato or sixties psychologists, the idea that madness might be a good thing meant re-valuing the role and powerful resonances of darkness in Greek-derived thought.[39] All over European languages and literature, Greek images of inner darkness ('black waves' of anger, 'dark' spirits, a 'shadowed' mind) penetrate talk of mind and feeling. They are what make us feel that black is a 'natural' colour for what we imagine inside us: mind, spirit, soul. The theologian Maritain called the mind a 'nocturnal kingdom'. Freud called the *id*, bottom section of his map of the psyche, its 'dark' part. In Auden's elegy for Freud, our unconscious desires are 'fauna of the night' mourning the great psychologist who wanted us 'to be enthusiastic over the night'. When Freud said 'dark' or 'black' about feeling, or when we do, it is ancient Greece talking. From the moment we learn to talk, we carry darkness at our core.[40] Increasingly, as modernism evolved, its images of mental blacknesss drew on ancient associations to femaleness, innerness, underworld, magic, madness, danger, prophecy, passion and knowledge. D. H. Lawrence called maleness the 'dark embryo' of civilization – as if manhood, male knowledge, the male journey and self-image, began in female dark.

All this is the ultimate source for the power which blackness wields in white fantasy: the Greek idea that you have darkness in you. What is in you is dangerously (even sexually, maybe) different from the light outside. Blackness is feeling, is self. Dangerous, violent, but creative; the deepest source of knowledge.

This was the imaginative background against which the fifties and sixties reappraised darkness, madness, wildness, drugs. Priding itself on its black origins, rock 'n' roll was an accelerating force in all that. Jazz, blues and their child, rock 'n' roll: whether you despised them like Malcolm Sargent or found them exciting like punters in the Cotton Club and a million sixties teenagers, those who called them 'primitive' were tapping into a stereotype which associated anything non-Western with beginnings; which saw Western white culture as the end-product of a civilizing process that started in the dark.[41] The stereotype 'black' did not change, but became something to learn from. Learning from the dark, like Greek tradition said.

IMPERSONATION

All This Darkness Once Was Mine

Plus the thought grew up that maybe this darkness was one's own property originally anyway. After Darwin, and the self-reassessments of evolutionary theory, the negro began to be seen as a first step: what whites had once been; the 'primitive' stage in white evolution.[42] 'Black' was shorthand for ancient-cum-authentic. The idea that all human origins come 'out of Africa' was around in popular myth long before recent testing of skeletons confirmed it. Add Freud, and you could now feel the primitive was 'originally' yours psychologically, too. It was where you came from. ('Hallo darkness my old friend', as Simon and Garfunkel sing in 'The Sound of Silence'.) Babies had a 'primitive' level of consciousness: the most exotic and primitive things now belonged to the deepest, earliest layer of yourself. Africa met newly primitivized ancient Greece in your own soul.

In the late sixties, rock dreamed itself into 'ethnic' music. The Beatles and Stones experimented with music from India and Morocco. George Harrison got a sitar teacher.[43] A short-circuit of associations about 'origins', based on popular psychology, grew up in rock. The origins of rock were black, jungle, primitive; so were human origins. Rock was youth culture, in touch with all human roots: the young child energy of each individual *and* the roots of humankind. Rock's origins, therefore, were those of all humanity, authenticated by the idea that the primitive was the dark heart of the civilized self. These ideas circulated in white rock culture like coins of the realm. Black bought you a right to the exotic. It was where you came from, inside you, like the black presence at the centre of American cities. Taking over blackness, rock was appropriating the origins of everything.

For the Greeks, the dark centre of yourself or of the world, the obscurity which could reveal to you the meaning of your journey and life, meant above all knowledge, whose ultimate source was divinity. Since the sense of divinity has drained away from a lot of our culture, we have translated that knowledge and sacredness into sex. Rock music began as phallus worship. In the sixties, it began to lead the white world's learning from the dark.

11 'Black': The Voice of Male Need

Suffering is Power

Identifying with the victim is one of the biggest things music can do. After the Germans left occupied Vienna in 1945, turning their guns on the cathedral in farewell, the first opera the Viennese put on in their restored opera house, listening to it in their thousands packed in the square outside, was Beethoven's *Fidelio*, which turns on imprisonment, tyranny and suffering. Its heart is an earth-shattering chorus of prisoners allowed to stumble up into daylight for a moment. In music, the voice of the victim is power.

Opera was supremely powered by women suffering, abandoned, dying – mainly for love. The highlight of Purcell's opera *Dido and Aeneas* is Dido's aria 'When I am dead', sung before she flings herself on the pyre. Torchsong, and the torch end of female jazz-blues, likewise: the voice of Billie Holiday is the archetypal aching victim. But the voice that powered rock music was quite different. The blues gave white popular song a whole new dimension in male suffering, with a wonderfully pedigreed historical as well as erotic authenticity.

White fifties teenagers did not care about the politics behind the blues which powered rock. They wanted the vitality and sex. But the next decade heard and valued the pain, especially in Delta blues. In Son House, for example, a key influence on Robert Johnson and a singer of 'drenching intensity',

> The sorrow of the blues was not tentative or ironic. Son's whole body wept as, with eyes closed, the tendons in his

powerful neck standing out with the violence of his feeling, he sang in an awesome voice the *Death Letter Blues*.[1]

The sorrow of the blues did not just mean losing your lover. It was closely lapped with defiance at the human condition which creates such suffering. Clapton and Keith Richards reworking Robert Johnson were part of a leviathan turnaround in popular expectations about where power is in voice, in music. What it comes from. The mindblowing textures, playing and voice were only part of the blues renaissance. Male pain: that was the big pull.[2] White fantasy responded to its own sense of blackness and sorrow which it found reflected in male blues, and leaped to readjust its ideas about how masculinity could express its own suffering: with aggression, defiance and rage as well as poignancy.

Desire and abandonment from operatic women, sex and misery from black bluesmen: male art was always good at identifying and ventriloquizing other people's pain. In imitating blues, as in writing for women, white men got off on identifying with a voice that was not theirs, whose power came from suffering. As figures empowering white male musical imagination, women and blacks – both supposedly closer to 'nature' than white men – were able to rise (musically speaking) over suffering. In man-made opera, a woman's voice is most powerful when she is most hurt. Her voice grows as her life is wrecked. 'Art is about heartbreak', the opera composer Tom Adès said to me,

> and when a man breaks down in an opera, he's finished, pathetic, at the end of his role, his power. A woman's power in opera is in her fragility. The more she breaks the stronger she gets.

What The Stones heard in Robert Johnson was a man's voice rising, musically, over every kind of pain.

There is an extra turn of the screw when men write sexual laments for women to sing about men, or whites copy a genre invented by blacks oppressed by white men. In each case, you are ventriloquizing a pain caused by people like yourself. Who could chart all the emotional echoes here? Is this denial of yourself, a back-folded cruelty, getting off on identifying with a figure which people like you have hurt, or supremacism, drawing power from the very aggression it dishes out, narcissistically imagining the pain of being on the receiving end? There are many different kinds of creative power. By impersonating the powerless – women, blacks – the powerful can tap into something hard to admit in their own persona: the power to say you are hurt.

In the sixties, cutting-edge male rock music left behind the big traditional musical route to vulnerability, which was writing for a female voice. Pop impresarios like Phil Spector could go on manufacturing that vulnerability for women's voices (as he did for, say, The Crystals' 'He Hit Me, and It Felt like a Kiss'); and women singer-songwriters could take it over for themselves. (Think of the brilliant pitches of hurt in Joni Mitchell's voice: the strength of naked vulnerability in Sinead O'Connor's 'Thank You for Hearing Me'; in Kate Bush and Tori Amos – who became 'President of Victims Anonymous' after being raped in LA.) But male songwriting teams like Richards and Jagger were powered by male blues aggression, frustration, urgent need. Maleness discovered its voice as angry victim rising above injustice, and never looked back.

On The Beatles' album *Abbey Road*, white boys step out into the road on the pedestrian crossing, trusting in the pedestrian's power of cocky vulnerability. The male crotch, centre of cock rock, is focus of male power but also vulnerability: the zero as well as the hero, the fears of losing power summed up in the crippled side of all those males round Venus. Her castrated father, who fell from power. Her lame, cuckolded husband whose fire is stolen. Her blind baby son. Her lover who is all armour, nothing else. When the black male voice empowered rock, blues defiance solved an age-old European tension between male vulnerability and male fantasies of omnipotence. It made male vulnerability, even impotence, aggressively sexy. Suddenly there was a way to suffer and be powerful at once. Rock music put on the global stage, for the first time, the voice of male need.

This need was not sexual only, but mediated brilliantly through sex. Heavy metal is still 'the choice for most America', as one rock critic put it: meaning most of twenty-something white male America.[3] Its enduring appeal is the blues-powered channelling of aggrieved aggression into sex. Rock became the way young men deal with feelings – especially sexual frustration, resentment, and rage – which the white world before 1956 didn't know how to hear. It said young male *Angst*, rage, lust and selfishness were not just OK: they were the basic equipment of the hero in the street.

The passionate totem of all this was the electric guitar, which amplified the sound of male feeling and sexualized the expertise which expressed it. For the first time in Western music, male feeling made a sound that a mass community felt was true, raw and unmediated by any codes. Needy, raging, exulting, rock music seemed (only seemed, but seeming is all) to epitomize urgent male feeling *as it really, universally was*. This power came from the symbolic force of the apparently powerless blues guitar. In William Faulkner's novella *Old Man*, about the 1927 Great Flood (remembered in Charlie Patton's two-part blues 'High Water Everywhere'), a white character complains that blacks – including a young man with a guitar – were rescued and he wasn't:

> 'Bastard niggers and one of them setting there playing a guitar but there wasn't no room for me. A guitar!' he cried: now he began to scream, trembling, slavering, his face twitching and jerking. 'Room for a bastard nigger guitar but not for me.'[4]

That bastard nigger guitar became the gold-standard, the line of élite descent, of 'natural' masculinity. In 1940, Tennessee Williams set his early play *Battle of Angels* in a prejudiced Southern town. His hero is a poet, fatally but innocently attractive to women, torn to pieces by the sheriff's dogs set on him by the jealous men. Seventeen years later, Williams reworked this as *Orpheus Descending* (1957). Val became a guitarist, for in those seventeen years rock 'n' roll had shot the guitar to stardom. This Val is far more potent, radiantly attractive, the only white who values anything black. Though he is still torn to pieces, he brings music and sex dangerously, healingly, into other people's lives, with a guitar autographed by the early blues greats, including Leadbelly. Cut to another doomed guitarist, Kurt Cobain. On Nirvana's 'Unplugged in New York', introducing their version of Leadbelly's 'Where Did You Sleep Last Night?', Cobain calls Leadbelly 'our favourite performer', and is longing to possess his guitar. 'This guy representing the Leadbelly estate wants to sell me Leadbelly's guitar,' he says, 'for five hundred thousand dollars. I asked David Geffin personally if he'd buy it for me.' The black guitar: magic ticket to the roots of male sexuality and the power of male need.

Not that classical music, or earlier popular song, had ignored male pain. But they mostly expressed it through codes that excluded somebody. The pain in troubadour and Elizabethan lovesong is not for everyone. The Provençal courtly code, and the cult of melancholy in sixteenth-century England which lies behind heart-searing Dowland songs, were élite games as elaborately coded as bridge bids; and the point of a code is that you do not notice your own. You see artifice and games-playing only in other people's conventions; you feel your own are natural. In opera, brilliant composers and singers wrote and performed male pain wholesale. Mimi dies, but *La Bohème* focuses not on her suffering but what the men feel about her: Puccini's subject is men's jealousy, longings and feelings of inadequacy. Peter Grimes, Rigoletto: opera is full of male need and pain. But except in Italy, none of this had popular, cross-class appeal. Popular songwriters of the thirties and forties wrote devastating songs of male pain – like Lorenz Hart's 'Ship Without a Sail' or Gershwin's 'One For My Baby', which got banned from American bars because it was so depressing. Sinatra sang those songs wonderfully. But this was adult stuff, experience looking back on loss, on mistakes. A grown-up code: not something which teenagers (once invented) could identify with.

Rock has elaborate codes of its own but they do not come, like Elizabethan music and opera, from a courtier class. They come over as male feeling straight from the heart or pelvis unfiltered by experience or class. (They *are* filtered, of course; but the codes stop you seeing it.) Via the blues, rock could present itself as something coming up naturally from the roots of the self, body or society, not coming down from above like Radio 3 or (until recently) the House of Lords.

Anger with the outside world, mistakes that are someone else's fault, are hardly new in music. Men have sung songs against oppression, nationalist and revolutionary songs, in a million communities all through history. But they were sung to local listeners. If they go on about masculine *Angst* and personal feelings as well as injustice, they do it in a specific, local scenario. The blues sounded, in the sixties, universal. That is why the Mississipi Delta shines 'like a national guitar'. Rock siphoned that universality off, putting hurt but defiant male feeling centre stage for the first time in Western music.

When you identify with a figure you and your culture find powerful, you buy for yourself the power you endow them with. For white sixties teenagers, singing black meant a flight from being who you were – suburban, middle-class, puny, of no account – into new strength, new energy. Whatever else this gorgeous new voice was, it was sexual first, supercharged by identification with black sexuality, laced with stereotypes about animality, instinct, free spirit which must absolutely not be constricted, primitive male sexuality, acknowledging vulnerability but triumphing over oppression. The empowering figure was no longer the woman – all that alien suffering and desire. It was a sexy black man, whose suffering was positive, angry and political. From there, the empowerment radiated out to include every angry misunderstood boy adventuring into the void of a hostile world – like a psychonaut, like Ziggy Stardust. The black hero was assimilated: the rock hero was up and running. The black voice empowered rock's feral leap to authenticate white masculinity.

Boy or Man? Oppression, Sex and Politics

The blues lyricists were in a sense America's first political poets. Male blues came from songs sung by men in prisons, men working in plantations, humping logs on Mississippi boats, building the mound along its length, all in conditions of peonage, pitiful wages, murderous bosses, contempt. 'A nigger didn't mean more to a white man than a mule,' said Big Bill Broonzey.[5] Blues defiance focused on what it was to be a man in the face of injustice and oppression which called you 'boy'. Male singers recorded in the twenties and thirties 'sound like men risking their necks to assert their right to be treated as men'.[6] When Muddy Waters sings 'I'm a man, I'm a rollin' stone' ('Hoochie Coochie Man', written by Willie Dixon), he is claiming not just sexuality but equality. Bo Diddley's 'I'm A Man' was a reverie-riff on that line. When Muddy sang it, he re-titled it 'Manish Boy'. It was about growing up male ('When I was a young boy... I had sump'n in my pocket... / Now I'm a man... I have lots of fun') but also about growing up free. Muddy and Bo recorded it in 1955, when Muddy was forty and Bo twenty-seven. Even then, black men were still called 'boys' in the South.

Sixties teenagers heard the blues, as fifties teenagers could not, as a song of defiance against oppression. They took personally that connection between anger and being a man: 'English white boys in the cockroach-free comfort of mother and father's home could get off on stud imagery from bygone times. The blues musicians' life was raw, glamorous, full of whores, liquor, violence, freedom. A bluesman was a real man.'[7]

Suddenly, blues spoke to anyone's pain. Peter Green, one of the most innovative sixties British blues guitarists and founder of Fleetwood Mac, grew up in London's East End as an apprentice butcher. As a Jewish kid in an anti-Semitic neighbourhood, he felt persecuted. He identified with blues because of that; and because of feelings about the holocaust.[8] When you identify with a song whose background breath is injustice and oppression, you align it with your own resentments – sexual, political, existential, historical, generational, whatever. The sixties blues renaissance coincided with civil-rights protest; the white world was suddenly listening to anger and guilt. British boys, mainly working-class but not only, liked the sex, virility, vitality, intense idiom and high-voltage volume of Chicago blues. But with an anger and edge that came from their own times, they also heard aggression, the refusal of oppression.[9] Plus, in Delta blues, they heard how a single song, a frail naked thing, emotionally and musically simple on the surface and immensely complex beneath, could turn on an audience of thousands by fusing personal and political intensity. All this, alongside the radioactive influence of Dylan and the sixties folk movement, empowered rock's development as protest. In the sixties, the Beatles, Stones and Hendrix rose as one to Dylan's challenge. In the seventies, you got Patti Smith on one hand, with her art-punk poetry and stinging début single 'Piss Factory' (1974), a defiant riposte to working-class drudgery; and on the other, singer-songwriters like Jackson Browne who increasingly used rock as political criticism. After visiting Nicaragua, Browne attacked American policy in Central America (*Lives in the Balance*, 1986). In good seventies tradition, Patti Smith's 1996 album *Peace and Noise* attacked America's handling of Aids and cult suicides and related them to earlier failures like Vietnam and the Depression.

But black music became a potent source of social criticism too. From the slickest, most unpolitical production stable around came Marvin Gaye's *What's Going On?* in 1971. Someone else wrote the title song; but when Marvin sang it, he made it his. It gave his own songs on the album a new political edge. 'What's Happening Brother?' is sung by a returning Vietnam soldier. (Marvin's brother Frankie had come back after three years in Vietnam; his twenty-one-year-old cousin was there for only three months in 1968 before he was killed. In a 1969 TV film, *The Ballad of Andy Crocker*, Marvin played the combat buddy of a soldier who returns from Vietnam to find everything changed for the worse.) 'Inner City Blues' reproaches America with Vietnam, brutal policing, poverty, inflation, crime, high taxes. The album's layers of religion, environmentalism and politics, plus the seamless jazz-inspired textures, made it an odd enterprise for Motown. Berry Gordy said it was crazy, uncommercial. The arbiters on his 'quality control' team wanted to bin it. But Marvin was a big Motown star, and insisted. It became the first Motown album to print lyrics, was Marvin's first album success, and coincided with radical changes of content and distribution in seventies black music. Sly Stone, Isaac Hayes, Al Green and Curtis Mayfield's Chicago band The Impressions all pioneered social awareness and criticism. (Al Green was an important activist, too.) Black albums, as well as singles, began to sell in large numbers.[10]

But sex was still rock's prime medium. When social anger flooded in in the sixties, there took place a powerful alchemy between politics and sex: the sexualization of politics, the politicization of sex. 'I Can't Get No Satisfaction' is both at once. Again, this link between sexual and social resentment came from male blues, where impotence and rage are social and political as well as sexual. The revelatory model, in whom male sexual grievance is the royal road to all suffering, was Robert Johnson. 'I'm the man that rolls, when icicles is hangin' on the tree/And now you hear me howlin' baby, down on my bended knee.' Life attacks him: 'blues falling down like hail'. Day is 'a hellhound on my trail'. A man must 'keep movin' '. Love would make life bearable – 'All I need's my little sweet woman, to keep my company' – but you wind up alone, 'Dogged and driven ever since I left my mother's home'. Women abandon you. 'Got up this morning . . . My little Bernice was gone.' They could heal a man's aloneness and drivenness, but they don't. 'Every man love that game you call love, but it don't mean no man no good.' Man's suffering is woman's fault. As he says in a song which went into The Stones's 'Satisfaction', 'A man is like a prisoner and he's never satisfied'.[11]

In Johnson, suffering is sexual, existential, social and ultra-male, all at once. 'People look at the dread in Johnson's lyrics as existential, but you've got to look at it in social terms too,' said the black guitarist Vernon Reid. The background weave to Johnson's landscape is social oppression. 'Run here baby, set down on my knee/I wanna tell you, about the way they treated me.'[12] Sex and the devil are real, but also an image: of society which rejects and hurts as women do, of a world teeming with icicles, crossroads, hellhounds. 'I bin mistreated baby an' I don' mind dying'.

This was the mix of eroticism, dread and musicality that inspired sixties singers to inject social and existential resonances into sexual anger. 'Satisfaction' (1965) was the Stones' first composition with social content. It began with a little riff from Keith, who recorded it and fell asleep. Mick, writing contemporary blues, heard in it 'an opportunity for anti-Establishment lyrics'.[13] Picking up the way Johnson uses sexual hurt as image of wider wrongs, the song yells abroad sexual *and* social anger – at 'useless information' on radio, boring TV, mendacious advertisements. In Roddy Doyle's novel *The Commitments*, soul music is presented to Dublin musicians as a winning mix of sex and revolution. 'Soul is a double-edged sword', says their leader:

> The first side is sex, righ'. An' the second one is – REVOLUTION! 'Say it once, say it loud, I'm black an' I'm proud.' They looked at him. 'James Brown . . . He sang tha'. And he made a fuckin' bomb. The Irish are the niggers of Europe, lads.' They nearly gasped; it was so true. 'An' Dubliners are the niggers of Ireland. An' the northside Dubliners are the niggers of Dublin.'[14]

Downtrodden themselves, they identify with downtrodden blacks whose music is 'all abou' ridin' ' (i.e., sex):

> That's wha' rock 'n' roll means. Did yis know tha'? (They didn't.) Yeah, that's wha' the blackies in America used to

call it. So the time has come to put the ridin' back into rock
'n' roll. Tongues, gooters, boxes, the works.

Sixties musicians were mesmerized by the political-cum-sexual spin of the Muddy Waters–Bo Diddley claim 'I'm a Man', or 'Manish Boy'. Many groups recorded it: The Yardbirds twice. A band led by one David Jones (who later changed his name to Bowie) called themselves The Manish Boys. The original Willie Dixon line, 'I'm a man, I'm a rolling stone', gave a leading rock magazine its title; Brian Jones, whose idols were Muddy Waters, Howlin' Wolf, Elmore James and John Lee Hooker, lifted it to name the group he founded, the most famous rock band in the world. 'Rolling' and 'Stone' are rock's most potently coupled words, partly because they belong with that naked claim, 'I'm a man'.[15]

But 'man' is a word with a lot of angles. Blues were made and sung by adult men; rock by boys, claiming manhood. For them and their male fans, 'man' stood not just for sex, but adultness; the power to judge the world for yourself and rampage through it on your own. When Elvis sang 'Tonight she'll know I'm a mighty mighty man', the repetition round 'man' simply spelt sex. (No hangovers from slavery there.) But the sixties picked up that male fusion between the sexual and the political. The foundation of rock was not only a white man singing in a black voice. If you look at Robert Palmer's *History of Rock*, the important faces in the first two thirds of the book are not only black but adult. The photos are a startling visual mosaic of heavily mature black men and willowy white boys whose body language is all about *saying* they are men. Not just white impersonating black, but boy impersonating man.

Teenage boys find sex a source of frustration and bitterness as well as triumph: male sexual resentment is one of the great forces driving rock's boy-made textures. 'Rock is always trying to work out relations with the opposite sex', said Paul Trynka. 'Not easy when much of the time you're feeling resentful, disappointed, and vengeful.'[16] For a sixties boy in a bedroom ruled by mum, whose girlfriend wouldn't sleep with him (or who didn't have one), the oppression he heard in blues was sexual first. Heard in that bedroom, reverberating in his head as he slammed the front door and walked down the street, 'I'm a man' meant saying you were sexual when you weren't sure how to be, to a world that didn't seem to want to know.

Teenage Protest and the Slave-to-Freedom Story

That was how sixties rock music channelled political–sexual blues pain into the politics of the young against the old: a war in which sex was the main weapon. Rock sex was not just sex. It was the force behind the 'zero to hero' zoom away from parents, the sound of the body which insists on fun and action, the antithesis of mum and dad's static life. Sex got you out of the house, where you were only a hero in your head, to a world where heroism might really come your way. In the fifties, Gene Vincent could sing 'Hey Mama, can I go out tonight? . . . Well, Mama, don't get mad.' Mum's anger still mattered; she still had a veto. Sixties rock laughed at her. 'One pill makes you bigger, one pill makes you small, and the pills that mother gives you don't do anything at all', sing Jefferson Airplane in their drug song 'White Rabbit'.[17] The Stones's 'Mother's Little Helper' ridicules her tranquillizers. No mention of the pills downed by their generation: parental pills insulate you from life, our pills pitchfork you into it. Mum, whose house you live in, does nothing for you compared to the big new force driving both you and the industry that defines the teenage world: where the prime oppressive force is a parent.

Dad got his innings a couple of decades later. Black Flag's album *Damaged* (1981), dominated by raging guitars, is anti-fatherdom personified. On the cover, the singer Henry Rollins glares into a shattered mirror. Blood is snaking down his fist where it meets the glass. He stutters out song-phrases while his father yells 'Do it again, boy!' 'Yessir,' he gibbers. Finally he retreats to catatonic isolation, yelling 'STAY OUT'. When the album came out in Los Angeles from Unicorn, on a distribution deal with the company MCA, MCA's distribution chief announced in horror, 'As a parent, I found this an anti-parent record'. 'ANTI-PARENT RECORD' stickers were pasted over the MCA logo on twenty-five thousand copies, boosting teenage sales 100 per cent.[18]

Parents and sex both get muddled up with resentment against coercive, rejecting, parental society. The last song of *Damaged* blames dad, but the first, 'Rise Above', gave the whole album its claustrophobic keynote of social rage and defiance to which the post-punk California generation thrilled. 'Such an incredible record', said Danny Weizman. 'So pure, such aggression to it, it somehow stood apart from the scene. *Damaged* is the suburban Southern California nightmare.'[19] Fifteen years later, Alanis Morissette's song 'Right Through You' (1996) took music executives who mispronounced her name and 'didn't wait for all the information before they turned me away', as an image for parent-like society which shut out her own generation. Her huge audience identifies with her as victim of a heartless world.[20]

Behind that romance of anger at oppression, which gave sixties rock such creative power, was male teenage frustration. It was this that hijacked the adult blues voice, witness of injustice in one particular place, to express its own personal resentments – partly socio-economic (at a time of profound social change in Britain), partly sexual, but muddled up all the way with resentment at parent-like control. One of its big targets was self-satisfied domesticity. Music originally sung to brandish your own humanity in the face of an oppressive world's denial of it became a generational weapon for the young against the old.

Politically, this take-over was outrageous. Nothing in the life of Mick Jagger, with a nice safe place at the London School of Ecomonics, was comparable to where blues came from. The boys re-making rock were better off by six million miles than the people whose music they used. But culture works by using what other people made. Creativity is ruthless. If you're able to make something new, and find something that helps you do it, nothing on earth will stop you. Unlikely connections get made everywhere. The sorrow of the blues authenticated everything. Look, says the blues, sparkling like broken granite at the bottom of rock ideology. Here's the real thing: oppressed powerlessness turned to strength by the alchemy of song. The voice of resentment, frustration, loneliness, the oppressed but invincible male self, telling the world's cruelty, justifies rock's increasingly virtuoso aggression, rejecting any confinement, parental, sexual or social.

Rock's story of itself is one of the great myths of getting free. From black Southern blues to white Elvis, Chicago blues to white Paul, Keith, Eric, black sound snaked its irresistible way up the Mississippi, from the Delta to Chicago and out to the waiting world: London, Berlin, Lebanon, Japan. It is a move from dark to light, like the Prisoners' Chorus in Beethoven's *Fidelio*, from black to white, 'Muddy Waters' to the Sun King. A white adventure, Huck Finn with Jim inside, empowering him. A boy's adventure; a growing up. On Mick and Keith's part there was a real, musicianly falling-in-love with blues style, but there was also an extra-musical love affair with the blues male self-image based on the slave-to-freedom story behind every black American voice.

Consciously or unconsciously, this love affair depended also on a grammar of maleness laid down in Greek myth. Rock music had enormous transformative power. Musically, it transformed blues; imaginatively, it transformed white ideals of maleness, both by exploiting black ones and by returning to ancient ideals embodied in heroes like Hercules and Theseus. Myths and music: both got changed in the transmission. But some blended spirit of heroic maleness, a spirit valued as 'primitive', carried on.

Fighting Back

Rock amplified that spirit as much as it amplified sound. The feeling it amplified was almost parodistically teenage male. Rock music is the voice of male growing-up, springing up out of confinement, enlarging something that longs to be noticed, bursting out of the home (or out of jeans bought with mum's money), translating the musical energy of an oppressed foreign culture into generational rebellion. Blues was music that wanted 'to be someplace else, but making the best of where you are'.[21] Sixties rock took from it an image of aggressive alienation. Trying to get away from (and outraging) the conventions of parent society was one of rock's own first conventions. Though for nineties teenagers, the revival of songs and fashions parents knew when *they* were young, made it harder.

Economics was an important dimension here. Materially, parents and parent culture had it all, and you didn't. Poverty, not having things, had been a vital link between country music and blues, the two main sources of rock music. The sixties made it a source of pride. Dylan (see 'Bringing it All Back Home') deeply rejected the poor-boy self-image he inherited in country music.[22] The sixties made not caring that you are a have-not in a world of haves the epitome of sexy cool. All you need, all the bluesmen needed, is your own male need and aggression. Rock music, the voice of growing up, is aggressive because it is fighting *back* against oppression. As if someone had murmured 'Down, boy, down', it stands up brandishing guitar, gun, microphone and cock to shout 'Look! I *am* a man!'

12 When the Guitar Became a Gun: Empowering Violence

Black is Bad, Bad is Cool: Leadbelly to Gangsta Rap

Rock is about fighting back: it has to go violent. In Homer, war comes first. First war, the *Iliad*; then adventure, the *Odyssey*. Rock did it the other way round. After inventing the group as the icon of adventurous growing-up, sixties rock increasingly turned to violence. The black stereotype through which they read the blues offered white boys a way of seeming 'bad' via the Western equation of violence and darkness.

This equation seems 'natural' now, but in ancient Greece, 'bad' was only one element of blackness symbolism. It was not antiquity but the Middle Ages and Renaissance which focused and developed that badness (especially in religious contexts) until 'black' stood mainly for evil. Judas (for instance) was born under 'the black star': Saturn, sign of melancholics, murderers and misery. See the 1967 Stax album from the black blues singer Albert King, *Born Under a Bad Sign* (written mainly by the black session musician and songwriter Booker T).[1] In the Middle Ages, this symbolism was unrelated to black *people*. But the idea that black meant 'bad' fitted white stereotyping of blacks all too well. It helped to empower racism, to map out the imaginative framework of white society within which American blacks had to make their new lives after slavery. Rampant sexuality was one term in the stereotype; violence another. In 1883, *Atlantic Monthly* said blacks were 'animal, half-savage, easily roused to fury' and white women were right to fear them.[2]

As the black hero became glamorous in the twentieth century, so did violence. As 'primitive' became exotic in the twenties, commercial companies began recording male blues in the thirties, and guitars got louder in the forties, violence entered performance as well as sound. T Bone Walker, a demonic showman, did tiger leaps across the stage, played the guitar with his teeth and behind his head. Howlin' Wolf thrashed orgasmically around on the floor.[3] Electric blues ('nobody couldn't hear you with an acoustic') presaged rock music's weapon-like battering at your ears, demanding entrance. Literally so when American Special Forces blasted General Noriega from his bolt-hole in Panama by playing heavy metal at top volume for three days non-stop, from loudspeakers in the garden. Heavy metal's fake war-sound defeated a real warrior.

But long before electric blues came Leadbelly, born in 1888. He spent years in Texas and Louisiana jails for criminal violence. In 1933, he was in prison for assault with intent to kill. The depression had muffled commercial recordings but the Lomaxes, father and son collectors, were wheeling their recording equipment into prisons to collect 'folk-songs' for the Library of Congress. They were delighted with Leadbelly, they played a song he composed in praise of Louisiana's governor to the governor himself, who pardoned and released this intelligent murderer. Leadbelly teamed up with Lomax to sing his 'folk' songs; Lomax published them (*Negro Folk Songs as Sung by Leadbelly*, 1939). Then they quarrelled. Lomax tried to stop Leadbelly singing his songs, but Leadbelly turned defiantly to commercial recording. As the recording industry picked up, his wildly successful records began commercial white valuing of black song and created a new white market: the folk audience, the people who later bought Woody Guthrie and Dylan. Leadbelly kickstarted commercial recording of American 'folk' song.[4]

He was also the first black performer to become popular through a mainly white market. For unlike twenties blues, Leadbelly was bought mostly by whites. Thirties blacks wanted to look forward, wanted new, urban blues. Country blues from the humiliating rural past were not what they wanted to hear themselves saying. Leadbelly was everything they wanted to shake off. But whites felt they were hearing the voice of living history, and adored the piquancy of his violent past. 'BAD NIGGER MAKES GOOD MINSTREL' trumpeted *Life Magazine*.⁵ A real black murderer singing 'folk-songs' to white audiences: radical chic *avant la lettre*, buying into other people's violence at no threat to yourself. For even then, violence was a big ingredient in the 'authenticity' white audiences looked for in jungle music. You could share 'Jungle Nights' in Harlem before scooting off back to Manhattan. From the fifties on, white kids enjoyed the sense of real-life risk in places where they heard black music.⁶ Black musicians kept innovating, twisting away from white imitation, giving social realism new lyric and musical shapes. Soul, funk, reggae and rap sang of real life with ever-new and ever contemporary energy. To white audiences, violence, danger and 'badness' were cool.

Rap began male. There are brilliant women rappers. But rap and hip-hop license violent misogyny more than any other genre. Niggaz With Attitude sing about a 'preacher's daughter' who offers to 'take a broomstick up the butt', gets raped by 'a gang of niggers', and 'licks out their assholes'. Rap violence started as a marketing device; it now often seems, to some listeners, the message itself. Critics from the black community worry that the brutality is undermining rap's black roots. Obscenity was always only one strand, though a very important one, in black music. 'The heart of this music was once desire. Now there is something close to hate at its core.'⁷ But that's what the white, as well as black, market wants. The rapper Jay-Z started dealing in crack at twelve, partly to help his mum after his dad walked out. It helped to finance his musical career but in his poignantly autobiographical album *In My Lifetime Vol. 1* his spooky song 'You Must Love Me' asked his family to stand by him despite the drug-dealing. 'The City is Mine' was an emotional song to his dead schoolfriend Christopher Wallace, the rapper The Notorious B.I.G. But fans thought Jay-Z had gone soft. For his next album, *Hard Knock Life 2* (1998), he brought back all the 'I fucked your bitch, I killed your brother' stuff: it sold 500,000 copies in America within four days of release and was number one for over five weeks. 'I showed a lot of emotion on my last album', he said.

> People weren't ready for that. There's no fear on the new album. It's a fearful life in the ghetto and that's what I showed. But some fans don't want you to question the ghetto mentality too deep.

In real life, he believes black-on-black murder and gangsta glorification is 'sick',[8] but he delivers what the market wants: hate, violence, brutality, packaged black.

Rap does not have to be violent. Black lyrics have always had brilliantly playful, jokey, quick metaphor. Rap runs on cheeky confrontation and rhyming wit. It is the hero as wordsmith, the man with all the rhymes, in control of language and repartee. Rhyming dictionaries sell like hot cakes in the ghetto. But the white market, as well as the black, adores the violence. They buy it, copy it and like it backed up by the real thing. Violence broke out in the US gangsta rap world in September 1996 when Death Row Records' star, twenty-five-year-old Tupac Shakur, symbol (said *Rolling Stone* in its memorial edition) of his generation's rage and *Angst*, was shot dead.[9] He had been in a fight with a man called Orlando Anderson, who was killed later in a shoot-out. In 1997, Jay-Z's friend B.I.G was shot in a drive-by shooting. In 1998, Ol' Dirty Bastard, founder of the Wu Tang Clan, was shot in a robbery. The Polygram President Eric Kronfield remarked that Polygram could not employ many African Americans as they were unable to hire people with criminal records. In reply, trip-hop singer Tricky put out a limited edition of 'Can't Freestyle' which attacked the racial policy of Polygram (parent company to Tricky's own Island Records), and Kronfield was fired.

Rap-linked violence hit Britain in 1998, by which time most UK rap records were bought by whites. The white DJ Tim Westwood, who hosted Radio 1's *Rap Show*, was attacked by 'black gangsters' at a 1998 gig. In 1999 he was wounded in a drive-by shooting that looked like gangland stuff. Was it anger that he refused to pay protection money?[10] While he was recovering, the New York DJ Funkmaster Flex took over his radio show and piled on the violence. Item three was 'I got the mind of a young Butch Cassidy/ Get fly, let 'em defy gravity/ Both fire rapidly lift you chest cavity.' Item five, 'You know my style. I put you there, in a wheelchair/ You cannot run from the hot one with shotgun./ When it hits you, you gonna do a 360, pretty swiftly/ Then nobody getting up, less they're in a wheelchair sitting up or spitting up./ Either way, I don't give a fuck.'

Defending the programme, Radio 1's controller Andy Parfitt said 'The term gangsta rap is outdated and meaningless ... The programme contained a mix of the latest and most popular rap music: love songs, humorous lyrics, reference to the realities of life in urban America.' Reviewers commented that item two ('Dress to impress/ Spark the bitch's interest/ Sex is all I expect/ Don't take 'em to the crib unless they're bonin''), was hardly a love song. Nor was item seven, about sodomizing women. If, they said, the Rap Show was indeed – as Parfitt claimed – 'recognized as the home of authentic hip hop', then the central note of that authenticity was callousness and violence.[11]

But this is what the white market currently wants. In 1998, Germany's top-selling rap artist was Nana Kwame Abrokwa, a twenty-eight-year-old Ghanaian; he sells two million CDs a year. In 1990, in Hamburg, he burst into the flat of his Turkish neighbours, beat three people to a pulp with a baseball bat, and was sentenced to three and a half years in prison. Eight years later, he had still not got to prison. He is rich and famous; his lawyers say it would be a shame to stifle his artistic talent. He is now a Christian, holding Bible classes between performances. 'I did some bad things,' he says. 'I know I got to pay the price.' But his songs go on being violent. His 1998 album included the line, 'Arnold Schwarzenegger-style I'll break your back and neck, believe me I've been though a lot of shit'. Meaning his crime, for which he still hasn't 'paid', except with cheques to lawyers.

Rap is top in Germany. The German market would like more of it, but heroes with authentic 'bad nigga' aura are thin on the ground. Johnny B says he shoplifted at sixteen in his home town, Gary, Indiana, but so what? A. K. Swift is a rising rap star. His songs speak of a rough childhood in gangster-infested Chicago, but he is married with kids in the suburbs, and does not rap about that. In Darmstadt and Kaiserlautern, record company scouts patrol US bases looking for mean-looking black GIs with rhythm.[12] White teenagers everywhere want their rappers black, American-speaking, ideally with a criminal record: the violence real, like in America. In rock ideology, violence is the bottom line of the authentic self which black seems to deliver. Back to Leadbelly, 1934: 'Bad nigger makes good minstrel'.

Impersonating Violence

Yet blues violence did not figure in rock 'n' roll's first phase, 1954 to 1962. Elvis and Little Richard were aggressively sexual, though a hint of sexual violence set rock 'n' roll apart from country or pop. Billy Goldenberg, musical arranger for Elvis's 1968 stage comeback, said he'd always felt 'something very raw, sexual and mean about Elvis. There's a cruelty... he's excited by certain kinds of violent things.'[13] But in the film *G. I. Blues* Elvis gets called a 'gentleman': not a label Led Zeppelin, for instance, would care for. (By 1968 The Stones had established menace as a big commercial power, so maybe Goldenberg was clinging to a bandwagon here.) The main shock of early rock was not only its black sexiness but also its defiant, mucking-around silliness. 'Awopbopaloobop Awopbamboom' and 'Ram Bunk Shush' (from the Ventures, 1961) yell out the teenage right to have fun and not mean things. Nonsense was a tradition from the start: a non-meaning which punk picked up on. 'De da da da, de do do do, that's all I want to say to you,' sings rock's *Guardian*-reading intellectual, Sting.

The violence came between 1964 and 1965. It began white, and coincided with the moment when rock lost that reader-friendly little extra, 'and roll'. Rock as we know it began with violence. Blues lyrics and legends gave white British apprentices all the elements that would reappear in rock violence: destruction, the devil, demonic guitar-playing, drink, drugs, weapons – and general 'badness' permeating a performer's life and, with any luck, death too. Charlie Patton, born in the 1880s, was expelled from Dockery Farm for bullwhipping a woman. In 1904 the collector Roy Carew, listening to factory workers in New Orleans, heard blues-fragments like 'Drink good whisky boy/And let the cocaine be'. Blind Lemon Jefferson's songs, whose success from 1926 on sparked off a rush of male blues recordings in the late twenties, ripple with bad liquor, shootings, hangings, jail. 'I wonder why they 'lectrocute a man after the one o'clock hour of the night./Because the current is much stronger, then the folkses turn out all the lights.' Booker Washington White's blues were sung in labour camp after he shot someone in a 1937 juke-house.[14]

Blues was 'devil's music'. Simply with his title 'Voodoo Chile' (1968), Hendrix laid blood-claim to the blues tradition. Peetie Wheatstraw called himself 'the Devil's son-in-law'. 'Casey Jones' (sung in the late twenties by Furry Lewis, who lost a leg on the railroad in 1916) was about an engineer who raced the devil. Ten years before Faustian Robert Johnson, alcoholic Tommy Johnson (whose 'Alcohol and Jake Blues' refers to home-brewed liquor made from paint-ingredients) sold *his* soul to the devil. Violent deaths – razor-wielding women, backstreet brawls, Chicago blizzards, seventeen stab-wounds in Sonny Boy Williamson's corpse in 1948, Robert Johnson's strychnine – added to the lyrics' glamorous violence. The aura of evil titillated juke-house audiences of the thirties just as it does gangsta rap and heavy metal audiences today.[15]

Powered by the sixties blues renaissance, aggression became the defining note in rock sound around 1965. The Who's manager Kit Lambert encouraged Pete Townshend to smash guitars as part of the act. Daltrey's snarly voice, Townshend's harsh guitar and defiant lyrics, Keith Moon's demonic drumming, gave them three hits that year, including 'My Generation' with its anthemic rock refrain, 'Hope I die before I get old': a hope which many rockers of that generation fulfilled. So, in the next decade, did the Sex Pistol Sid Vicious, who often quoted it, who lived and died by it.[16] Teenage audiences suddenly wanted bad image, violent playing. The Stones became rock's paradigm 'bad boys' – a much fought-over title ever since. Their manager Andrew Oldham encouraged a blankly menacing image offstage as well as on. By today's standards, this rested on pretty flimsy stuff, like Mick saying 'We'll piss anywhere, man' to a garage attendant upset by Bill Wyman peeing on his wall. But the media gleefully helped, especially in 1967 when some of The Stones were sentenced on drug charges and jailed before appeal and Keith told the judge, 'We're not old men. We have no interest in your petty morality.'[17]

Onstage, their music (Keith's wolfish rhythm-guitar, Mick's swaggering 'black' voice) and themes were increasingly menacing, the dramatic personae more arrogantly aggressive. On *Their Satanic Majesties Request*, 'Midnight Rambler' is a rapist with a knife. 'Street Fighting Man', with its harsh timbres, came out of Mick's appearance at the 1968 demonstration against Vietnam in Grosvenor Square. He was taking the piss: London Town, he snarls, is no place for street-fightin' man. Jagger's whip-play with the microphone, twisting torso and twisting lips were exhibitionism playing sadism. After Brian Jones went to satanic festivals in Morocco, the occult came in with the ritual and satanism of 'Sympathy for the Devil' (1968). Mick's Lucifer was accompanied by grunts, screams, and a pounding beat: he ended by screaming out his demonic power over every object of desire. 'I want ya, baby!' Performing this in Los Angeles, he terrified his designer, Ossie Clarke:

> I never designed another costume for Mick. It was as if he'd become Satan and was announcing his evil intentions. He

was revelling in this role. Frightening, truly frightening. The more the audience's reaction intensified, the more Mick baited them.[18]

The Gun Guitar: Weight, Goths and Heavy Metal

The Stones did not sing about holding hands like The Beatles. Their sex was aggressive, with violence round the corner. As boys started going *en masse* to their concerts, violence sang out in the names of other groups, song-titles, lyrics, in the public image of performers; in the musical textures of MC5, The Who, Iggy and The Stooges. From 1965 the guitar became a gun as well as a penis. Keith Richards often held his guitar as if he were firing it. Wilko Johnson machine-gunned the audience with his at the climax of Dr Feelgood's act. From wanking to repeat fire, music became war as well as sex. From the 'hardness' of cock guitar to weapons symbolism, 'heavy metal' was born; about 1970. Led Zeppelin came out of British blues. In 'Whole Lotta Love' (1968), their singer Robert Plant shot off volleys of ear-splitting sexual–military grunts and hoarse exhilarating yells, inspiring generations of heavy-metal bands.

Simultaneously Jim Morrison and The Doors mingled murder and sex in California. Their apocalyptic 'The End' (1967) is about an Oedipal killer. Flinging himself into the audience, Morrison literally got over the 'weight' of his persona and his subject. Violence was now part of the rock hero's image and relationships with his audience, his body, his guitar. You hurled aggression at the audience, and savaged your own guitar. Sometimes its destruction had a musical point. Hendrix left the amp on as he burned his beloved guitar at Monterey in 1967: the burning sound, the snapping strings, were part of the music. But sometimes the destruction had the purely symbolic point of orgasmic self-destruction. As Morrison keeps singing, 'This is the end.'

This was when murder, rape, Satan, voodoo, savagery, death and destruction walked wholesale into rock and set up house there. Long afterwards the gravel-voiced Australian singer Nick

Cave, investing in doom-drenched lyrics which blend the Bible with the American Deep South, sexual despair and sex-murder, parodied sixties violence-'n'-satanism in his 1994 album *Let Love In*. His murderer is a melodramatic vision of Stephen King's *The Stand* ('He's a god he's a man... Hidden in his pocket is his *red right hand*'). But it also sends up Jagger's 'Midnight Rambler' and Jim Morrison's killer, tapping into the vision of male sexuality they began: murderous, malevolent, outlawed, omnipotent.

Black magic became especially big business in heavy metal. Led Zeppelin's guitarist Jimmy Page was obsessed by the necromancer Aleister Crowley; Black Sabbath, the other begetters of heavy metal, looked at long film queues, thought 'Let's sell ourselves as Gothic horror', and imported the whole paraphernalia of horror movies into rock. The Gibson SG guitar played by Tommy Iommi (who lost two fingertips in an electric welding machine) groaned and gnashed like a massive torture machine; their crashing chords supported lyrics about war, destruction, drugs and the occult; their whole sound, look and concept upped the ante on rock shock.

Metal group names were chosen to shock. Paul Rodgers had been lead vocalist with the sixties band Free (a classic hippie name). In 1973 he formed Bad Company, who expressed their 'badness' in ponderous rhythms and hoarse voices. Lyrics got increasingly (and often comically) murderous: see Metallica's seminal metal album, *Kill 'Em All*. Motorhead, a hardcore group formed in 1975, had a 126-decibel live sound with songs like 'Overkill' (1979) and 'Bomber' (1979). Their 1982 album was *Iron Fist*. The New York group Anthrax, a pioneering thrash band of the early eighties which led to nineties heavy metal, had fun with *Fistful of Metal* (1984), *Armed and Dangerous* (1985) and *Attack of the Killer Bees* (1991). Some of them then formed a splinter group called Stormtroopers of Death. The Australian group AC/DC, heavy-metal elder statesmen (the ones used against Noriega in Panama), brought out 'Big Gun' (from the Schwarzenegger film *Last Action Hero*) in 1993. Menacing metallic destruction, evoking machine-like killing, defines the musical texture. In 1998, police in the British Home Counties attributed a spate of pet killings – dead cats, returned mutilated to their owners – to heavy-metal fans.

The themes which would dominate the gothic underworld of 'shock rock' began here. Goth culture proper began in the seventies. Siouxsie Sioux used 'gothic' to describe the new direction of her band the Banshees; Anthony Wilson, former manager of Joy Division and head of Factory Records, said they were gothic compared to the pop mainstream of 1978. For thousands of teenagers, eighties Goth culture became a global community of fanzines sharing rebelliously macabre fashion.

Many of these magazines are touchingly full of ads for Addams Family black chic: of anxious pride in being different from conventional teenagers; in being Goths together. Advice about how to handle your misfit nature, how to express it in your clothes, flies across the ocean from Cornwall to New Zealand. But the subculture 'industrial gothic' is much more aggressive. Its fans are 'rivetheads'; much of the music is more male, electronic, depersonalized and violent. Nineties Goth idols include the six-foot-six transvestite Marilyn Manson. (His name marries Marilyn Monroe and the murderer Charles Manson.) He has called himself 'the most evil man in America'; his themes are suicide and satanism; his misogynist autobiography *The Long Road Out of Hell* was a bestseller on both sides of the Atlantic.

Another Goth totem band is the Seattle-based KMFDM, who took their initials from *'Kein Mitleid für die Merheit'*, 'no pity for the majority', and who toured with a group called Thrill Kill Kult. After albums called *Angstfest* and *Nihil*, KMFDM chose the anniversary of Hitler's birthday to release their 1999 album *Adios*. That was the day that two Goth boys who used to sing Marilyn Manson lyrics (including 'I kill who I don't like') and painted their faces white and nails black in Manson's honour, who admired another German Goth band, Rammstein (whose songs include 'Punish Me' and 'You Hate') and called themselves the Trenchcoat Mafia, carried guns into their school under long black coats and sprayed their fellow students with bullets, killing seventeen; because they felt humiliated by the athletic élitism of their Denver high school. The blackness of all that violence symbolism had become unbearably real.

Rock darkness was summed up in the 'weight' metaphor of 'heavy metal'. 'Heavy' could mean anything in the seventies: bad, good, scary, intense, significant, wonderful, woeful, confused; or a real drag. In the late sixties it became a code word for the vital link which rock music increasingly stood for between violence and male sexuality. That was the moment, so Paul Trynka told me, when

> the music got heavier *and* lyrical content got heavier. That was when people started to shorten 'rock 'n' roll' to 'rock music'. It wasn't 'popular music' for family entertainment. Whites started to get heavy as Howlin' Wolf, started to measure up to the sheer density, weight of sound, and conviction of black music.

The 'weight' of 'heavy' metal was the armour of Mars: warrior violence, expressed in musical 'attack' and connected deeply to themes of 'darkness'. Most heavy metal guitarists are white. Yet musically, heavy metal is indebted most to Jimi Hendrix. It was he who mixed musical weight with pure guitar innovation, who took on musically the challenge of Vietnam. The white rock that is the most violent in its textures, its black symbolics, its death and shock themes, its narcissistic male swagger, is descended musically from a black guitarist.

Musical praise in CD notes or rock reviews comes straight from the violence section of a pornographer's manual. 'Whiplash', 'hard', 'urgent': the metaphors are comic, but they do pinpoint the appeal. *Vox* magazine, for example, described one song (called, mockingly, 'Stay Happy') as 'hairy-bollocked rock with dig-in-deep hooks'.[19] The evil and violence may be parodied, but say something real to teenage boys desperate to give their sexuality 'weight' in the world. To throw your weight around, throw it at other people (as Goths throw their 'blackness' at their classmates); to matter to other people even to the point of destroying them: the core of all this is the solipsistic credo of Jim Morrison in 'An American Prayer': 'Death and my cock are the world.'

Precipitating Violence? From Altamont to Colorado

White boys had wanted to be black since the sixties. Black was cool. Darkness of music and theme was nicely shocking to adult white society. The knee-jerk white reaction to black music, however highly worked, is that it is authentic – and violence (in rock mythology) is the most authentic thing of all.[20] But the most transgressive areas of rock – Trent Reznor's 'dark world of sex, pain and rock 'n' roll', the vampire and dead-baby imagery of heavy metal – drew not on black culture but white fantasy. It was not black music or performers but a pack of white *ideas* about blackness and badness that gave rock its violence, its kaleidoscopic black iconography, from Dylan's leather jacket which upset folk fans at Newport in 1965 to the Trenchcoat Mafia.

Most rock violence was skin-deep designer display, a marketing device like the satanist trappings of Black Sabbath. (When London punk came in, its violence was designed to be theatrical; but fan violence, violence on the street, was cool: and two, at least, of the Sex Pistols enjoyed a fight – their image and stance played into a strand of British Fascism which punk could not control.)[21] Whenever The Stones came into contact with real violence, they retreated. Jagger left the Vietnam demonstration and wrote 'Street Fighting Man' with its *faux*-pathetic question 'What can a poor boy do, 'cept sing for a rock 'n' roll band?'. Marianne's memoir may not be unbiased, but she does describe Jagger in tears in jail, Jagger evading the issue when Brian Jones was found dead in his swimming-pool the week after The Stones replaced him in the band. The Stones did a memorial concert with great display of grief in Hyde Park; Marianne Faithfull suggests Brian's death solved a predicament for the band, and was almost a relief.[22]

For The Stones, the split between designer violence and the real thing was most glaring in their last concert on their 1969 American tour. Criticized for ticket prices, they decided this show would be free. With blind romanticism (and echoes of Walt Whitman), the San Francisco rock scene had been idealizing the local Hell's Angels. *Rolling Stone* called them 'magnificent incarnations of the beast in all of us'. Local bands told The Stones to hire Hell's Angels to police the concert. The Stones knew British Hell's Angels, who had protected their stage in Hyde Park; Bay Area Angels were something else. Biker violence was escalating; the Stones did not know the 'chapters' of Angels they hired were bitter rivals.[23]

The site, Altamont, was a deserted stadium east of San Francisco. From dawn, it was smothered in people 'like a moonscape of crushed auto bodies'. Local bands played first. From the moment Santana started, the Angels began rampaging, stamping on the peaceful audience. When Jefferson Airplane opened, Marty Balin reproached the Angels for brutality and got punched unconscious. The Grateful Dead refused to play.[24] Then The Stones began: Jagger wrapped his cloak around him and the band struck up 'Sympathy for the Devil' . . . The Angels went berserk, the sickening sound of their smashing pool cues competing with the music.

Angels clubbed a naked girl who had rushed the stage, and threw her into the crowd in front of Jagger. 'Rape, murder, it's just a shot away' sang Mick as Angels killed one of his audience:

> I saw him as he came down, burying a long knife in the black man's back. Angels covered the black man like flies on a carcass . . . Five others joined, kicking the boy's head in. Kicked him all over the place.[25]

Jagger told the audience at the end,

> We gonna kiss you goodbye and we leave you to kiss each other goodbye. We're gonna see you, we're gonna see you again, all right? . . . Well, there's been a few hang-ups you

know but I mean generally I mean you've been beautiful... you have been so groovy... Kiss each other goodbye.

Much later, the Stones saw Altamont on film:

> They watched the screen intently and our camera recorded their faces, which were expressionless. When the film ended there was a long silence, then Mick asked us to show it again... Again, Mick showed no expression on his blank face. He didn't say a word to anyone. He didn't look at Keith or anyone else, and he said nothing to us about the film itself. He just got up and walked out. So did the others.

That was Altamont. Four dead (one murdered, two run over, one drowned in a ditch), hundreds injured, and four blank faces. Jagger did not sing 'Sympathy for the Devil' live for six years.[26]

The Stones 'were playing a dangerous game that came to life'. 'They never took the ideas they toyed with as seriously as their fans.'[27] Altamont threw Jagger a terrible irony. He had got where he was, and gathered the power to lash thousands of people into Dionysiac frenzy by impersonating a black voice. But the boy murdered while he sang about murder was also black.

The violence bluff had been called, and shown to be vacant. Jagger did not cut a heroic figure. Sexuality and theatricality is not all there is to a hero. Imitating black energy, acting the devil, singing about beating women, does not mean you can control a violent situation. The pose collapsed with the California hippie dream. San Francisco bands blamed the Stones' arrogance, but to more objective American commentators the whole psychedelia experiment was politically naïve, based on 'derivative romantic themes like the return to innocence, the invocation of primal authority, the mysteries of blood'. As in Nazi rhetoric, the mythic themes lugged with them romantic links between violence and authoritarianism which the stoned, armed Angels exemplified.[28] Thirty-five years before, America romanticized a black murderer as the authentic voice of American folk-song.

Now it thrilled to Hell's Angels as 'the beast in all of us'; and looked on, helpless and stoned, as Angels murdered a black man in a mostly white audience.

To the eyewitness Joan Didion, the hippie mile of San Francisco called Haight-Ashbury, epicentre of psychedelic rock – where teenage girls dropped acid for their four-year-old daughters – looked like 'the desperate attempt of a handful of pathetically unequipped children to create a community in a social vacuum'. Beneath the hash cloud, violence was now very close to the surface. While *Rolling Stone* drooled over Hell's Angels, Charles Manson was collecting his Family from the waste products of the American dream. One of his girls said at the trial. 'We are what you have made us.' There was some 'mystical flirtation with the idea of "sin" around', said Didion; an eerie 'demented seductive tension, building in the community'. So when news of the Sharon Tate murders broke in August 1969, 'no one was surprised'.[29]

Altamont was sparked off by a British band. It showed up the theatricality of their violence; but the American violence itself was homegrown. The Stones had trailblazed a theatrical link for rock between sex and violence; afterwards, in *Sticky Fingers* (1971), they retreated to sex, drugs and autobiography ('Wild Horses', 'Sister Morphine', 'Dead Flowers').

Goth bands KMFDM and Rammstein retreated in the same way in 1999 when their music was linked to the deaths at Columbine High School, Colorado. 'We only show violence during our gigs; we make it the subject of our lyrics,' said Rammstein, 'but we definitely refuse to practise violence or propagate it in any way.' Sascha Konietsko, bandleader of KMFDM (who in one song boasted 'I'm a radical pig, I abuse and exploit'), posted condolences on his band's website, offering 'heartfelt sympathy' to the parents of the dead. 'From the beginning, our music has been a statement against war, oppression, fascism and violence against others,' he typed.[30]

Here is another aspect of rock's problem with authenticity. Not just a boy singing about being a man, not just white singing black, but your relation to your own violence. Are you really refusing 'to propagate violence in any way' if you make it the subject of your song? If it is real to your fans but not you, what does that say about your relation to your music? Or to your fans?

Hendrix and Vietnam

At the heart of the disparity between British and American experience were two prime American issues, racial injustice and Vietnam. Even The Stones were connected to Vietnam via their recording company. 'All the bread we made for Decca,' said Keith,

> went into making little black boxes that go into American Air Force Bombers to bomb fucking Vietnam. When we found that out, it blew our minds.[31]

They could retreat after Altamont because they were British. But as they were dramatizing rape, murder and evil on a sexy global stage, three million American boys were meeting it all for real. 776,000 of them fought in Vietnam; 321,000 were wounded, 58,000 thousand died. While Jagger introduced himself in Los Angeles as Lucifer in Ossie Clark's gorgeousness in 1969, nearly a million boys were living on the edge of mutiny in an army full of drugs, dying because others were stoned, humiliated and forced into senseless violence by their own officers:

> Daylight came and we found we'd killed a lot of fishermen and kids. The fucking colonel says, 'Don't worry about it. We got body count!' I know the colonel got his fucking medal. They had award ceremonies, y'know. I'd be standing like a fucking jerk and they'd be handing out medals for killing civilians. I actually puked my guts out. You know it's happened but – see, it's all explained to you by captains and colonels and majors: 'That's the hazards of war. They

were in the wrong place. They were suspects anyways.' And we was young fucking kids.³²

The peak year for desertion in Vietnam was 1971. Doctors who treated these 'young fucking kids' later, found they had reached psychological and moral breaking-point in Vietnam. Officers forced on them a violence no one wanted to hear about back home, degraded them so they'd vent their rage on the enemy, encouraged them to run berserk to avenge dead friends. For months they lived only to kill:

> I became a fucking animal. I started putting fucking heads on fucking poles. They wanted a fucking hero so I gave it to them. They wanted fucking body count, I gave them body count. But they don't have to live with it. I do.³³

The boys reacted by murdering officers. Twenty per cent of officers who died in Vietnam were killed by their own men. There were at least 1,013 documented killings or attempted killings of officers. (Called 'fragging', from 'accidentally' fragmented grenades.) The boys felt utterly betrayed by those they were dying for: their leaders and government. They felt the officers were heartless, crooked, treacherous, self-indulgent. They returned damaged, but when they sought help in the seventies, doctors said they were paranoid schizophrenics or manic depressives. War trauma? Forget it. Only in the mid-eighties did doctors realize (or acknowledge) that their still appalling state had been caused by Vietnam.³⁴

There was a disproportionately high number of blacks in Vietnam. Increasingly, blacks saw the war as a plot to destroy black Americans. 'We started feeling the government didn't really want us back, that there needed to be fewer of us back home.' Twenty years after, many veterans still felt their defeat meant God was against America, and they themselves were 'shit'. They lost any American belief that God was on their side.³⁵ Black or white, returning soldiers brought back into their own and the next generation a load of guilt, hostility, alienation; the personal knowledge that government can sacrifice young men in a wrong cause, and then give up on them.

   Hendrix became an experimental guitarist in the early sixties when a judge sentenced him to military service instead of jail, for joy-riding. He joined a parachute regiment in Kentucky, sixty miles from Nashville, two hunded from Memphis and the Delta. In 1962 he asked his father to send his guitar, began jamming with other musicians and visiting Nashville at weekends: not for country music but joints south and east of town which played blues. It was the first time he'd seen recording studios and he swore that afterwards he'd come back to make a record. He began experimenting on his guitar, imitating sounds, working them into tunes: guns on the firing range, plane doors slamming, the wind-rush of a parachute-jump.[36] In 1969 at the Woodstock Festival he used those sound-experiments for a shock version of 'The Star-Spangled Banner', which smashed its melody to smithereens. Fractured music, fracturing any trust in patriotism. He bent the notes, mangled the keys: war sounds, siren-sounds broke through and made the tune hideous. Next year he used it again. But before playing it, he tried a new piece which he dedicated 'To all the troops fighting in Harlem, Chicago – and, oh yes, Vietnam. A little thing called "Machine Gun".' Feedback like dive-bombing planes shook the stage; guitars screamed like women; the drum's rat-tat-tat was so loud the audience flinched:

Machine gun tearing my body
O machine gun tearing my buddies apart.

When he segued from that to 'Star-Spangled Banner', the audience erupted.[37] A moment which gave another twist to white patronage of the Leadbelly phenomenon: a 'good nigga' minstrel showing up the badness of white American society.

   Hendrix faced the violence head-on. Not by manufacturing satanic personae or playing at evil, but going musically into a real issue at a truly violent time and doing something creative with it in how he played, not what he wore. He also linked it to 'troops' of black activists as well as soldiers in Vietnam. If all a hero could do was make his guitar explode the hollowness of patriotism, distort and mirror the violence of power, implode those dead stars spangling over murder, hypocrisy and evil, he did that. Being a hero isn't just having violent power, whether musical, creative, physical or sexual. It's what you do with it.

Theatrical violence has mutated since The Stones, but it still works wonders. Keith Flyte of The Prodigy, bulging with leather studs that would not disgrace a pit bull terrier, had himself carried onstage at Glastonbury Festival. The Prodigy, white blokes from Essex with a neolithic warrior image, keen to align themselves with gangsta rap charisma, could not face a spot of English mud. Rock flirts with violence but runs from it in real life. Dennis Cooper, novelist and rock critic for *Spin* (the American version of *New Musical Express*), wrote a 1998 novel called *Guide* about obsessive rock fandom, rock's maleness, predatory violence, rape and murder. One character drugs Alex, young bass guitarist for an English band called Smear, and fucks him 'harder than he'd fucked anyone in his life'. Cooper confessed he was thinking of Alex James, Blur's deeply gorgeous bassist. 'Smear' lyrics are real-life Blur lyrics. *The Idler* magazine set up an interview between them, Alex agreed to meet Cooper – then he failed to show. Rock manhood is not made for that much reality. Its currency is myth.

13 Heroes Are Violent, Dark, Against – Especially in the Theatre

Where Did Rock Violence Come From?

Today, the violence in rock seems a 'natural' part of its masculinity. But was it so obvious that a musical form that began with 'Maybelline' and 'Rock Around the Clock' would flower in fifteen years to a genre where you snarl out destruction, smash guitars on stage and dress like a cartoon war-lord? Could you have forecast that Elvis would lead so quickly to heavy metal? How did the violence get in there?

There were a thousand causes, psychological, social, political, economic. Blues tradition, plus white symbolic uses of blackness, meant that rock 'n' roll could explore violence through black stereotypes fixed in white fantasy. But the violence really came from that white fantasy itself. The hangings, jails and woman-beating in 'the devil's music' of Blind Lemon Jefferson and Robert Johnson, the ho-fucking and brother-killing in Jay-Z, Niggaz with Attitude, Nana Kwame Abrokwa, is pretext, not cause: violence sought out and used by white imagination.

The causes lie not just in the historically created landscapes of white fantasy – mythic white America, the land where rock was born, plus the different faces of maleness round the Greek goddess of sex – but also in rock's own theatrical nature. Rock is a song of myself that is also the song of someone else; its apparent naturalness depends on impersonation. It is a theatre of the self, and theatre has been concerned with violence from the very beginning. Rock's whole hero complex, its choreography of male dominance, its shocking vulnerability and overweening show-offery, draws on the roots of European theatre.

Why Does Sex Choose Violence for her Lover?

The sex and violence connection shows up in the two males closest to Venus, Eros and Mars, young desire and war. Between them, they sum up the ways in which teenage males (animal as well as human) challenge the world, i.e. adult society. The rock god package, tied up in tinsel by Elvis, made sure of the sex; the increasingly loud snarl of mid-sixties British rock injected the violence. As the sound of the male teenage body, rock is the perfect vehicle for aggression. In Greek hero stories, as in many *rites de passages*, a boy becomes a man, a man lays claim to world attention, not through sex but by killing. Davy Crockett, to bring back white America a moment, 'killed him a b'ar when he was only three'.

The relation between Venus and Mars is an ancient link-up between sex and violence. As I said (chapter 3), this does not make it absolutely inevitable psychologically. Yet a recent historian, collating war letters from hundreds of soldiers from the twentieth century's biggest wars, suggests that many men do find a sexual thrill in war-killing. When one First World War officer got a direct hit and 'saw bodies or parts of bodies go up in the air... it was one of the happiest moments of my life'. The first time he stuck his bayonet in a German soldier's body, wrote another, 'it was gorgeously satisfying'. A postcard from a captain in Korea says it was 'super', wiping out the enemy. 'Big masturbations afterwards!' These men often used sexual metaphor to describe killing. 'Like the best sex ever' and 'I had a hard-on' were common variations on a theme.[1]

So maybe that link is inevitable after all. But it is also a deep part of white Western myth; and it is myths as well as biology which determine what we call natural. Rock music is (originally) male music to do with sex; and sex makes a deep forbidden bond with male violence. A bond far stronger, and more exciting to think about and paint down the centuries, than her contract with creativity.

Why is the God of Theatre Violent? Why Does Orpheus Provoke Violence?

Then you add the theatre. Greek theatre (which means our own theatre) began as music. A tragedy was a through-composed music-drama like a Lloyd-Webber musical or Strauss opera; its poet was also a composer. He often sang and acted in the play, as well as writing and directing the music. But its god was Dionysus. Hundreds of tragedies turned on killing and death. Medea kills her children, Orestes his mother; Oedipus stabs his eyes out with brooch-pins off the still-warm corpse of his wife, who hanged herself on discovering she had married her son. Pentheus is torn apart, his mother carries his torn-off head onstage; Ajax falls on his sword. Hippolytus is carried in dying of multiple injuries after a chariot crash, Hercules is carried on writhing in agony, because his clothes are drenched in corrosive poison, and gets burnt on a pyre. All this violence people do to each other and themselves: we only have a fraction of the tragedies performed at Athens in the classical age and some lost ones were even more violent. In the lost *Lycurgeia* (a trilogy by Aeschylus), Orpheus refused to honour Dionysus and worshipped the Sun on a mountain: Dionysus sent maenads to tear him to pieces. Then king Lycurgus insulted Dionysus, who maddened him as he was pruning vines. He hallucinated, saw his own son as a vine stalk, and lopped off his head and extremities. His people then tied him to horses, and as they galloped away he was torn apart.[2]

The plays which handled myths of Dionysus himself show how intrinsic violence was to him. Someone always gets torn to pieces. In one myth, giants tear Dionysus himself to bits, and there was a legend that Euripides, most emotional of the three great tragic poets, was himself torn to pieces by dogs. Tennessee Williams's play *Orpheus Descending*, whose first title was *Battle of Angels* (chapter 11), has the shape of a Dionysus myth, a fatal package of music, 'battle' and sex. Orpheus gets torn to pieces because women follow him as moths follow flame. The figure who gets torn apart is always male and Dionysus's women, maenads, his mad followers do the tearing. You cannot have a male maenad: the word means 'mad*woman*'. But the figure who inspires them to madness and violence is the young male followed by crowds of women. He maddens them; but also mirrors the figure they destroy.[3] The gods of music and theatre are the two gods of violent dismembering.

Tragedy began in violence and whenever the theatre renews itself, violence tends to have a hand. The 1932–3 'Manifestos' of Antonin Artaud argued passionately for a newly primitive 'theatre of cruelty'. Theatre was moribund; it must find 'a language half-way between gesture and thought', whose 'dynamic expression in space' would be based 'on spectacle before everything else'. This spectacle had better be violent. (Artaud's first project was the conquest of Mexico.) 'The theatre will never find itself again,' he thundered, 'except by furnishing the spectator with the precipitates of dream, in which his taste for crime, his erotic obsessions, savagery, chimeras, even cannibalism, pour out.'[4] Dionysus reigned in thirties Paris as in fifth-century BC Athens.

Why *is* the god of wine, ecstatic dance, illusion, madness, destruction and violence, the enduring god of theatre? Because, I think, Dionysus made such a perfect link between violent action and violent feeling. The point of his rituals – as in those mystery religions (chapter 2) – was violent change in consciousness and feeling. The tragedies turn on conflict between people, but also on inner conflict: distraught emotions like jealousy, grief, fury, vengeance and madness fight it out inside people with deeply anxious ideas of right and wrong. All those violent acts and torn-up bodies are the result of desperately torn-up minds: they body forth violent *feeling*, which Greek in any case expressed in terms of physical damage. Feelings wound, pierce, hit, burn, bite and tear the mind. The god of tragedy is a linking principle between madness and murder, between violence in the mind and violence people do to each other.

Greek theatre was masked. Is there something violent about

impersonating someone else in itself? You wear a mask on the stage just as people in daily life are masked to each other. Violent, maybe murderous, feelings get hidden. Under the aegis of Dionysus, Greek theatre put on the map the possibilities of violence in the mismatch there is, in life, between the inside and outside of a person. One barbarian supposedly said how odd Greeks were to 'set apart a place in the middle of the city where men got together and told each other lies'.[5] He meant the political centre, the *agora*, but it could just as well have been the theatre. The theatre is where you pretend to be someone else – and our capacity for pretence, for masking feelings from each other, for taking on different roles, is a source of delight and excitement, but also deeply dangerous.

All this sets the 'Dionysian' side of rock in a bit more context. Rockers began identifying themselves with Dionysus in the sixties, says Robert Palmer; when rock claimed its territory of crowd ecstasy, phallic energy, drugs and altered consciousness. Palmer has a photo of heavy metal fans making 'the sign of the horned god', whom they identify with Dionysus. Discussing violence-and-death themes in the later sixties, especially Jim Morrison, Palmer points to Dionysus again. Morrison's life and lyrics follow impeccable Dionysus lines: the beautiful, out-of-control performer who sends women out of their minds, dives madly into their midst, binges self-destructively on drink and drugs, and then dies young.

Morrison himself was keenly aware of the violence of Greek myth, the 'faces from the ancient gallery' which we pick and put on like masks to play a violent role. 'The killer awoke before dawn,' he chants in 'The End'. 'He put his boots on. He took a face from the ancient gallery and he – walked on down the hall.'[6] That 'face' is Oedipus, about to kill his father and rape his mother. But it could be any violent hero, or Dionysus himself, who was perfect shorthand for the violence developing in sixties rock. From Jagger's 'Midnight Rambler' and Lucifer, and The Who's 'Hope I die before I get old', many stars worked on a doomed, violent relation with the world; it was cool to idealize

Hell's Angels and Charles Manson. When Sid Vicious first landed in jail (as a Sex Pistol) for throwing a beer mug which cut a lot of faces at a concert, he started reading about Charles Manson.[7] Star drug deaths and car crashes spiralled on for two decades, keeping pace with fans' desire for real violence behind the façade, which took wing from punk to rap. The stars' self-contradictory relations with their own violence, and the violence of their fans, exemplified at Altamont, came out in the disengenous disclaimers by Rammstein, KMFDM and Marilyn Manson about 'only showing violence', 'not practising or propagating it in any way'. Deliberately or not, they took on the 'face' of Dionysus, whose followers tear those who oppose him to bits.

Uses of 'Blackness'

Palmer calls the violence themes begun in sixties rock 'dark' – as in Morrison's visions of apocalyptic blackness, which draw on William Blake's *Songs of Experience*. 'Some are born to sweet delight, some are born to endless night'. Black Sabbath, Black Flag, and the whole blackness iconography of heavy metal and Goth music, bear him out. All that blackness is a macho cliché of this area of rock. Palmer explains it by the 'shadow' side of Dionysus.

But *Greek* images of Dionysus were not 'dark'. Greeks did think anger and madness were dark, and madness was certainly a Dionysus speciality.[8] But plenty of other gods, like the Furies, Hecate and Pan, went in for madness too. Madness was not his monopoly, nor did it make him a 'dark' god in Greek terms. In Greece, 'dark' gods were chthonic gods, who belonged to earth (*chthon*): underworld gods like the Furies. Palmer's 'darkness' image for Dionysus is post-Greek. It comes from our own medieval symbolism, developed in the Renaissance, our own sense that 'black' spells violence, misery, danger and death. This is one reason why it is so useful to have 'dark' *people* as a source of these things in the lyrics, or the legends behind them. This is blackness used to mask, but also legitimize, white violence.

Epic Heroes: Power-Packed Bodies

Greek heroes belong with violence. As the rock hero grew from sex god to a darkness-and-destruction warrior, he also became more Greek. Western poetry got off on violence from the beginning. Simone Weil called Homer's *Iliad* 'the poem of force'. Great swathes of it are taken up with spears pushing teeth through the bridge of the mouth into eyes and brain, swords raping the gut, or prodding the ribs of a wife weeping over her dying husband. Homer runs on moments of breathtaking compassion, but the background is gory details of physical violence and death, and the very word 'hero' has physicality at its heart. It is the hero's body which destroys or saves other bodies. His body is what makes him matter.

The earliest type of hero, Homer's epic hero, comes in two modes, battle and adventure. The hero of Homeric battle is a glamorous ferocious warrior-king, whose power is killing power. Achilles is the best because he kills best. The adventure-hero, Ulysses, James Bond, Luke Skywalker, has all that and intelligence too. He outwits as well as overcomes the monsters, giants, and witches. But physique matters to the journeying hero, too. He is wanted by women, strings bows other men cannot, wins fights, defeats enemies. Ulysses blinds the Cyclops and his Greek name comes from *odussao*, 'I bring harm'. Which is what heroes do to those who oppose them. He gets his palace back by butchering his wife's suitors.

Homeric battle and adventure set in concrete for all time the adventure-hero who overcomes all opposition, dangerous terrain, dangerous animals, dangerous men. He galloped through later European legends like *Beowulf* or King Arthur and on into sci-fi iconography and the heroics of the boys' bedroom and toyshops today. Non-combative qualities (intellectual, sexual, moral) match his fantastic physicality but his centre of heroism is that wonderful body. The power to save his own, and destroy what is against him.

His physicality is picked up in another Greek meaning of

heros, which played a bigger role in everyday life in ancient Greece. These *heroes* were invisible daemons who afflicted you with physical troubles like boils and piles. Aristophanes wrote a comedy about them. The air of classical Athens was stiff with them. You made offerings to them at little shrines through the city, where they were supposedly buried. *Heroes* belonged in the earth. They were 'chthonic' demons and their business was human earth: the ills-prone human body. Some were said to be Homeric heroes, heroized after death like canonized saints. If you annoyed them, they responded with the boils and piles treatment. Honouring them with libations was a kind of protection money: they protected the patch of earth they lived in, and defended you in it, if you behaved yourself. When the Athenians fought the Persians, the hero Theseus hurried to help. Like Homeric heroes, their big thing was violence. These demons usually became heroes (were 'heroized') because they had killed a lot of people in their life.[9]

The epic hero, then, the lowest stratum in our notion of a hero, has the basic ingedients of a rock hero. The importance of body, the glamour, the violence.

Tragic Heroes: Self-Destruction Centre Stage

Under the aegis of Dionysus, the tragic playwrights invented a new kind of hero. They took over stories Homer told, so their heroes are often the same characters, same names, family relationships, life stories – Ajax, Agamemnon, Odysseus – but gave them a different nature, with different issues to face. Tragedy, unlike epic, asked questions about individual versus society, about self-restraint, right and wrong, and choosing between two evils.

You might think rock music, which began in fun and sex, has not much to say to tragedy. But Altamont and Colorado called the bluff of rock's theatricality, and showed up what Palmer calls the 'dark' side of its Dionysiac nature. The two things do have music in common. But still, rock stands, surely, for fun, excitement, freedom, dancing in the street, and tragedy is about – well, tragedy? Yet the concept of tragedy flourishes in Western culture like wild yeast, and settles on any areas of violence or pain it can find. As rock evolved its violence, the tragic hero wrapped himself like clingfilm round the figure of the rock star. It was the tragic hero who brought Dionysus into the modern world. Tragedy was acted in his precinct and would not exist as a concept in modern minds but for the cluster of Greek connections that said 'Dionysus'. So the relationship is two-way: without tragedy, we would have a very different idea of Dionysus. Directly or indirectly, our modern sense of him comes from one of Euripides' tragedies. Robert Palmer's picture of Dionysus would be quite different if Euripides had never written the *Bacchae*.[10]

The motif central to Dionysiac religion, to tragedy and to a lot of rock music, is human assertion in the face of destruction. From the blues suffering-to-defiance story, rock went on to explore pain and evil as well as sex and fun. As Henry Rollins and Black Flag explored evil via My Lai and Charles Manson, so Velvet Underground explored suffering and self-destruction. Their song 'Heroin' gives self-destruction a Christ-like destiny. 'When the smash begins to flow, When it shoots off the chopper's neck, When I'm closing in on death... I feel just like Jesus' son.'[11] Late sixties rock put the hero into heroin and developed a sense of tragic destiny and tragic pain alongside the violence.

Many Greek tragedies (and later ones) end in physical destruction. 'Look, all of you, at this wretched body' bellows Hercules as the poison-soaked mantle eats into him like acid. 'Another spasm burns and shoots through my ribs – this terrible pain gnaws through me.' Hippolytus lies on a bier, his 'young flesh' pierced like Velvet Underground's addict. 'Sharp pains dart through me, spasms of agony leap through my brain.'[12] At the end of many plays a machine rolled out the dead through the backdrop. Dead Agamemnon, dead Clytemnestra and Aegisthus; dead Jocasta, with Oedipus standing over her, fresh-blinded eyes dripping. The *sparagmos* of Pentheus at the hands of Dionysus' maenads – his body torn up and scattered in bits over the hillside, collected by his grandfather, his mother holding the head – is an image for the emotional tearing-up of a tragic climax. Grief and guilt are tragedy's main currency. Creon, Theseus and many other tragic heroes cause the death of their own sons. Orestes, his mum's blood on his hands, is chased offstage by Furies. Hecuba has seen her city, husband and children destroyed; she takes revenge on the man who betrayed her last son by blinding him and killing *his* children.

You cannot be a hero without something against you. Epic heroes have human, monstrous or magical enemies, but a tragic hero has fate and gods against him: his enemy is the human condition. He is the all-star model for modern, existential explorations of the self. The tragic world is full of irreconcilable conflict which is an inextricable part of being human.

Greeks explained this conflict by multiple gods, who represent different elements in human experience but are often (unfortunately for us) interested in disastrously different bits of the human organism or human society. Sophocles' *Antigone* packs in all the great clashes – woman against man, individual against group, family against state, young against old, living against dead. Our bodies, psyches, institutions, allegiances and feelings are the gods' battleground, where they play out their rivalries against each other. Tragedy brings out the point of a theological system of multiple gods: to express and make bearable our sense of inner conflict, or conflict in relationships.[13]

Tragedy often stages someone fighting back against fate, against gods. Ajax squares up against a goddess; Pentheus battles against Dionysus; Fate is against Oedipus from the start, but he does his best to cheat it. It is hopeless to try – but it is that struggle which makes a tragic hero. In Greek tragedy, as in Racine or Shakespeare, tragic heroes are famous figures, usually royal. They are not going to win: they are going to get destroyed. But they stand up anyway – for human energy, for self-assertion against whatever odds. Tragedy was the first civic shaping of this fight; the Western stage was invented to show it off. The tragic hero is who the stage was invented *for*.

These associations flicker through modern responses to the rock star. He became the twentieth century's icon of fame and fortune whom the odds, as rock 'n' roll's history proclaims, are traditionally stacked against. *Time Out*'s 1998 celebration of 'Thirty Years of Rock' ran through some key deaths: 1969, Brian Jones; 1970, Joplin and Hendrix; 1971, Jim Morrison; 1974, Mama Cass; 1977, Elvis; 1978, Keith Moon; 1979, Sid Vicious; 1980, John Lennon plus John Bonham of Led Zeppelin; 1981, Bob Marley; 1983, Karen Carpenter; 1984, Marvin Gaye; 1986, Phil Lynott; 1991, Freddie Mercury; 1994, Kurt Cobain; 1995, Richey James of the Manic Street Preachers; 1997, Michael Hutchence. You could add Billy Murcia of the New York Dolls in 1972, Marc Bolan in 1977.[14] That is an awful lot of people from one career dying young by accident, suicide, alcohol, drugs and murder. A far higher proportion than larger professions – say, hairdressers, cab-drivers, builders or nannies. The tradition goes back to legendary blues deaths. In Geoff Nicholson's rock novel *Flesh Guitar*, the guitar hero revisits the dying Hendrix of 1970 and Robert Johnson, convulsed with strychnine in 1938. But it also reflects the Western tragic hero.

On a rock stage, the star has darkness round him like a Rembrandt portrait; he is human and small against a larger dark. Exposing your genitals up there to ten thousand people is not only sexual swagger: in some mad way, it lays bare the source of human energy and life, spotlit but alone in the dark with a lot of odds against you. Of course there's joy, rudeness, energy, fun, glamour, thrills; but also threat and frailty. Back to Sting: 'Being on stage is a fucking war'.

The stakes are very high. The surviving Sex Pistols came into monarch-like wealth. Nineties TV interviews with John Lydon and Steve Jones for the television history of rock, *Dancing in the Street*, were shot in front of their own swimming-pools and parquet halls, in lunatic contrast with their first television interview, where Bill Grundy, the smart-suited interviewer goaded a bunch of T-shirted boys to say 'dirty words' and laughed at them. Sid Vicious only joined the Pistols after that, but it was he more than any of them who encapsulated their message of goaded desperation: and within two years, desperate on heroin, he killed his girlfriend and died on bail from an overdose. Death by drugs, suicide, murder or accident on the one hand; global fame and fairy-tale wealth on the other.

Falling: Alone in the Dark

The tragic hero's power, pain and violence matter intensely to other people, yet he is essentially alone. In Sophocles' play *Women of Trachis*, Hercules is burnt to death. 'This grief is common to all citizens', the play declares in its last words. A tragic hero is a soloist, counterpointing a group. The chorus stands in for the audience; it represents civilization and order, so it always opts for a nice, safe way of doing things. Like a rock star, the hero is intemperate, extreme. The chorus want to soft-pedal wild emotion, the hero goes right in.[15]

John Lydon said he modelled his Sex-Pistol persona Johnny Rotten on Olivier's demonic over-the-top performance as Shakespeare's Richard III. 'Anyone can be *nice*,' says Lydon scornfully, in the TV version of Palmer's *Dancing in the Street*. A tragic hero is both less and more than a man. Like talismanic rock stars, he is beastlike, godlike. 'Michael Hutchence will be remembered for his animal presence,' said one obituary.[16]

The tragic hero explores what being human is by being both less and more than human; he plumbs areas of experience no one else has touched. Think of rock group names. Animals, Beastie Boys, Shadows, Beatles, Stones: the jokily bestial, elemental echoes are not coincidence. At the end of *Oedipus at Colonus*, Oedipus disappears across 'unseen fields', image of the uniquely unbearable things he has done and suffered. One modern paradigm of this is the astronaut, who dares (as in the split-the-infinitive-split-the-atom introduction to *Star Trek*) 'to boldly go where no man went before'. David Bowie turns this into a psychonaut, inventing a persona, Ziggy Stardust, an alien hermaphrodite messianic pop deity through whom he explored (from 1972 to 1973) the uncharted space-landscape of male campness; his identification with Ziggy led to near-breakdown and he announced in July 1973, at the end of the *Aladdin Sane* tour (a punning reference to madness), that he would give no more live shows. He had (he said later) 'this compunction (*sic*) to parody rock and make it very vaudeville – or whatever it was that some of us were doing'.

Bowie became an icon of camp defiance, fellating Mick Jonson's guitar onstage. Following on from The Rolling Stones' cross-dressing floaty scarves, side by side with seventies glam and punk groups like Queen, New York Dolls, and KISS (and later Prince), Bowie flouted conventional rock maleness by transvesticism and make-up.[17] In his most apocalyptic scenario, Ziggy flirts cosmically with suicide ('we had five years left to cry in'); David Bowie presented this silhouetted under one splash of spotlight, darkness all round: a visual hieroglyph of the human condition, tragic version of. In 'Space Oddity', Major Tom calls to Ground Control, 'I'm stepping through the door; I'm floating in a most peculiar way.' Ground Control calls back: 'Your circuit's dead, there's something wrong.' In the later 'Ashes to Ashes', Ground Control has finally heard from him: a 'message from the Action Man'. But they dismiss it. 'We know Major Tom's a junky, hung out on heaven's high, hitting an all-time low.'

Major Tom's movements sum up the career curve, the daring and the fall, of Morrison, Brian Jones, Marvin Gaye, Sid Vicious, Michael Hutchence, Kurt Cobain ... High, low, falling from a height, are ancient stage images for the tragic hero, the famous man who 'falls' from his success. Oedipus blinds himself when he realizes what he's done. The chorus look at him and sing:

> I see human beings are nothing: just dead generations.
> All you get from life, or the gods, is just to seem happy –
> And then, having done that seeming, fall away.

In medieval Europe, tragedy's 'fall' resonates with Adam's Fall. Chaucer calls tragedy,

> The harm of hem that stood in heigh degree
> And fillen so that ther nas no remedie.[18]

Bowie came out of stage tradition. In the sixties, he belonged to Lindsay Kemp's Mime Troupe; in the seventies, his wife Angie encouraged him to use all that in his music. Bowie was not tragedy, of course; very much not. (He was horrified when the badly released *David Live* came out in 1975. 'It was the final death of Ziggy,' he reflected later. 'That photo on the cover! God, it looks as if I'd just *stepped out of the grave!*') But theatricality was his watchword.[19] He used it parodically, infusing into the psyche of the day key characteristics of the tragic hero who is always in danger of falling, of losing contact with 'Ground Control' – ordinary reality, conventional restraint. A hero 'cut off', like his 'Rock 'n' Roll Suicide', from audience or chorus, from anyone who might tether him to safe ways of being and feeling. 'The first work of the hero', says Joseph Campbell in his reverie on the mythic hero, 'is to retreat ... to causal zones of the psyche where the difficulties really reside, and there clarify the difficulties, eradicate them for himself (i.e. give battle to the nursery demons of his culture), and break through to undistorted, direct experience.'[20]

Bowie got this into his songs unscathed (more or less). Others lived it and were wrecked. Its loneliness ('It's time to leave the capsule if you dare', says Bowie's 'Space Oddity') comes over in Kurt Cobain's suicide note (chapter 20). The way the hero takes on the world is dangerous. Like Bowie's 'Major Tom', Rollins and Cobain were conscious of heading into darkness where other people never go.

Yet the hero needs other people as a foil: the group to be lonely against. Like rock stars, the tragic hero needs an audience. You can't be a hero without one; just as you can't sustain a rock career without a fan base.

Sacrifice

The tragic hero needs other people because he suffers *for* them, on their behalf. He exists in the dative, the 'giving' case in grammar, the case that means 'to' and 'for'. He is violent; he fights against the human condition; but he also represents it 'for' us, for audience and chorus. Just as the star does for fans, magazine-readers, the media. Rock heroes, like tragic heroes, are living myths *for* other people. They are extreme, for other people. From their passions, pain and triumphs they produce some kind of truth: for other people.

As set up in the sixties, your archetypal rock star leaves a stage littered with smashed guitars, a life littered with discarded women. Jagger's public profile is inextricable from photo shots of girlfriends and wives. The mythic sexual destructiveness and appetite speak to, and for, other men.

As with tragic heroes, this destructiveness is often self-destructive. By punishing Antigone for loyalty to other gods than his, Creon destroys his own wife and son. Because he refused the goddess Athena's help and rudely said he'd fight without her, thanks very much, Ajax went mad – and then killed himself in shame.[21] The rock hero's self-destructiveness, symbolized in guitar-smashing, expresses the Dionysian package of drugs, group ecstasy, violence, publicity and *sparagmos*. Witness Brian Jones in his swimming-pool, Morrison in his bath, Hendrix on his bed, Marvin Gaye shot by his dad, and the string of rock 'survivors' who had long periods of self-destructive drug and drink dependency, like Eric Clapton or Peter Greene.

A tragic pall of sacrifice, of being on the edge and diving into uncharted darkness for the sake of other people, hangs round the rock hero. Hercules destroyed monsters and became 'the saviour of Greece'; to save Thebes, Oedipus looked for the source of plague and found it was himself. The ultimate male romance is the hero who makes his dangerous journey into the black outer space of psychic experience *on behalf of everyone else.* The frostbitten explorer leaving camp at night to save the expedition.

In this paradigm, the rock hero lives his life for his audience and fans. He sings, has his hair cut, eats breakfast, gets divorced, declares his sexuality, under their gaze. Every detail is mythically important. For them he incarnates the lonely human condition on the dark stage. When Hendrix sacrificed 'something dear to him' at the 1967 Monterey gig, set his guitar on fire and left the amp on, the audience heard, in the snap of guitar strings as they buckled and burnt, the music of sacrifice, of self-destruction:[22] an idea satirized in Nicholson's *Flesh Guitar*, when the amp is left on while a guitar is run over on the road.

But rock self-sacrifice does not necessarily save other people. Fans identify with you, live through you. At twenty-seven, Kurt Cobain embodied the anger and desperation of a whole generation. When he put a twenty-bore shotgun in his mouth in 1994, anguished fans killed themselves too. The dative bond, made by living for other people, implicates them in your destruction. As they said at Hercules' funeral pyre, 'This pain is common to all citizens.'

The self-destructive heroism set up in the sixties was deeply tied to some do-or-die ideal of male bodies. You find it in athletes. I once taught Homer in translation to a white eighteen-year-old called Gary from New Jersey, son of a truck driver, who was about to take up a baseball scholarship at an Ivy League university. His heroes were a black team called The Brothers; he wrote a wonderful essay on the battle values of Homeric heroes. His favourite, Diomedes, was, he said, a great fighter but also a great team man who got on with things without making a fuss. Gary had been told that if *he* went on with baseball, his knees would be crippled before he was thirty. Fine, he said, I'll die at thirty in the gutter. But I'll be a great player first. Heroism and prowess were what mattered; never mind the future.

Hendrix's guitar virtuosity helped to make male instrumental prowess the focus of heavy metal.[23] But his insight into that self-destructive heroic mode of 'being on the edge' for other people, compounded by his death, contributed to metal's madly intense maleness. ' "Foxy Lady" is about the only happy song I've written,' he said once. 'I can't write no happy songs.' Despite the fun end of rock, the glitter and sex and money, the heroic mode that emerged at the end of the sixties was glamorously tragic.

Punk loathed all that tragic virtuosity as pretentious, out of touch, élitist. But in one of pop's many contradictions, successful punks embarked on heroic myth as thoroughly as The Stones they reviled. One history of punk compares the life and death of Sid Vicious, who followed 'the grisly James Dean archetype' of youth, speed, death and sex, to a mythic hero 'blasted from within and without, crucified like Prometheus on the rock of his own unconscious'.[24] An attraction of some punk shows was the blood running down the fingerboard from players unused to the guitar, or who slashed their arms with razors mid-concert.

The glamour of all this self-pain for others' benefit taps in to what Greek tragedy did for *its* society. It's hard to think this now, but Sophocles, Euripides and co. were challenging things, pressing on areas of conflict in the psyche of the society they were part of. They may be untouchable classics these days, folded away on the top shelf in a language practically nobody reads, but they influenced everything. Tragedy is at the back of all theatre, from Shakespeare to soap. Its art was transgressive and violent. That was why the city stopped for days while the plays were on. The conflicts they staged upset people, flouted assumptions about politics, the state, human relations, gods. They went into the secret violence of the family, questioned ideas of piety, right and wrong, and sometimes upset people so much, their plays were banned: like many famous rock records, like rock 'n' roll on American radio at the start. Their art involved destruction, self-destruction and a single figure pitted against morality and fate. It mattered to everyone. (Well, everyone who mattered, i.e. men.)

It seems a long way from that to questions in the 1997 British Parliament about The Prodigy's 'Smack My Bitch Up'. But rock was not the first mass musical genre to get transgressive with its own society and make an impact through violence and pain. Tragedy got there first. Tragedy too was about confrontation, young against old, man against woman, and laid down the ground-rules for rebelling against fate. Tragic heroes typically 'Fight against god' or 'Kick against goads'.[25]

Greek tragedy sees this rebellion as both mad and necessary. It will never work. You cannot rebel against gods, like Prometheus; cheat fate, like Oedipus; be dismissive of gods, like Ajax: you simply get punished. Other characters, minor ones like a chorus, a wife, sister or restraining friend, try to stop you. But in doing it, you stand up for being human.

Rock 'n' roll was about that rebellion too. In the nineties, it became harder for rock to keep that rebellion alive, but founding heroes like Jim Morrison still live on. 'No matter what they tell us,' intone even Boyzone (to words by Lloyd Webber) in 1998, 'No matter what they do, No matter what they teach us, What we believe is true.' Give or take a few profundities, this is the Greek tragic hero's stance. What we believe is true – and stuff the authorities, the rest of the world, gods, parents, or society.

14 America: The White Romance with Violence

Impersonating America

Rock is black impersonating white, boy impersonating man, and the whole world impersonating America. Rock 'n' roll was born – born male – just as it was clear that America ruled the earth, when it was picking up world pieces after the Second World War. What else would its voice be but American? From then on, whatever you were, British, French, Japanese, Greek or Dutch, wherever you were (Belfast, New Delhi, Glasgow, Hamburg), the song of rock maleness was not in your own voice but America's. The Liverpool Beatles sang American: 'I *wanna* hold your hand'.

This voice was American in all its connotations, from Route 66 to the streets of Memphis. Behind it were not just the blues but cowboys, lawlessness, outsiderdom. In the sixties, Ray Davis of the Kinks slipped London English into rock 'n' roll; in the seventies, David Bowie did it again and paved the way for British punk. But mainly, through the sixties, America was *it*. At every level, rock sexuality was powered by ideas of a maleness that was not actually yours. The dream of black said you too could be violent, your naughty-boyness was truly 'bad'. Sixties satanism led to the black magic and gore of heavy metal, custodian of the violence The Stones began, or the bad-boy image the Australian AC/DC projected in their multi-million-selling *Back in Black* (1980), or Black Flag's album *Damaged* (1981), praised for being 'raw, dark and pure'. As rock diversified, each genre upped the ante on shock. Punk's way, for instance, was swastikas and nuclear war.

Britain was the main catalyst for rock's theatre of aggression, and could capitalize fine on its own violence, as punk showed. But rock 'n' roll came from racial interaction in America, not Britain. Britain developed its own idealized understanding of the blues, British music benefited enormously from relations with Jamaica, from reggae and ska. (Maybe the distance of the source helped to make their violence less real.) But it was in white America that violence became really glamorous. It was a white American, Jack London, who wrote *The Call of the Wild*, the title whose words sum up the appeal of drums to white jazz and rock fans (and another, Norman Mailer, who summed up the romantic appeal of the outcast in his famous essay 'The White Negro'). It was white Americans who appropriated black music as the landmark American art of the twentieth century. The American Hell's Angels who murdered a black at Altamont were white. The wildness of rock 'n' roll came most deeply, I guess, from myths of maleness in the white American psyche.

Gun Law: Outviolencing Nature

The fifties and sixties, when rock began, were also the great decades of cinema's elaboration of frontier mythology. All over the world, Westerns made the gun the icon of white American violence and virility: a maleness which identifies with the dangers both of its land, and with the wonderful weapon by which that land was 'won'.

Oklahoma! was Broadway's first exploration of the rural American soul. Set 'in Indian Territory', it presents a community on the brink of statehood, making awkward moves to civilize itself. The back history to the musical is the Louisiana Purchase of 1803, when Oklahoma, part of the land bought from France, was believed worthless; then the Treaty of Dancing Rabbit Creek in 1830, which deported there the Choktaw, Chickasaw, Seminole and Creek tribes from Virginia and Georgia. The Choktaw called it *okla humma*, 'land of red people'. They were told they could have it 'for as long as the grass grows and the rivers run'.

That lasted thirty years. In the 1860s, the red earth was found to be fabulously fertile; in 1889, the US government threw 'Indian Territory' open to white settlers. The musical, set just before Oklahoma became a state in 1907 (by which time it already had 100,000 white farms), makes the land and the gun central to white American masculinity, both its nasty side (epitomized by Jud Fry) and its youthful virile goodness summed up in Curley, the hero.

In the musical (first performed in 1943), two songs home in on guns and virility. The first is a male chorus. When the seducer Ali Hakim is warned off a girl by her dad ('Shift your face,' snarls dad, 'or I'll fill you so full of buckshot you'll walk like a duck the rest of your life'), the male chorus is outraged. 'It's getting so you can't have any fun. Every daughter has a father with a gun!' Ali finally marries another girl. He explains miserably, 'I wanted to marry her – when I saw the moonlight glinting on her father's shotgun.' All this good clean fun depends on the sex and guns connection. The other song is from Jud, the self-outcast hired hand. Jud has dirty fingernails and postcards. He festers alone in his 'smoke-house'. The only thing he cleans is his gun, which goes off in his first confrontation with Curley. Afterwards, in the strange aria 'Lonely Room', Jud ponders his pornogaphy-strewn hut where he fantasizes about the heroine, Laurey, 'Her hair acrost my face like rain in a storm'. One humorously, the other dangerously, both songs stress virility's dark, dirty guns–sex link. The film cuts both numbers, but does make the famous dream sequence, 'Laurey Makes Up Her Mind', spell out two alternative faces of male sexual violence. Clean, outdoorsy Curley; smoke-house Jud with 'sump'n wrong inside of him'. In Laurey's dream, Jud kills Curley. In the story, Curley kills Jud and all ends happily, for the improvised jury find him innocent. Curley belongs to the land and the land he belongs to (and therefore his virility) is grand. White America's vision of its own male violence is self-justified, clean, outdoors. Darkness and smut define the outcast, Jud. 'America will never develop a Boy George,' said Kim Fowley. 'America needs to have John

Wayne masculinity in everything it does.'[1] But from Leadbelly to Prince and Snoop, it likes black America to act dirty.

All this danger is linked to the violence of the continent itself. European cities are not built on geological fissures, tornadoes don't toss three-bedroom semis in Edinburgh over the rainbow into Oz; there are no hurricanes pushing you off the motorway from Brussels to Paris. The American continent, its original inhabitants and animals, gave the American soul a more-than-Europeanly violent idea of nature, and produced a corresponding ideal of masculinity. You had to be violent, to cope with all that violence of nature. Hence the gun-lobby argument. In a violent world, you have to be armed to defend yourself.

Europeans hear a deeply non-European pride in talk of Curley's grand land. Marlborough Country is man-size country. Its dangers, the rattlesnakes, grizzlies and Injuns, are part of the romance of American virility. The 1998 film *The Horse Whisperer* reworks Nicholas Evans's bestseller, which drew on the autobiography of the horse-tamer Monty Roberts. Roberts stressed his childhood revulsion against his cowboy father's violent bronc-busting methods: he gets amazing results without violence. But the movie hero wrestles a large horse to the ground with a rope and sits on it like a sofa. Roberts disowned the film as a misrepresentation of his ideas, but the scene represents Hollywood manhood perfectly: virility out-violences animal nature. In Evans's follow-up tale, *The Loop*, Montana farmers resent the reintroduction of wolves and hire an illegal wolf-killer. At the climax (shades of Greek tragedy) the redneck rancher leading a pack of drunks with guns shoots his own son who is trying to save the wolf-cubs in their den.

From *Oklahoma!* to gangsta rap, guns have been as essential to America's virility as violence is to its land; and to its male teenagers' dreams. Incredibly, thirteen American kids die every day in gun-related incidents. Or so English papers were saying in August 1999. The rise of school shootings in the late nineties was devastating. In 1997, three in Kentucky, two in Mississippi;

in 1998, two in Oregon, one in Tennessee, one in Philadelphia. In 1999 came the trenchcoat-clad teenagers of Denver, Colorado.

The Colorado shootings happened just before the National Rifle Association had its annual meeting. Its president, the film star Charlton Heston, agreed to scale down the meeting in sympathy. 'But', he added, 'we must stand in unshakeable unity even at this time of anguish'. He suggested it was trenchcoats, not guns, that needed banning in schools.[2] A hundred and ten years after white settlers took Oklahoma from the Indians, there was still intense congressional resistance from both political parties to tougher gun-laws. In 1994, Clinton forced a ban on assault weapons on to the statute book against the opposition of the NRA; he then lost twenty Democratic seats in congress and blamed the gun lobby. 'The NRA is the reason the Republicans control the house', he said. The 1999 killings forced party governors in several states (Arizona, Illinois, Ohio, Utah, Virginia) to side with gun-control advocates. James Gilmore, a Republican senator who once posed with a shotgun for an NRA ad, signed a state law banning the keeping of guns in the cars of school pupils.[3]

Yet it is impossible, apparently, to weaken the gun-romantic's belief in a man's totemic right to carry guns. Ostensibly to use on 'nature' and in self-protection. More deeply and symbolically, this is masculinity using arms to bolster the male nature idealized by Hollywood: an emblem of virility when some aspects of the thing itself seem undermined and movie directors use guns as a cliché not of virility but male sexuality under threat. One month after the Colorado killings, with a president desperate for gun control 'to keep guns out of the hands of children', the Senate did approve stronger restrictions on guns, but a month later the House of Representatives voted by 280 to 147 votes to reject a gun-control bill.

What happened? One compound provision simultaneously required safety devices to be sold with all handguns, and weakened background checks on people buying weapons at gun shows. The National Rifle Association backed this provision and sent last-minute letters asking for support to all congressmen. Many Democrats voted against because of the check-weakening clause; many conservatives voted against because (incredibly, to a European) they did not like the safety-device clause. One Georgia Republican, Bob Carr, announced that if the Ten Commandments had been posted up in school, and Thou Shalt Not Kill displayed in the classroom, the Colorado tragedy would never have happened.[4] Little realizing that it is exactly his brand of self-justifying rule-imposing violence which rock ideology, from The Stones to Black Flag to Patti Smith, reacts against. 'I grew up', said Chrissie Hynde,

> in a part of the US that had the highest suicide and homicide by gun rates, and produced a high percentage of serial killers. Jeffrey Dahmer was a local. I put it down to some weird energy from the Indian burial grounds there, plus this deep, burning racial hatred there seemed to be in the hearts of people around me, and fear of anything that wasn't the perfect American family you'd see on the cover of *Life* magazine in 1953. Rock to me was survival instinct... All the music I listened to talked about freedom. I saw slavery all around me in the white suburbs – slavery of the mind.

And reaction can be negative as well as positive. As Brenda, one of the Manson Family, announced to adult America at the Manson trial, 'We were brought up on your TV'.[5]

Charlton Heston invoked the Second Amendment of the Constitution, the right to bear arms, again three months later when a guy who had suffered big losses on the stock exchange killed twelve people in a random shooting in the financial district of Atlanta, Georgia. 'Americans are not going to give up their right to firearms,' he declared. Another NRA spokesman, Bill Powers, said gun ownership was even more necessary with nutters like that around. 'A lot of people in Atlanta feel good they could protect themselves.'[6] The rationale is self-defence; but must (mustn't it?) come from the consciousness that the land was taken ('won') by violence against Indians, and belongs to other people originally brought there, and maintained as slaves, by violence.

In the big American gun tragedies, it is the clean kid who has 'sump'n wrong inside'. Curley, not Jud. The Colorado massacre happened in a premier school in a 93 per cent white suburb, with street-names like Belle Flower and Strawberry. Male teenage 'gun-cleaning' and gun-dreaming, like Jud's, is done in 'lonely rooms' by surburban kids: dreaming (as in Paul Simon's song 'My Little Town') 'of glory, twitching like a finger on the trigger of a gun'. As the captain wrote after killing in Korea (chapter 13), 'Big masturbations all round!' The American dream crashed when it found that Curley *was* Jud, in disguise: your own golden boy was also the dark, rattlesnake-writhing, heavy-metal war-lord lurking in the smoke-house of every teenage bedroom; the toad at the bottom of the happy, sanitary, family well.

That violently grand land, with its frontier myths, wild geology and fauna, lies behind the clichés of American masculinity. Westerns and gangster movies shaped the way Europe imagined America – and all this went into the violence of sixties rock, that music with the triumphal male American voice. No wonder British Keith Richards began holding his alternative virility symbol like a gun.

Getting in Touch with Evil: 'Charlie' Manson and Black Flag

There were more immediate factors, as well as deeper cultural reasons, for sixties rock to plunder links between sex and violence. Tony Palmer's film *All My Loving* shows Eric Clapton demonstrating the link between guitar-playing and aggression by 'power chords'. Footage from the Vietnam war accompanies the violent power riffs. But the violence that gathered in rock in the early sixties was more general than that. It had an important emotional as well as social dimension, and arose from a sense of being, like a Greek hero, against an enemy: parents or parental society. Rock aggression is reactive; as if violence has been done *to* you first. The violence emerged before Vietnam, fuelled (as in the early eighties, when Black Flag in Los Angeles spoke violently for teenagers who felt they were victims of California's unreal, undeliverable silicone-and-avocado dream) by the generation gap; by teenage resentment at powerlessness in an unreal, unjust world. In the sixties, political fury about Vietnam simply joined the aggression already catching fire in rock behaviour, performance and themes.

In America, the violence was exacerbated by the inrush of drugs. In 1967, 50,000 young people came through San Francisco. New psychedelic highs like STP gave you a three-day bad trip, and San Francisco General Hospital was treating 750 bad trips a month. Then heroin came, and doubled drug casualties.[7] Britain had mad injustices of its own: class, race, economy, generation. But Black Power and Vietnam were American issues first, and it was particularly in America that 'the peace and love decade' – when Martin Luther King was shot, police shot students on campus and Vietnam began – took hold:

> It was a country of bankruptcy notices and commonplace reports of casual killings ... Adolescents drifted from city to torn city, sloughing off both the past and the future as snakes shed their skins, children who were never taught and would never now learn the games that had held the society together ... It was not a country in open revolution. It was not a country under enemy siege. It was the United States of America in the cold late spring of 1967, and the market was high ... and it might have been a spring of brave hopes and national promise, but it was not.[8]

California was the crucible of everything: peace-and-love, drugs, 'darkness' and counter-culture. From 1965 to 1970, the hippie community in the Haight-Ashbury area of San Francisco was the eye of the psychedelic storm. Music, drugs and the freedom slogan were its heart. Jefferson Airplane was the raunchy, adventurous band: in 1968, Grace Slick sang from their album *Crown of Creation* on the Smothers Brothers TV show wearing black make-up, clenching her fist in support of Black

Power athletes in the Olympic Games. The premier psychedelic band was The Grateful Dead, the stoned, meandering side of hippy music. One of them had taken part in Stanford University's LSD tests; the LSD chemist Stanley Owsley was in charge of their sound.[9]

But the psychedelia dream sprouted poisonous weeds. 'San Francisco', says Joan Didion, 'was where the social haemorrhage was showing up.' Such a blur of guns and drugs swirled round the guitarist Carlos Santana that he had to keep away from his own band. Hell's Angels were as much a part of the scene as hippies. At Joan Baez's 'School for non-violence', students debated whether the 'Vietnam Day Committee' at Berkeley University should reason with Hell's Angels. 'The Angels just shrug and say, "our thing's violence".' Romanticizing the outlaw was another cliché of Hollywood Westerns, just as romanticizing the 'barbarian yawp' of the proud white male body was one of Whitman's. Out of the rock scene's long romance with Hell's Angels came Hunter S. Thompson's rhapsodizing book *Hell's Angels* and *Rolling Stone*'s belief that they embodied 'the primordial energy of brute force, the excremental vision and freedom of the outcast'. By 1969, the Haight-Ashbury dream was out of control. By 1970, after Altamont, the Summer of Love was over.[10]

The figure most associated with its collapse was another Jud Fry. Charles Manson was a crank guitar-playing prophet with visions of death-to-the-rich, on the fringe of the California rock scene. He took demo tapes round studios and lived for a while at the Malibu home of Dennis Wilson, leader of the Beach Boys, who called him 'The Wizard'. In 1967, Manson founded his Family of male domination, sex and occult ceremony at the edge of Death Valley. In 1968, the world heard about it when his Family butchered Sharon Tate, pregnant with Roman Polanski's child, and the next night another wealthy couple, the LaBiancas.

In Southern California, the murders left a horrific mythic legacy. Images: Tex Watson led the killers into the house saying 'I'm the devil, I'm here to do the devil's business'; Susan Atkins, who smeared 'PIG' on the door in Sharon's blood, wanted to cut out the victim's eyeballs, regretted not ripping out the foetus to take as a trophy to Manson and pronounced killing Sharon the most exciting sexual experience of her life. The trial: in grotesque parody of the All-American Family's family snaps, the Manson Family's pictures feature laughing, muslin-clad bright-eyed faces: in one, they could be any young adults gathered for a picnic; but they were also these chanting, shaven-headed girls with an X cut into their foreheads, haunting the courtroom. Manson did a ten-foot leap across the court holding a pencil as if to stab the judge; the prosecutor Vincent Bugliosi wondered aloud if a glance from Manson, as he sat there staring, eerily self-possessed, had paralysed his watch.[11]

This legacy surfaced ten years later when Black Flag, based in Los Angeles, violently attacked the California dream in Manson-obsessed iconography. 'We get an arcane and emotional value from Manson,' said Chuck Dukowski in 1982. They called their tours 'Creepy Crawls', after the Manson Family's habit of breaking into rich houses and rearranging furniture. Unlike Marilyn Manson after the Colorado killings, Black Flag refused to criticize or censor the violence their music aroused. Their flyers, pasted all over town – sometimes on every locker in every high school – showed human beings trapped like cockroaches in a brutal mix of political satire, sex, scary mysticism and caricatures of the Manson girls.

These were drawn by Raymond (brother of Black Flag guitarist Ginn), who designed the band's logo and suggested its name. (From an insecticide.) Raymond adored Manson iconography. His 'Fifth Beatle' print showed Manson as a dwarf silhouette over The Beatles' shoulders – for Manson's Family had been famously obsessed with The Beatles and coded their murder-commands from tracks on *The White Album*, especially 'Helter Skelter'. 'Manson is a great American hero,' said the singer Lydia Lunch. 'He is the ultimate American poet. How could you not be into the man who singlehandedly ended the Summer of Love?' Her own song with the New York band

Sonic Youth, 'Death Valley 69', is a crashing spiral of guitars 'COMIN' *DOWN!*', recalling both The Beatles' 'Helter Skelter' and the Manson Family's crashing descent, physical and spiritual, to the twisting canyons of Barker Ranch in souped-up dune-buggies, bolted together from stolen car parts.[12] It was cool to call Manson 'Charlie'. Diminutive, familiar: our hero, our pet murderer. Manson T-shirts sold like cherries all through the eighties. His songs were featured by Guns 'N' Roses (and in England by various Manchester-based bands like Indigo Prime, whose credits include 'Charlie's 69 Was a Good Year'). Marilyn Manson helped himself to Charlie's name. The name 'Charlie' and the T-shirts let you iconize away what he actually did, while claiming the glamour of its badness for yourself.

Manson's own voice and thoughts reached the eighties rock scene direct from the prisons where he was held, through Black Flag's manic singer Henry Rollins. Rollins wrote to Manson in prison. By the end of 1983 they were in regular correspondence. Manson sent Rollins Polaroids of himself with an 'X' (turned into a swastika) cut in his forehead, plus tapes of himself singing to guitar. Rollins was entranced. 'This five-foot four guy, sitting behind bars, *terrifies* people!' He played the tapes on tour in the Black Flag van and negotiated to release them commercially. (He sent best-quality cassettes: Manson sent songs back on the worst quality possible, having made a small profit in prison.) The record company SST planned to release them under the title *Completion*. The style is country music: set, so Manson announces at the beginning, in 'The SST Recording Studio'. But there are prison sounds in the background: flushing lavatories, shouting, TV gameshows. The first three songs are sweet-voiced ruminations; the fourth is terrifying. The guitar-picking changes to jagged chords, the voice becomes inchoate like an animal at bay; Manson gnashes his teeth. 'Burnin' . . . fire . . .' he grinds out. In the end, threatening phone-calls stopped SST releasing the recording.[13]

Rollins was also obsessed by iconography from the most infamous Vietnam massacre. He and Tom Troccoli talked for hours about Coppola's film *Apocalypse Now* and its mission, 'Search and Destroy'. Those were the words the American soldiers of Charlie Company heard from their officers, before they entered the village of My Lai; Rollins had them tattooed on his shoulders over a black sun containing a glaring face. Body and mind, he became a walking inventory of the two most famous crimes of the immediate American past. 'A lot of what Black Flag is about', he explained, 'is looking at the evil that lies within human nature.'[14]

Vietnam vets brought their alienated resentment home to their younger brothers. Along with public outcry against the war and films like *Apocalypse Now*, this resentment validated the teenage belief that the adult world is bad and mad. But the bitterness of one generation is the horror-currency of the next. Heavy metal's 'darkness' is stage demonism, voices between grooves on a CD hissing 'worship the devil' repetitively backwards. Post-punk Rollins is unusual in identifying so directly with embodiments of evil like Manson and My Lai, but his notion of going into evil because you feel evil around and within you is globally popular. It may be stagy. But it is what millions of boys want to hear.

The 'darkness' that began in sixties American rock did not surface only in California. Avant-garde Velvet Underground, based in New York, was one of the most influential mid-sixties bands. Musically, they had beautiful moments, but were also brilliantly harsh and nihilist. They got attacked for spoiling the peace 'n' love party. 'The only thing this'll replace', said Cher when they first played in Los Angeles, 'is suicide.'[15] Their album with the German singer Nico, *The Velvet Underground and Nico*, was the first 'bad trip' album. Their street-real lyrics about dying for your next shot of heroin ('Waiting for the Man'), shooting speed ('White Light White Heat'), sado-masochistic sex ('Venus in Furs'), orgies with transvestites and sailors ('Sister Ray'), were light-years away from the happy acid-trip of The Beatles' *Sergeant Pepper*, released the same year, or the flowers of The Grateful Dead. They put centre stage everything you looked away from on the street – the twitching junkies, the trash, the menace. Nico did not get on well with them and left soon after, but shared a lot of the vision. When she toured with a band of her own in the eighties (keeping her fix in her knickers, so the gentlemanly Italian police never found it), the top video to relax to, for male members of her band, was open-heart surgery: 'There was a particular sequence they liked, a configuration of clamp and catheters, peeled flesh and subcutaneous fat – a collage of bloodstained scalpels.'[16]

The Black Excuse: An Echo, Mirror, Shadow of Yourself

Rap is currently the most violent area of rock. What does it say about the relation of white fantasy and black reality that rap is bought *en masse* by whites who use 'black' – from trenchcoats to Satan – as casual currency to express the violence and weight that turns them on in rock?

Earlier on, I used anthropological and psychoanalytic language of 'self' and 'other' to talk about orientalism. In rock as in Greek myth, international relations or commercial competition, 'other' is always what you measure yourself against. Any myths, ancient Greek, gun-lobby American, or the newer ones of rock, help you define your own identity through stories which sum up certain ways of thinking about yourself, by contrasting self with someone, or something, other. But what is other? Greek thought tends to see it in divinity, nature, women or barbarians. (Greek literature, being male, takes male as the model 'self', who belongs to that ideal social unit, the political and military male band.) Ever since teenagers were invented in the fifties, they have forged their own identity by sharing stories, styles, frameworks, personas, images and attitudes which contrast them with adult society. Adults are the other *they* define themselves against. Within the larger society, white uses black in the same way. Hence (I'd say) the teenage rush to blackness, to identify with what adult society thinks is alien. Processed by adults but aimed at teenagers, empowered by blackness and using it as a mask to express its own violence, rock is theatrical blackness: a blacking-up which takes black violence parodistically over the top but also expresses and disguises white violence.

Over the centuries, male Western song has been empowered by two different figures which set off its own maleness. First, the abandoned, yearning woman; then the black man whom it saw as sexier and more violent. White men, heroes of their own culture, had real-life power over both these other figures; whom they also defined themselves against. Self finds itself by exploring what it is against, as echoes come back *at* you, from the cliff face.

In myth, Echo is unantagonistic and desiring. You can turn your back on her. She is part of you, because she sings your words and shows how wonderful you are. But she is also someone else, female and alien. You imagine her negatively, female against male: she is what you turn away from; or keep, like Jagger's girl, under your thumb. For Narcissus, echo and mirror do the same thing: reflect back his self-image. White male song has in its time pressed both black man and desiring woman into service as its own echo or mirror. But when it empowered itself from black maleness, it took on a different negativity. Black became the shadow: anarchic, full of sex and violence: a power-packed darker self. Identifying with it means being against a whole lot of things in nice, safe white society: against what you have come from. You are backing the darkness in yourself against other people's light.

PART 3 Relationship and Artifice:
Misogyny, Cross-dressing and the Fans

15 'Counter' and Contradiction

Counter-culture: Dylan and the Problems of Protest

A lot of rock is about that 'self and other'. When it involves sex, this makes for desire, union, identification, as well as regret, accusation, rejection, separation. But when it involves society, you get mostly rejection and accusation: the classic heroic 'against'.

Rock has always seen itself as counter-cultural. It was born by battling, entering American airwaves against opposition. It was teenagers getting free. It was 'just this noisy rage and anger', said Richard Hell. 'It was about energy and fuck the adults.' Fuck their clothes, behaviour, ideals, education, conventions, their rule-bound, keep-the-butter-in-the-fridge homes. From white kids (Elvis among them) defying parents to listen to black radio, it snowballed until 'The whole frantic thing was a denial of barrenness of feeling in middle-class respectability.'[1] Rock 'n' roll was teenage self-definition by rebellious rejection.

A very simple rejection, by today's standards. No more 'School Days', let's have fun. The 1979 film *Rock 'n' Roll High School*, starring the Ramones, ends with a school in flames. 'Roll over Beethoven and tell Tchaikovsky the news,' sings Chuck Berry. The 1958 film *High School Confidential* was teenage anarchy played out against the brick wall of school life. 'Let's shake things up', sings Jerry Lee Lewis, flashing briefly on screen as a truck driver.

The sixties made all this political, and institutionalized the counter-culture. Drawing on the blues' slave-to-freedom story to justify rebellion, playing up the sound of fighting *back*, the sixties turned rock 'n' roll into a medium whose message, textures and lyrics were all a big self-justified *against*. But protest songs first appeared in folk music. With the waning of rock 'n' roll energy in the early sixties, folk music was increasingly a channel for teenage againstness and its magus was Bob Dylan. You could say rock music (and the sixties themselves) only really began once Dylan opened everyone's eyes to the political resonances of rebellion. Sixties rock was political in a way rock 'n' roll was not.

Dylan began all this between 1963 and 1964. 'In a way it was like the beginning of rock,' said Robbie Robertson, guitarist in The Band, who accompanied Dylan for eight years. At the August 1963 'March on Washington' rally, when Martin Luther King gave his 'I have a dream' speech, Dylan himself sang 'Only a Pawn in their Game', while Peter, Paul and Mary sang his 'Blowin' in the Wind'. By 1964, he was singing at voter-registration rallies in Mississippi. His new songs appeared in activist magazines like *Sing Out*. He attacked arms dealers ('Masters of War') and defended human rights for starving miners or murdered black servants. He also hymned teenage freedom, telling mothers and fathers throughout the land their sons and daughters were beyond their command. He became the voice of his generation's political conscience and personal freedom. But he did not want to be stuck doing that. Between 1964 and 1966 he began mixing blues, protest, folk and rock textures and 'went on a spree unlike any other in pop history'.[2]

In June 1964, his album *Another Side of Bob Dylan* moved into more personal territory and provoked possessive reproach from the editor of November's *Sing Out*:

> You said you weren't a writer of 'protest' songs but any song writer who tries to deal honestly with reality is bound to write protest songs... Your new songs seem to be all inner-directed... maybe a little maudlin and cruel...[3]

Folk investment in protest and sincerity crystallized round the form Dylan had perfected. Form and content: both were sacrosanct. But like Euripides in tragedy two thousand years before, Dylan kept experimenting with subject matter, angles and musical ideas that his audience felt should be kept out. He played electric guitar (*Bringing it All Back Home* had one side acoustic, one side electric guitar); he played in bands. The Animals did a million-selling rock version of the 'House of the Risin' Sun', which he had sung on his first album. The Byrds, the first folk-rock group to get into the pop Top Forty, had a big hit with an electric version of 'Mr Tambourine Man', and Dylan played sessions with them in 1965. Meanwhile, though only the co-tenants on his Harlem block cared, an obscure electric guitarist then called Jimmy Hendrix was playing that album obsessively day and night. 'Jimmy just loved it to death', said his girlfriend Fay. 'We nearly got put out of our apartment because of Bob Dylan.'[4] In content, approach, and texture, folk and rock were coming together, and Dylan was where they met.

As in the forties, the flash-point was electricity. Muddy Waters then made blues electricity spell sex. A decade later, electricity invented the teenager and stood enticingly for city rather than country, for the slick, not the sincere. To the sixties folk audience, electricity meant commerce, not feeling. Dylan came out of the folk tradition, energized by Woody Guthrie but created as a market partly by Leadbelly. No electricity, please, we're folk: 'authentic' stuff from the furrow and the heart. The close-to-heart acoustic guitar said it all.

In fact, many songs Leadbelly sang in the thirties, like 'Goodnight Irene', came out of white Tin Pan Alley. If your notion of authenticity involved cotton-picking and sun-bleached furrows, these songs were inauthentic.[5] But they had helped create the blues-folk standard of authenticity. In 1965 many white blues or folk enthusiasts looked at electric blues with repugnance. Dylan's own early songs were against not just the parental world but the commercial values it seemed to foist on the young. An electric guitar was a red-rag icon; commerce polluting the values of protest, of sincerity.

So the initial folk reaction to Dylan's move to electricity was fury. This first erupted at the Newport Folk Festival in 1965. The Festival offered two kinds of music: songwriters singing protest songs, plus 'traditional' stuff: ballads, blues, bluegrass, spirituals, worksongs. One black group chopped a log on stage while singing. Both categories despised electric guitars as symbols of pop culture. When Dylan appeared in his 'sell-out' black jacket, playing electric guitar, backed by the rock guitarist Mike Bloomfield plus the Paul Butterfield band, he met a wall of rage. Alan Lomax, son of Leadbelly's original patron, got into a fight with Dylan's manager, Albert Grossman. It was suddenly not at all surprising to find two legendary chiefs of the music industry rolling in the dust and the revered Pete Seeger taking an axe (borrowed, no doubt, from the log-chopping worksingers) to the all-important electric cable.[6] At twenty-four, Dylan turned these famous, rich grown-ups into backstage backwoodsman, pitting a neolithic weapon against the Goliath of modern technology.

When Dylan sprang on them his new rock song 'Like a Rolling Stone', the audience exploded:

> Dylan with his amplified accompanists seemed to be embracing the world of commercial music from which they'd made a conscious effort to turn away.[7]

This scene was repeated elsewhere that year at Forest Hills, New York and throughout Dylan's American tour. Next year, 1966, shouts interrupted the electric part of his show in Dublin; and also in London's Albert Hall and Manchester – where one voice bellowed 'Judas!' Dylan flung back, 'I don't believe you!' – a quote from a song he had already sung, 'You're a Liar': which he introduced by saying (ominously, to those who wanted him to stay as he was), 'It used to go like that and now goes like this.'

To the protest movement, he seemed a double traitor. On the one hand, he had turned his alienation and anger inward, serving his psyche rather than society. On the other, he was using sound, textures, technique and personnel from a world which folk music felt threatened their authenticity.

But the long-term effect was not to abandon protest or the claim to authenticity. It just moved the lot into rock. 'Like a Rolling Stone' became the first Dylan A-side to sell over a million copies. It is a relentless put-down of a privileged girl. The snare drum and tambourine build batteringly up to the howling question, 'How does it feel?' It was personal and dramatic. But its title was doubly inflammatory to a folk audience. Rolling stone? The phrase harked back to the blues-figure hallowed by folk tradition (and by Dylan's early persona), but recalled both Muddy Waters (progenitor of the electric band, traitor to the acoustic guitar) *and* the raw, bad emperors of commercial rock, The Rolling Stones: whom Dylan was now measuring himself against. As The Stones knew, of course. In *Stripped*, a mostly acoustic trawl through their back catalogue, they do 'Like a Rolling Stone': Mick gives it the cheekiest introduction he could. 'Here's a song', he announces, 'that Bob Dylan wrote for us!'

Dylan's albums *Another Side of Bob Dylan*, *Highway 61 Revisited* and *Blonde on Blonde* had enormous, immediate impact. The Stones themselves, along with Hendrix and the Beatles, began to look for more social content in songs. 'Satisfaction', their first song with social content, also came out in 1965. By 1967, after the drugs trials and jail, Jagger was saying,

> Teenagers the world over are being pushed around by half-witted politicians who attempt to dominate their thinking and set a code for living.[8]

As teenagers joined movements for human rights against police repression and Vietnam, folk and rock merged. Authenticity shifted to electricity. What made you authentic was opposition. You wanted to be heard (as in Muddy Waters's 'Nobody couldn't hear you with an acoustic'). You could find yourself, be yourself, in opposition to what you came from: older generations, older music ('Roll Over Beethoven') and the world around you.

The protest strain in rock has never looked back. Iggy Pop

said he based The Stooges' music on 'the attitude of delinquency and general mental grievance I'd gotten from the dropouts I was hanging out with.' The Manic Street Preachers, 'Wales's rock 'n' roll radicals', were brought up in the shadow of the 1984 miners' strikes and crushing unemployment. They were socialist and saw themselves and their music as part of the Situationist tradition. They began 'intense, arrogant and angry'.[9] But in the seventies ('the Me Decade', as Tom Wolfe called it), protest became increasingly personal and homed in on the immediate agents of teenage oppression, parents. Rock had always been anti-parent, but now became more personally so. Henry Rollins spotlights how his father 'damaged' him on Black Flag's album *Damaged* (1981). 'Dad' orders the son to sing the national anthem. 'Son' ends with a snarly retreat into self-isolation. The point is the American dream gone wrong, poisoned in the well of the family home. Its mangling of the national anthem is poles apart from Hendrix's 'Star-Spangled Banner' twelve years before. That was political attack. Rollins's is private: the national anthem as instrument of family torture. When MCA later branded *Damaged* as 'anti-parent', their distribution chief declared in the *Los Angeles Times*. 'It didn't have any redeeming social value. It certainly wasn't like Bob Dylan.'[10] And to combat the anti-parent push a 'Parents' Music Resource Centre' was set up in California, aiming to censor rock lyrics. In 1985 Frank Zappa, whose group was called the Mothers of Invention, spearheaded a campaign against this centre, testified before a Congressional Committee and released *Frank Zappa Meets the Mothers of Prevention*.

But in the best hands, anti-parent rock also attacked the hurts suffered by those parents who made you suffer, showing up the system which imposed the hollow ideals that betrayed your parents into pushing that system at you. Bruce Springsteen songs are hurt by, but also for, dad. The son wants 'to walk like a man', to follow dad's footsteps in the sand. But dad has failed to live up to his own ideals of manhood. 'Factory' is all disenchantment, with dad 'walking through them gates in the rain'. Dad 'worked his whole life for nothing but the pain', and now 'walks these empty rooms looking for something to blame'. Fighting is the only way dad can vent anger: 'Just you better believe, boy, somebody's gonna get hurt tonight.' The son sees the anger as useless and unfulfilled. Springsteen's fathers are trapped men, a dull mute force in the house. Their goal of manhood is an empty prize, a primitive loyalty which cages them. He sympathizes with dad hurt by a remorseless system, but today is 'Independence Day'. They 'ain't gonna do to me what I watched them do to you'.[11] He *has* to break free, from dad and his code. He does what teenage does, what heroes do: dramatizes himself against someone else.

Being Against What You Depend On

Teenage opposition has one big built-in self-contradiction. You are against what you come from, but economically and emotionally you depend on it. Your bedroom, fortress against your parents, belongs to them: walls, bricks and all-important electrics.

This contradiction – opposing what you depend on, depending on what you are against – gets into everything. Your relation to earlier rock music, your audience, and the older generation represented most importantly, once you are a successful band, by your managers and record company.

Every rock generation sees the last as the establishment and tries to undo it, to define itself by attacking 'the other'. The biggest 'others' are the old: their sound, their image, their style of sexuality: and how they show themselves male. The seventies rebelled in several ways against the macho, virtuoso rock players of the sixties. One way was disco, created by people marginalized by their colour (black), class (working) and sexuality (gay), but adopted by the rich partying class who wanted glamour and dance. In the seventies, disco provoked rockist fury. In a 'Disco sucks' campaign, there were mass record-burnings in Chicago very like the 'Judas' cries hurled against Dylan. Glam rock upstaged guitar virtuosity (which took itself boringly seriously) by smooching into effeminate, theatrical dress, parodying the showiness of sixties musicians like Jagger and Hendrix, taking it all glitteringly over the top. In its DIY ethos of dress and music, punk rebelled against rich rock stars isolated from their fans, playing only to vast impersonal stadiums; against fetishized musicianship, peace and love. The Sex Pistols were against everything, the Silver Jubilee, the system that loaded Britain with unemployment, the previous rock generation (Mick Jagger was top of Johnny Rotten's list of hates). When Rotten first met Malcolm McClaren, he glared and said 'I hate hippies'. In punk, it mattered more how you held the guitar, and what else you did with it, than how you played. Fifteen years later, at the beginning of the nineties, came grunge, created by the first American generation to realize they would never have all their parents had. They too were against the millionaire rock-star pose, which they saw as hypocritical and self-contradictory: an act that pretends to be against society and actually does better from it than anyone.[12]

Movements against tradition usually end up enriching it. By being against sixties rock, punk re-energized rock tradition. Out of disco's danceableness came nineties rave culture. But the new has to be deliberate attack: to get its energy from opposition.

The dilemma of being against what you depend on increasingly got into bands' relationships with the people they depend on most: their audience. When the Beatles and Stones were speaking loudly for youth culture, they were already living in a privileged, smoking-club atmosphere, cut-off from the street, sending out from hotel rooms for all they wanted. How, from all that, could they identify with the 'ordinary youth' who were identifying like mad with them? 'We want the world and we want it now,' goes the refrain to Jim Morrison's 'When the Music's Over', in which the rock star who already *has* everything – fame, women, money – offers his life as a distorting mirror to his hungry teen audience. But what they wanted, he already had.

The argument was that if you played youth music, you inevitably represented youth. But as with the gap between the staged violence of The Stones or Rammstein and the real violence of Altamont or the Trenchcoat Mafia, there were many possibilities of delusion and let-down in all this. Rock's theatricality means it plays a major part in the teenage enterprise of trying out roles to discover 'who you really are'. What you listen to defines you. The songs on record create something inside the fans, yet the records were created in a studio by technicians and synthesizers as well as musicians. On tour, musicians get a chance to draw meaning from the to-and-fro with the audience, but fans want them to re-create the same show over and over. They want to see and hear for real what has made them what they are.

So glitches crop up between the musicians' impulse to experiment, to go for self-expression, and the crowd's longing to see and hear them the way they belong to them on their Walkmans, in their bedrooms, in their heads.[13] The groups' very lovedness makes them less themselves. They depend on recording to reach the fans, but it gets in the way of live relations. Recording, with its disguises and orchestrated effects, can create a false relationship, an illusion of intimacy. Those who love the slickness of pop love the artifice of it. But as sound became layered and more sophisticatedly manipulated, so did the fan–star relationship.

This relationship has two big points of contact, the record and the gig. Over the decades, the balance of power between these shifted. In the sixties and seventies, the touchstone was the live relationship.[14] In punk, Gaye Advert of the Adverts told me,

> the problem was to make it sound as good as it did live. We'd stand there listening, thinking, That's a really nice sound. And then it never came out.

Today, the technology the Adverts did not have is available on the street. It is that technology which counts. The commercial fan base, 'the hallowed teen gurl crowd that turns your band into millionaires if you press the right button,'[15] is increasingly young; too young, often, to go to gigs on their own. What they want to hear in concerts is what they already know: the CD.

Concerts become a plug for the merchandise. Many groups use backing tapes to make 'live' sound match the recording. You stand there and mime. Recent gadgets tune your voice as you sing, but you have to be careful: if you are a quarter tone out, will it tune you up or down? You have to specify a key before you start.

Some groups feel the sophistication of technology makes for greater spontaneity. Studio technology 'frees you up to try things that no way could you have dreamt of doing five years ago'. And it works live, too. 'We've got to where the technology serves us as opposed to us serving the technology', said Shirley Manson.[16] But it depends how good, and how real, you are in your music. Increasingly, pop recordings bear out what Louis MacNeice said about poetry: 'the truest' is 'the most feigning'.

From the late sixties on, live relationships with the audience became laced not just with artifice and theatricality, but antagonism. Performances began to threaten the audience and incite brutality. Jagger as Lucifer 'baited' the audience, said Ossie Clark. Pete Townshend machine-gunned them with his guitar: a tradition that goes on into the nineties, when KLF 'machine-gunned' the audience at the Brit Awards and dumped a dead sheep at the door. The Dead Kennedys, the link between the UK punk bands of 1976 and late-eighties US hard core, did one concert in Los Angeles when 'twenty seconds into the third song, the guitarist took his guitar, smashed someone's head, then dove in after'. The relationship was increasingly ambivalent.[17] The group was no longer dative, 'to' or 'for' the crowd, but often playing *at* it. Masochistically, audiences loved being mown down by the noise and the chords. But they also began hurling things back, meeting violence with violence. At punk concerts, spitting was a big part of the two-way relationship with the players. 'It was all right,' Gaye Advert told me, 'if it was a nice audience. You'd just hope they didn't spit at you too much.'

But they were not always nice; and spitting was not all. Beer cans and used condoms were favourite missiles. When Black Flag played in Milan,

This skinhead pissed in a cup and – swoosh! – just DOUSED Chuck. I thought it was beer, then I saw his face make this most... agh! He turned totally white and had this look of terror. He put his bass down and ran behind the amp and was sick.

Jim Morrison began leaping into the audience in 1967 and Iggy Pop followed. In the early eighties, Henry Rollins both intimidated audiences and became their whipping boy. 'I remember people putting cigarettes out on his back, throwin' shit at him... he had sores all over him.'[18] Rock antagonism against the audience was returned in spades. The hero's *against* was turned on the audience too – and the audiences hurled it back.

Over that Counter: Selling or Sell-out?

Within thirty years of its birth, rock dominated American musical taste. To take figures from one year nearly twenty years ago: Radio Information Centre figures for Autumn 1983. By then, rock had half the FM and AM radio audiences in America's hundred top markets while jazz had less than one per cent of the top ten markets. Rock had thirty per cent (fifty, if you include rhythm and blues) of American record and tape sales while jazz and classical music both together only had ten per cent. Rock was doing very well in the world – how do you square that with its againstness? The big teenage contradiction is sharpest in the rock group's relation to its own success: to its management, and money.

'Counter culture' has more than one meaning. You may sing about 'countering' society, but that shiny counter at Virgin Megastore with your CDs on it reflects the very thing you say you're against: the parent-like commercial system. This is where accusations of sell-out, and anguish over authenticity, kick in. The counter is where you and your image get sold, according to the rules of people ten or twenty years older.

As grunge ideals emphasized, the centre of that contradiction is your relation to the previous generation's money and power. The Stones, aged twenty-four, were shocked to find their records supported the arms trade, but what did they expect? They said they made no concession to commercialism, but the system made them millionaires for saying they despised it.[20] This was the self-contradictory legacy: the rolling-in-it rock star yelling defiance at the system which enriched him.

The Sex Pistols crusaded against it in their single 'EMI' and album *The Great Rock 'n' Roll Swindle*. Yet they ultimately replicated it themselves. Punk was in an especially sharp double bind. You wanted to reach people, to play literally on the same level as your audience. Record companies helped you, but you had to buy in to their values. 'We didn't realize', said TV Smith, lyricist and singer for the punk band the Adverts, 'that after you've done one thing, it gets taken over. The record companies and music press want you to stick to that format.' 'But who decided the "format" of a punk song?' I asked. 'Wasn't that a contradiction in terms? Punk was about inventing new things. There should have been no limit to that.' 'That's what we thought, yes,' said TV.

> We enjoyed finding out what we wanted to do. But something happens between being creative and going out into the public. You get told, 'This is what you've done and this is what we want you to do next.'

Rock culture, like teenage life, depends on parental economics. Your songs may be against the market-place, but you won't sell them unless you join it. The rock sociologist and critic Simon Frith pointed this contradiction out twenty years ago. The ideology is freedom, but commercial practice means the freedom is self-deluded. (Or hypocritical.) Since the fifties, adult record-producers have dominated teenage music, creating stars, giving them the personality and music they decided – as in the packaging of Cliff Richard. Rock is financed and distributed by adult commerce; rock musicians are bought by a company, men older than themselves; their voice is chosen, image shaped, interviews influenced to an increasingly sophisticated agenda.[21] When you join the market-place, you take its production values on board.

One distinction sometimes made between rock and pop, Mat Snow told me, is between 'artist-led' and 'production-led' work. A pop producer creates and packages a group or singer, like the Spice Girls. He chooses the face and image, trains and directs the voice, decides the personality profile and publicity, chooses lyrics, emotional atmospherics, video-look. That is pop: the producer in control. Most people, TV Smith told me, unless they can handle the technology entirely themselves,

> need producers and mixers to get their sound to sound like something else, an ideal. People might say, for instance, 'Go for a Spice Girls kind of feel', and so on. What the producer and mixer do is capture certain kinds of sounds.

Ideally, a rock artist does everything him or herself; writes the lyrics, directs the music, directs the sound and look, plays the guitar (maybe) and sings. Bruce Springsteen, Prince, Bjork. But in one of the most competitive industries in the world, it is hard to insist on your own values. And even if you do, there is a further contradiction. Not only do you depend on the adult system you are against; you cannot help imitating it. As Simon Frith pointed out twenty-five years ago, the male supremacism and narcissism of most male rock lyrics are hardly 'counter-cultural'.[22] Believing you were against tradition became the biggest rock tradition. And rock culture, the whole rock establishment, also reflects some major – and to a woman, vital – conservative features of the society which rock ideology was created to attack.

16 The Comforts of Misogyny

Misogyny? Really?

'Look in thy heart and write', said Philip Sidney in *Asphodel and Stella*. But what about looking into someone else's heart and writing that? At the heart of rock maleness breeds something women find incomprehensible, which men seem to have an oak-aged, myth-hallowed need for but tend to gloss over, deny or mysteriously fail to register: supremacism, which shades easily into misogyny.[1] The way rock culture and music handles all this demonstrates its conservatism: the way it clings to the structures of the society it defies.

Misogyny is as old as the hills – or the Greek islands. The earliest written misogyny I know is Semonides, an island poet from seventh-century BC Amorgos, who satirized wives in animal-terms (mare-women, ferret-women, monkey-women, for instance) as variously greedy, promiscuous and lazy; they eat up your money and possessions and sap your strength. The first woman – Eve in the Bible, Pandora in Greek myth – corrupts the pristine male world. Women come after men, and are the origin of evil. Pandora opens her box and lets diseases loose on the world, Eve opens Eden to Satan. In Greek myth, all the disease and nightmare demons, underworld persecutors, punitive and polluted forces like the Furies, are female.

Why have men, who have always held the advantage in the balance of power, said so loudly that women are bad? Where, on earth, does misogyny come from? Some theorists pin it on male fears of female sexuality. The little boy in awe of mother's power (and her insides, where he came from) turns into the ruling male, making sure that women's secret power does not threaten male order.

Greek myth backs this lot up. The Furies are textbook incarnations of those fears. A thousand myths show women destroying men, mainly through that tendency to open things better kept closed. The literature hums with stories and comments about women's dangerous openness – to nature, wildness, demons, darkness and, above all, passion. The tragic poets exploited all that brilliantly. In Euripides's *Bacchae*, the royal house falls when its women run mad on the mountain; in *Hippolytus*, a boy dies because his stepmother desires him. With Medea, Clytemnestra and Hecuba on board, Greek tragedy specialized in women whose passions destroy men. Reinventing Greek tragedy, opera too demonized destructive female power: Carmen the gypsy, Semiramis the Babylonian queen.[2]

So much for myth. But where would you look psychologically for the roots of misogyny? Where do you start to broach, in rock, this apparently unnecessary bit of male lumber?

Baby – and Resenting Male Need

Well, what about the infantilizing endearments? When I asked Yoko Ono what she thought about rock's babyizing words, she said,

> It's to do with childhood. The strength of rock 'n' roll is the energy of a baby, almost, saying 'We're trying to communicate!' I think that's its deep power, really.

Does rock's 'deep power' come, then, from the way you learn to love and hate as a baby?

'Baby' is pop's favourite endearment. It came into popular white music from black culture in the twenties and thirties. In its original context, it was interchangeable with 'Mama' and 'Daddy'. Where's your mama gone, where's your baby gone? Mama and baby were the same person – your lover. But history of a convention does not explain what it is up to today. Origins, say anthropologists, do not determine function. 'Baby' came from black culture, but white pop did not have to use it. It gave up the 'lover' meaning of 'mama' and 'daddy', but It hung on to 'baby' because it meant something. 'Baby' is used now because it expresses something now.

Well – what? Why such a family word, when 'family' is part of the system male rock wants out of?

'Baby' can be sung by men or women. (White culture kept the interchangeability to that extent.) But boy using it to girl is a million times commoner. It is the template, and suggests a need to downgrade: to treat girls as chicks, dolls, birds, little bits of fluff. Protect her, scold her, rock her, hold her; pick her up, put her down, pat her back, make her cry. Do what you like, she is a plaything, an infant. As you were, when a woman first held you. Having begun life in a woman's power, you've got to tip power back the other way. If rock's fundamental voice is a boy saying he is a man, of course it is going to downgrade girls to infants.

That would be the argument, anyway. Is 'baby' such a frail thing to hang it on? It is pop's big word. 'Baby Come Close', 'Baby Come to Me', 'Baby Don't Go', 'Baby Don't Go Too Far', 'Baby Don't You Weep', 'Baby Get Lost', 'Baby I Don't Care' (a likely story), 'Baby I Love You', 'Baby I Need Your Loving', 'Baby I'm a Want You', 'Baby I'm Burning', 'Baby I'm Lonely', 'Baby I'm Yours', 'Baby It's You', 'Baby Let Me Follow You Down', 'Baby Let Me Hold Your Hand', 'Baby Let Me Take You Home', 'Baby Make it Soon', 'Baby Now That I've Found You', 'Baby Please Don't Go', 'Baby What You Want Me To Do', 'Baby Won't You Please Come Home' – these are a tiny fraction of song-titles beginning with it. (As for titles where the word eels its way somewhere else into the line, forget it. Check them out yourself, in a catalogue.)

After 'baby' comes the imperative mood ('Baby Scratch My Back'), the jussive ('ordering') subjunctive ('Baby Let's Play House'), a where's-my-sympathy plaint ('Baby It's Cold Outside'), or a pathetic little plea. ('Baby can I hold you tonight?'

Boyzone are inquiring on my radio this minute.) Coax, complain, cry, command: this is how mothers and babies operate together. When lovers talk in baby talk, say psychologists, they are not talking like babies but like mums talking *to* babies.[3]

The album *Let Love In* (1994), from the Australian singer Nick Cave (chanting 'Do you love me?' obsessively at beginning and end), homes brilliantly in on male fury at this need, this violent helplessness, connecting infantile vulnerability to women with murderous violence against them. Cave begins in imperative mood and goes on via devilry to death. First the boy has power, then mum does; first the woman, then the man. His charcoaly bass introduction, 'Do you love me *like I love you*?', is pure menace. He feels ragingly little. 'I seemed so obsolete and small.' He tried ('I really tried') not to hurt her. But (with a knifewaving edge to the voice, a downward-curving tune and threatening accompaniment) 'I was a cruel-hearted man.' She's still in him ('moving through me even now') but has 'blood running down the side of her legs'. 'She's nobody's baby now.' His voice lays her to rest on the bottom keynote. In 'Loverman', he is 'a devil waiting outside your door, howling with pain, crawling up the wall'. He is the devil trying to get in ('Let Love In'). He pesters like a baby, 'I'm your loverman. I am and I am and I am'; 'Give him more give him more'. Like a child, he feels both weak and evil, 'a devil lying by your side'. In 'Jangling Jack', he cries 'Mummy, mummy? Please don't leave me I'm here all alone.' In the last song, the name of the bar he's in describes himself. He is a sorry dog:

> Sorry sorry sorry, I'm sorry that I keep bobbing up . . .
> I'm sorry I've forgotten how to fuck,
> I'm feeling very sorry in The Thirsty Dog,
> I'm sorry that I'm always pissed I'm sorry that I exist,
> I'm feeling very thirsty in The Sorry Dog.

Its hilarious sinisterness does not undo the connection he pinpoints in his edgy bass between infantile dependence, furious resentment of any such thing, and terminal violence. 'I've always enjoyed writing songs about dead women,' he has declared. 'It's something that crops up that still holds some mystery, even to me.'[4] Or, as his dark master Edgar Allen Poe said, 'The death of a beautiful woman is unquestionably the most poetic subject in the world.'

One of the most-played pop classics, Sting's 'Every Breath You Take' (1983), fizzes with resentment at dependence on a woman. Sting wrote it during his divorce from the strong woman who had supported and encouraged him into stardom. Now *he* was leaving her, very publicly, for someone younger. But the message ('every smile you fake, every vow you break, I'll be watching you') is vicious possessiveness. Accompaniment and lyrics are a soft hieroglyph of fury and need. 'Can't you see you belong to me, how my poor heart aches with every step you take?' The sinister plucky steps of the introductory guitar and synthesizer, the cat's-tread, spymaster menace of the chord progressions. have been taken for tenderness. Other singers have sampled the song to express constancy. 'It's about need,' a man once explained to me with tears in his eyes. But its deep power is poison: a fine-drawn tension between possessiveness, furious resentment at need and Sting's genius for tightly controlled romantic song. Sting himself called it a sinister, evil song veiled in a romantic setting.[5]

A lot of the sex war in early blues music is driven by men's anger at their need for women and resentment at women's power – summed up in Blind Lemon Jefferson's 'Crawlin' Baby Blues' (1929). 'The woman rocks the cradle and I swear she rules the home'. (In country music too, men's longing and feelings of inadequacy – what Johnny Cash's 'Man in Black' calls 'the hopeless hungry side of town' – are women's fault.) Lonnie Johnson's thirties recordings ache with a brooding misogyny he handed on to Robert Johnson, whose light, high voice makes it all the more sinister. 'Me an' the devil were standing side by side/And I'm goin' to beat my woman until I get satisfied.' If it was up to him, he sings (to a loonily cheery guitar accompaniment), 'the little woman I'm lovin' wouldn't have no right to pray'. He despises the women he needs: 'I can't see no reason why/I can't leave these no-good women alone.' As with all rock's againstness, wrong has been done *to* him first. 'If I send for my baby and she don't come/All the doctors in Hot Springs sure can't help her none.' (Nick Cave, your songs start here.) 'An' if she gets unruly, thinks she don' want do/Take my 32–20 and cut her half in two.'[6]

Back to seventh-century Greece, to Pandora and Eve; to men projecting evil on to women. Whatever's wrong with the world is women's fault.

Fifties rock took from blues mainly the sex and fun. Despite the little edge of meanness in Elvis's voice, despite the cockproud swagger, songs he sang did not attack women. On 'Hardheaded Woman', say ('A hard-headed woman and a soft-hearted man/ been the cause of all the trouble ever since the world began'), he is all defence. Bill Haley was bouncy and didn't want to offend anyone, Little Richard was stylish, sexy, suggestive; Chuck Berry's most popular songs hymned schoolroom rebellion.

Supremacism and misogyny rolled explicitly into rock in the sixties, along with the violence. As with the violence, the main inspiration was blues misogyny – which also inspired heavy metal in the early seventies. Led Zeppelin has its own version of the Fall. 'Many people talkin' but few of them know/the soul of a woman was created below', they howl in 'Dazed and Confused', mingling ancient associations of women and the underworld with fantasy over female anatomy. Just as King Lear does, when he's mad:

> But to the girdle do the gods inherit
> Beneath is all the fiend's;
> There's hell, there's darkness, there is the sulphurous pit.[7]

Steven Tyler of Aerosmith heard Led Zeppelin do that song in 1970. 'They literally brought me to tears', he said, 'with the middle section. The dynamics and power were unbelievable! It was foreplay, fucking and climaxing. Led Zeppelin was like great sex. It was so heavy it made me cry.' (He cried again later when Page disappeared with his own girlfriend, but 'Page was such a motherfucker onstage I couldn't hold it against him'. Staging aggressive male sexuality is far more important than the girl you've been sharing a home with.)[8] A triumphally brutal musical staging of male supremacism, which aligns femaleness to hell, is 'like great sex'.

The savageness of blues misogyny came from a savage social and economic background: grown men felt humiliatingly insecure in a society where work had ex-slavery connotations, women got work more easily. Victims outside the home, men wanted power in it. 'White folks say, "Why you guys hold your things?" "Cause you done *took* everything else, motherfucker."'[9] But white boys used all that for theatre, for staging teenage fantasy. As David Coverdale, vocalist in the metal band Whitesnake, explained, 'I find coloured boys seem to be able to come out of the closet and sing exactly what they're thinking about.' In heavy metal, blues themes became 'a combination of lust and misogyny dangerously close to the glorification of rape'.[10]

If you put the babyisms next to the resentment, need, and brutality, the fantasies that women come from hell plus the come-close-fuck-off attitude to women of sixties on-the-road rock, it does all add up, wouldn't you say, to at least the possibility that rock misogyny begins at the maternal breast: in a baby boy's resentment of mother's power?

Trapped in an Alien World: That Magical Female Element

But there must be more to misogyny than fearing mum's power and resenting need. One bit of it is fear of being trapped.

Sixties rock increasingly identified women as anti-freedom. Women stood for smothery restriction. The Canadian group Guess Who saw American warmongering and the Vietnam war as women's fault. 'American woman, stay away from me'. In his hit 'Gimme Hope Jo'anna' (1987) the Anglo-Guyanese Eddy Grant personified apartheid as female.[11] Femaleness spelt society:

THE COMFORTS OF MISOGYNY

which sixties rock dramatized itself against. Femaleness and society nail the rebel down. Girls are objects of desire but also of hostility and ridicule; something to hunt, show off to, put down, flee. They try and trap you into marriage. Girls who refuse sex are repressed and get cursed for it. Girls who don't are sluts, or trying to trap you, or both. 'Just What You Want, Just What You'll Get' (1966, from John's Children), sets this paranoia to a brutal military beat. 'Don't think I don't know just what you want/ EVERYTHING!/ Don't think I don't know just what you'll get/ NOTHING!'[12]

Bruce Springsteen, mapping the blue-collar male soul, sums up this mindset up more compassionately fifteen years later. Women are little and frail. In nine out of twenty tracks on *The River* (1980), they are 'little girls'. Men want to protect them. But marriage denies them the freedom at the core of maleness. They marry, get a union card, get responsibilities. Women are the end (in both senses) of male wanderings. In 'Racing in the Streets', the hero wins a 'little girl' as a prize; but doesn't keep her. Women are commitment: what men define themselves against. Wandering and 'straying' makes men feel like men, but all that is left of that is the right to 'fool around'.[13]

All that is in lyrics. In rock life, women will mess up your male comradeship. Being in a band is men's work, sweat and toil. Girlfriends are regarded with suspicion. 'There was enormous pressure on me,' Yoko Ono told me. 'I didn't even have to *say* very much, I was just there. That was already a threat.' (Still, she did also tell me 'I think of creativity as a feminine attribute', which might have ruffled a few Beatle feathers in 1969 when she got into trouble for pinching George Harrison's chocolate biscuit at rehearsal, or 1971 when Lennon left her off the credits for his song 'Imagine', when he'd pinched the idea from her book of poems, *Grapefruit*. 'Those days I was a bit more selfish,' he said. 'She's just the wife and you don't put her name on it, right?') In Aerosmith, 'I felt incredibly rejected and alienated', said Steve, 'by Joe's relationship with this girl. The minute she came along I was suddenly not Joe's friend any more.'[14] Girls stifle men's friendships and creativity. They tie you; they are anti the rock ideal: male freedom.

These engulfment fears have a glaringly obvious symbolic side. Forget mothers: what about the mindblowingly simple sexual worry is that once you get in, you'll never see that centrepiece of rock poetics, your own cock, again? It'll be swallowed up in Charybdis, the female whirlpool. Getting into women is the model of all male adventuring into danger. The world is full of places you enter and may never come back from. Ariadne gives you a 'clue' (the old word for her thread) to the labyrinth; women guide you into shadowy interiors, mysterious palaces or forests. But whatever you find there, will you ever see the light again?

Then there is the sea, woman's magical element, birthplace of Venus. The hero skims over it, meeting mainly female dangers *en route*; island goddesses like Calypso who 'cover' him in her cave. If girls are just girls, you can take them over the sea, dump them on islands and get out. But if they are goddesses (or if your feelings turn them into goddesses) they are more at home in that sea than you are. They can help you or drown you. Ulysses is fine. Goddesses give him magic girdles and food, tell him how to make rafts and get home. But Narcissus? Echo loves him: can't she save him when he dips his gorgeous face too near the water? Somehow this female image of a resonating hollow is counterpart to the watery mirror which pulls him under.

Woman as engulfment you have to escape merges with woman as emblem of imprisoning society in Jagger's 'Have You Seen your Mother, Baby, Standing in the Shadows?' Girls turn into their mothers. The end result of that girl whose knickers you want to get into is society, domesticity and, once again, *mum*. Girls may be magic, but magic 'turns' one thing 'into' another. Women into goddess, girls into mum. Bruce Springsteen, with his genius for hitting the mythical nail on the head, asks 'Is that you, baby, or just a brilliant disguise?' (*Tunnel of Love*, 1987). Girls are the domestic trap in brilliant disguise. Tempting on the surface, like the top half of a mermaid; singing enticingly, like Sirens. But below belongs to the sea. If you come on to Sirens, you wind up on the rocks.

Penetrating the Alien World: Secrets of Venus

These fears, resonating against myths of women's veils, of women's fakery, of their insides being totally different from their surface, find a perfect image in astronomy. From Babylonian times, men have identified the brightest close planet to Earth as the goddess of love. Venus is Earth's girl-next-door: brilliant and available, but also the hardest planet to see into. Its brightness is a mirror-shimmer, reflected from a dense and endless aeolian transport of loose grit, a moving dust-cloud which angles the sun's dazzle down to Earth.

Earth has a hot mobile 'mantle' covered by a rigid crust. Its lithosphere is segmented into slowly moving plates like the overlapping toolings of medieval armour.[15] Men's images of their own planet melt into an armoured vision of themselves. But to male eyes, Venus is utterly female. Astronomers have found it hard to 'penetrate her secrets'. Galileo, the first to look through a telescope, was the first to see all her phases. But he could not see in because (we now know) of that swirling cloud. Bright from afar, a mystery up close; so very near (in planetary terms), Venus is almost Earth's twin in size, density and mass, yet very alien; the perfect cosmic image for how men see women. Impenetrability and femininity hang together. That place whose dazzling swirly veil you want to penetrate is as alien as Hades or the sea. Women are a different, maybe a hiddenly hostile, element.

Mythically, one of the secrets of Venus is the way she gets you to desire her. By mascara? By faking? Maybe misogyny is just despairing fury that women are not only men's fantasies but have a life (and sexuality) inside that men cannot know. Maybe it punishes women for being able to feel differently from how men want them to, for turning into mothers who put the children first, then get you out of bed to look after them. Above all for being able to fake *when you can't* (or couldn't before Viagra came along), for the fact that you never know if they are faking or not. Maybe men hate women for being fake twice over: manmade fantasy *and* real bodies, horribly able to fake desire. Unlike men, women can fake not just desire but (the great male worry) orgasm. How do you know she's really come? In the film *When Harry Met Sally*, the heroine demonstrates in a restaurant exactly how easy it is to fake an orgasm. ('I'll have what she's having,' says a watching woman diner to the waiter.) If this made-up package of desire on which your maleness depends is fake, what about you? Maybe misogyny is resenting your need that her desire for you, and pleasure in you, should be real.

Like the idea of Venus born from her dad's castration, misogyny reflects vast tracts of male anxiety and anger. Fears of getting engulfed, resentment of your own need, of how women draw you in to an alien place... Whatever, misogyny does seem to be something many men need. If not all the time, then at moments. It has an uneven relationship to sexism and supremacism. You can hate women without bossing them about; you can be misogynist but not supremacist. But you cannot have sexism and supremacism – which rock music is full of – without a dash of misogyny, somewhere.

Heavy Metal: Parody – or Theatre of Misogyny?

Whether you explain all this psychologically, politically or economically, social-wise or selfish-wise, the end result is desire that turns into hatred of what you desire. Which is, I suppose, the supreme case of being against what you depend on. In male myth, the doubleness of both women and desire (chapter 6) reflects the two sides of that contradiction.

Men often soften misogyny. They call it pet names like 'boysy' or 'laddish'; they wave it away. If rock is a boy saying 'I'm a man', men tend to reverse the process when asked to think about misogyny. 'I'm not sure it's misogyny you get in heavy metal,' one male rock expert told me. 'It's more bone-headed bemusedness.' But 'Knockin' down the door, pull you to the floor' (from Great White), though it may be bone-headed, is not exactly bemused. From women's point of view, not just fantasies of violent rape but parodies of those fantasies are as misogynist as the thing itself.

Heavy metal camps up the misogyny–macho display. Monster Magnet's 1998 London Astoria show had one song-formula, 'a slow prelude of simple guitar figures and doom-laden drums erupting into thrusting power riffs', while the singer Dave Wyndorf parodied the rock god. His pecs glistened under their leather, he rolled around on the floor simulating orgasm with a beer bottle, cackling as if at his own absurdity.[16] But camp lets you have your fantasy and eat it too. You laugh, but still believe in and belong to what Wyndorf parodies.

Though punk changed women's role in rock, sexism was just as important in some areas of it as in The Stones. In fact, since feminism was then on the rise, the anti stuff was more virulent. Malcolm McClaren, punk's British architect, saw punk as violence against a smothering mother-culture. When Sid Vicious was tried for knifing his girlfriend, McClaren wanted to relaunch Sid's career by getting him to record 'Mac The Knife'. The Stranglers, the next most commercially successful British punk group, were notorious for their misogyny. 'Sometimes' was about beating up a girlfriend. The singer-guitarist Hugh Cornwell explained, 'I think a lot of men like to dominate women. A lot of women like to be dominated.' 'Ugly', about strangling a girl after sex because of her awful acne, ended with the chant 'MUSCLE POWER'. 'London Lady' slagged off a fading groupie, hanging round stars like a vampire: the guitarist Burnell defended it by saying 'that's no way for a chick to be'.[17]

When The Prodigy brought out 'Smack My Bitch Up' (1997), they said they were anarchists. But violence to women is the opposite of anarchy. It is as old and conservative (or more so) as the House of Lords. The video of that song staged a laddish night out (drugs, drink, strippers, vomit), and at the end you discover it was a woman doing it all. It is still male fantasy but, as in Aristophanes' *Lysistrata* of 411 BC, the joke is women doing what men do. (Only in Aristophanes, this is stopping war, not sicking up.) There were public calls for the posters of 'Smack My Bitch Up' to be banned for inciting violence against women. The group said they were misunderstood. They 'credited their audience with enough intelligence not to literally interpret or act out the lyrics'. They said the song 'didn't mean anything', didn't incite violence to women, was not even about women; it was about intense experience.

By denying their theatre of misogyny meant anything, they had it both ways. Male critics said they'd made a pantomime of twisted masculinity and were beautifully intense. 'The dodgy politics are flambéed to a crisp.' They were cuddly chaps, incapable of smacking a biscuit, let alone a woman. The whole thing brought out a disingenuous male defence of rock misogyny and state-of-the-art laddishness. It was all about masculinity in crisis. The 'hos' and 'bitches' of gangsta rap, the misogynist clichés of white rock, send masculinity up, and women who do not like it are uncool moralists who cannot handle irony. Twelve-year-old girls wanted the single for Christmas, delighted to shock parents by repeating 'it didn't mean anything'. And everyone made money. With sales of seven million, The Prodigy were British dance music's most influential band. Misogyny is big business.

Is heavy metal really (or only) irony: a parody that 'doesn't mean anything' of masculinity in crisis? Let's put some of heavy metal's lyrics beside what they get up to in private. In 1984 you got Whitesnake's album *Slide It In* and Ted Nugent's album *Penetrator*. Nugent, son of an army sergeant, was one of metal's founding fathers: his songs seldom stray from aggression and misogyny. Great White had lines like 'Gonna drive my love inside you, nail your ass to the floor'. We get a glimpse of what such lyricists were doing off-duty from a woman musician now known as Jarboe who sings with Swans, an American experimental rock group. In the early eighties she was working her

THE COMFORTS OF MISOGYNY

way through college in Atlanta. She sang in lounge bars, and then got a job as a sexual entertainer for visiting celebrities. She specialized in 'big name rock 'n' rollers'. Her (then) name was on the tour 'riders' of groups' contracts, listing her along with the liquor allocation as what the group would get in each town. In the course of her work, Jarboe got a glimpse of misogynist fantasies in action:

> I was hired because I had the ability to endure. When I first got involved it was sort of mild. But I wound up doing things like being urinated on, being tied up. I don't want to name a lot of names – I was burned with a cigarette on my left breast; I still have the scar. I was bound and gagged, with a group standing round me spitting on me. A lot of this had nothing to do with sex; it was about using you as an object; treating you like shit.

The men she met were 'spoiled beyond belief, fetishistic to the point of being babies. That was the world I saw: very pompous, money-is-no-object, very exploitative of tremendous numbers of women.'[18]

This was the era of arena rock, 'of AC/DC, Van Halen, Kiss and Judas Priest'. AC/DC revelled in a bad boy image: Angus Young playing guitar in schoolboy cap and short trousers. Kiss was inspired by superhero comic books; their act involved giant hellhounds with glowing eyes. Van Halen, one of the leading metal acts of the eighties, had a brilliant guitarist, Eddie Van Halen himself. Judas Priest, essence of British metal (their leather-clad singer came on stage on a motorbike), was formed in Birmingham. Their 1981 album *Point of Entry* reached the British Top Twenty; *Screaming for Vengeance* sold over two million worldwide in 1982. In 1990 a teenage fan committed suicide after hearing one of their records, but a Nevada court ruled they were not responsible.

The fact that violence to women is a cliché and can be satirized does not undo its misogyny. A pantomime dame is mimicking a real thing, an ironic cartoon does not do away with the reality of Tony Blair, a child's war-game is still about war. All the armoury of heavy metal – from rape to studs (in every sense, leather, brass and wishful thinking), is Mars, the war-god, screwing Desire (or burning Jarboe's left breast), and masquerading as Eros, the naked baby in a school cap like AC/DC, dreaming comic superheroes like Judas Priest. The schoolboy dimension does not stop it being misogynist: it capitalizes on the unreality of rock.

In this case it is not a boy impersonating a man, but men impersonating boys. 'Boysy', laddish: misogyny seems to turn on exactly that swing-door between boy and man which rock 'n' roll's first stagings of masculinity enacted. Misogyny exploits the possibility of being both. But instead of a boy impersonating a man, you get a man impersonating a teenage boy, the most ill-informed about and least sympathetic form of maleness to women, the laddish form of maleness which absolves itself from responsibility. The Prodigy, and defences of 'Smack My Bitch Up', reflected the rise of nineties laddishness, which smoothed over beer-and-birds sexism by calling misogyny irony. This was the 'Aren't we awful?' cool of being non-politically-correct. 'If you're a girl going to football,' said a radio DJ one afternoon in 1999, 'we want to hear from you. Chris wanted to call this slot Totty Footie, but *I* don't think we should.' The laddish hallmark is that having-it-both-ways mix of grinning put-down and smug disclaimer. An otherwise wonderful blues historian 'nearly' called his chapter on contemporary women musicians 'Chicks with Picks'. It would have been tasteless, he said, 'but not too wide of the mark'.[19] What mark would that be, precisely? Misogyny may start by feeling vulnerable to mum and resenting her power, but in action it is a man claiming the irresponsible invulnerability of a boy.

The misogyny of heavy metal, the guns of rap, are Mars throwing his weight around. But they are also Mars playing Eros, hiding, as Eros hides behind Venus' veil, behind the artificiality, theatricality and impersonations of rock. Heavy metal is the war-god's armour, the archaic core of the reactionary male dream within rock, constantly renewed for anyone who needs it, even when they disguise their need by laughter. By focusing *ad absurdum* on the cock-proud legacy developed by The Stones, heavy metal brought out the misogyny at the heart of rock.

Being Against What You Desire: Not Just Teenage, Male

It is comforting to be boy and man at the same time. From the sixties on, rock amplified ultra-traditional sexist fantasies, staging the maleness endemic in the very archaicness it wanted rid of in parent society. Rock culture expects its fans to stay teenage in a bit of their mind when they grow up.

You go for that rebel yell as a teenager and hang on to it in middle age. You may be in your thirties or forties with a partner and kids, but you still like feeling you're part of the rebellion of rock. 'There's a symbiotic relationship,' said Mat Snow, 'between rock culture in its widest sense, and self-perceptions of people who are no longer young. Most men my age, thirty-nine, have long-term partnerships and children but still like to feel they're participating in quasi-rebellious rock culture.'

'Sentimental music', says Nick Hornby's rock-obsessed hero, 'has this great way of taking you back somewhere at the same time that it takes you forward, so you feel nostalgic and hopeful all at the same time.'[20] Listening, identifying, you go back and forward at the same time, can be thirty-five going on seventeen. But seventeen doesn't have to resolve the contradictions of its fantasies. If you stay teenage in a bit of your mind, that validates everything. But from women's point of view, forty-year-old men clinging to the teenage boy mindset has an element of – well, to put it softly, disingenuousness.

Rock is a very male-dominated industry: the proportion of women in powerful positions in rock journalism, management and production is a tiny fraction of women in other areas of journalism or management. It has traditionally been hard for women to break into rock; according to many women, a conservative, defended misogyny still operates in it at nearly all levels.²¹ If they are right, here too rock culture replicates traditional structures of the traditional parent world. Selling is close to sell-out. 'Roll over Beethoven'? Things are changing a bit now, but rock is far more woman-excludingly hierarchic than the classical music world, which these days would never put up with von Karajan remarking 'A woman's place is the kitchen, not the symphony orchestra.'

When I went to college in the late sixties, one pub we went to had a men-only bar. It was a smoky little hole, full of the hostile silent eyes of older men, and has long gone: it was one of the farcical archaic things we were all going to change. I didn't know then that a new, far more wide-reaching men-only club was being formed by my own contemporaries – who thought they were demolishing the very structures of soul that brought that bar into its defensive being.

The Harmony of Misogyny

Myths make things feel natural. So does harmony. The cat's cradle of ancient and modern myth that goes into misogyny helps men feel securely male. Apart from musical styles and techniques, the really new thing about rock was the teenage psyche. But the really *ancient* template was misogyny. Rock misogyny validates not growing up. It is traditional and comforting; you know where you are with it. Janus-like, it lets you be boy and man, modern and ancient, forward-looking and backward-looking, at once. Under its aegis you can be romantic and tender with women, and let rip all the pop slush you want about needing her, and never letting go. For you are the strong one, you're the hero. In 'The Glory of Love' (1986), the male voice sings 'I'll be your hero ... I'll be the man who will fight for your honour'. He compares himself to 'a knight in shining armour'.²² In love, sex, war, the world, men know the rules and impart them to their baby, their 'little girl'.

Misogyny is as comforting, in fact, as the basic harmonies of traditional blues-rock or country music. Rock is famously built on three chords which act as a cradle, a safety-net under the way rock takes on the world. You can play them angrily; if you are a brilliant musician like Hendrix, you can lunge out from them into wild tonalities; can make your melodies, rhythm, volume and pitch say how against the world you are. But you still depend on the house of harmony to come back to, as a teenage rebel's bedroom is still part of the parental home. And heavy metal's harmonies are the most reactionary and safe of all. The supremacist sexual politics are the best example of both teenage contradictions built into rock culture: replicating the system you say you are against, plus being against what you depend on.

You can turn that contradiction round. Being against what you depend on is also depending on what you are against. In some areas of rock, this contradiction becomes a key condition of maleness. Needing what you belittle becomes denigrating, spitting on and despoiling what you desire.[23]

Hence the weird political paradox, that the most important original music of the century which gave women the vote and empowered them as never before, validated the aggressive, misogynist and supremacist side of male sexuality as no Western music ever had before.

17 Dylan: Creativity, Misogyny and Echo

Staging Maleness, for Echo

Maybe men need misogyny for more than comfort. It seems to have a deep connection with male creativity. For male love poets (though maybe not gay ones), the female Muse is still a real force. Woman is where poems 'come from'. Robert Graves said in *The White Goddess* that the Muse inhabited the different women you love, and had affairs with ever younger women in order to write poems. 'Stealing green leaves to light an alien fire', he called it in a late poem. His daughter said 'He needed them for his poetry. His obsession to keep writing poetry the way he felt was right, was his way of being loyal to himself.' Her mother 'was aware of the importance of his work'.[1]

It is also important, apparently, to control the sounds coming from your female source of inspiration. For your words to be heard, you've got to silence her. 'That's where the violence comes in,' one male poet told me (the only man I know who works out of challenging moments of misogyny in himself). 'To achieve the poem, you've got to silence them.' 'You say it best, when you say nothing at all' runs the 1999 hit (from the film *Notting Hill*) by Ronan Keeting of Boyzone. A cutely wise male boy voice, singing his own words, about how well she says she loves him *when she doesn't talk*? In 'Love Minus Zero/No Limit', Dylan praised the woman he married by saying 'My love, she speaks like silence'. When Marianne Faithfull met him, they were alone, and romance was in the air: what happened? She sat there awestruck and mute; he wrote 'an epic' about her. (Then she told him she was pregnant and about to marry someone else; he tore the poem up and threw her out.)[2]

Wordsworth remembered making owl-calls across the valley as a boy and getting answering echoes back. Seamus Heaney uses that as an image for the way a poet finds his voice:

> My own voice cheered me, and, far more, the mind's
> Internal echo of the imperfect sound.

The poet, says Heaney, 'is drawn into himself even as he speaks himself out; it is this mesmerized attention to the echoes and invitations within that constitutes his poetic confidence'.[3] But remember whom Echo fell in love with, whose voice she echoed. Heaney's 'echoes and invitations' home in on the closeness of creativity to narcissism. Silence and space around the creating man let his own words come back to him more authoritative, more enticing. The arch-narcissist Walt Whitman puts it in wonderfully over-the-top sexual terms. He celebrates 'the smoke of my own breath', the 'echoes, buzz'd whispers, love-root', 'crotch' and 'sound of the belch'd words of my voice'. Echo is the great turn-on: your own voice coming back to you.

Singers often picture their voice as theirs and not-theirs. Placido Domingo feels his is 'both separate from me and dependent on me'.[4] The separateness, a real thing out there in the world as well as in yourself, makes you confident. A real owl (maybe) calls back to Wordsworth; a real woman desires Narcissus. Confidence and delight in your creativity depend on the reality both of the thing outside, and of the thing you make.

Something giving back the sound you make: the Greeks could have done anything with that. Echo was just a word: they could have given it any story, any sex. But they made her a parable of hopeless female desire for a man who loves his own image. Her voice, like his reflection, comes back to him: it is his 'acoustic mirror', as one critic calls the female voice in film.[5] The poet gets pleasure and confidence from her voice. Echo is all voice – his.

Greek myth suggests men's self-image depends on images of

women and their desire for you; male creativity too, apparently, depends on a bit of femaleness somewhere. An Echo, a Muse. Hearing female desire for you, hearing your voice coming back from her. 'I'll be your dream I'll be your wish I'll be your fantasy, I'll be your hope I'll be your love I'll be everything that you need', sing the softly echoey voices (nearly all those words on the key note), from Savage Garden in 'Truly Madly Deeply' (1998).

Echo taps into men's desire to get a sound back from women in, most basically, sex. When Duke Ellington was twelve, he and his friends used to take girls down to the reservoir:

> we'd be in hearing distance; the object was to see who did the greater job as a man. If the girl's reaction was greater, then he was a great fucker, because this chick was hollering and screaming 'Hello Daddy!' 'Oh baby I'm coming,' and all that shit.

This sound, tally of your manhood, was so important some boys cheated:

> We found out some cats were pinching the chicks to make them holler, and one was slipping the chick quarters![6]

But you get it in other forms too. One theory of opera is that it is the 'angel's cry', the cry men want to hear from a woman in sex. In opera as in sex, men are in control. The high notes of the soprano at the aria's emotional climax, are the *jouissance* of a woman with a man – a conductor or director – in charge. Opera's centrepiece is the soprano voice, 'the queen's throat', the 'diva's mouth'. Nearly always produced, as in pop, under male 'direction'.[7]

Or you get that sound in response to your own creativity and display. In a rock concert, female throats ten thousand strong deliver back at you a howl of desire. Sociologists call it 'uncontrolled erotic sobbing'. Marianne Faithfull, watching The Stones at a Bristol concert, put it more dramatically:

> From the first notes of 'I'm A King Bee' an unearthly howl went up from thousands of possessed teenagers. Girls began pulling their hair out, standing on the back of their seats, pupils dilating, shaking uncontrollably. Snake-handling frenzy filled the hall. Clinical Dionysian mass hysteria was breaking out everywhere. Mick effortlessly reached inside them and snapped that twig.[8]

Narcissus and Echo: the pair are a weird parody both of sex and of a creative set-up. The man making an impression, the woman registering it in sound. 'You were at school,' said Eric Clapton,

> and nobody wanted to know you. Then you get into a group and you've got thousands of chicks there. There you are with thousands of girls screaming their heads off at you. Man, it's power ... *phew*![9]

The big twentieth-century boy fantasy: spotlight, fame and screaming girls. But what does misogyny have to do with it?

Up on stage, the star faces not only screaming girls but what he once was: male fans, yelling back at him his former fantasising self. 'When people ask how far I've come in this racket, I always say twelve feet – from the audience to the stage', said David Lee Roth of Van Halen.[10] Heavy metal is about staging maleness for, particularly, those boys. 'It's little to do with women, really,' a male friend of mine keeps telling me. But it is and it isn't. 'The stud-strut of heavy metal', says a distinguished rock critic, 'is a ritual by which men celebrate each other ... The woman is essential as part of the intercourse kit, not as an individual.'[11] Metal stages maleness for men but uses women to do it; that's where the misogyny comes in. It has lots of fun fantasies like decapitating chickens that have little to do with women, but rape is one of its presiding demons. Before a 1970 Led Zeppelin gig at Madison Square Gardens, Steven Tyler of Aerosmith found the stage and nineteen thousand seats empty:

> I walked onto the stage and lay down with my head hanging backward off the edge, overwhelmed with delusions of

rock 'n' roll grandeur, imagining I was roaming the land raping and pillaging, an ambassador for rock. And I said to myself, *Someday a band of mine is gonna fill this fuckin' place*.[12]

Muddy Waters recorded Willie Dixon's seduction song 'You Need Love' (telling a woman she lacks experience and love, and he can help) in 1963. Six years later, Led Zeppelin turned it into 'Whole Lotta Love', a cock-proud slam. 'I'm gonna give you every inch of MAH LURVE,' howls Robert Plant, and roars out the woman's orgasm for her. Any feeling she will have is 'not for her benefit but the price of his admission to alpha-male society'.[13] Her sounds are created by him. They are his achievement.

'*Man*' – and Sixties Illiberalism

From the beginning, the sexuality and freedom of rock 'n' roll were going to mean almost opposite things for the girls and boys who responded to it. For girls, it began with the fun of responding, not making. The freedom on offer for most of them in the pre-Pill, beehive-hair world of the fifties was freedom to leave their parents' hive to clone it with a guy of their own. Teenage daughter, teenage mom, there's hardly a difference: the housework and home environment are the same – as fifties song lyrics like the Chordettes' hit 'A Girl's Work is Never Done' (1956), make clear.[14] Sexuality was passport to a series of conventions called freedom, not a goal in itself.

Hence the importance of girl songs like the Shirelles' 1960 hit, 'Will You Still Love Me Tomorrow?'[15] What will happen if I do have sex? was not a question girl voices had asked in pop before. For girls, rock expressed tensions about sexual, social, and emotional freedom which careers as wives and mothers were not going to resolve. They responded wholesale to the music, they screamed at Elvis and danced. As in other aspects of the lives they were heading into, its unchallengeable maleness was almost invisible. Rock was the male body; of course. Its delights, its dangerousness. This was also the era of *Psycho*, of hinting at untamed forces beneath the skin – of society, of the psyche, of maleness. The girls' role was to be the thrilled audience and echo of male danger.

But things changed very quickly for girls after the Shirelles.

Back, a moment, to 1865, when there were no women competing with men for making a noise, casting a vote, getting jobs or school and university places – and no male songs banging on about keeping girls under your thumb or sneering at any who refused you sex. But by 1965, when possibilities of more freedom for girls were unfolding, young male psyches suddenly needed misogyny as they never had before. 'Man' became word of the decade – and not only because it was cool to sound black. In addition to Muddy Waters's original claim 'I'm a man', The Stones's first (1963) Top Twenty hit was Lennon and McCartney's 'I Wanna Be your Man'. Unlike The Beatles' softer version. Jagger's swaggery delivery underlined the arrogance in 'wanna' – and, course, 'man'. 'Little Red Rooster' and 'Under my Thumb' established the rock ideal of the cock-proud man who can free up repressed women and dominate wild ones.[16] The Stones led (but a hundred groups followed) male sneers at women for being prudish or frigid if they refused sex. 'I know, I know you'll probably squeal and cry', snarls even Hendrix at a reluctant chick in 'Are You Experienced?'

But to who in your measly little world
Are you trying to prove that you're made out of gold?

And *he* was nice to groupies, and did not humiliate them like some.

The Stones set out the grid-lines of rock sexism, a lyric ideology in which (as one sceptical male critic observed) 'a chick's place is not only in the home but between the sheets and a feminist is more fucked up than fucked over and better off plain fucked'.[17] Female subordination with sadistic topping was standard fare: on the Hollywood billboard for *Black and Blue* was a bound, gagged woman with the slogan 'I'm black and blue with the Rolling Stones and I love it'. 'Brown Sugar' eroticized racism. The trader in 'brown sugar' ('Scarred old slaver knows he's doin' alright, he used'ta whip the women just around midnight') tells the girl he's whipping 'I'm going to hurt you till you break'. 'I do occasionally arouse primeval instincts,' Jagger conceded with a shrug, 'but I mean most men can do that. They can't do it to so many. I just happen to be able to do it to several thousand people.'[18] From 'Bitch' to the 'Some Girls' catalogue of 'willing and submissive' American, French, Italian and Chinese girls, the theme is the cock's right to humiliate and crow about it. 'Yesterday's Papers' ('Who wants yesterday's papers, who wants yesterday's girl?') was 'a horrible public humiliation' for Chrissie Shrimpton, Jagger's girlfriend when he met Marianne Faithfull. 'Under My Thumb' ('Under my thumb is a squirming dog who's just had her day') was also about Chrissie. 'When he got her where he wanted her, he didn't want her any more,' said Marianne. Sixties Stones lyrics burn with lust but also contempt. 'Look at that stupid girl,' they hoot. If girls mention *their* feelings, they get told 'Doncha Bother Me No More' or 'Baby Baby Baby You're Out of Time'. And everyone, *everyone*, dancing to the lip-smacking sadism (as one critic calls it) of 'Brown Sugar' would stamp and join in on those four whiplash beats.[19]

Any justification for all this was triumphantly double. First, chicks liked it. Great White break down the door and knock you to the floor ''cause you need it so bad'. The narrator of the sixties novel *Groupie* gets told,

> You want your clothes ripped off and your face punched. You want me to scratch away your feelings because feelings are a drag. Because they interfere with sensations, and deep inside chicks are all sensations. So how about being honest and admitting it?[20]

Secondly, men gotta be free. 'It's good to indulge the beauty of a girl you've never seen before,' said Hendrix, but she's not the last. You see a green coat and purple shoes prancing in the corner so you fall in love in a *second*! You go down on her – anything! But after fifteen minutes you're in another part of the street. Any time, man. It's your life. Freedom's the key word.[21]

Along with the narcissistic romance of the open road which basically meant the right to leave every girl the minute after sex, the main expressions of this male freedom were supremacism and putting women down.

It was all extraordinarily retrogressive and unequal, especially for a culture that said it was progressive. Yet another paradox of the era whose peace and love brought violence into rock: youth was 'liberated' but male rock became atavistically *il*liberal to women. 'Put on the Dead, get on the bed, and spread', was the male command in the peace-love-and-freedom of Haight Ashbury. Liberation meant women liberated to have sex with supremacist men. In one year, the rate of venereal disease in San Francisco went up sixfold.[22]

The paradox was summed up by the Plaster Casters, the Chicago girls who made casts of rock stars' erections. As a rock star tells his British girlfriend in *Groupie*, 'They plate you until you're hard, then thrust it into soft plaster and wait until it sets. It's bastard getting your hairs unstuck.' For a few years the Plaster Casters 'were considered avatars of sexual freedom – and artists, to boot'.[23] Liberated women, free to practise the art of making men hard for ever, showing the world how great male erections are. The freedom rock was about was male. It involved trying to re-make the cage girls thought they were climbing out of, by crimping them into stereotypes (girlfriend, mum) and despising them for it.

Eventually this set women a creative challenge of their own, to write and sing their own 'against'. Some women did try it in the sixties. Grace Slick, Lesley Gore (who sang 'You Don't Own Me' in 1963, though the song was written by two men), above all gutsy, tragic Janis Joplin who shipwrecked herself trying to do what Memphis Minnie did, and behave 'like a man'. Walking out of LA's Sunset Sound Studio in September 1970 with a male crew, she wondered which of them should drive. She looked at all the guys. 'Who's got the biggest balls?' she asked. After a moment she answered herself. 'I do.'[24] But for most sixties girls, the main rock role was fanning flames of male supremacism, being Echo to Narcissus. When they screamed at Mick Jagger, they identified with the antagonism to society, the bid for freedom at the heart of this rampant expression of what society always said was ticket to *their* freedom – male sexuality. But rock was dedicating that antagonism, freedom and sexuality to being against *them*, too. To the right to enjoy them and be rid of them. Freedom was Mick and Keith writing, playing and recording with white-hot creativity till six in the morning with the eyes of the world upon them, or touring with groupies, while Marianne paced the house she shared with Mick, 'alone or with Anita, bored to tears, feeling useless and ornamental'.[25]

It's Not Me, Babe: Dylan's First Girlfriend

Bob Dylan seemed, at first, to have more equal ideas. On *Another Side of Bob Dylan* (1964), 'All I Really Want to Do' weaves a brilliant yes-and-no relationship with Willie Dixon's 'I Just Wanna Make Love to You', recorded by Muddy Waters and the Stones. It ticked off manipulative things Dylan said he did *not* want to do to a girl and ended 'All I really want to do/ is, baby, be friends with you'. But at the end of that album came 'It Ain't Me Babe'. In it Dylan goes through the conventional catalogue of romantic qualities women want from a man – to be always strong, ready to die for her, be a lover for life – and rejects them all. 'Go 'way from my window', he begins, and at the close of each verse intones, 'It ain't me you're looking for, babe.'

I hate this song. I can't really even listen to it, whether he sings it or Johnny Cash. The way they both spit out 'babe' at the end of the line sounds utterly vicious. Maybe it doesn't come over to everyone as misogyny straight up, but it does to me. The girl is free to say similar things back. But if, as the song says, she wants someone to look after her, she's not going to, is she? The point of the sixties take on free sex was that only the man was free. In that cruel-whine voice, Dylan delivers each clause as a triumphant nail, skewering her emotional coffin.

Over the next twenty-five years, Dylan became more supremacist to women, which puts 1964's apparent liberalism in a sourer light. In his Christian phase, he ticks off a girl for not fucking him. God wants Dylan to have what he wants, 'Our Father would not like the way you act'.[26] The Dylan egotism always had a cruel streak. 'It's All Over Now, Baby Blue' is a giant of a song, wonderful, mesmeric; but also the last word in patronizingness, sung to a woman who can't keep up with him, babe.

His first serious girlfriend was also the first person who convinced him he could be what he wanted, a rock star. They went everywhere together; she encouraged and supported him. When he metamorphosed from small-town kid to 'Bob Dylan', he got rid of her. Her name was Echo Helstrom.[27] Bob Dylan was empowered on to his starry creative road by a girl called Echo.

When Creativity Came

Dylan had a huge impact on rock in the sixties. He influenced everyone – Stones, Beatles, Hendrix, the lot. He built a bridge between pop and underground bohemia, the beat poets, the folk movement. He gave rock a newly intellectual focus. Above all, he made it newly creative. He joked about it – in London, according to Marianne Faithfull, he put rolls of waxy British lavatory paper, 'just the right width for song lyrics', in his typewriter – but it was *the* overwhelming Dylan thing.[28]

The hierarchy of modern musical values still comes from the nineteenth century, which put musical creativity and innovation way above reproduction and tradition. We respect the creativity of performers, but we do think composers are somehow higher.[29] Before Dylan and The Beatles, pop singers were lightweight not just because they were pop, but because they were not creative. Behind them was a manager, record company, publishing company. In the late fifties there were two main sources of songs. One was pinching black hits, the other was writers whom the publishing house employed. House writers often worked in twos like Jerry Leiber and Mike Stoller. They were white and Jewish but began by writing for black artists like The Coasters. ('The black and the Jewish communities worked together a lot in old R and B and doo wop,' the singer-songwriter and pop historian Louis Philippe told me. 'It's a very interesting sideline of pop history.') They also wrote hits for Elvis ('Jailhouse Rock', 'Treat Me Nice'), and hundreds for other artists. In the sixties, the house tradition was dominated by Don Kirshner, publisher of Aldon Music. In the Brill Building on Broadway, he got over four hundred hits between 1961 and 1967 from a team of exceptional writers: Carole King and Gerry Goffin, Jeff Barry, Eddie Greenwich. These songs were mainly for male solo singers (teen heart-throbs like Bobbie Vinton) or girl groups like the Shangri Las. There was an almost Marxist division of work: songwriters, arrangers, producers; and singers. In the first rockabilly phase of rock, some men (Buddy Holly, Eddie Cochran) did write their own material. But most early sixties teen idols (with rare exceptions like Neil Sedaka) sang songs other people wrote.

But in country music and blues, the two main genres rock 'n' roll came from, singers (Robert Johnson above all) did write their own songs. Chuck Berry wrote his own words to 'Maybelline'. In 1954, Johnny Cash was crossing and recrossing the country on tour in a fat Plymouth. While his band-mates Luther Perkins and Marshall Grant (the Tennessee Two) kept the engine going, he wrote 'Get Rhythm' on the back seat. The rest of that tour, he wrote 'Give My Love to Rose' and 'Big River': songs which flashed on the radio to teenage Dylan in Hibbing, Minnesota, and were a revelation to him. They seemed 'just words turned into bone'.[30]

Dylan was drawing on all this when he exploded all ideas of rock's inferiority to classical music by singing his own songs.

He and The Beatles turned the pop industry inside out. 'They were writing their songs,' explained Louis Philippe. 'From that moment, things changed completely.' By 1968 it was common practice for big bands to write their own material. But that change was uniquely swift, with no parallel I can think of in music history. Though singing songs other people wrote went on through the sixties – the Brill Building's powerteams, Motown, Phil Spector – by the end of the sixties the ethos that now reigns was firmly in place. To be real in rock, you write your own songs – or say you do. It is so important that journalists can be sued for 'image-damage' if they question whether singers have written their own music.

Even The Beatles, who were so incredibly important themselves in all this, were influenced by Dylan. They met him in August 1964. He turned them on to marijuana, and they 'started writing much grittier lyrics', as the journalist Al Aronowitz, who was at that famous meeting, recalls. (The *quid pro quo*, of course, was that Dylan went electric.) The Beatles took in Dylan's work, depth, and persona along with the hash. 'I started being me about the songs,' said Lennon. 'Not writing them objectively but subjectively.'[31] The Stones began as blues purists. For them, bluesmen like Robert Johnson were a model of creativity as well as sound. But The Beatles and Dylan were the living challenge. More than any other single man, Dylan made rock creative in the eyes of the world. He also helped to broaden its content. Rock musicians found new ideas for songs, wider than conventional love themes, in folk-songs. They began making songs out of personal obsession rather than 'giving people what they want'.[32]

Dylan was the arch-influence. He turned country music into folk, acoustic to electric, 'sincerity' into the urban flamboyance and artifice of rock. In *My Generation*, the 1996 anthology of rock 'n' roll reminiscences by seventy-odd Irish writers and film-makers, Dylan is the beloved common influence. Chris Smith, Secretary of State for the Arts (from the sixties generation) compared him favourably in 1998 to Keats. Dylan is the hero of creative maleness. But to many women's ears, the whiny, insistent masculinity of his voice also carries an edge of supremacism and misogyny. He is brilliant. But it is nearly always men who go on about him. And the sixties he spearheaded was also the moment misogyny got really under way in rock.

Rap Misogyny, White Theatre

In the nineties, that tradition is still strong but its main focus, apart from heavy metal and the so-called parody end of things, is rap. In The Prodigy's title *Smack My Bitch Up* 'Bitch' (especially after 'smack') comes from the rap lexicon. 'Back off, bitch,/just because I'm struggling/Just get on your knees and then start juggling/These motherfuckin' nuts in your mouth', sings Warren G. 'I'll serve your ass like John McEnroe/If your girl steps up, I'll smack the ho', sing House of Pain. 'Guess who's back in the motherfuckin' house/Got a fat dick for your motherfuckin' mouth' sings Snoop Doggy Dog. Perhaps the most provocative misogynist of all to date is 2 Live Crew.

It is as if rap freeze-frames all the misogyny that came into rock in the sixties: has become the corralled repository of rock misogyny. As in blues, this ferocity may be due to relationships specific to black life in America and Britain. It is still easier for black women to get jobs than black men. In Britain, 'The fracture between the black woman and black man is so commonplace some women live their lives in a cloud of fear and loneliness.'[33] You could argue that the misogyny of the genre comes from specific cultural need. But why, then, its white appeal?

White rappers who do their stuff well, like Eminem, have been accepted by the black rap community. But a lot of white uses of rap, like Prodigy's art, comes not from black social reality but white fantasy. Like The Stones flirting with violence, it is designer misogyny, borrowing other people's pain and fury to stage white maleness.

And yet the fantasies it speaks to are clearly real. The largest market for misogynist rap is fourteen-year-old white boys in bedrooms in the American suburbs. Back to Paul Simon's trigger-happy boys, 'dreaming of glory' – i.e. misogynist fantasy – or the vision of rape and pillage that visited Steve Tyler in the empty auditorium at Madison Square Gardens. Why should male teenage fantasies (which rock stars are able to play out) involve nailing women to the floor and peeing on them? Can psychologists – or Greek myth – say?

18 Misogyny on the Hoof

Groupies: Is Misogyny Sexy?

Is it sexy, this misogyny? 'Whole Lotta Love', Jagger's sneers, Snoop Doggy Dog? Why do millions of women who danced to The Stones in the sixties and seventies still adore this music whose message they would not put up with for a minute in real life? When I ask if The Stones were misogynist, their words vary but the formulation is spookily, get-off-the-hookily the same. Yes, but – it doesn't matter. Yes, but – it's irrelevant. Yes, but – it's not conscious. (What?)

They like the music because it is sexy. 'How it hits the hormones', one says. But why is it sexy? Could you take the sexism out and it still be sexy? Or is supremacism coded into the actual musical texture and shape: the power chords, foursquare harmonies and in-out, 4/4, up-down, on-and-on-till-the-climax-comes beat of prime-cut blues-rock as The Stones flung it down on the green English sward in the mid-sixties?

The first essay I know that raised any of this, a 1970 piece (by a man), explained rock's sexist appeal by musical continuity. Coming from traditional music – blues and country music, which themselves harked back to even more traditional African tribal music, and British-cum-Celtic ballads – rock's sexual energy was traditional and sexist, promoting traditional sexist dominance.[1] This argument is not about lyrics, but whether male domination is encoded into specific cadences and harmonic progressions. Thirty years on, the musicological jury is still out on this. Wildly divided, in fact. The avant-garde (mostly feminist) says yes, the old guard no; fascinated observers sit subtly on the fence.[2]

But harmonies apart, there *are* the lyrics; plus, in the auditorium, the radioactive physical presence. Truman Capote called Mick Jagger's act 'about as sexy as a pissing frog', but girls – like those Marianne Faithfull watched in Bristol – have gone hysterical for him in their multi-thousands. At him, not the cadences; though cadences helped.

Is misogyny sexy? The sixties groupies' answer is an enormous 'Yes'. Girls had always mobbed teen idols; Sinatra and Duke Ellington were surrounded by women. Little Richard's band had a great time backstage in the fifties. But it was the sixties (and the Pill) that institutionalized girl worship of male singers into a mass sexual offering. Expensively educated, beautiful girls from Kyoto to Cologne, Honolulu to the Home Counties, turned instantly into anxious, jealous sex-slaves-of-the-moment for thin, spotty boys with guitars.

Groupie (1969) was a fictionalized picture of its female author's sixties adventures. Blow jobs are everywhere. Jealousy and competitiveness regulate groupie protocol and hierarchy: stage-door groupies, suburban groupies, London hopefuls and elderly super-groupies of twenty-two. But the UK is amateur compared to America. There, says a male musician, 'Chicks come up to you after and say, Can I kiss you sir, would you like to ball me sir?' A good CV is essential:

> You usually started small and ended up with the biggest, if you made it. By that time the ones you had when you were small had made it big, so you'd have a few good names to your credit.

It was a career ('to your credit'). And, as Aerosmith's memoirs testify, girls took it very seriously indeed:

> This beautiful girl had been hanging around. I woke up and realized I was being done by this girl and John was doing her from behind. When she was finished, she crawled up – *What now?* – and whispered in my ear, 'Where's the rest of the band?'

Jagger was the summit. One American groupie

> scored with hundreds of rockers but after each would tell her friends, 'He was alright, but no Mick Jagger.' One night in Los Angeles, there he was! Mick Jagger himself! She moved in and bagged him. Next day her friends asked how it went. 'He was alright', she said, 'but he was no Mick Jagger.'[3]

Sixties songs were an unprecedented explosion of male creativity and teenage power. When else in the history of the world had teenagers, or just-post-teenagers, been able to write, perform and have such extraordinary global influence through song? But for these women, achievement was clocking up names 'to your credit'.

Female ambition and originality poured into making it with these male creators:

> Another girl liked to sprinkle glitter over herself. You could always tell someone had been with the Glitter Queen if he came out of a room sparkling.

For women, to link up with the travelling roadshow was to be a handmaiden.[4]

Early seventies Los Angeles had a formidable super-groupie scene at the English Disco. Black-lipsticked groupies like Sable Starr, Lori Lightning and 'Gas Chamber' Nancy treated the word 'groupie' as an honour. 'Lori and Sable introduced themselves as the world's greatest groupies.'[5] On tour in eighties California, Black Flag kept a sexual 'Corn Score' on the van's sun visor. Early in the group's history, one girl called Holly had sex with them all. Ever after, the post-gig goal was 'getting a Holly'. 'I'd find 'em,' said Mugger,

> get 'em in the van and say, Hey, you wanna do one of my friends? Everyone would have a go and the girl would wave her underwear out of the porthole when she was done.

When one Holly had her period, the boys washed together

afterwards in park sprinklers.⁶ In that Tokyo hotel where the LA Guns stayed in the nineties, 'hordes of groupies with five inch spike heels, leather up to the crotch, amazing bras and ultra-flamboyant make-up and hair' waited in the foyer. Remember the woman musician from another band, who saw the 'hundreds of little white notes' taped to the guitarist's door? The guy came in with three or four girls:

> I heard him say, 'You can stay if you lay on the floor. *You* get over there!' One girl asked 'Let me get in bed with you.' He said 'Well you can if you don't move.' I heard him try out a Spinal Tap number on a guitar.⁷

It sounds like a medieval king's bedroom – and it doesn't stop. In Dublin in 1998 after James Brown (age sixty-five) had sung, I watched a crouching band-member gather up the 'take me' notes like flowers from a hundred waving hands in the front row. A sure-fire path to admittance, I was told, is to come to the gig in wet T-shirt and no bra, and sit on the shoulders of someone tall. Most men, say women rock stars, accept as a matter of course. Shirley Manson is married, and has a good working relationship with the men in her band. When girls in 1999 offer themselves to them,

> I want to scream at them, 'What the fuck are you doing? He's dipped in every yolk for the past year.'

'Any guy in any band will take any girl who offers herself', says Chrissie Hynde. 'Doesn't matter if she's a farmyard animal.'⁸

On the men's part, it is unquestioning acceptance. Some keep a score card. (Fifty million is attributed to Jagger.) You have to fend them off. Before the last gig of Led Zeppelin's 1973 American tour, their manager sat in the suite refusing phone offers:

> No, tell her we don' want any fuckin' chicks tonight no matter how fuckin' well weird they are... No, we don'

have any fuckin' back passes for a chick with a fuckin' trick pussy ... The boys are so fucked they're about to drop.[9]

There's no interest, of course, in what the girls feel or think. John Cale of Velvet Underground said blankly to a colleague in the eighties,

> When you're playing Northern California they come up to you out of the past and say 'Remember that blow job I gave you in 'Frisco in '67?' What are you supposed to say? What do they want?[10]

When one rock journalist joined Van Halen in Detroit, the band was about to do a radio interview. David Lee Roth and Alex Van Halen picked two girls from the fans at the door and carted them off to the radio booth. 'Welcome to the top,' said Roth, cupping their bottoms. 'You've finally hit the big time.' The bands' entourage got the girls to bare their breasts, and launched into the interview. Roth stood one girl against the window, her back to the fans below, and sang 'Everybody Wants Some' while hoisting her skirt above her waist and running his hand up and down her leg. Later on, the journalist was about to interview Alex himself, when Roth burst into the room with a blonde. He asked them to clear out, saw the tape-recorder and changed his mind. 'We'll give you an in-*depth* perspective of Van Halen.' He ordered the girl, 'Tell him what you think of us'. When she didn't understand, Alex laughed; Roth stared at the woman he was about to make love to in disgust. 'Tell the tape recorder what you think of us,' he repeated. 'C'mon babe, don't waste the man's time.' The girl took the mike nervously and said she enjoyed Van Halen's show very much because they were rock and roll and made you want to groove. And also, she said, smiling at Alex and Roth, 'every *one* of the guys in this band knows how to get *down* – that's for *god*damn sure.' At the end of her speech, Alex Van Halen laughed and asked 'Can you *believe* the mentality of some of these girls?'[11]

To Van Halen, observes this journalist, as to many male

musicians, servile women are 'a matter of endless fascination'. After seeing enough naked women and hearing enough abasing morning-after anecdotes for a whole article on sexism and porn-rock, he told Roth the group did not hold women in high regard. Roth looked surprised. 'What do you mean? I like women *very* much.' He said they did not *force* women to do anything, or sing about that. 'I'm in this job to exercise my sexual fantasies. When I'm onstage, it's like doing it with twenty thousand of your closest friends.'[12] And he was the frontman for the band whose 1991 album *Unlawful Carnal Knowledge* was an international bestseller.

But some men, like those bands with Jarboe, want to humiliate and hurt. In the novel *Groupie* the boyfriend wants the girl hero to squirm in jealousy:

> 'That hurt, didn't it?' 'Yes,' I said. 'I know, because I could feel my words hitting you, pow, pow, pow, crashing into you like great rocks of pain... Aren't you crying yet? You should be by now...' Grant launched into this thing about his power scene.[13]

Offering yourself to men who despise and humiliate you ('can you believe their mentality?'), who sing about beating up women or killing them after sex, does slightly hint that women find misogyny sexy. Created as one of the most male arts of all time, as chauvinist as domestic law in ancient Athens, the epitome of Greek heroic maleness expressed in technical and sexual prowess, rock flares forth the certainty that creativity is man's work and women will always worship at the shrine of what archaeology calls the phallus and Tokyo groupies The Rock God. And there are no male groupies. 'I've never been approached and I've never met a female rock star who has,' said Chrissie Hynde. 'They'd be terrified of being turned down.' The industry and the rock god cliché *depends* on the response of 'the hallowed teen gurl crowd that can turn you into millionaires'.[14] They are the kingmakers, they buy, they make everyone's reputation.

It is an oddly mythic balance of power. Classic rock sexual

politics means 'powerful sexy men and powerless girls on their knees sucking off the stage-hand for a glimpse of God', as a male fan of Courtney Love put it. The blow-job – a silenced woman on her knees pleasing a man ('plating', the commonest word in *Groupie*) – is the classic service.[15] But though that girl on her knees is silent, she is not, as Monica Lewinsky demonstrated, entirely powerless. She is keeping supremacism on the road. It couldn't live without her. Men can be 'rock stars' *because* girls tape 'little folded notes' to their door and come forward to be groupies. This male industry runs on girl-response, the politics of Narcissus and Echo. An Echo who gets off, apparently, on misogyny.

Exclusion: Women DJs, Journalists, Managers

If women want other sorts of power in rock, they face a few more worries than *Groupie*'s main worry – whether sperm is fattening or not. Women working in the industry suggest that the ancient male feeling that women do not belong in Eden, is alive and well out there. Men who do not exclude women, or do it genuinely unconsciously (charmingly, I'm sure), may not realize its force.

The pop industry is fairy-tale huge, technical, handles unbelievable amounts of money and, in the words of one man high up in it, 'is a pretty boysy world'. In one eighties study, out of 1,019 pop managers, two were women.[16] These statistics continued when the more low-key, casually smart nineties manager came in: the slightly older contemporary of his artists, calculating their careers and images over five years. Nigel Martin-Smith, who masterminded Take That. Tom Watkins (Pet Shop Boys, Bros, East 17), Marcus Russell (Oasis). Simon Fuller (Annie Lennox, and the Spice Girls when they were making their name). All men – yet being a manager requires qualities people generally think women are good at, like taking care of artists, their clothes, feelings, how they present themselves: skills managers do not need in industries, where women *are* in top management.

Things are changing. In 1999, the heads of 'International', 'Creative', and 'Special Projects' in Virgin Records were women, and there were two in that holy of holies A and R ('Artist and Repertoire') which signs the new talent. The Spice Girls did eventually go to a woman manager, but only 3 per cent of Britain's really senior managers anywhere are women, and rock has not yet contributed at all to that statistic.[17]

Another way of being in charge, an increasingly high-profile way, is choosing, playing and introducing records for radio and live dance. The DJ and MC (Disc Jockey, Mike Controller) are rising steeply in the glamour stakes. Fourteen-year-old boys once dreamed of being on stage with a guitar. Now they dream of MC-ing, 'scratching' and 'mixing' records, talking over them. 'I am a DJ, I am what I play', sang David Bowie. 'I've got believers believing me.' They have immense power over the records' popularity and fate, and over their audiences. See Cleveland's song 'Last Night a DJ Saved My Life'. The girl is 'saved from a broken heart'. He proclaims that mixing is everything: DJs are omnipotent. One musician, playing in an all-women band in a London club, watched a male DJ bait the feminist audience there for her own band, and ruin their evening by playing the most sexist lyrics he could find.

All this power is a firmly male preserve. There are very few female MCs in London at present. In 1998 some women tried to break the male DJ hold in clubs with a collective called 'London's Most Wanted'. 'You've got to have the confidence to try,' Emma Feline said,

> though you know there are people absolutely *willing* you to mess up that first mix. Lots of people still think women are for dancing half-naked on the podium and little else. There is too much sexism in our industry. We aim to change that.

'The top people in the industry are all men,' said Donna Dee. 'That can't be right.' Women DJs find male promoters laugh in their faces, male bouncers in clubs hide their record boxes, male organizers hire them with casting-couch expectations.[18]

Then there is journalism. Rock criticism began in the mid-sixties. People say it was Dylan who created a need for commentary which would get to grips with rock's new depths, but it was not only Dylan. There were other factors at work. Rock culture and youth culture were changing everything: how you talked, how you ate, how you dressed, relationships across generations and among the young; politics, foreign policy, racial policy. Culture criticism was born to cope with all that. New magazines ran rock essays by writers like Greil Marcus and Lester Bangs.[19] But they – and the great cultural commentators (Hunter Thompson, Tom Wolfe) – were all male, except the brilliant Joan Didion.

That was the sixties; in the nineties, in Britain anyway, most rock journalists, editors and publishers are still men. 'We try and use more women,' *Mojo* told me, 'but they're hard to find.' There are four daily national broadsheets: only one has a woman rock critic. A 'Writing Rock' panel I went to at 1998 Cheltenham Literary Festival's 'Rock 'n' Roll Day' was four men, appointed by a man. Comments from the floor suggested that women felt excluded from reading even the best rock magazines. (By what? Tone, format, coverage? It wasn't clear – but the feeling was.) Many women journalists say they feel rock journalism is a male network. They report male editors criticizing women who get off with male rock stars, congratulating men who have sex with female stars.[20] They also have difficulties with male musicians. In the seventies, the Stranglers treated journalists as groupies:

> We were drawing lots on who was going to screw this female column writer and someone said, 'But it'd be like chucking a sausage up the Mersey Tunnel.'[21]

More recently, one woman was ticked off by her male editor for ending an interview with a star who told her to do the interview sitting on his knee and said she must be having her period when she refused.[22]

As for how you write up women's rock: a 1995 article by a man said there were enough books on gender in rock ('enough' was five) and 'women in rock' was no longer an issue.[23] Yet when I talked to Shirley Manson of Garbage in 1997, she said,

> There's this huge fuss about women in rock but I don't feel anything has changed. I think it's just the flavour of the month. The whole industry is run by men. Until that changes – well, how *can* you change an attitude and an atmosphere? It's nonsense.

She said she admired women journalists who interviewed her, but

> a lot of male journalists I've come across can't write. It amazes me how they've gone on for so long. Very few are accomplished writers. Though to be fair, more men interview you, so you see more flaws in male ability.

Lynn Breedlove, a member of a Californian lesbian band, says,

> we're always being viewed through the eyes of male rock journalists writing for a male audience. Not all are getting the idea. A woman at the *Voice*, Carol Cooper, wrote a great review putting us in the context of traditional rock 'n' roll. I thought it was really well done, but that's a rare article.[24]

Male journalists cannot realize how much radical rethinking lies behind strong, successful, original work by women in any genre whose monuments, and main role models, are aggressively male. Rethinking not just about form, style and content, but about where you start, the relation your voice will have to the male tradition, *and* what that tradition says (and even more, what it implies) about everything you are – namely, a woman, the object of male song. Like Eurydice. Women poets have the same problem but rock singer-songwriters like P. J. Harvey have it a million times tougher. 'I've been asked endlessly about being a female in a man's world blah blah blah and it's tedious,' said

Chrissie Hynde, one of the main role models herself for women guitarists of the eighties.[25]

Institutions and expectations are shifting, but rock is still, self-confessedly, a boysy place. And 'boys' do not realize how something that feels to them ordinary and innocent becomes misogynist exclusion when you're on the receiving end.

Unlike poetry, rock is a blatant staging of maleness. (Poetry does it more hiddenly.) For five decades, before most women now in rock were born, rock has been singing variations on 'I'm a Man'. If you are not a man, you have to put hard thought and imagination, your own self and life, into making something new. The project is complicated and personal. It must be easy to think people will not understand if you explain. Women journalists expect male editors to think male readers will not want to know.

'Breasts Are a Big Problem': Guitars Again

Then there's performance.

You cannot divide playing from singing and writing; most people do at least two of the three. But each has its own problems, and it is women playing guitar that calls out the most direct misogyny. The guitar is the magic badge of male rock. Problems of how to hold this instrument, which men treat as an extension of their own bodies, sum up problems women have of finding their own position in man-made tradition.

A guitar is most easily played at chest or waist level, where your fingers fall naturally on the strings. That is where jazz and classical guitarists hold it. Rock guitarists hold it at cock level and have to adapt the fingering to suit. The strap began getting longer when players like T-Bone Walker played guitar behind their head or with their teeth, and longer still as the guitar hero evolved. Eric Clapton took it down, Hendrix took it further. So if you're a woman, what do you do? You play best higher. You can record like that; but you feel it looks wrong on stage, because of male tradition. But if *you* hold it crotch-level, you are imitating men, and that's not what you want. You want to find your own stance. Then there's breasts. Depending on the guitar (some women modify guitars to fit) it can be painful or embarrassing. One breast squashed, the other hanging over the curve...[26] In the end, you have to ignore both the physical problems and the symbolism. 'Over the past five years,' Paul Trynka told me in 1998,

> women have stopped worrying and just done it the way they felt. That's a change. They've worried less about imagery, just gone out and done it.

Even more importantly, women have changed how they use the right hand. Rock style is 'everything on a down stroke'. Up to the seventies, most women used an up-and-down folk-stroke. This changed in the eighties, said Paul:

> More women play the guitar rock style now. This affects the music profoundly: it becomes really precise, less loose: more urgent, more aggressive. One could see the change. Early Elastica played folk-stroke; it would be loose and floppy. You'd see them a year later, playing guitar in a totally different way, more punk as much as anything; and that's common now.

There are now a lot of well-known individual players, though they tend to play bass rather than lead. Jennifer Batten, a studio musician who teaches at MIT and plays electric guitar for Michael Jackson among others, is enormously prized. Chrissie Hynde, a trailblazing woman guitarist and singer from the seventies, says 'There was something about the electric guitar. It was the violin of our generation. The sound of a chord to me was *everything*.' Shirley Manson, for whom Chrissie was a vital role model, says 'Chrissie can play the guitar cooler than any woman on earth'.[27] Yet guitar magazines think men, almost exclusively. August 1996 *Guitar* had eighty pictures of men playing, two of women, and one a nearly naked, worried-looking babe in an ad for guitar straps, captioned 'Don't Drop That Guitar'. A 1996 issue of *Guitar School* had seven articles on players. The only piece on a woman (Sinead Lohan) was headlined 'I Can Play, Really'. The message 'women can't play, especially not electric' flares out even in ads, or pieces on professionals. 'As a woman player, you'd think she'd go for a dainty acoustic but no, her current instrument is a black Godin Acousticaster.'[28] Boys' colour, too.

Women's Bands: Punk – and Lynn Breedlove's Black Cock

These days, of course, there are women's rock groups everywhere. Punk changed everything. Two of the great seventies inspirations, Patti Smith and Chrissie Hynde, flowered in it. Smith evolved from the New York art rock scene. Her first album, *Horses*, came out in 1975. By 1977 she was hailed in the US along with the Ramones, The Clash and the Sex Pistols as the cream of punk,[29] and inspired many women into punk bands. Chrissie Hynde came to London in 1977 when there were many groundbreaking women bands and people 'just took the music for what it was'. With its DIY, anyone-can-do-it ethos, punk offered women opportunities just to get on with it.

Role models were vital, said Paul Trynka:

> When you start playing you don't just think, 'I've got these feelings to express and this instrument will do it.' You find somebody and want to copy them. They're so important to you, you want to be like them. You get to the point where you can copy them adequately; then you think, 'Oh I want to do *this*, as well.'

Late seventies women's bands provided models for eighties women. Chrissie Hynde was a key inspiration for Kristin Hersh, singer-songwriter-guitarist who formed the Throwing Muses with Tanya Donelly in 1986, and challenged female stereotypes on her first solo album, *Hips and Makers* (1994), with lines like 'Oh no you don't put me in that box' from 'Houdini Blues'. 'Chrissie was so jumpy and screechy ... She made an incredible mark. She's a landmark all by herself.'[30]

Punk's irony and anger helped women players: it attacked conventional sexuality as it attacked everything. Women shed stereotypes like snowflakes. Punk 'turned every yes into a no'. There were songs about jobs, class, race, cigarettes, murderers, traffic-lights, impotence (ATV's 'Love Lies Limp') and masturbation (The Buzzcocks' 'Orgasm Addict'). Women's bands like the Raincoats and Slits tore into pop culture's gender clichés. In 'Ping Pong Affair', the Slits' singer ditches evenings with her boyfriend for nights of smoking and masturbating. When Vox Pop played in Los Angeles, a woman strode naked on stage, pulled a Tampax out of her and hurled it into the crowd. 'Grown men, skinheads, turned white and ran away.' Forget romantic role-play: punk wanted other dealings with desire. The one thing you could not write was a love song.[31] Twenty-five years after 'Gary Gilmore's Eyes', TV Smith has a flourishing solo career but still, he told me, 'I've never written a love song'.

In Britain, bands like the Slits produced figures like Naomi Cherry, who kicked off a whole new musical direction to women's rock. So did American heavy bands like Pixies, Throwing Muses, Hole, or Kim Gordon playing bass guitar in Sonic Youth (where bass was a lead instrument). They all offered strong, successful models, said Paul Trynka, and a lot of current female performing comes from there. 'Girls saw women playing guitars, looking cool while being aggressive, and thought "I can do that."'

Yet punk rocked with a double tongue over misogyny. When I asked Gaye Advert if punk made things different for women, her response was pretty cautious. 'Ye-es,' she said, 'in the same way as it did for everybody.' Women punk musicians like Siouxsie Sioux, or Poly Styrene and the X-Ray Spex were very influential at the time and long after. 'Siouxsie made me feel things were possible,' Shirley Manson told me in 1997. But Malcolm McClaren said 'Punks are not girls'. Punk grew out of sixties garage bands, whose songs aggressively targeted women, and punk's 'we hate everyone' included feminism. As in the Stranglers, and their infamous misogyny.

In America, Tanya Donelly (who formed the grunge girl group The Breeders and the mixed-sex Belly, as well as Throwing Muses) thinks it was Riot Grrrl consciousness, not punk, which made girls pick up guitars. 'Punk pretty much excluded women,' she said. 'Punk was very white, and boy-oriented. It's taken a while to change that.'[32]

The seventies fractured rock into many very different paths and this too worked to the advantage of women guitarists. The woman singer-songwriter, the folk-rock singer with an acoustic, flourished. So did women's punk and heavy rock. Having listened to Black Sabbath and Led Zeppelin as a teenager, Joan Jett pioneered American women's heavy rock in the late seventies. From 'I Love Rock 'n' Roll' (1980), her women's group the Runaways (begun in 1975) had huge hits through the eighties.[33]

Punk had a lively afterlife in nineties American women's rock, thanks to figures like Kim Gordon, Kristin Hersh and Courtney Love. The San Francisco lesbian punk band Tribe 8 shocks audiences by the way it mocked cock rock. The singer Lynn Breedlove peels off her top, gets men in the audience to kneel and suck her large black rubber penis, then cuts it off. This began just with the sucking:

> Everybody was fighting over who was going to be the most punk rock, who was going to suck my dick. They went O my God it's so horrible, it's so punk rock, it's awe-inspiring. Mayoral races in Bloomington Indiana have revolved round the fact that people have sucked my dick. Some think it's the most outlaw and punk thing possible. But a lot of people think it's great.

She introduces her song 'Radar Love' by saying 'Rock on with your cock on... dress for success, wear a white penis':

> I whip my dick out in 'Radar Love' and masturbate, and the group are wanking the necks of their guitars, *'wank, wank'*... We're spoofing men, the narcissistic aspect of rock 'n' roll, how the focus is on the penis all the time.

The first time she cut it off, Lynn just happened to have a knife on her. With the audience excitedly screeching after a lot of sucking, 'I was going like "Yeah, then I'll whack it off!" To myself I was like "My ten-dollar penis! What am I going to do? I'll have to get another one."' These days, the San Francisco sex store Good Vibrations gives them rubber cocks free.[34] Her cock satirizes cock rock, of course. It is the ultimate shock. But it also makes the simple statement that playing rock is wearing a cock.

Many more American independent bands (like Babes in Toyland, L7, Bikini Kill) offered role models for eighties women rockers. There are many underground women's bands in Britain too, including feminist ones who set up their own record label, like Stroppy Cow. 'There is a whole music world', said one woman guitarist, 'beyond *Top of the Pops*'. At this less talked-about, grass-roots level, women face obstacles which men's bands do not. They see the misogyny of male audiences and technicians day to day. Working conditions, especially lavatories and dressing rooms, are geared to men – young men, who do not care what a toilet looks or smells like. Organizers and male bands resent women asking for anything different. (It just shows women can't play.) Audiences throw things. They throw them at male bands too, but they do not also yell 'Show us yer tits' and 'She can't play'. Promoters, engineers, technicians and DJs do not hassle them with sexist obstruction. Many boy-bands feel girl hangers-on threaten their male bonding in the studio and on the road; they also resent women musicians.[35] In Manchester in the early nineties, Liz Phair was on with a male band, 'about thirty-five of them backstage, all hostile as shit'. They gave her 'really ugly stuff, like do I pay my band-mates with sex?' Apart from hostility, there is show-off sexism. Men admire a woman's guitar, then play very fast on it themselves all over the neck. Technology is another male preserve. Women who do not manage their own electrics find male PAs leaving amp levels at a mark which suits the male band, or changing the balance of their instruments without asking. Women who do, find technicians refusing to make room for them at the control desk.[36]

But the eye of this sexist storm is instruments. Drums sometimes, but mostly guitar. You don't change gender stereotypes – threatening misogynist defences *en route* – by singing, but by playing.[37] When Gaye Advert played bass in the seventies, her *look* was for a while the most copied anywhere. Glossy black hair, big dark eyes: girls wanted to look like her, magazines put her on the cover. But what she was *doing* was playing guitar. Gaye was trailblazing for other women, said TV Smith,

> and she got criticized in a way men didn't. She was just as competent as the others, but was always singled out. You'd get a guy criticizing her for putting weight on, saying 'She's been eating cream buns', saying she couldn't play – they didn't say that about the others. 'Nice-looking but can't play', they'd say.

'Or they'd say I could play,' said Gaye, 'but sounded surprised about it.' Did she go home in tears? 'No,' she said. 'Wanted to thump them. It was just quite nice when it stopped, really.' She cared about the music and the sound, but hated the hassle. She is now, twenty-five years on, a successful manager in Social Services.

Women guitarists get mocked by women ('A girl in a dress with a guitar looks weird, like a dog riding a bicycle,' said the columnist Julie Birchill) and others who you might think would be on their side. That blues historian who nearly called his woman guitarist chapter 'chicks with picks' said the phrase would have fitted

> the self-conscious stance occasionally taken by younger women guitarists. They face a problem, that blues rhythm is equated with male strut. Some members of their mostly male audience are never going to get over the fact that those are *girls* up there, walking that walk (often in short skirts

and spike heels, no less). Sometimes I think these women guitarists have never gotten over it themselves.[38]

How does this guy, so nuanced, so informed about male black–white relations in blues history, react to women of his own generation with guitars? They have not gotten over their problem – of being women, no less.

Performing on guitar, the core act of rock, is whipping out your cock. Which is why Tribe 8 whip it off. The male response to women guitarists, apparently, is misogyny in action. The electric guitar was made to proclaim male supremacy. As penis gun, it is aimed at women. Women 'can't play' because they belong on the target end.

19 Cross-dressing, Castrati, Camp

Impersonation, Again

Rock 'n' roll began in impersonation, and so it went happily on. Boys impersonating men, middle-class impersonating working-class, British impersonating American, white fantasy (shaped by Greek myth) plundering heroic 'faces' in Jim Morrison's 'ancient gallery' but masking itself in black maleness. Always one lot of people imitating the voice of another, in a tradition so conscious of masquerade that singing someone else's songs is singing 'covers': a voice, a sexuality, freedom and feelings that are not yours. Part of rock's fun is 'tension between reality and fakery'.[1]

But part of the anguish it addresses – the '4 REAL' issue brought out in Richey Edwards' self-mutilation – belongs here too: in rock's own staginess, its gift of fantasy. Rock's yen for authenticity, the way it equates identity and power with style, its scorching contempt for the wrong music, clothes, trainers, or hairstyle, depends on investing *musical* style in a very specific (but constantly changing) fantasy ideology.

Musical style has always been muddled up with ideology. Style changes have been ferociously attacked ever since Euripides gave a single sung syllable more than one note and late-fifth-century Athenian purists tore into him as decadent. Stravinsky's *Rite of Spring* met furious catcalls and missiles at its first performance. But music never carried such fierce ideology as when specific chords, textures and tempi got to bear the urgent weight of teenage longing to show yourself male.

Music is like fantasy, made up. Rock music is sexual fantasy's winged chariot. ('I'm in this game to exercise my sexual fantasies,' says David Lee Roth.) Yet this fantasy *means*, to some people, almost too much. In no other society ever has music been the currency of such particular collective sexual fantasy. If this is fantasy, are *you* fake for resting your identity on it? Are the feelings you invest in it true? The gun tragedies in Colorado and elsewhere, the listening-to-heavy-metal suicides, suggest that for some fans the disparateness between fantasy and reality is quite literally unbearable.

To cope with its own artificiality, to use it and test it, rock music drew on the place where professional impersonation began: the European theatrical tradition with its teasing joy in the deliberate suspension of disbelief, the mystery and glamour of a made-up world. And a big part of it is the sexiest impersonation of the lot: men cross-dressing as women.

America and Britain have different traditions of impersonation. America has blackface. Britain has cross-dressing. Boy actors played women on the Elizabethan stage, and Shakespeare had a great time cross-dressing the cross-dressers. Rosalind, Viola and Helena in *All's Well* were played by boy actors; when they disguise themselves, they are boys impersonating women impersonating men. The film *Shakespeare in Love* turned that inside out: the stagestruck heroine dresses as a boy in order to act. When she plays Juliet in her own clothes, Queen Elizabeth (herself well-schooled in playing a man's part) averts scandal by pretending Juliet's femininity is a brilliant illusion. The film underlines the sixteenth-century morality behind this, which forbade the stage to women, but cross-dressing goes back way beyond English sensibilities and specific local moralities. Impersonating women on stage began with the Western stage itself, in the fifth century BC.

The first woman's role we know is the Persian Queen in Aeschylus's tragedy *The Persians*, the earliest surviving drama (472 BC). That, and the thousands of passionate female parts which came after (Clytemnestra, Medea, Antigone, Phaedra and the rest) were sung by masked male actors. Not because it was immoral to have women on stage, but because art was important, and male.

Cross-dressing goes back beyond even theatre. Achilles and Hercules, the two supremely physical heroes of Greek myth, both had cross-dressing episodes. Hercules was forced to be a slave of Queen Omphale. Achilles' mother dressed him as a girl to save his life, to avoid the draft for Troy. His cover was blown when Ulysses turned up disguised as a pedlar selling ribbons, brooches and a sword – which Achilles seized. Historically, there was cross-dressing in Greek cults, too: especially cults of Venus. Men wore women's dresses and pretended to be in labour, women wore men's dress, armour or beards.[2]

Cross-dressing is ancient and sexy. When male rock stars borrow intensities and invitation from female illusion, some antique theatrical power is at work: and it began right at the start of rock 'n' roll. Though it began male, it kept at least one foot in the feminine (as it were) camp. Little Richard dressed his band, the Upsetters, in fancy gender-bending frills in the fifties. They found this had amazing pulling-power with girls, who threw clouds of knickers at the stage. 'We'd be playing and dodging panties,' said the drummer. 'When they landed on my cymbals I'd pick 'em up with a drumstick and wave 'em in the air.' Little Richard foreshadowed everything: Elvis oozing into gold lamé and mascara in the late sixties; the cross-dressing of Alice Cooper, Boy George and the New York Dolls in the early seventies; the high heels and face paint of heavy-metal Kiss; Iggy Pop, who cross-dressed (as he rolled on broken glass and waved his equine cock about) just to see where it took him. Queen was formed in 1970 ('*ever* so regal', said Freddie Mercury), the year glam rock began.[3]

On the black side of Little Richard's legacy, Michael Jackson reshaped his face with plastic surgery to as near a white girl's as possible. Prince, 'a godlike hermaphrodite, like Presley, like Jagger', cross-dressed like seraphim, and used glam tradition to the hilt. He understood trangression like no one else: the central tease of his *Controversy* is 'Am I black or white? Am I straight or gay?' His tarty, nebulously ringletted star-child image got girls into bed by pretending he was one of them.[4]

Men can cross-dress in voice as well as body can cross-dress, too. Black singers never needed to emphasize their maleness by staying in lower registers: Robert Johnson goes as high as a mezzo. On Prince's album *Sign o' the Times* (1987), vocals in four songs are attributed to 'Camille': Prince's own voice, electronically tampered with, androgynized. His biographer calls 'If I Were Your Girlfriend' (where Prince imagines being part of the girlie intimacy his lover has with women) 'a landmark in Prince's quest to wriggle out of the gender straitjacket'. No coincidence that Sinead O'Connor, Cyndi Lauper and Sheena Easton sang Prince songs so successfully. Part of his musical project was to 'hey, come inside of you, girls' every possible way, including their feelings and voice.[5] He distanced himself from norms of masculinity with hair-dos, clothes, falsetto, creating disguises within a disguise for an elusive pop identity matched by his name-changes from 'Prince' to 'The-Artist-Formerly-Known-As' and then a hieroglyph of male and female symbols, which the disrespectful media dubbed 'Squiggle'.

Ever since Jagger, that sexual butterfly in gauzy scarves, British rockers have been famous for cross-dressing. The Stones wore drag in the promotion film of 'Have You Seen Your Mother, Baby, Standing in the Shadows?' They were acting female, not playing gay, though their velvets and eyeliner created a gay aura, a London mode of flirting with female looks which sometimes shocked Americans. 'No men wore make-up in America, apart from drag queens,' says Tony Visconti. 'After a few days I realized this wasn't Kansas any more.' Blurring sexual roles was part of the creative mix of the time.[6] Glam upped the ante in the early seventies. Everyone was into theatricality; everyone suddenly thought they were bisexual. Oxford undergraduates went to tutorials with glitter on their eyes and pearls in their ears. As for voice: in the late seventies the Bee Gees, once soaring Australian tenors, were reinvented as blue-eyed disco stars singing 'Saturday Night Fever' in falsetto.

Rock mines sexual energy of all kinds. But androgyny, so essential to camp, has a special charge. 'Mick was a flirt, a tart,' says Marianne Faithfull. 'His androgynous quality gave it an edge.' Jagger himself said, 'What I do is a sexual thing. I dance, and all dancing is a replacement for sex. What really upsets people is that I'm a man not a woman. What I do is much the same as a girl's striptease dance.'[7]

Androgyny and cross-dressing do not do away with misogyny. Jagger's misogyny flourished alongside his floaty scarves. The homo-erotic sub-theme to his relationship with Keith, says Marianne Faithfull, engendered a collective misogyny.[8] But women could use what men began. The androgynous, made-up role was tailor-made for them. They were the ones it imitated. Patti Smith's hero was the male poet Rimbaud; she was the close friend of Mapplethorpe and onstage had 'her own version of the androgyny that gave Jagger such power'. When she sang Van Morrison's 'Gloria', full of male fantasies about being seduced by a temptress, she rewrote the notion of a man singing in a female voice. Eighties women parodied male camp further. In 'I Need a Man' (1987), Annie Lennox impersonated a man impersonating women, parodying Jagger's caricatures of bluesmen *and* of women. The lesbian singer k.d. lang parodied men in drag with androgynous intimations of her own gayness: on a nineties *Vanity Fair* cover, she wore a moustache while barbering a male-clad Cindy Crawford. When Madonna in 'Vogue' (1990) copied black drag queens in their 'voguing' cult (documented by the 1987 film *Paris is Burning*), she was the ultimate female impersonator.[9]

Quest – and Made-up Women

A woman pretending to be a man pretending to be a woman, a boy pretending to be a woman pretending to be a man: Shakespeare used all those double-drag camp ambiguities for Viola in *Twelfth Night*. But he used something else as well. Most male plots in which a woman dresses as a man turn on a quest. Quest is traditionally a male thing. In most male stories, women go on a quest dressed as men, and the result is getting hitched to a man. In the English ballad 'Polly Oliver', Polly enlists as a soldier to 'follow her love'. She nurses his wounds, the doctor praises her, she breaks down and reveals herself; then 'the captain took joyfully his pretty soldier bride'. Much the same emotional scenario as Beethoven's *Fidelio* and *All's Well That Ends Well*. Female cross-dressing means woman's quest. She heals and saves him, reveals her womanhood; then the union. (Well, re-union, in *Fidelio*.)

Not at all what Lennox and Madonna had in mind. Their point was parody. They were homing in on the way that women themselves are fictions. Women have always had to impersonate men's *idea* of women, the way men have written them into fiction, song and dream. Greek tragedy invented 'woman' as dramatic fiction, making 'her' voice and feeling central to Western theatre. With a 'female' chorus, the whole theatre seethed with 'women' written and acted by men. Character, mask, persona: all those theatrical concepts were façades, invented by men using an idea of femaleness, its made-upness. *Charakter* meant the 'stamp' on a coin which told you where it came from. It was first heard on the stage in Aeschylus's play *Suppliant Women*: Greek women born abroad come back to Greece, and the *charakter* of their dress says they are foreign. This is the first talk of dramatic 'character'.[10] *Persona*, a female word, was Latin for dramatic 'role' because it originally meant 'mask' – which the voice 'sounds' (from *sonare*, 'to sound') 'through' (*per*). Like actors, women are 'made up'. They play a part in order to please. *Mascara* means 'mask'. A woman is a perfect dramatic role, a voice (like Echo) that comes through an opening in a made-up façade. And the theatre's god was the most androgynous god of all. 'Your hair is like a woman's,' says the brittly macho King Pentheus in the *Bacchae*, to the effeminate Stranger he thinks is Dionysus' priest but is really Dionysus himself in disguise. The god replies by getting Pentheus to dress as a woman and worry if his hemline is 'straight', before he destroys him.

Remember Venus' veil, source of all desire: how Cranach painted it as the same cloth as Eros's blindfold? Women cover up their inside with veils, mascara, white samite, or foundation from the ground floor of Harvey Nichols. It makes them look like goddesses. But their attraction, which makes love blind, is made up. 'She fakes, just like a woman,' sang Dylan. According to Marianne Faithfull, he wrote that song for the gay poet Allen Ginsberg, so it has a double charge of sexual impersonation.[11] Women fake; but the blueprint to which they fake is drawn (just as plastic surgery today is done) by men. Just as Billie Holiday was asked to black up to impersonate white ideas of black – 'I had to be darkened down so the show could go on in dynamic-assed Detroit,' she says[12] – so women have to impersonate (or anyway, they get on better in a man's world if they do) men's ideas of women.

I Am a Cliché: Impersonating Women's Voice

The history of women's *voice* on the Western stage gives another dimension to the male ideas of a dramatic link between women and artifice.

Greek tragedy created women's voice as male ventriloquy; opera, reinventing tragedy, took this loonily further. Castrati were invented, in fact, by the Church in the sixteenth century. They sang the angel-voiced soprano parts in choirs, because women could not sing in church. But opera took them over enthusiastically. From the seventeenth century, when opera began, until the late eighteenth century, they not only sang women's parts, they *were* Italian opera, and the first international stars. Their charms were argued over in drawing-rooms from Russia to Portugal, Dublin to the Ottoman borders. They sang show-off florid music in show-off florid costumes and wonderfully ornate settings: with *that voice*. There is a whole mythology round the uncanny sound and impact of the castrato voice. It was full, sweet, immensely powerful – but above all artificial, and this was what Goethe adored:

> In these representations, the concept of imitation and art is more strongly felt. Their performance creates a conscious illusion. A noble pleasure is given, in that they are not women, but only represent women. They present a nature foreign to them.[13]

'They present a nature foreign to them.' Many writers have explored opera's artifice: its disguises, its secrecy and masquerade, women singing men's roles *en travesti* (in trousers; hence 'travesty') and its glittery play with the mismatch between voice and body, appearance and reality.[14] Castrato tradition underlies and expresses the lot. What *does* it say about male fantasies of women and need to impersonate them, that boys were *mutilated*, unmade as men and turned into artificial women, to sing in women's voices?

As the law changed in Italian states (Mantua, for instance, in 1608), women singers gradually took over from castrati. But they were still directed by men, as their roles and music were written by men. Hence the great diva battles of the nineteenth century: for who knows better how to sing a woman onstage, a woman or a man? Whose fantasy were they impersonating, and for whom?

Outside opera too, men decided both *how* women's voices sounded and (give or take a few inspired women) *what* they sang until, really, the mid-seventies. Even Bessie Smith, who took a lot of things into her own hands, sang mostly men's songs. Men produced, recorded, distributed her. Carmen's arias destroy Don José – but who wrote the original story? The male novelist Mérimée. Who wrote the opera? Who conducted and directed her? Whose *idea* is it that she has that sexy power?

Male creativity may silence its Muse to produce its own words, but Echo re-produces your own male voice. When a castrated man impersonates a woman, the very sound this 'woman' makes is male. When real women sang, men directed the timbre and volume of the voice. From Mozart to Verdi, Wagner, and Strauss, male composers have very firm ideas about the sound they want, but in their letters they worry most about the voices of sopranos. Divas fought conductors, but their job was to serve men's vision of woman.

In nineteenth-century ideology, poetry and thought were male, but 'Music is a woman', says Wagner, in *Opera and Drama*: opera is sex between male words and female music.[15] Female voice needs male control. In pop, men control it through technology. At Motown, Berry Gordy was a genius at finding the right emotional setting for a voice. When he recut the Miracles' 'Shop Around', he switched from drums to brushes for a softer, feathery feel, knowing exactly how to give a voice the right injection of plaintive yearning or vulnerability.[16]

Producers do this to male voices too, but the star story is finding the ideal female voice. That key audition: the moment in Billie Holiday's autobiography when she fails to get a dance job and the pianist says 'Girl, can you sing?' Or Ronnie, aged seventeen, from Spanish Harlem, auditioned by the youthful impresario Phil Spector. 'When Phil first heard my voice he kicked over the piano stool. He said "That's the voice I've been waiting for." ' She and the Ronettes then had amazing hits: 'Be My Baby' (1963) was Spector's biggest ever. But controlling her voice went much further. In 1966 he married her, shut her in a twenty-three-room Beverley Hills palace, said her voice was finished, stopped her going out or having visitors, and when abroad he would phone, then go to sleep on the phone, so she could not talk to anyone else. In 1999, their court case is not yet settled. Their relationship sums up his relation to women's voice as its mad disciplinarian controller (just as Balanchine in the New York City Ballet was the all-powerful dictator of women's bodies). Spector's girl songs, like the Crystals' 'He's a Rebel' and 'He Hit Me (It Felt like a Kiss)', are devoted imprisoned female hymns to maleness.[17] Men have harnessed all their technical, musical, professional and imaginative powers to impersonate, 'produce' and control a woman's voice in man-made song.

But what kinds of thing should it say? What most favourite soprano arias, most women's pop songs till the mid-seventies, say, in words but also in their timbre, melody, harmony and soft, longing, vulnerable, seductive, yearning atmosphere, is that she wants him, is wretched without him. 'The problem with operas', director Graham Vick told me, 'is they're written by men, full of romantic notions that women can't live without them.' The man-made Greek deity of sex and desire is a woman. Echo is her aural image: the voice of helpless female desire for men.

According to the Marquis de Sade, the sound men most want to hear is a woman's cry which tells you the power you have to affect her. The sound Duke Ellington and his mates used to compete for.[18] Women's lovesong is that cry made song. 'Bet you think this song is about you, don't you?' sang Carly Simon in 'You're So Vain' (1972, backed by Jagger's vocals). Yes he did, and he was right. Women's lovesong *is* about men. The difference between that and male lovesong is that until the mid-seventies (Carly was unusual), it was mostly written by the very people it was about, and cast them in the best possible light. In Gershwin's 'The Man I Love', 'He'll be big and strong, the man I love.' Credits by Narcissus, Inc. Or Wishful Thinking.

Give or take a few divas, women performers co-operate in male production of women's voice. Of course. Wonderful music – you want to sing it, give your whole self to it. 'It's a performer's basic instinct,' said the soprano Josphine Barstow, 'because you're a human being and a lonely human being, to try and get the audience's sympathy for your character.' You make the song and feeling yours. You cannot think you are serving a man's version of woman's desire. 'I wouldn't look at it that way,' Josephine Barstow told me. 'It's not my job. If as a performer I think, "I'm expressing Verdi's desire not Violetta's", it's not going to work. I have to express Violetta's desire, try and work out where I think *she's* at.'

Any musician serves the music as best they can. But songs have words as well, and when you are singing you have to make them yours. Sheryl Crow was once asked if the hurt lyrics of the song she sang, 'Leaving Las Vegas', were autobiographical. 'Yes!' she said. No way! said David Baerwald, who actually wrote them. He was inspired by *Leaving Las Vegas*, a book by his friend John O'Brien that became an Oscar-winning film.[19] Singers internalize songs men write; they have to reproduce, dramatically and vocally, the image of woman men have made. Just as iconic geniuses of the female image, like Marilyn Monroe and Madonna, internalize male fantasy in order to re-produce and incarnate it. Madonna parodically, Marilyn tragically – as the ideal Echo.

In pop, this tradition carries heftily on (the Spice Girls were a triumph of male image-manipulation and marketing) alongside the eighties and nineties explosion of really creative women's song. But this whole history, this enforced impersonation of male fantasy, the faking men ask for and then attack, is what Madonna and Lennox were getting at in their cross-dressing. Until the mid-seventies, most women pop singers, like classical singers, were 'working within a man-made notion of how women should sound'. They had to. When punk blew every stereotype to bits, and the stereotype of the made-up woman along with it, punk women attacked that notion bitterly. 'Oh bondage up yours,' yelled Poly Styrene, whose name sent up the artificiality of the stereotype. 'I am a cliché.'[20]

The Truest Poetry is the Most Feigning

But it was exactly this polystyrene quality, the artificiality of 'woman', that attracted male singers into cross-dressing. The fun and point of glam was its theatricality, its denial of authenticity. It wanted a slice of the sexiness and seductiveness men had invested in their image of women: above all, that secret source of desire, that liftable veil. Once the rock god was well established as the object of display and desire, he could be dressed, like Dionysus, as a woman. It is artificiality that camp plays for: and artificiality goes with femaleness. Following Jagger's footsteps, glam rock staged a maleness capable of faking, in Dylan's words, like a woman.

Electricity and the Truth of Artifice

Rock managed all this by electricity. No electricity, no rock. And electricity, the founding energy, is all about bodies. The 'attraction' of 'bodies', caused by friction, was the first electrical property ever discovered. This was what gave electricity its name: from *electron*, 'amber', which pulls 'light bodies' (said scientists) when you rub it. Benjamin Franklin's 1740s theory of electricity posited an electric 'fluid'. We still talk of current and connection. Electric music means flow between bodies, shared energy, people in touch. Its language is a bunch of relationship-making metaphors – input, current, charge. The radicalness of rock was 'live' relationship, sexual voltage, the frictional flow between thousands of bodies in the audience, the magnetic pull between audience and star.

So back, once again, to the endless implications of electricity, and what it does to music, performers and listeners. We can go right back, this time, to legends of the first electric American music. The first amplified bluegrass violin happened, apparently, by hazard, in 1789 in Dunwich, Massachusetts, when Captain Obadiah Pickman Grunte was playing 'Leather Britches' under an elm tree. Lightning struck the tree and hurled him against stone walling with copper ore in it. A hollow log touching the wall amplified the vibrations. Twenty miles away, punters at the 'Bull and Stool' heard 'a mightie scream and huge fidyle playing a reele', and danced till the echoes died away at dawn.[21] Even in 1789, electricity meant bodies sharing excitement.

Electricity, which empowers rock, defines it in two main ways, recording and amplification, and its main gifts are artificiality and omnivorous volume. These two belong together but pull in different directions, and can lead to opposite experiences for listeners. Amplifying brings you in, makes you closer to the music and other listeners. In the stadium you give yourself up, lose yourself in a swirling explosion of sound. Live rock means entering and sharing something fantastically larger than yourself. But recording gets truth by artifice. It brings you sound, but mucks it about first. What makes the music, fakes it. When you listen to a recording, you are in control of its volume rather than its volume overwhelming you. You can switch off; or listen with headphones, not sharing *anything*, cut off from other people in a closed circuit of voice, fantasy and ear in electronic solipsism, as a headphones hero whose body is not related to others but an echo-chamber for the fantasizing mind. The different drugs associated with different rock music reflect these two relationships. The E generation takes Ecstasy for communality. Everybody strokes everybody, saying how lovely they are. Quite different from the private shoot-up hymned by Velvet Underground.

Guitars went electric because they wanted to be heard by more people – the dancing-in-the-street, community side of rock. But electricity changed the sound. The medium, even artificiality itself, became the message. Evolving technology – feedback, distortion, wah-wah pedal, Moog synthesizer – made rock the sound of electricity and it sidelined the instruments. Musical virtuosity could be less important than electronic skills. Kraftwerk, the seventies German group begun by an organist and woodwind player keen on avant-garde jazz, started electronic experiments (using music from Stockhausen to Pink Floyd) with tape loops, drum machines, synthesizers, vocoders. *Autobahn* (1975), their international breakthrough album, inspired early eighties British electro-pop bands, Afrika Mombaataa and electric hip-hop and was sampled by nineties techno. Rock is increasingly recycled, collaged, layered. Technologies of production and reproduction make each track a miracle of sonic innovation, which gets the play of tension and release (on which all music depends) without any instruments. You can sit down with a mixer desk and a panel of buttons in your bedroom, lift a CD track there, a film-track here, add synthesized drums, and there's your pop song. Electricity turned imitation into carnivorous innovation: as in the metaphor of 'sampling' other people's work.

That moment when a synthesizer could produce the exact sound of drums and guitars marked a profound change in the relationship between musician and listener. If you could get a drumbeat and guitar riffs out of your synthesizer, who needed to learn to play? Technology also puts the voice in question. If you can manufacture its emotional appeal, reverberation, texture and pitch, whose voice is it, the singer's or the sound engineer's? Elvis Presley's voice was a gift to Sam Phillips, but he recorded him in several different songs, blues, ballad and country material, until the 'Sun sound' emerged. For the epoch-making early singles, Phillips enhanced the urgency of that voice with meticulous flutter, reverberation and echo. What were you responding to? Singer or producer? The voice, or the recording? The shaping art is that of producer, mixer, sound engineer.[22] What physical body is the voice is coming from? The lithe styled boy in the photo whose voice is as airbrushed as his face? Or the computer-keyboard out of sight?

'Authenticity' comes from Greek *autos*, 'self'. When Dylan upset his fans at Newport by going electric, he was denying them the currency of honest giving, from one intimate self to others, on which they felt 'country' tradition was based. By the end of the thirties, when the name 'country and western' had taken over from 'hill-billy', that music had been controlled by major record companies. It was sold as 'sincere', 'real' music, even though it was utterly unreal and incongruous for American city-dwellers who heard it on radio.[23] Two generations of belief in sincerity lay behind the values which said the less encumbered and artificial the sound, the truer the feeling and relation between singer and audience. Dylan was challenging values that felt god-givenly American. 'Country' was the deepest truth.

But Dylan was going after a new truth, one that belonged to the city, to electricity. In electric music, truth is in the faking, the possibilities of creating new sound. Dylan's move produced 'folk rock', which in 1960 would have been a contradiction in terms.

(He did not mean to. 'Folk rock? I've never even *said* that word. The word "message" strikes me as having a hernia-like sound.') But more wide-reachingly, he was responding to the new relationship to sound; a new authenticity of sound based on the vistas of artificiality opened up by 'electric'.

Prince was an electronic as well as gender-bending tease of genius. (One of his favourite games was winding up the press: asked in 1981 what his ambition was, he said 'Senility – I'm close to it now'.) His flirty cross-dressing in image, clothes and hair mirrored the way he flirted with the glowing artificiality of electronic sound. Subverting pop illusions with a slyly serious frivolity that matched Dylan's, he seemed to ask: What *is* a pop song, this conventionally criss-crossed electronic envelope of emotion – in which what is fake is real, what is real is fake, where sincerity is artificial and 'image' everything? He could spoof, explore and ironize all that in electronically contrived musical textures: cross-dressing, and crossing wires between truth and falsehood in the very sound.[24] Am I black or white? Am I straight or gay? He was deep-dyed in glam tradition. He knew exactly what it did, how it used femaleness; he had a ball making the artificial true.

20 A Love Affair With Love

We Were Pointing at Each Other: Fan, Fantasy and Star

Rock operates in 'terrain between fantasy and reality'.[1] What matters most, emotionally (and commercially), is its relationship with the fantasy of listeners and the reality of the street.

Street? Rock dances in it, comes from it, celebrates it. It is where fans come from – and, supposedly, the star. Pretending to be working-class when you are not, like Jagger, is a big rock tradition. 'When all this is over,' says David Lee Roth of Van Halen, 'I'm going back into that audience, back to the streets.'[2] Fans feel they have that in common with you. Rock creates royalty up there in the spotlight, but its ideology is fiercely democratic: the hero was here on the floor where you are, once. It would never have taken off without American fantasies (which the story of the blues embodies) about coming up from the bottom. Part of the dream is how the rock god got there, that mythic move from obscurity to light. Much of The Beatles' appeal in America came from their working-class roots: the democratic American soul saw them in blues terms, Liverpool's cheeky answer to élite supercilious London.

A lot of this relationship is visual. Stars are not just voices but pin-ups for teen bedrooms. Image-manipulation is all-important. 'In my day,' said Chrissie Hynde, meaning the seventies, 'if a stylist told you what to wear for a photo, you'd hear a resounding "Fuck off". The whole idea of being in a band was that you could be exactly the way you were.' Today's new stars know they are paid to be in the fantasy business and are deeply careful of their image. (Though there is a big division between musicians who make that image part of their music, and stars who do what marketing men say.)³ Boys have to offer the illusion of availability. 'We thought, "We've had it with the groupies" once we got married,' said McCartney, but The Beatles' appeal survived. The band Take That, though, all had girlfriends in their heyday and pretended not to. Dreamwise, they have to seem *possible*. Sexually, visually, they are a fantasy pizza base for fans to place their toppings on. Hence the anxiety when Steve Gately of Boyzone came out gay. 'A secret that will break so many hearts' mourned the *Mirror*. His mother expected a backlash from the disclosure.⁴ But it was beautifully press-orchestrated, and within a month Boyzone simply sprouted a new gay following. Everything rides on the star's phantasmagoric availability to enough people. As Shirley Manson puts it, 'It's your "duty" as a popstar to give them something that's irrelevant to you' (she was talking about autographs, but it could just as well be a fantasy-friendly image) 'in exchange for the fact that they are maintaining your lifestyle. You could be cleaning toilets for a living.'⁵

The big change in the star–fan relationship came in the early seventies, rock's first postmodern phase. Musical formats splintered, the guitar-hero was ironized and undermined by the two great rivals, glam rock and punk.

Glam parodied rock and made it a tart. But where glam attacked the theatricality and inauthenticity of the guitar hero from an iridescent high, punk attacked by coming down to floor level. Like glam, punk offered teenagers new ways of reinventing themselves. Instead of the Jagger–Richards stud male, you got, in glam, a queen, an alien. In punk, you got a ragingly dysfunctional, DIY-dressed boy.

The fan–star relationship runs on a quality of promise, a dream of exchange. Both glam and punk turned the spotlight on to fans, and both were white movements, turning their disparate backs on imitating black. They wanted to give fans something they could share, rather than (as with stadium rock) marvel at. Glam showered the world with fakery which fans could do too.

It was their turn to be stars; they could flaunt allegiance to glam by parading their own glitter. If Narcissus has become a shimmery mirror, you can be mirrors together, reflecting each other's sequins into infinity. 'At one point,' said a male Bowie fan, 'doing "Breaking Glass" David points to a member of the audience who then has a pointing match with him. And at one of the gigs, that was me. *We were pointing at each other!*'[6]

Punk got that 'pointing at each other' by the opposite route. Refusing the hypocritical overblown pop-culture that had sold the young so short, it drew attention to its own artificiality ('Poly Styrene'), but made it utterly rebarbative, in a lunging effort to re-find authentic rawness. Its answer to the fans' longing for interchange was taking the stage away. Punk wanted to be on a level: de-bourgeoisify, de-hierarchize, break roles. Men could give up macho posing or push it to extremes. Sid Vicious (following Iggy Pop) made dysfunctionalism an art form.[7] Musicians wore the same tatty lumber as fans. 'We wore ordinary clothes, we hadn't got anything else,' said Gaye Advert. Punk was the values of trash, of making your own records, of *not being able to play.* DIY on every front – spiritual, sexual, social, electronic, musical.

The Sex Pistols were against any conformity. Especially (since they were in the music business) conformity of voice. Punk declared war on rock's conspiracy of impersonation (American, black): it wanted to destroy artificiality in sound as well as the spatial demarcation of a raised stage, and the whole social code that stage embodied. The Pistols attacked the medium of conventional sound as well as its message: they wanted to undo the politics of voice. 'Voice' was conformity, sweetness was compliance. There they were at No. 1 in 1977 *snarling* 'and we don't cayyyyyyyyyyyyyyyyyre', in a visceral attempt to unseat the smugness of voice. Punk was vocal chaos, screaming off every scale in fury at this grey, claustrophobic, unjust world.

And the physical side of the star–fan bond? From Jim Morrison to Iggy Pop and Henry Rollins, diving into audiences said, 'I'm part of you, I'm yours, I'm in you.' Punk wanted to democratize that relationship, do away with distance. Fans responded by spitting. You left the stage slithering, like a just-born cub, in your fans' mucus.

One movement of the *Zeitgeist* which punk reflected was interactive theatre. The Austrian dramatist Peter Handke wrote *Offending the Audience* in 1966, but it first came to Britain in 1970. The abuse it flung at the Royal Court audience could have been a Sex Pistols manifesto:

> You are the subject matter. You are the centre of interest. You are being acted upon. The front of the stage is not a demarcation ... We and you form a unit. You are looking at us, you are being looked at. Instead of saying *you*, we could say *we* ...

'Kids want threatening noises,' explained Johnny Rotten, 'because that shakes you out of your apathy.'[8] Handke's conclusion is a clairvoyant summary of Rotten and Vicious with *their* audience:

> We will insult you because insulting you is one way of speaking to you. By insulting you we can turn you on. We can tear down a wall ... You were the heroes of this piece. You were a hurricane, you swept everything before you, you savages, rednecks, fiends – you killer pigs.

Remember the used Tampax thrown at a Los Angeles audience (chapter 18)? You can't get much more intimately, or aggressively interactive, than that.

But removing the stage, levelling things between yourself and the audience you were screaming at, did not work. Punk changed a lot of things, but not the hierarchic division between audience and star. Jagger headed Rotten's list of hates, yet Rotten – as Jagger gleefully pointed out – almost became him. In 1977, two torn pictures of a snarly, squinting Rotten were collaged on the front of *Rolling Stone*. 'The Sex Pistols have copped out,' said Jagger (who has graced that cover more often than anyone, nineteen times since *Rolling Stone* began). 'If I were Johnny

A LOVE AFFAIR WITH LOVE

Rotten I wouldn't even talk to *Rolling Stone*. I'd tell them to go fuck themselves.' In the eighties, who were the two groups cherished as all-time role-models by the Charlatans in their 'we are fucking rock' bosoms? The Sex Pistols and Rolling Stones.[9]

Punk wanted to do away with the hypocritical theatricality of stadium rock, and found it had created an artificiality of its own, a style, a look, a copyable stance. Punk style came down to the show of shock: which is what nineties punk Lynn Breedlove counts on, when she whips out her black cock and gets you to suck it.

Ever Get the Feeling You've Been Cheated?

The fan–star relation can be overwhelming on both sides. On the fan side, tidal waves of obsession – families dedicating a room in their house as a shrine to Marc Bolan where everyone from gran to grandson listens to Marc at least once a day; women making love with their husbands pretending it is Barry Manilow ('after, when I realize it's not him, I cry to myself'); schoolgirls positive their photos of Nick Rhodes (from Duran Duran), Sellotaped to their school desk, look back at them and smile:

> He's looking at me and can see me and hear me through the magazine. When I stare at one picture and look away quickly I can see from the corner of my eye that his lips are moving and he's smiling.[10]

That photo is hallowed by more eyes, more desperately intense belief, than any icon these days in a church.

Fans also resent the stars' power over them ('They're really time-consuming, my fantasies'), and the inequality of the relationship. ('I know Nick Rhodes exists and I'm spending money buying things for him, *but he doesn't know I exist*.') But they also feel their particular star deserves all they can give:

> They represent the success story up there... You're

absolutely gullible. It's almost pathetic, that idol thing. But then Bowie was extraordinary and deserved all that idolatry.

One twenty-five-year-old, reflecting on her teen fan past, said,

> Kids of sixteen and eighteen take it all in because they really do worship these people. That's how I think it's dangerous. Because kids lose their own identity. The star up there expresses something very real for you and so you mistake that thing for yourself. You mistakenly think you can live his life.

She thinks it can leave scars:

> Stars can damage people by their life styles and the money they throw around and the kind of images they present. I actually believed I could have a relationship with David Bowie. This was *his* influence and it was rather damaging. He's got a lot to answer for.[11]

What fans yearn for is reciprocity. Not only sexual: we are not talking only girls. At twenty-two, Bernard had edited a Bowie fanzine but never met Bowie. Going to a gig was not a chance to hear good music but 'a marvellous experience to share two hours with him'. Yet the payback was pathetic:

> For the Hammersmith show, me and some other fans got an arrangement of flowers in the shape of a red shoe. And we put a card on it with everyone's names. So that, you know, they were then a name to Bowie – which is nice. It's nice for people to know Bowie's read their name.[12]

Fans are desperate to possess their stars, but cannot, so they take revenge in dreams, trying to control this figure who has such power over their soul. One girl had fantasies of spanking Boy George. 'I've wondered', she said, 'how would *I* feel, if people had fantasies about me?' She would hate that, 'but I suppose the stars are there for people to fantasize about'.[13] He is a screen. He will never know you. Yet he is in you; he defines you.

And the star? How is it, being a screen for projected fantasies, getting paid for 'being there for people to fantasize about'? Being a screen was perfect for Charles Manson. 'I am what you project your fears onto,' he announced at his trial. But many stars find it difficult. You're fine if you utterly believe in what you are doing. Prince knows the reality is artifice: he revels in it. Dylan was fine when reinventing the truth of rock, but in 1978, a year after the Sex Pistols topped the charts, he said 'Rock 'n' roll ended in 1959. There's no more rock 'n' roll. It's imitation. It has turned itself inside out.' But that same year Bruce Springsteen said he believed passionately in the 'reality' and morality of his show and his songs:

> You have to go the whole way because that's what keeps everything *real*. It ties in with the morality of records. There's a certain morality of the show, it's very strict.

The *Rolling Stone* interviewer clearly preferred artificiality; he found Bruce a bit too good to be true. 'The advantage of the sanctimony and rhetoric of punks', he said, 'is that such flaws humanize them.'[14] But passionate belief in what you are doing is a great protection.

Some stars are more aware of needing protection than others. If you have self-destructive fragilities within you, if you feel manipulated and resent it, or (like Richey Edwards) long for 'real', it can all turn frighteningly blank. The Sex Pistols were brought together aged twenty by Malcolm McClaren, who orchestrated press coverage and stressed the violence of their image. But Johnny Rotten wrote the songs. Their energy was his; their magnetic negativity ('No Feelings', 'Pretty Vacant', 'No Fun') was his own rage, disillusion, resentment, frustration, claustrophobia. They were passionately meant and British fans identified passionately, responding with equal rage against the 'vacancy' of their own lives, the 'no fun' there glaringly wasn't on the hundred-per-cent-unemployed housing-estates where they grew up. McClaren wanted the Pistols to live up to their image, trash hotel rooms, get beaten up. Rotten believed in what he was: McClaren was selling it as style.

For the Pistols' American tour, McClaren picked the South, because Southern audiences might hate them, be violent and produce brilliant press coverage. That tour was the end of the Pistols. By then Rotten was not speaking to McClaren anyway. An early gig in San Antonio was just what McClaren ordered: 2,200 Texans, Mexicans and Indians fighting each other, throwing beer cans and bottles of Jack Daniels at the band. Sid hit one with his guitar. Fine. But the last show in San Francisco was the most lacklustre they ever played, and their last. 'I don't like rock music,' said Rotten in an interview beforehand. 'I don't know why I'm in it. I just want to destroy.' It was 'a zombie performance', according to reports. 'The worst I've ever seen.'

As encore, the Pistols did 'No Fun'. Rotten announced it in a speaking voice, as though commenting on the whole event. 'This is no fun.' Half-way through, he stopped. 'Oh bollocks,' he said. 'Why should I carry on?' He sat on the stage and looked at the audience. 'Ever get the feeling you've been cheated?' he asked. Later he explained, 'I meant myself, not them.' His feeling, his relation to what thousands of people were howling at him for doing, had gone.[15] The danger is that you'll feel blank as a screen because you are one. What's there is other people's stuff, not yours. 'With all this attention, you become a child,' said Jagger once:

> You can't talk about anything apart from your own dopey life. It's very dangerous. But there's no way, really, to avoid that.

As Kurt Cobain's suicide note said,

> I haven't felt the excitement of listening to as well as creating music... for too many years now. I feel guilty beyond words about these things. When we're backstage and the lights go out and the manic roar of the crowd begins, it

doesn't affect me the way it did Freddie Mercury, who seemed to love and relish in the love and admiration from the crowd which is something I totally admire and envy. The fact is, I can't fool you, any one of you. It simply isn't fair to you or me. The worst crime I can think of would be to rip people off by faking it and pretending I'm having 100 per cent fun.[16]

If you want not to fake, if you believe you really are what fans' fantasies create, you're lost.

It seems to be worst for men – for many reasons. That '4 REAL' *Angst* about male authenticity; the fact that rock invented this theatre of maleness and each new generation wants to challenge it – son against father, Kronos against Heaven – but then finds, like the Pistols with the Stones, it has somehow reproduced it. Also because (as groupies tirelessly demonstrate) the star–fan relationship is a male–female template. But for women musicians, the theatre of maleness built into rock is something to struggle against; and challenge is what rock does best.

The star–fan bond is a relation of need on both sides. Male fans like Bernard are what the star was, remind him of his envious past self. But the mythic blueprint always makes the longing female. Orpheus pulls everyone to him with his voice; Narcissus is so gorgeous, everyone adores him. These male myths of omni-adoration, all-magnetic song and looks, yell out how the male self-image depends on other people, above all women, wanting you. Though she never draws near him ('I know he exists, but he doesn't know I exist'), Echo's devotion creates Narcissus, just as that 'all-hallowed teen gurl market' creates the star.

Sex and Soul: Looking and Being Looked At

The fan–star relationship is based on the fans' quest for relationship, yet quest is traditionally a male thing, the 'love 'em and leave 'em' open road, away from relationship into selfhood.

Ulysses goes home not just for Penelope but his palace, possessions, position in the world.

In female quests, women are searching for a lost man, like Leonora in *Fidelio* or Aretousa in the sixteenth-century Cretan epic *Erotokritos*. Off they go to rescue him: physically (the English ballad 'Sweet Polly Oliver'; *Fidelio*), spiritually (Helena in *Alls Well that Ends Well*), legally (Portia at the end of *Merchant of Venice*) and emotionally. In Hornby's *High Fidelity*, the girlfriend gets a new job, returns to the hero and makes him use his rock anorak skills successfully. Women save men to unite with them. The way Ariadne helps Theseus with the labyrinth says it all. Tie this string to a rock, darling. When you go in, you won't get lost – you'll have a fixed point to come back to. Namely, me.

These man-made myths – what do men get out of them? The thought that *if* men get lost on their journey away (as of course they won't, they are blokes, they can handle anything), women's desire and quest for relationship will come to their aid. 'I always think women are going to change and redeem me', mutters Hornby's hero.[17]

In most of these stories, the questing women cross-dress – as if men telling such a story can only bear women to be active when they pretend to be men. But on two Greek quests, women go as themselves. The goddess Demeter searches for her kidnapped daughter, and Psyche searches for her bridegroom, Eros.

Both stories played a sacred role in one of the ancient 'mysteries'. As an initiate, you were searching for new meaning in your life. The climax of the darkness, confusion, lights and sound you encountered was being shown a sacred object, the 'mystery'. In Demeter's 'mysteries' at Eleusis, it was an ear of corn. In Dionysus' mysteries (as in shows by Jim Morrison and Iggy Pop), it was a giant erect penis, in a basket. This experience changed your life; the story was how it did it.[18] Psyche and Eros were perfect for it: their story is the search for love. Plato used that 'mysteries' mix – darkness, psychic search, revelation and transformation through desire – to illustrate his theory of how Love brings about revelation in your being.[19]

The story? We had it earlier, but here it is in more detail, including parental persecution.

Psyche is human, so beautiful that Venus is jealous. But Venus' son Eros falls in love with her, defies his mother and whisks Psyche off to his palace. Psyche believes he is a monster. (This is a pre-run of 'Beauty and the Beast'). He forbids her to see him and makes love to her in the dark at night. She comes to love him, has to see what he looks like, does so when he is asleep and wakes him up. When he sees her looking at him, he flies off to Venus, who imprisons him in a tower. Psyche wanders the earth searching for him; Venus pounces on her and sets her some impossible tasks; Eros escapes and rescues Psyche just as she's failed the last one. They are reunited with the blessing of the gods.

This story reappears in folk-tale, but the Greek myth packed extra power because of the names. Eros means Desire; Psyche means Soul. Since ancient times it has been endlessly reinterpreted by painters, poets, religious allegorists. (The Renaissance took it to signify the human soul's search for God.)[20] As Love's love affair with Soul, the everlasting human quest for love, it is the theme of most pop songs. As a myth of mutuality, it deals in the relationship between pop's two commonest words, 'you' and 'me'. It talks about Soul having sex with invisible Desire; about breaking rules, losing love, suffering, getting love back. It also speaks to anxiety about male potency: Desire takes wing, shrivels away, when the female Soul inspects it.

In Greek tradition, male religious poets often personify all human vulnerability and grief as female; like the soul in relation to its harsh male lover, God, in what one critic calls 'a type of bereaved cross-dressing'.[21] Just as the female voice traditionally represents 'the human voice', Psyche is female but represents 'the human soul': female and yearning and lost, questing – as women on quests always do – for relationship. But this woman is searching for Desire itself.

Any good myth has a lot of meanings. Desire and Soul embody the themes of nearly all pop lyrics and 85 per cent of rock. 'Soul' is Psyche's music. It celebrates 'Sexual Feeling' – its carnality, its spiritual passion. Eros turns up in his Roman guise, Cupid, all over Soul music. 'Cupid's Boogie' was an R & B hit in 1950 for Esther Phillips, who became a soul singer deeply admired by Aretha Franklin. (In 1973, Aretha beat her to the Grammy Award for Best R & B Vocalist and promptly handed it to her as the better candidate.) Sam Cooke, a wonderful precursor of soul, wrote 'Cupid' in 1961: it became a 1970 hit (produced in Jamaica) for Johnny Nash; the Moonglows – reinvented as the Detroit Spinners – reworked it in 1980 as 'Cupid (I've Loved You for a Long Time)'. The *Average White Band*, which imitated black soul, had a 1982 album called *Cupid's in Fashion*.

Most pop lyrics are myths of erotic yearning. In Tom Stoppard's play *The Real Thing*, the hero thinks 'You've Lost That Lovin' Feeling', by the Righteous Brothers, is 'the most haunting, most deeply moving noise ever produced by the human spirit'. No opera singer – certainly, no 'woman called Callas in a foreign musical', as he describes the most passionate star-soprano of all time – can possibly compete. Yearning for lost love, the centre of Psyche's story, is *it*. The ethereal voice and gnomic lyrics of Green, Welsh-born singer and songwriter with Scritti Politti, gave them several hit singles (including 'Perfect Way', an American No. 1 in 1984) on their 1985 album *Cupid and Psyche*.

Like rock tracks, myths get sampled, recycled, used for different things, and you can use Eros and Psyche to underline rock's yearning not only in its songs, but in the relation between its fans and their star. The personifications of desire Greece handed down to us are double. Rock fans seeking the star are caught like Psyche between desire's two Greek faces: Venus, the jealous no-saying mother, Eros, the shimmeringly unavailable adolescent boy.

Initiates in the ancient mysteries supposedly emerged feeling

'I am a stranger to myself'.[22] The search for desire is also a quest for identity: hence the hope in current pop psychology that when you discover your sexuality you 'know who you are'. Psyche's search for Eros is a quest for the 'who am I?' revelation which happens when you fall in love.

Being teenage is anyway a quest – for sex, for love, for who you are. Rock music helps in that on a world-wide scale. Music is 'one of the means by which we make ourselves who we are';[23] rock created a teen culture aiming to find all that out. Partly through the melody, harmony and rhythm of desire, partly by re-evaluating your relationship through the landscape around you; in which, like Psyche, you have impossible tasks pressed on you by a persecutorily parental world. Seventies teenagers, fed up with pop that seemed nothing to do with what they were, found the Sex Pistols speaking to their disenchantment offered new ways of seeing and being. 'It was as if we'd been living only symbolically till then,' said a male friend:

> Their sound came in and shattered the mirror, made you free. You could say to your parents, 'See, I'm not you. This is torture to your ears but music to mine.' It was a choice of identity. 'This is where *I* am.' The music you listened to was a choice you made, like putting safety pins in your blazer and spiking your hair with gel. My brother's wall was covered with posters of Johnny Rotten.

For girls, it is much easier to be in love with a poster than one of the real, spotty, squeaky-voiced males around. ('Boys smell a lot', says my thirteen-year old daughter.) It is a controllable dream, plus you can share passion for it with other fans, and find your own identity not so much through desire but activities like cutting out photos, comparing scrapbooks, going to gigs on the bus together: far more important, in the end, than the actual star. 'The excitement was not about the Bay City Rollers; it was about ourselves.'[24] For boys, the choice is allegiance, role-models, hitching your identity to a star. 'We admired Lennon because he was *dead cheeky*,' said a friend born in 1953:

> That's why I put him on my wall. We liked the way he was rude to people. We wanted to egg him on, we wanted him to fight our battles for us. That boy feeling, which Gary Glitter got in 'Do you Wanna be in My Gang?'

Another friend, born in 1968, said listening to the Pistols 'could identify you as nothing else could. Their sound made it possible to think of living a life you really wanted.'

This myth of Sex and Soul is about seeing: seeing the truth of desire, of yourself; like the revelation of sacred objects in the mysteries or the teenage revelation of seeing life through your own sexuality and music, not through your parents' eyes. Looking is a battleground of teenage identity. How you look, how stars look, 'good' looks (in every sense) are crucial. What you wear, safety pins, glitter, the right kind of trainers, says *who you are*. Stars' posters matter as much as their sound. They look back at you from the wall. 'He's looking at me through the magazine.'

They also challenge parents. A decade apart, at different ends of Britain, both these friends' posters were torn down by furious parents and replaced by religious pictures. Devastating as it was then, that tearing down showed the parents had already lost out to Johnny Rotten and John Lennon. It was the rearguard action of jealous Venus, who knows her winged son will eventually fly away to join Soul. One useful thing about this myth is that Psyche and Eros always win.

In myths of me and you, looking is always a risk. Orpheus looks back and loses Eurydice, Narcissus ignores Echo, drools over the pool and drowns. Eros vanishes when he sees Psyche looking at him. But in this story, as in pop's optimistic backdrop, things work out. Never mind parental jealousy and restriction: Soul sees Desire, suffers, gets it back. In most star–fan obsessions, the star is a benign image for fans in their quest for identity. 'The Pistols got us out of the house, to dances, and into the arms of women,' said my friend. Rock's deepest role is to give musical voice to teenage rage, resentment, frustration, vulnerability, claustrophobia, yearning tenderness and the breaking of parental rules.

But this myth is a mutual lost and found. It has things to say about both sides of the star–fan bond. In the end, stars need fans – to fantasize, arrange roses into gigantic red shoes, stare at posters or photos in school desks – far more than fans need stars. Even the god of love needs love. As men (like Nick Hornby's hero) need women to rescue them, so Eros needs the human soul to yearn for him, to find him out. And for all their glamour, Jim Morrison, Jagger and Robbie Williams need fans to do the desiring. 'An autograph', says Chrissie Hynde, 'is signing a contract that says, "I will never waitress again".'[25]

Rock is a huge man-made mythology of sex and soul, a love affair with love and desire. But rock myth or Greek myth, the male soul and its mirror image, rock god, cock hero in his starry glory, depend on women's desire.

21 A Dream of Being Male

The men now in charge of the world (give or take the odd female head of state) are the first world-rulers who were teenagers in the modern sense. Who grew up to rock culture, modelled themselves on ideas of black maleness. based their approach to the world on a specific mix of antagonism, sex and fun: who were shaped by the rock mythology of being male. Wherever they grew up, America, Britain, Holland, Germany, Japan, they 'sang into broom handles, imitated Elvis with tennis racquets, practised the pelvic wiggle' like their contemporary Salman Rushdie. 'Elvis had the same impact in India he had everywhere. The first record I ever bought was *Heartbreak Hotel*.'[1]

The rock mythology that formed them, so keen to show itself male, is full of a terrible unresolved relation to blackness both in society and itself; and also full of male teenage selfishness, contradiction, violence, misogyny, narcissism, supremacism, resentment, anger, darkness and fantasies of omnipotence. (Have I missed something?) It has also been *the* key force in the last half-century of young energy, humour, creativity, originality, warmth, intelligence, scepticism, sex and fun. It radiates a longing – shared as you dance and listen – for only the moment to matter; and history, or the future, not at all. It runs on intense belief in the moment and the street, in enjoying yourself in your age group and fuck anything that went before, plus a passionately democratic hope. Wherever you live, it can be a force for finding *meaning* in your life.

It is changing all the time. Rock has changed from against and alternative to dominant and mainstream; it now means a million different things. 'Rock is stylistically very connective', Mat Snow told me. 'It's really hard to say what has not been drawn under the rock umbrella.' It is wildly more electronic, verbal and female than anyone could have dreamed in 1965. At the yearning end of things, fourteen-year-old boys keep mixing decks in their bedroom, not guitars. Forget air guitar: on the school bus they practise rapping and MC-ing, when not spitting at cars or spraying the girls with Lynx.

Male singers know what the new kingmakers want. Jim Morrison sang 'the little girls understand'; what today's little girls understand is light-years away from what they wanted in his day. Physically, they seem to want something more like themselves. Those palomino fauns called Brad Pitt, Matt Damon and Leonardo DiCaprio look like fourteen-year-old girls. The current 'teen gurl' ideal of maleness is a floppy-haired filly. At Christmas 1998, Italy's leading teen magazine *Kiss Me* debated the relative charms of Matt Damon and Leonardo DiCaprio and decided they were equally good-looking but Leonardo ('our boy', in Italy) had 'superior human qualities'. As for glistening pecs, leather trousers, guitar riffs – if fourteen-year-olds notice them at all they are simply (that lethal teenage put-down) 'sad'. Since the rise of 'chart factories' like Stock Aitken Waterman and Virgin Records, today's young male singer, whose calculated image is the utter opposite of the freewheelin' rocker on the open road, is eroding any distinction ever dreamed of between rock and pop.

I asked two men if the rockist game was up. The thirty-year-old said (like Dylan in 1978), 'Definitely. Rock's over. I live in a culture of sampling. All I ever hear is borrowing.' The forty-five year-old said 'No way! Rock's still there, it's diversifying, you have classic rock, Oasis, Asian rock like Cornerhouse, good lyrics, innovation, Massive Attack...'

What with energy, talent, new musical ideas bursting out all over, and a capacity to startle in new places, rock looks set to go on.

Rock began as music which both focused and freeze-framed a stage of growing up. Each generation spends its formative years in a different sonic atmosphere, something shared, enveloping them from radio and tapes in canteens, kitchens and shopping centres as well as poster-plastered bedrooms and smoke-machine-lit dance floors. The music of each decade, destined to be drenched in a million different nostalgias and memories of your own teenage, is music that means more, more intensely, than anything else possibly could, to kids discovering how overpowering meaning is.

Rock gets this effect in weirdly different ways. It is both personal and generational. Each decade, it reinvents ways of speaking to teenagers, and everyone looks back on something different. What was around when you were growing up affects how you hear what's new. On Massive Attack's *Mezzanine* (1998), forty-eight-year-olds brought up on The Stones go for the guitar solos: thirty-two-year-olds who grew up with punk get excited by its drums and bass, 'because it's so dementedly urban'.

But whatever the twenty-first century does with rock 'n' roll, 'I'm a Man' will still insist on being heard. It is what white kids hear in gangsta rap; what The Prodigy, with all their famous irony, are saying to their generation.

Women's rock is so strong now, I think, because it can play with that theatre of maleness, make it fantastic, genuinely ironic, interesting, poignant and playful: can question it by angling their own persona against it. 'What caused the jump from loving rock to doing it?' *Mojo's* interviewer asked Chrissie Hynde and Shirley Manson. 'Desperation and fear', said Chrissie:

> Rock to me was survival... As Bob Dylan said, when you've got nothing you've got nothing to lose. That made me fearless. Because nothing was worse than staying where I was.

'I agree', said Shirley:

> I grew up in a really nice city with a wonderful family but I never felt comfortable, ever... I was a target for

bullies, so at school I became really aggressive. I couldn't depend on teachers to defend me, I couldn't communicate with my parents because they would belittle the problem, I didn't really have any friends; I used to lock myself in the bedroom and listen to Chrissie's records, and at that age there's this kind of love for whoever you're listening to – 'She understands me, she'd like me if she met me.' It's an alternative reality.

For both sexes, rock is there like this as a shared world to go into. It offers you power to change how you are in the claustrophobic, unjust world you have landed in. But women's rock, though now (as for Shirley) it has its own role-models, also does what male rock did in the sixties – empowers itself by what is 'other', what it is against.

In the ocean of history, rock's fifty years are a small salt drop. Like David Bowie says, 'Heroes – just for a day'. Maybe all this will soon *be* history, kicked upstairs to some *passé* House of Lords of masculinity in the sky. But this was what rock made: a music of maleness to dream against the world. A wild, mainly well-meant dream of making everything – families, societies, politics and that nuclear minefield called sexual relationships – new, newly meaningful, newly fun.

In a lot of that, it succeeded beyond belief. For millions of teenagers all over the world, every new generation, rock put fun and hope – hope of *ways out*, hope of *'this is where I am'* meaning something to somebody else – on the map as nothing else did. It created crucial ways of sharing inner worlds – everything from lust, grief, pain, rage and dirty jokes to irrational optimism and gorgeous nonsense – through the body. It took on all the darkness and the light. It could do all that because, while it made completely new things, invented, discovered and shocked, it also flirted heavily back to one of the oldest, most unreconstructed and monstrous statements of male heroism we've ever had.

Those Greeks have a lot to answer for – look at the wreckage under the wheels of the rock 'n' roll chariot. Rock music gave the world a new way of saying 'I'm a man', new models of what it took to be primitive masculinity. Bursting with energy, violence, sexuality, it also brought to impatient, enriching, antagonistic, laughing life a bunch of immensely old ways of saying the same thing. It was ultimately Greek mythic ideals of relationship, quest, triumph and danger, of exploring self through impersonating other people, which powered this sci-fi mix of ancient and primitive, male and female, ultra-sophisticated electronics and crazed rawness, violence and darkness, all this theatrical dream of being male, in our time.

Notes

INTRODUCTION

1 Interview by N. Strauss, *Rolling Stone* 29 June 1995.
2 See Pfeil, *White*, p. 78: Whitely, *Groove*, p. 101.
3 Cook, *Short*, pp. 9, 12.
4 Robb, *Charlatans*, p. 248.
5 Cook, *Short* pp. 7–8, 17, 131–2; Frith and Goodwin, *Record*, p. 369.
6 *Faithfull*, pp. 50–51; see below, chapter 15 with nn. 2–8.
7 Marcus, *Basement*, pp. xii, 20–31.
8 Davis, *Blues*, pp. 132, 141, 144, 168–70; Lively, *Masks*, p. 216.
9 Palmer, *Dancing*, p. 77.
10 Reynolds and Press, *Sex*, p. 356.
11 Farrell, Guinness and Lloyd, *Generation*, pp. ix–xi *et passim*.

CHAPTER TWO

1 Burkert, *Mystery*, pp. 89, 93–5.
2 Palmer, 'Essay on the Fifties', 'Rolling Stone', *Covers*, p. 189.
3 *Hit Parade* (Britain), January 1957.
4 Frith, *Sociology*, p. 177; Nicholson, *Duke*, p. 242–7.
5 O'Brien, 'Sisters', p. 78.
6 Like the 1951 'Sixty Minute Man' from Clyde McPhatter and the Dominoes. See Pattison, *Vulgarity*, p. 33.
7 *New Musical Express*, 23 September 1956.
8 Gillett, *City*, p. 14.
9 First record contenders ranging from a 1944 jazz jam session to 'Rocket 88', Jackie Brenston's 1951 boogie. Possible first hits include Presley's 'Heartbreak Hotel' (1956), Muddy Waters' blues recordings (see Davis, *Blues*, p. 208) and Bill Haley and the Comets' 1955 'Rock Around the Clock'. See Dawson and Propes.
10 See P. Guralnick, sleeve notes to *Sunrise Elvis Presley*, RCA 1998.
11 Goldman, *Elvis*, p. 129; Davis, *Blues*, pp. 8, 290: Marcus, *Mystery*, p. 152. Grossberg, *Conservatism*; Pattison, *Vulgarity*, p. 53.
12 Prown and Newquist, p. 11.
13 Gillett, *City*, pp. ix, 190.
14 Shapiro, *Waiting* p. 97.

NOTES

15 Goldenrosen, *Buddy*, p. 90; *Faithfull*, p. 233.
16 Davis, *Blues*, p. 178.
17 Shaar Murray, *Traffic*, p. 133.
18 Prown and Newquist, p. 10; Davis, *Blues*, pp. 103, 175–7.
19 Davis, *Blues*, pp. 192, 103, 196. He took the nickname of another performer, J. T. 'Funny' Papa Smith, who recorded the two-part 'Howlin' Wolf Blues' in the late twenties. For his first hit, 'Moanin' at Midnight' (1951), he was still in Memphis. He moved to Chicago in 1953 to be nearer the Chess label.
20 Nicholson, *Duke*, pp. 243–6, 258–66.
21 Dove, *Rosa*, p. 91.
22 Savage, *Dreaming*, p. 9.
23 K. Le Gendre, reviewing Johnson and Taylor, *Slave*, *Independent on Sunday*, 11 July 1999.
24 Mailer, *Miami and the Siege of Chicago* (1968), see Kureishi and Savage, *Pop*, p. 336.
25 Riesman, *Quarterly*, pp. 359–71.
26 Davis, *Blues*, p. 209.
27 Marcus, *Basement*, p. 68.
28 Hornby, *Fidelity*, pp. 26–7, 137.
29 Marcus, *Basement*, p. xvi.
30 Kureishi and Savage, *Pop*, p. 45; Reynolds and Press, *Sex* p. 332; *Guitar Player*, p. 29.
31 Lomax, *Land*, pp. 342–3.
32 Pattison, *Vulgarity*, pp. 11–12, 215–16.
33 Young, *Nico*, pp. 191–2.
34 Juno, *Angry*, p. 30; below, chapter 18, n. 7.

CHAPTER THREE

1 See Empedocles (Kirk, Raven and Schofield, p. 287); Sappho (*Greek Lyric I*, p. 184).
2 Hesiod, *Theogony*, 127, 159–87. Hence Aphrodite's titles 'Cytherea' and 'Paphian'.
3 Homer, *Iliad*, 18. 401; 1, 592; 20. 36; 21. 242–80.
4 Lyrics by Fields and McHugh, 1937; DuBois, *Body*, pp. 110–19; Padel, *Mind*, pp. 100, 110–12, 117.
5 Fragments 31, 48, in *Greek Lyric* I, pp. 80, 95.
6 Apollonius of Rhodes, 3.275–98; Virgil, *Aeneid*, 1.688; 4.2; 4.689.
7 John Danyel, *Songs*, 1606: 'Fire, Fire, Fire, Fire' from Thomas Campion's *Third Book of Ayres* (c. 1618).
8 Homer, *Iliad*, 1. 606; 18.370–420, 470, 590; 21.357; 20.36–7; *Odyssey* 8.267–367.
9 *New Musical Express* interview, 20 July 1996.
10 Frazer, *Fire*, p. 90.
11 Bachelard, *Fire*, pp. 52–3; Frazer, *Fire*, pp. 36–7, 74, 76, 80.
12 Frazer, *Fire*, pp. 194, 217; Plato, *Protagoras*, 320D–321E.

13 Frazer, *Fire*, pp. 22, 36, 45–6, 67, 71, 77–8, 110, 210, 217, 220–4.
14 Frazer, *Fire*, pp. 23, 43, 45–6, 49, 115, 220–3.
15 Frazer, *Fire*, p. 192.
16 Hesiod, *Works and Days*, 70; *Theogony* 570–93.
17 Homer, *Odyssey*, 8. 310.
18 Homer, *Iliad*, 19. 357–63.
19 Homer, *Iliad*, 18. 480–615, 19. 369–90.
20 Palmer, *Dancing* p. 176.
21 Sappho, *Greek Lyric* I, pp. 185, 369.
22 Euripides, *Hippolytus*, 528–32.
23 Zeitlin, *Other*, pp. 257, 123–72.
24 Leader, *Letters*, pp. 1–2.
25 *Symposium*, 203B.
26 Sandford, *Sting*, p. 239.
27 Palmer, 'Masculinity', pp. 100, 109, on 'The Boss'.

CHAPTER FOUR

1 Davis, *Blues*, p. 209.
2 Prown and Newquist, p. 8.
3 Oakley, *Devil*, p. 128.
4 Oakley, *Devil*, p. 178; Davis, *Blues*, p. 145.
5 Davis, *Blues*, pp. 124–33; S. LaVere, *Robert Johnson, The Complete Recordings*, Columbia 1990, cover notes pp. 7–23.
6 Davis, *Blues*, p. 133.
7 Richards 'Well, This is It', and Clapton 'Discovering Robert Johnson', in *Robert Johnson: The Complete Recordings* (Columbia 1990), Introduction, pp. 25–6.
8 'From Four Till Late', recorded 1937; for the roots of Johnson's art, see Davis, *Blues*, pp. 127–32.
9 Lomax, *Land*, pp. 360–1.
10 'Travellin' Riverside Blues', 'Phonograph Blues', 'Me and the Devil Blues', 'When You Got A Good Friend', 'If I had Possession Over Judgement Day', 'Ramblin' On My Mind', 'Dead Shrimp Blues'.
11 See Davis, *Blues*, p. 123; Lomax, *Land*, p. 360; Oakley, *Devil*, p. 130.
12 Stewart-Baxter, *Rainey*, p. 8; Davis, *Blues*, p. 72.
13 Garon, *Woman*, p. 10; Placksin, *Jazzwomen*, pp. 41–116; 145, 184, 93.
14 Oakley, *Devil*, p. 199; Davis, *Blues*, p. 142; Garon, *Woman*, pp. 11, 38, 42, 45, 57, 59; Lomax, *Land*, p. 361.
15 Dawidoff, *Country*, p. 10–11.
16 Ibid., p. 13.
17 Ibid., p. 18–19.
18 Ibid., pp. 182, 185–6; 204–7.
19 Ibid., pp. 53–63; *Guitar Player*, p. 268.
20 Dawidoff, *Country*, pp. 63, 66.
21 Ibid., pp. 63–6.
22 Davis, *Blues*, pp. 198–9, 201.

NOTES

23 *Guitar Player*, p. 198; Dawidoff, *Country*, pp. 39–40; Prowne and Newquist, pp. 9, 11.
24 Davis, *Blues*, p. 164.
25 Prown and Newquist, p. 21; Davis, *Blues*, p. 84.
26 Interview by John Kelly, *Irish Times*, 23 May 1998.
27 Palmer, *Dancing*, p. 193–5; Prown and Newquist, p. 27; Davis, *Blues*, pp. 222–3, 226.
28 Prown and Newquist, pp. 49–50; Shaar-Murray, *Traffic*, p. 16; Hopkins, *Hendrix*, pp. 182, 191.
29 Hornby, *Fidelity*, p. 42.
30 Prown and Newquist, p. 8.
31 Bayton, *Frock*, pp. 105–6, 122–5.

CHAPTER FIVE

1 Homer, *Odyssey*, 5. 208–20.
2 'Babes in Toyland', *Spanking Machine* (1990), see Reynolds and Press, *Sex*, p. 264; Padel, *Mind*, pp. 99–105.
3 Homer, *Odyssey*, 12. 186, 192.10. 226; *King Lear* 1.3.37.
4 R. Carpenter, 'All You Get From Love Is A Lovesong'; H. Arlen and T. Koehler, 'I Got A Right to Sing the Blues'.
5 Bacchylides 16. 30, Ovid, *Metamorphoses*, 2. 858–75.
6 Herodotus, *Histories*, 1.1–3.
7 See Calasso, *Marriage*, pp. 3–4.
8 Euripides, *Medea*, 251, 389, 1079.
9 McClary, *Endings*, pp. 86–8, 92–6; cf. Poizat, *Angel*, pp. 41–5, 128, 155
10 Many noble Athenian women, says one Aristophanes character, took hemlock from shame at Euripides' play *Bellerophon* about Stheneboa's adulterous passion. That word *gamous* shocks even the god Dionysus. 'Sssh!' he says in horror (*Frogs* 849–50, 1043–5).
11 Carson, *Glass*, p. 128.
12 Holiday, *Lady*, p. 168; Padel, 'Possession'; Padel, *Mind*, pp. 106–13; Grieg, *Tomorrow*, pp. 134–5.
13 Reynolds and Press, *Sex*, chapter 1 and pp. 230–31.
14 Lyrics by Burke and Webster.

CHAPTER SIX

1 Homer, *Odyssey*, 5. 335–53, 455, 462.
2 Bacchylides 16; Homer, *Odyssey*, 5. 276; 10.505; 12. 26, 39–141.
3 Strauss, *Correspondence*, pp. 367, 371, 456.
4 Reynolds and Press, *Sex*, pp. 192, 207, 212, 285.
5 *New Musical Express*, 16 September 1978; Gray, *Venus*, p. 112.
6 Apollonius of Rhodes, *Voyage of the Argonauts*, 3.275–902; Homer, *Odyssey*, 4.219–26.
7 Homer, *Iliad*, 14. 198–224.

8 'Venus and Amor', Art Museum, Princeton University.
9 Posner, *Watteau*, pp. 23, 73, plates 7, 34, 36.
10 Bachelard, *Fire*, p. 52.
11 Brooks, *Desire*, p. 27.
12 Showalter, *Anarchy*, pp. 145, 148, 176.
13 Baudelaire, 'La Mort des amants':

> Nos deux coeurs seront deux vastes flambeaux,
> Qui réfléchiront leurs doubles lumières
> Dans nos deux esprits, ces miroirs jumeaux.

14 See Plato, *Symposium*, 178B; Goldhill, *Foucault*, pp. 9, 148–9.

CHAPTER SEVEN

1 Robb, *Charlatans*, p. 249–50.
2 *Faithfull*, pp. 72, 79. 'Marianne, don't forget the Grail,' said Richards to her, long after.
3 Sandford, *Sting*, pp. 55, 63, 70–2.
4 Gilmore, 'The Sixties Essay', in 'Rolling Stone' *Covers* p. 193.
5 Prown and Newquist, p. 32. Cohn, 'Pop From the Beginning' (1969), Kureishi and Savage, *Pop*, p. 226–7.
6 Lomax, *Land*, p. 406.
7 *Faithfull*, p. 70.
8 Gilmore, 'The Sixties Essay', in 'Rolling Stone' *Covers*, p. 193.
9 *Guitar Player*, pp. 64, 67.
10 Frith and Goodwin, *Record*, p. 373.
11 Palmer, 'Essay on the Fifties', in 'Rolling Stone', *Covers* p. 189.
12 Hornby, *Fidelity*, pp. 52, 73.
13 Flipper, 'Brainwash,' Subterranean Records 1981.
14 Christgau, 'Stupid', p. 368.
15 See Raphael, *Bollocks*.
16 'Ticket to Ride', produced by Jack Daugherry, arranged Carpenter 1969.
17 'I take one everywhere I go. I carry it on the plane – it'll go in the overhead. I couldn't not. It's like I forgot my teeth or shorts.' Dawidoff, *Country*, p. 40.
18 Peter Green, 'Ramblin' Pony', Decca 1967; Rolling Stones, 'Midnight Rambler'; Nick Cave, 'Red Right Hand'.
19 See Padel, *Mind*, pp. 7–8.
20 'A Woman Waits For Me'; see *Song of Myself* 24, 527; 52. 1331–4; *Children of Adam*, 'I Sing the Body Electric'. Pattison, *Vulgarity*, p. 51, argues that rock is heir to American romanticism and blossomed particularly in the South because the white South was steeped in nineteenth-century romanticism.
21 Whitman, *Song of Myself*, 20. 380–415; 48. 1281–2, 17ff; 24. 527ff. See *Leaves of Grass*, p. 899, against slavery.
22 *Faithfull*, pp. 133–4, 188, 194.

NOTES

23 Interview on Rocking Eddie Murphy's memorial programme for Elvis, Shannon Side, Northern Sound Radio, 16 August 1998.
24 Cohn, *Awopbopaloobop*, p. 23; Melly, *Revolt*, pp. 36–7, Frith and Goodwin p. 392.
25 Hopkins, *Hendrix*, pp. 189, 215.
26 Shaar Murray, *Traffic*, p. 8.

CHAPTER EIGHT

1 See Hoare, *Soul*, p. 122; Palmer, *Dancing*, p. 15.
2 Said, *Orientalism* is a massively larger thesis than this, of course, and begins with Europe's 'invention' of 'the Orient'; see Thornton, *Painting*, p. 18 *et passim*.
3 Marcus, *Victorians*, p. 200; Lively, *Masks*, p. 148; Croutier, *Veil*, pp. 173–9; Thornton, *Painting*, pp. 4–5 and all illustrations.
4 See Said, *Orientalism*, p. 54.
5 See the argument of Hall, *Barbarian*.
6 Aristophanes, *Thesmophoriazousae*, 1175–1225.
7 Lively, *Masks*, pp. 145–8.
8 For various reasons why, see Pattison, *Vulgarity*, p. 47.
9 Roediger, *Whiteness*; Davis, *Blues*, p. 168.
10 Turner, *Trouble*, p. 36; Gillett, *City*, pp. 17, 143.
11 Frith, *Sociology*, p. 177–9; Gillett, *City*, p. 17; Kamin, 'Jazz', p. 99.
12 Gillett, *City*, pp. 190–1.
13 Malcolm Bradbury, *Independent*, 3 February 1996, reviewing Douglas, *Honesty*.
14 Nicholson, *Duke*, p. 137; Lively, *Masks*, p. 212; see the argument of Douglas, *Honesty*.
15 See S. Lasker's cover notes on the album, 'Duke Ellington and his Cotton Club Orchestra: Jungle Nights in Harlem (1927–32)'; Lively, *Masks*, pp. 99–100, 156, 206–13.
16 Lively, *Masks*, p. 205.
17 For more on this, see Rubin, *Primitivism*.
18 Lively, *Masks*, p. 207.
19 Tull, *War Child* (Chrysalis); Patti Smith, *Easter* (Arista); Pattison, *Vulgarity*, p. 50.
20 Marcus, *Mystery*, p. 156.
21 Stearns, *Jazz*, p. 282, Hoare, *Soul*, p. 118–19.
22 18 June 1933, Nicholson, *Duke*, p. 136.
23 Frith, *Sociology*, pp. 178–81, see argument of Cutler, *Popular*; Hoare, *Soul*, p. 122; Turner, *Trouble*, p. 119.
24 Gillett, *City*, p. 11.
25 Doyle, *Commitments*, p. 134.
26 Hoare, *Soul*, p. 209; Dyer, 'Disco', p. 414; see Turner, *Trouble*, p. 92; and, of course, the whole brilliant volume Palmer, *Dancing*.
27 See whole argument of Wilson, *Earth*.
28 Nicholson, *Ellington*, pp. 310–13.

29 Gillett, *City*, p. 8; Davis, *Blues*, p. 173; P. Guralnick, cover notes for *Sunrise Elvis Presley* (RCA 1999).
30 Lomax, *Land*, p. 340.
31 Palmer, *Dancing*, pp. 63, 237–8.
32 Palmer, *Dancing*, p. 15.
33 Turner, *Trouble*, p. 19; Gillett, *City*, p. 242; Frith, *Sociology*, p. 178. Hoare, *Soul*, pp. 134, 152; Doyle, *Commitments*, p. 57.

CHAPTER NINE

1 Palmer, *Dancing*, pp. 47–9.
2 Shaar Murray, *Traffic*, pp. 184–5, 193; Palmer, *Dancing*, pp. 47–96.
3 Gillett, *City*, pp. 11, 119–52; the story is related in Whitcomb, *Ball*; see argument of Hamm, *New World*; see bibliography in Pattison, *Vulgarity*, p. 245.
4 Dawidoff, *Country*, pp. 10, 196; Marcus, *Mystery*, p. 156.
5 See the discussion in Shaar Murray, *Traffic*, pp. 84–105.
6 Barbara McMahon, *Evening Standard*, 16 March 1999.
7 Palmer, *Dancing*, pp. 27–8, 43.
8 Marcus, *Mystery*, pp. 138–40; check it out on *Sunrise Elvis Presley* RCA 1999 (two CDs); Pattison, *Vulgarity*, p. 87.
9 Marcus, *Mystery*, p. 154.
10 Shaar Murray, *Traffic*, pp. 83, 86.
11 Marcus, *Mystery*, pp. 153–5; Davis, *Blues*, p. 209; Palmer, *Dancing*, p. 28.
12 Gillett, *City*, p. 28; Davis, *Blues*, p. 173; see discussion by Marcus, *Mystery*, p. 147.
13 Marcus, *Mystery*, p. 145; Palmer, *Dancing*, p. 24.
14 Gillett, *City*, p. 29.
15 See Palmer, *Dancing*, pp. 46, 51.
16 Gillett, *City*, p. 14; Pattison, *Vulgarity*, pp. 34–5.
17 Turner, *Trouble*, pp. 38–9.
18 *Faithfull*, pp. 70, 225, 333.
19 D. St Hill, *Pride Magazine*, May 1999, p. 17.
20 Lively, *Masks*, pp. 199, 214.
21 Shaar, Murray, *Traffic*, pp. 82–3; Hopkins, *Hendrix* p. 269.
22 Gillett, *City*, p. 122.
23 Shaar Murray, *Traffic*, p. 86.
24 Hill, *Prince*, p. 96.
25 Turner, *Trouble*, p. 64.
26 Gillett, *City*, p. 390.
27 Shaar Murray, *Traffic*, p. 96.
28 Palmer, *Dancing*, p. 275; Savage, *Dreaming*, p. 116.
29 Sandford, *Sting*, pp. 63–5, 107, 168.
30 Shaar Murray, *Traffic*, p. 97.
31 Interview, L. Markwell, *Independent* Magazine, 22 May 1999.
32 Shaar Murray, *Traffic*, pp. 86, 97–8.
33 Shaar Murray, *Traffic*, pp. 40, 49, 54, 98–9.

NOTES

34 A. Bozza, *Rolling Stone*, 29 April 1999, pp. 43–5; D. St Hill, *Pride* magazine, May 1999, p. 18.
35 *Guardian*, 20 July 1999, p. 3.
36 Walton, *Black, White, Blue*, pp. 65–6, 142.
37 Turner, *Trouble*, p. 83.
38 P. Wallin, *Today*, 14 August 1993; A. Duval Smith, *Independent*, 18 March 1999; St Hill, *Pride* magazine, May 1999, p. 19.
39 Shaar Murray, *Traffic*, p. 103.
40 Shaar Murray, *Traffic*, p. 91.

CHAPTER TEN

1 Hopkins, *Hendrix*, pp. 172, 192; Hill, *Prince*, p. 3; quoted in Baldwin, *Price*; Christie, *Independent*, 18 June 1998.
2 Hopkins, *Hendrix*, pp. 104–7, 118; D. St Hill, *Pride Magazine*, May 1999, p. 20.
3 *Aerosmith*, p. 156.
4 See Gillett, *City*, p. 18–21.
5 Palmer, *Dancing*, p. 140; Pattison, *Vulgarity*, p. 59; White, *Richard*, p. 40.
6 'Rock 'n' Roll Personality Parade', *New Musical Express*, 1957, p. 5.
7 Gillett, *City*, pp. 10–20; Davis, *Blues*, p. 158; Palmer, *Dancing*, p. 15.
8 Hopkins, *Hendrix*, pp. 152–8, 172, 191; Didion, *White*, pp. 21–5.
9 *Cream*, August 1981, p. 39; Turner, *Trouble*, p. 83; *Independent*, Thursday Review, 2 July 1998; Pattison, *Vulgarity*, pp. 114–16.
10 Whitcombe, *Ball*, Preface; Hopkins, *Hendrix*, p. 152.
11 Davis, *Blues*, p. 113; for the classic 1978 article, see Frith and Goodwin, *Record*, pp. 373–4; 'So what', from the British punk *Anti-Nowhere League* (WXYZ 1982).
12 Pattison, *Vulgarity*, p. 115; Hopkins, *Elvis*, p. 153.
13 Hill, *Prince*, p. 3; Hopkins, *Hendrix*, p. 269; Shaar Murray, *Traffic*, chapter 4, for a nuanced account of black musicians' relations with white audiences.
14 Professor Howard 'Stretch' Johnson, dancer with the Cotton Club Boys in 1932: see Lively, *Masks*, p. 214.
15 Lively, *Masks*, p. 219; Holiday, *Lady*, p. 61; Shaar Murray, *Traffic*, p. 87.
16 Hill, *Prince*, p. 198.
17 Ibid., pp. 3, 90, 96. Ward, *Soul*, relates white views of black music and black 'progress'.
18 Frith, *Sociology*, pp. 421, 423.
19 Hill, *Prince*, p. 90.
20 Marcus, *Lipstick*, pp. 96–7, 108.
21 See Shaar Murray, *Traffic*, p. 97.
22 Hill, *Prince*, pp. 2–3, 69–72, 78–80. 129–30.
23 Ibid., pp. 72, 97.
24 Ibid., pp. p. 77, 82–6.
25 Ibid., p. 85.
26 Ibid., p. 69.

27 See Shaar Murray, *Traffic*, chapter 3.
28 St Hill, *Pride Magazine*, May 1999, p. 17.
29 Pattison, *Vulgarity*, pp. 30, 36–7, 49–51; after Frazer's *Golden Bough* came the charismatic Cambridge classicists Gilbert Murray and Jane Harrison.
30 Palmer, *Dancing*, pp. 147–8; Euripides' *Bacchae*, ed. Dodds; Dodds, *Irrational*, chapter 3; Padel, 'Space' and *Gods*, chapter 3.
31 S. Reynolds, *Guardian*, 4 June 1977.
32 Plato, *Phaedrus*, 244A-E, 265A-B; Dodds, *Irrational*, chapter 3; Padel, *Gods*, pp. 82–9.
33 Padel, *Mind*, p. 73; Padel, *Gods*, pp. 47–54.
34 *Iliad*, 1. 104; Padel, *Mind*, pp. 25, 68, 99; Padel, *Gods*, chapters 5–7.
35 Padel, *Mind*, pp. 72, 101.
36 Padel, 'Possession', *Mind*, pp. 101.
37 Homer, *Odyssey*, 11. 12–17, 93–6; Plato, *Symposium*, 201D-12A; Parmenides: see Kirk Raven and Schofield, p. 242; Padel, *Mind*, pp. 71, 112.
38 Nick Cave 'Do You Love Me?'; Padel, *Mind*, pp. 99–102.
39 Laing, *Divided* pp. 50–1; Padel, *Gods*, pp. 55–61, 95, 110; Padel, *Mind*, p. 71.
40 Auden, Maritain: see Padel, *Mind*, p. 76.
41 Cook, *Short*, p. 44.
42 See the brilliantly researched and organized argument of Lively, *Masks*, chapter 3.
43 Palmer, *Dancing*, p. 160.

CHAPTER ELEVEN

1 Lomax, *Land*, p. 18.
2 Blues revival: Davis, *Blues*, pp. 211–12.
3 Gilmore, *Night*, p. 205.
4 Davis, *Blues*, pp. 97–8.
5 On a 1946 recording session for *Blues in the Mississipi Night*, see Lomax, *Land*, pp. 233–313; Davis, *Blues*, p. 108.
6 See Oakley, *Devil*, pp. 23–33, 124–209.
7 Celmins, *Fleetwood*, p. 11.
8 Ibid., p. 23.
9 Birchall, 'The Decline and Fall of British Rhythm and Blues'; Eisen, *Rock*, p. 96.
10 Turner, *Trouble*, pp. 118–37.
11 'From Four Till Late', 'I'm a Steady Rollin' Man', 'Walkin' Blues', 'Drunken-hearted Man,' 'Hellhound on my Trail', 'If I Had Possession over Judgement Day'.
12 In an issue of *Musician* dedicated to Robert Johnson, 1991.
13 Heatley and Leigh, *Song*, pp. 22–3.
14 Doyle, *Commitments*, pp. 9, 35–9.
15 Chapman in *Mojo*, July 1999, pp. 64–84.
16 Doyle, *Commitments*, p. 8; Frith and Goodwin, *Record*, p. 369.
17 Davis, *Blues*, pp. 216–7, Reynolds and Press, *Sex*, p. 21; Jefferson Airplane, *Surrealistic Pillow* (RCA 197).

NOTES

18 Parker, *Rollins*, pp. 75, 82–6, 96. See below, chapter 15 n. 10.
19 Parker, *Rollins*, p. 96.
20 Grills, *Alanis*, pp. 18–20.
21 Davis, *Blues*, p. 256.
22 Spitz, *Dylan*, p. 270.

CHAPTER TWELVE

1 Padel, *Gods*, chapter 6.
2 Anon., *Atlantic*; Logan, *Betrayal*, p. 244; Oakley, *Devil*, p. 22.
3 Davis, *Blues*, pp. 163, 191.
4 Oakley, *Devil*, p. 71; Davis, *History*, p. 170; Shaar Murray, *Traffic*, p. 131.
5 Davis, *Blues*, pp. 164–71.
6 Frith, *Sociology*, p. 180.
7 See argument of Bayles, *Hole*, p.
8 Michael Odell, interview, *Guardian*, Review, 4 Dec 1998, p. 15.
9 *Rolling Stone*, 31 October 1996, 'Rolling Stone', *Covers* p. 257.
10 *Guardian*, 20 July 1999, p. 3.
11 Andy Kershaw, 'Shooting from the hip', *Independent*, Weekend Review, 31 July 1999.
12 *Independent*, 16 March 1998.
13 Colin Escott, sleeve notes to *Memories: the '68 Comeback Special*, BMG 1998.
14 Oakley, *Devil*, pp. 66, 128–32; Davis, *Blues*, pp. 97, 114, 122.
15 Davis, *History*, pp. 91, 104–6, 129–30, 184; Shaar Murray, *Traffic*, p. 148.
16 Savage, *Dreaming*, p. 530.
17 Booth, *True*, p. 17.
18 Hotchner, *Blow*, pp. 345–6. Pattison, *Vulgarity*, p. 175; Whitely, *Groove*, p. 78.
19 *Vox*, June 1998.
20 See Savage, *Dreaming*, p. 488.
21 Savage, *Dreaming*, pp. 222, 240–2.
22 *Faithfull*, pp. 172, 180.
23 Hoskyns, *Diamond* p. 210.
24 Ibid., p. 210.
25 Booth, *True*, p. 47–8, 91–2; Hotchner, *Blow*, p. 20.
26 Hotchner, *Blow*, pp. 347–8; Whitely, *Groove*, pp. 84–8.
27 *Faithfull*, pp. 186–7.
28 Hoskyns, *Diamond* p. 210; Didion, *Bethlehem*, pp. 120–2, 128.
29 Parker, *Rollins*, p. 59; Didion, *White*, p. 42.
30 Younge and Ellison, *Guardian* 23 April 1999.
31 Hotchner, *Blow*, p. 373; Whitely, *Groove*, p. 89.
32 Sheehan, *Lie*, p. 741; Shay, *Achilles*, pp. 28, 171, 150–3, 213, 224. The peak year of desertion from the army was 1971.
33 Shay, *Achilles*, pp. 83, 202
34 Ibid., pp. 7–9, 110, 125–7, 138, 150–4, 158, 165–9. The author, a trauma-physician, has treated many Vietnam vets. Over a third met all criteria of

the American Psychiatric Association and World Health Organization for Post-Traumatic Stress Disorder (over 70 per cent had at least one symptom): a hostile, mistrustful, estranged attitude to the world; massive feelings of emptiness, hopelessness, being on the edge.
35 Shay, *Achilles*, pp. 32, 143, 146–8.
36 Hopkins, *Hendrix*, pp. 40–8.
37 Ibid., pp. 255–6; 277.

CHAPTER THIRTEEN

1 See argument of Bourke, *Killing*; P. Kingston, *Guardian*, 26 May 1999, pp. 2–3.
2 See Padel, *Gods*, pp. 10, 24.
3 Padel, *Gods*, pp. 23–9.
4 Bentley, *Stage*, pp. 53–7.
5 Herodotus, *Histories*, 1.153; Padel, 'Space', p. 337.
6 Palmer, *Dancing*, p. 183.
7 Savage, *Dreaming*, p. 222.
8 Padel, *Gods*, chapter 5.
9 Knox, *Heroic*, pp. 42, 56.
10 Palmer, *Dancing*, p. 155; Winkler and Zeitlin, *Dionysos?* pp. 3–5, 10, 97–129, 336, 340.
11 See Palmer, *Dancing*, p. 233.
12 Euripides, *Hippolytus*, 1351; Sophocles, *Women of Trachis*, 1079.
13 Padel, *Mind*, pp. 44–8.
14 *Time Out*, 7 October 1998; Hoskyns, *Glam!*, pp. 74, 105.
15 Padel, *Gods*, pp. 132–3, 241–6.
16 Steiner, *Antigones*, p. 120; Padel, *Mind*, pp. 150–2, 161; *Independent*, 24 November 1997.
17 Hoskyns, *Glam!*, pp. 48, 27, 32–3; Whitely, *Groove*, p. 91.
18 Sophocles, *Oedipus Rex*, 1187; Chaucer, *The Monk's Tale*, 2–3, 2951; Steiner, *Death*, p. 11–16.
19 Hoskyns, *Glam!*, pp. 22, 48, 98.
20 Campbell, *Hero*, quoted by Savage (*Dreaming*, p. 123) to illustrate the anarchically creative side of John Lydon when he joined the Sex Pistols.
21 Euripides, *Hippolytus*; Sophocles, *Ajax*; Euripides, *Bacchae*.
22 Palmer, *Dancing*, p. 228.
23 Ibid., p. 228.
24 Savage, *Dreaming*, pp. 505 (quoting Campbell, *Hero*), 530.
25 Padel, *Mind*, p. 127; Padel, *Gods*, pp. 202–4.

CHAPTER FOURTEEN

1 Hoskyns, *Glam!*, p. 111.
2 *Guardian*, 22 and 28 April 1999; *Independent on Sunday*, 24 April 1999.
3 Martin Kettle, *Guardian*, 28 April 1998.

NOTES

4 Internet report from M. Kettle in Washington, *Guardian*, 19 June 1999.
5 Parker, *Rollins*, p. 59; Chrissie Hynde interview, *Mojo* July 1999, p. 52.
6 *Independent*, 31 July 1999, p. 3.
7 O'Brien, *She Bop*, p. 102.
8 Didion, *Bethlehem*, p. 84.
9 Hoskyns, *Diamond*, throughout, but especially p. 15.
10 Hoskyns, *Diamond*, pp. 206, 210–11, 213, 214; Didion, *Bethlehem*, pp. 49, 85.
11 See Whitely, *Groove*, pp. 83–4; Parker, *Rollins*, p. 58.
12 Parker, *Rollins* pp. 46, 55, 145–6.
13 Ibid., pp. 173–4.
14 Ibid., pp. 147, 158, 172, plates pp. 144–5.
15 Palmer, *Dancing*, p. 177–80.
16 Young, *Nico*, p. 124.

CHAPTER FIFTEEN

1 Palmer, *Dancing*, p. 262; Davis, *Blues*, p. 209; Shapiro, *Man*, pp. 124, 135.
2 Light, *History*, pp. 301–3.
3 Quoted by Glover, p. 12.
4 Hopkins, *Hendrix*, p. 70.
5 Davis, *Blues*, p. 169–70, n. 1.
6 Davis, *Blues*, p. 221–2 (quoting Sawyer, *King*); Marcus, *Basement*, p. 12.
7 Glover, p. 22.
8 *Faithfull*, p. 148.
9 Palmer, *Dancing*, p. 176; S. Hills, *The Times*, magazine section, 6 March 1999, p. 26; above, chapter 11.
10 Al Bergamo, *Los Angeles Times*, 27 September 1981; Parker, *Rollins*, pp. 86–7, 96; above, chapter 11, n. 19.
11 'Walk Like A Man', *Tunnel of Love*, 1987; 'Adam Raised a Cain', *Darkness at the Edge of Town* (1978); 'Independence Day', from *The River* (1980); Whitely, *Groove*, p. 103.
12 Prown and Newquist, pp. 95; 153; 242.
13 Frith, *Sociology*, pp. 166, 172–3.
14 Hoskyns, *Glam!*, p. 109.
15 Robb, *Charlatans*, p. 48.
16 *Mojo*, July 1999, p. 56.
17 Whitely, *Groove*, pp. 84–5; Parker, *Rollins*, p. 113.
18 Dez Cadena, Mike Watt, Geordie Grindle, quoted in Parker, *Rollins*, pp. 112–13.
19 Pattison, *Vulgarity*, pp. 9–10.
20 Frith, *Sociology*, p. 164.
21 Frith, *Sociology*, pp. 162–3, 188; Rogan, *Starmakers*, pp. 14–19, 382–92.
22 Frith, *Sociology*, p. 174.

NOTES

CHAPTER SIXTEEN

1. Reynolds and Press, *Sex*, chapters 2–3.
2. For classicist material and discussions of all this, see references, arguments and bibliography in Padel, 'Possession'; *Mind*, pp. 99–113, 159–62.
3. Leader, *Promises*, p. 10.
4. Reynolds and Press, *Sex*, p. 28.
5. Heatley and Leigh, *Song*, p. 36; Sandford, *Sting*, pp. 123, 28, 131.
6. Davis, *Blues*, pp. 123, 206; R. Johnson, '32–20 Blues', 'Drunken-Hearted Man'.
7. Davis, *Blues*, p. 85; Shaar Murray, *Traffic*, p. 61; *King Lear* iv. 6.
8. *Aerosmith*, p. 55.
9. Shaar Murray, *Traffic*, p. 58 (quoting Richard Pryor).
10. Shaar Murray, *Traffic*, pp. 59 (quoting 1984 interview in *New Musical Express*), 62.
11. Frith and Goodwin, *Record*, pp. 369–90; Reynolds and Press, *Sex*, pp. 3–12; Shaar Murray, *Traffic*, p. 64, points out Dylan and Jagger both used women to illustrate the stagnancy of society. 'Like a Rolling Stone' and 'Play with Fire' sneer at rich girls who offend the boy's (fictitious) working-class integrity; compare the real thing in Jarvis Cocker's 'Common People'.
12. Whitely, *Groove*, p. 20; Reynolds and Press, *Sex*, p. 89.
13. Whitely, *Groove*, p. 104.
14. *Aerosmith*, p. 165; Heatley and Leigh, *Song*, p. 134; Reynolds and Press, *Sex*, pp. xiv, 20, 32, 216 (and 2–155 generally); Whitely, *Groove*, pp. 20–2, 109.
15. Cattermole, *Venus*, chapter 1.
16. F. Sturges, *Independent*, 18 December 1998; Whitely, *Groove*, pp. 41–3.
17. Reynolds and Press, *Sex*, pp. 34–40.
18. Davis, *History*, p. 249.
19. Juno, *Angry*, pp. 13–14.
20. Hornby, *Fidelity*, p. 58.
21. S. Frith, 'Girls don't make it in rock', *Cream*, October 1971; *Let It Rock* (special issue, July 1975). Sexism in lyrics till mid-seventies, 'Popular Music', in King and Stott *Life*. For more recent stuff, Reynolds and Press, *Sex*, Chapters 2–3; see below, chapter 18, nn. 18, 21–6, 31, 41–5.
22. By David Foster and Peter Cetera: it appeared in *The Karate Kid II* and was a big hit for Cetera.
23. Easthorpe, *Man*, p. 120.

CHAPTER SEVENTEEN

1. Graves, 'At the Gate', *Collected Poems*, p. 541; interview, Hester Lacey, *Independent on Sunday*, 24 January 1999.
2. *Faithfull*, pp. 45–8.
3. Heaney, *Preoccupations*, p. 63; *Government*, p. 153.
4. *Independent*, 23 April 1998.

NOTES

5   See argument of Silverman, *Mirror*.
6   Nicholson, *Duke*, p. 11.
7   See arguments of Clément, *Opera*; Poizat, *Angel*; Koestenbaum, *Throat*; Leonardi and Pope, *Mouth*.
8   Whitely, *Groove*, p. 86; Jenson 'Defining Fandom', in Lewis, *Adoring Audience*, p. 15; Faithfull, p. 70.
9   Shaar Murray, *Traffic*, p. 71.
10 Gilmore, *Night*, p. 204.
11 Shaar Murray, *Traffic*, p. 60.
12 *Aerosmith*, p. 56.
13 Shaar Murray, *Traffic*, p. 60.
14 See Grieg, *Tomorrow*, pp. 21–5; Douglas, *Girls*, chapters 3–4.
15 Grieg, *Tomorrow*, chapters 1–2; Douglas, *Girls*, pp. 84–98.
16 Shaar Murray, *Traffic*, p. 58; above, chapter 11.
17 Christgau, 'Stupid'.
18 Cohn, *Awopbopaloobop*, p. 140; Frith and Goodin, *Record*, pp. 374, 382; Hotchner, *Blow*, p. 165; Whitely, *Groove*, pp. 69–73, 77, 93; Shaar Murray, *Traffic*, p. 72.
19 Frith, *Sociology*, p. 174; Hotchner, *Blow*, p. 39; Shaar Murray, *Traffic*, p. 64.
20 Fabian, *Groupie*, p. 54.
21 Christgau, 'Girl'; Hopkins, *Hendrix*, p. 98.
22 O'Brien, *She Bop*, p. 102.
23 Shaar Murray, *Traffic*, p. 71; Fabian, *Groupie*, p. 170.
24 Shaar Murray, *Traffic*, pp. 66–7; O'Brien, *She Bop*, p. 98.
25 *Faithfull*, pp. 87, 134, 159.
26 'Oh Sister', 1976.
27 Spitz, *Dylan*, p. 57; Shaar Murray, *Traffic*, p. 65.
28 *Faithfull*, p. 45.
29 Cook, *Short*, pp. 9, 82.
30 Dawidoff, *Country*, p. 185.
31 Frith, *Sociology*, p. 166; Palmer, *Dancing*, pp. 99–101.
32 Laing, *Electric*, pp. 78–9; Frith, *Sociology*, p. 185.
33 McCleod, 'Rising', p. 123.

CHAPTER EIGHTEEN

1   Christgau, 'Stupid', p. 366; Whitely, *Groove*, pp. 50–64.
2   Cook, *Short*, chapter 7; see McClary, *Endings*, Introduction, chapter 3 *et passim*.
3   Pattison, *Vulgarity*, pp. 114–19; Fabian, *Groupie*, pp. 14, 30, 38, 109, 170.
4   *Aerosmith*, p. 161; see the story of Etchingham, *Gypsy*.
5   Bebe Buell, quoted in Hoskyns, *Glam*, p. 78.
6   Parker, *Rollins*, p. 88.
7   Juno, *Angry*, p. 30; above, chapter 2, n. 34.
8   Interview, S. Simmons, *Mojo*, July 1999, p. 56.
9   Yorke, *Zeppelin*, pp. 182–4. Jagger and the fifty million story (current well before he impregnated his Brazilian model), Juno, *Angry*, pp. 58, 198.

10 Young, *Nico*, p. 191.
11 Gilmore, *Night*, pp. 201–3.
12 Gilmore, *Night*, p. 203.
13 Fabian, *Groupie*, p. 109.
14 Chapter 15, n. 15.
15 Internet alt.fan.courtney-love; see Whitely, *Groove*, p. 62.
16 Rogan, *Starmakers*, p. 400.
17 Ibid., p. 402; King, 'Feminism', p. 54.
18 *Guardian*, 29 July 1998; Bayton, *Frock*, p. 127.
19 A. Gill, *Independent*, Review, 18 December 1998, p. 12.
20 Evans, *Girls*, p. xv; Sullivan, in Cooper, *Girls*, pp. 140, 144.
21 Reynolds and Press, *Sex*, p. 34–5.
22 Evans, *Girls*, p. xvi; Sullivan, in Cooper, *Girls*, p. 144.
23 Ibid., p. xiii.
24 Ibid., p. xiv; Juno, *Angry*, p. 53.
25 Juno, *Angry*, p. 190.
26 Bayton, *Frock*, pp. 117–23, with illustrations; see her article in Whitely, *Groove*, pp. 44–5.
27 *Mojo*, July 1999, pp. 54–6.
28 Bayton, *Frock*, pp. 215–16.
29 Johnstone, *Patti*, p. 93.
30 See argument of Gaar, *Rebel*; Raphael, *Bollocks*, pp. xiv.
31 Marcus, *Lipstick*, pp. 77, 213; Reynolds and Press, pp. 307–10.
32 Raphael, *Bollocks*, p. 177; Rogan, *Starmakers*, p. 326; Reynolds and Press, *Sex*, p. 90.
33 Juno, *Angry*, p. 69.
34 Ibid., pp. 60–7.
35 Frith, *Sociology*, pp. 164, 174; Bayton, *Frock*, pp. 132–7, 195, 202–3.
36 Raphael, *Bollocks*, p. 231; Bayton, *Frock*, p. 122–33, Whitely, *Groove*, pp. 46–7.
37 Bayton, *Frock*, p. 13.
38 Davis, *Blues*, p. 249; Raphael, *Bollocks*, p. xi.

CHAPTER NINETEEN

1 Frith and Goodwin, *Record*, p. 423.
2 Robertson, 'Betrothal', p. 34.
3 Palmer, *Dancing*, p. 140–1; Hoskyns, *Glam!*, p. 100.
4 Hill, *Prince*, p. 155; Hoskyns, *Glam!*, p. 109.
5 Hill, *Prince*, p. 77, 128–41, 200–2.
6 Hotchner, *Blow*, p. 164; Whitely, *Groove*, pp. 76–7; Hoskyns, *Glam*, pp. 12–13; *Faithfull*, p. 133.
7 Whitely, *Groove*, p. 67; DeCurtis, *History*, p. 182.
8 *Faithfull*, pp. 133, 145; see Sontag, 'Camp'.
9 Johnstone, *Patti*, p. 69–74; Whitely, *Groove*, pp. 199–202; Reynolds and Press, *Sex*, pp. 294–6, 318–22.
10 Aeschylus, *Suppliant Women*, 202; Padel, *Gods*, pp. 146–7.

NOTES

11 *Faithfull*, pp. 48, 55.
12 Holiday, *Lady*, p. 61.
13 Heriot, *Castrati*, pp. 13, 24.
14 E.g. Koestenbaum, *Throat*; Blackmer and Smith, *Travesti*; Leonardi and Pope, *Mouth*.
15 Wagner, *Opera*, p. 111.
16 Palmer, *Dancing*, p. 24; George, *Motown*, pp. 31, 86.
17 Ronnie Spector, interview Adam Sweeting, *Guardian* 8 January 1999; Holiday, *Lady*, p. 34.
18 Poizart, *Angel*, p. 138.
19 *Independent*, 22 November 1996.
20 Frith, *Sociology*, pp. 174–5; Savage, *Dreaming*, 418, 442, 486, 496; Marcus, *Lipstick*, p. 77.
21 Phillips and Kosek, *Bluegrass*, p. 111.
22 Cook, *Short*, pp. 11, 17–19, 42.
23 Gillett, *City*, p. 8.
24 Hill, *Prince*, pp. 72, 98, 128.

CHAPTER TWENTY

1 Frith, *Sociology*, p. 421–3.
2 Gilmore, *Night*, p. 205.
3 'Rolling Stone', *Covers*, pp. 118, 185.
4 *Mirror*, 16 June 1999.
5 *Mojo*, July 1999, p. 54.
6 Frith and Goodwin, *Record*, p. 488; Hoskyns, *Glam!*, pp. 34, 102.
7 Marcus, *Lipstick*, pp. 77, 81.
8 Savage, *Dreaming*, p. 122.
9 Robb, *Charlatans*, p. 236; 'Rolling Stone', *Covers*, p. 92.
10 Vermorel, *Starlust*, quoted in Frith and Goodwin, *Record*, pp. 482–7.
11 Frith and Goodwin, *Record*, pp. 424, 482–7, quoting Vermorel, *Starlust*.
12 Frith and Goodwin, *Record*, pp. 485, 488–9.
13 Ibid., pp. 422–3, 486.
14 'Rolling Stone', *Covers* p. 96: *Rolling Stone*, 24 August 1978.
15 Savage, *Dreaming*, pp. 356, 362, 448–59.
16 'Rolling Stone', *Covers*, pp. 104, 230.
17 Hornby, *Fidelity*, p. 58.
18 Burkert, *Mystery*, pp. 89, 93–5; above, chapter 2 n. 1.
19 Burkert, *Mystery*, p. 93.
20 Allen, *Mysteriously*, p. 292.
21 Paulin, *Moment*, p. 281; Padel, *Mind*, pp. 157–61; see further Warner, *Monuments*, p. 86 et passim.
22 Burkert, *Mysteries*, p. 89.
23 Cook, *Short*, p. 119.
24 Frith and Goodwin, *Record*, pp. 375, 399, 401, 405–6, 409.
25 *Mojo*, July 1999, p. 54.

CHAPTER TWENTY-ONE

1 Interview, *Guardian*, 17 April 1999.

Bibliography

Abbaté, C., *Unsung Voices: Opera and Musical Narrative in the Nineteenth Century*, Princeton University Press, 1991
Aerosmith with S. Davis. *Walk this Way: the Autobiography of Aerosmith*, Virgin Books, 1999
Allen, D. C., *Mysteriously Meant: The Rediscovery of Pagan Symbolism and Allegorical Interpretation in the Renaissance*, Johns Hopkins Press, Baltimore and London, 1970
Anonymous, 'Studies in the South', *Atlantic Monthly*, lxix, February 1983
Bachelard, G., *The Psychoanalysis of Fire*, trans. A. Ross, Routledge, 1964
Baldwin, James, *The Price of the Ticket: Collected Non-Fiction 1984–1985*, Michael Joseph, 1985
Bayles, M., *Hole in Our Soul: The Loss of Beauty and Meaning in American Popular Music*, University of Chicago Press, 1997
Bayton, M., *Frock Rock: Women Performing Popular Music*, OUP, 1998
Bechet, S., *Treat It Gentle*, New York, Hill and Wang, 1960
Bentley, E., ed., *The Theory of the Modern Stage*, Penguin, 1968
Blackmer, C. and Smith, P. J., eds, *En Travesti: Women, Gender, Subversion, Opera*, Columbia University Press, 1995
Booth, S., ed., 'The True Adventures of the Rolling Stones', *Granta*, Penguin, 1984
Bourke, J., *An Intimate History of Killing in Twentieth-Century Warfare*, Granta, 1999
Brooks, G., *Nine Parts of Desire: the Hidden World of Islamic Women*, Penguin, 1996
Burkert, W., *Ancient Mystery Cults*, Harvard University Press, 1987
Calasso, R., *The Marriage of Cadmus and Harmony*, Vintage, 1994
Campbell, J., *The Hero with a Thousand Faces*, 1948, Paladin, 1988
Carson, A., *Glass, Irony and God*, New York, 1995
Cattermole, P., *Venus, The Geological Story*, UCL Press, 1994
Celmins, M., *Peter Green, Founder of Fleetwood Mac*, Sanctuary, 1998
Christgau, R., 'Look at That Stupid Girl' (1970), in Kureishi and Savage, *Pop*, pp. 365–9.
Clément, C., *Opera or the Undoing of Women*, trans. B. Wing, Virago, London, 1989
Cohn, N., *Awopbopaloobop Alopbamboom: Pop from the Beginning*, London, Paladin, 1970
Cooper, S., ed., *Girls Girls Girls*, Cassell, 1995

Cook, N., *Music: A Very Short Introduction*, Oxford, 1998
Croutier, A. L., *Harem: The World Behind the Veil*, Bloomsbury, 1989
Cutler, C., *File Under Popular*, November Books, 1985.
Davis, F., *The History of the Blues*, Secker and Warburg, 1995
Dawidoff, N., *In the Country of Country*, Faber, 1997
Dawson J. and Propes S., *When was the First Rock 'n' Roll Record?*, Boston, 1992
DeCurtis, A., ed., *Illustrated History of Rock 'n' Roll* (3rd edn), Random House, New York, 1992
Didion, J., *Slouching Towards Bethlehem*, (1968), Flamingo, 1993
– *The White Album*, Flamingo, 1993
Dodds, E. R., *The Greeks and the Irrational*, University of California Press, 1952
Douglas, A., *Terrible Honesty*, Picador, 1997
Douglas, S., *Where the Girls Are: Growing Up Female with the Mass Media*, Penguin, 1994
Dove, Rita, *Poems: On the Bus with Rosa Parks*, Norton, New York, 1999
Doyle, Roddy, *The Commitments* (1988), Minerva, 1991
DuBois, P., *Sowing the Body*, Chicago, 1988
Dyer, R., 'In Defence of Disco' (1970), in Frith and Goodwin, *Record*
Easthope, A., *What a Man's Gotta Do: The Masculine Myth in Popular Culture*, Paladin, 1986
Eisen, J., *The Age of Rock*, New York 1970
Etchingham, K., *Through Gypsy Eyes: My Life, the Sixties and Jimi Hendrix*, London, 1998
Evans, L., *Girls Will be Boys: Women Report on Rock*, Pandora, 1997
Fabian, J. and Byrne, J., *Groupie* (1969), Omnibus, 1997
Faithfull, M. with Dalton, D., *Faithfull*, Little, Brown and Co., New York, 1994
Farrell, A., Guinness V. and Lloyd, J., eds, *My Generation*, Lilliput Press, Dublin, 1996
Feinstein, E., *Bessie Smith*, Viking Penguin, 1986
Frazer, J., *Myths of the Origin of Fire*, Macmillan, 1930
Frith, S., *The Sociology of Rock*, Constable, 1978
Frith S. and Goodwin A., eds, *On Record: Rock, Pop and the Written Word*, Routledge, 1990
Gaar, G., *She's a Rebel: the History of Women in Rock 'n' Roll*, Blandford, 1992
Garon, P. and B., *Woman with Guitar: Memphis Minnie's Blues*, Da Capo Press, New York, 1992
George, N., *Where Did Our Love Go?: The Rise and Fall of the Motown Sound*, Omnibus, 1985
Gillett, C., *The Sound of the City: The Rise of Rock 'n' Roll*, New York, Pantheon, 1984
Gilmore, M., *Night Beat: A Shadow History of Rock 'n' Roll*, Picador, 1997
Glover, T., sleeve notes to *Bob Dylan Live 1966*, Columbia 1998.
Goldenrosen, J., *Buddy Holly: His Life and Music*, Bowling Green KY, Popular Press, 1975

BIBLIOGRAPHY

Goldhill, S., *Foucault's Virginity: Ancient Erotic Fiction and the History of Sexuality*, Cambridge, 1995
Goldman, A., *Elvis*, New York, Avon, 1981
Gray, J., *Men Are From Mars, Women Are From Venus*, HarperCollins, 1993
Greek Lyric, Loeb Library (Harvard/Heinemann), trans. D. Campbell, 1982
Grieg, C., *Will You Still Love Me Tomorrow?*, Virago, 1989
Grills, B., *Alanis Morissette: The Story*, Quartet Books, 1997
Grossberg L., *We Gotta Get Out of This Place: Conservatism and Popular Culture*, Routledge, 1992
Guitar Player Book, The (by the editors of *Guitar Player Magazine*), Grove, New York, 1979
Hall, E., *Inventing the Barbarian*, Oxford, 1989
Hamm, C., *Music in the New World*, New York, Norton, 1983
Hardy P. and Laing, D., *The Da Capo Companion to 20th-Century Popular Music*, Da Capo Press, New York, 1995.
Harrison, D. Duval, *Black Pearls: Blues Queens of the 1920s*, Rutgers University Press, New Brunswick, 1988
Heaney, S., *Preoccupations*, Faber, 1980
– *The Government of the Tongue*, Faber, 1988
Heatley, M. and Leigh, S., *Behind the Song: Stories of 100 Great Pop and Rock Classics*, London, 1998
Henrichs, A., 'Loss of self, suffering, violence: the modern view of Dionysus from Nietzsche to Girard', *Harvard Studies in Classical Philology* 88 (1984): 205–40
Heriot, A., *The Castrati in Opera*, London, 1956
Hill, D., *Prince: A Pop Life*, Faber, 1989
Hoare, I., ed., *The Soul Book*, 1975
Holiday, B., with William Duffy, *Lady Sings the Blues* (1956) Penguin, 1984
Hopkins, J., *Elvis: A Biography*, Simon and Schuster, New York 1971
– *The Jimi Hendrix Experience*, Plexus, 1996
Hornby, N., *High Fidelity*, Gollancz, 1995
Hoskyns, B., *Beneath the Diamond Sky: Haight-Ashbury 1965–1970*, Bloomsbury, 1997
– *Glam! Bowie, Bolan and the Glitter Rock Revolution*, Faber, 1998
Hotchner, A. E., ed., *Blow Away; The Rolling Stones and the Death of the Sixties*, New York, Simon and Schuster, 1990
Johnson, C. and Taylor, Y., eds, *I Was Born A Slave: Vols I and II, An Anthology of Classic Slave Writing*, The Library of Black America, Payback, 1999
Johnstone, N., *Patti Smith*, Omnibus, 1997
Juno, A., ed., *Angry Women in Rock: 1*, Juno Books, New York, 1996
Just, R., *Women in Athenian Law and Culture*, London, 1989
Kamin, J., 'Parallels in the Social Reactions to Jazz and Rock', *Journal of Jazz Studies* 2 (1974)
King, J. and Stott, M., eds, *Is This Your Life? Images of Women in the Media*, London, 1977
King, O., 'Why we still need feminism' (*On the Move, Feminism for a New Generation*, ed. N. Walters, Virago 1999, pp. 48–61)

Kirk, Raven and Schofield, *The Presocratic Philosophers*, CUP, 1983
Knox, B., *The Heroic Temper*, Berkeley and London, 1964
Koestenbaum, W., *The Queen's Throat: Opera, Homosexuality and the Mystery of Desire*, New York, 1993
Kureishi, H. and Savage, J. eds. *The Faber Book of Pop*, Faber, 1995
Laing, D., ed., *The Electric Muse*, London, 1975
Laing, R. D., *The Divided Self* (1960), Penguin, 1965
Leader, D., *Why Do Women Write More Letters Than They Post?*, Faber, 1996
– *Promises Lovers Make When it Gets Late*, London, 1997
Leonardi, S. and Pope, R., *The Diva's Mouth*, Rutgers, New Jersey, 1997
Lewis, L. A., ed., *Adoring Audience: Fan Culture and Popular Music*, Routledge, 1992
Light, A., *The Rolling Stone Illustrated History of Rock*, ed. A. DeCurtis and J. Henke with H. George-Warren, Plexus, London, 1992
Lively, A., *Masks: Blackness. Race and the Imagination*, London, 1998
Logan, R., *Betrayal of the American Negro*, New York, 1965
Lomax, A., *The Land Where The Blues Were Born*, Minerva, 1994
Marcus, G., *Mystery Train*, Plume/Penguin, 4th ed., 1997
– *Lipstick Traces*, Penguin, 1989
– *Invisible Republic: Bob Dylan's Basement Tapes*, Picador, 1997
Marcus, S., *The Other Victorians*, Corgi, 1969
McClary. S., *Feminine Endings: Music, Gender, and Sexuality*, University of Minnesota Press, Minnesota, 1991
McClary, S., *Carmen*, Cambridge Opera Handbooks, Cambridge, 1991
McCleod, I., 'Still Rising', in *On the Move, Feminism in a New Generation*, ed. N. Walter, Virago, 1999, pp. 121–34
Nicholson, S., *A Portrait of Duke Ellington*, Sidgwick and Jackson, London, 1999
Oakley, G., *The Devil's Music*, Harcourt Brace Jovanovich, New York, 1976
O'Brien, L., *She Bop: The Definitive History of Women in Rock, Pop and Soul*, Penguin, 1995
– 'Sisters of Swing, Segregation and 1940s/1950s Pop', in *Girls Girls Girls*, ed. S. Cooper, Cassell, 1995
Padel, R., 'Women, Men and Horses', *Encounter*, November 1980
– 'Women: Model for Possession by Greek Demons', *Images of Women in Antiquity*, eds A. Cameron and A. Kuhrt, London, 1983, pp. 3–19
– 'Making Space Speak', in Winkler and Zeitlin, *Dionysus*, pp. 336–65
– *In and Out of the Mind*, Princeton University Press, 1992
– *Whom Gods Destroy*, Princeton University Press, 1995
Palmer, G., 'Bruce Springsteen and Authentic Masculinity', in Whitely, *Groove*, pp. 100–17.
Palmer, R., *Dancing in the Street*, BBC Books, 1996
Parker, J., *Turned On: A Biography of Henry Rollins*, Phoenix House, 1998
Pattison, *The Triumph of Vulgarity: Rock Music in the Mirror of Romanticism*, OUP, 1987
Paulin, T., *Writing to the Moment: Critical Essays 1980–1996*, Faber, 1996
Pfeil, E., *White Guys*, Verso, 1995

BIBLIOGRAPHY

Phillips, S. and Kosek, K. eds, *Bluegrass Fiddle Styles*, Oak Publications, New York, 1978
Placksin, S., *Jazzwomen, 1900 to the Present*, Pluto Press, 1985
Poizat, M., *The Angel's Cry: Beyond the Pleasure Principle in Opera*, trans. A. Denner, Cornell University Press, 1992
Posner, D., *Watteau: 'A Lady at Her Toilet'*, Allen Lane, 1973
Prown, P. and Newquist, H. P., *Legends of Rock Guitar*, Hal Leonard Corporation, 1997
Raphael, A., *Never Mind the Bollocks: Women Rewrite Rock*, Virago, 1995
Reynolds, S. and Press, J., *The Sex Revolts: Gender, Rebellion and Rock 'n' Roll*, Harvard, 1995
Riesman, D., *American Quarterly* 2 (1950)
Robb, J., *The Charlatans: We Are Rock*, Ebury Press, 1998
Robertson, N., 'The Betrothal Symposium in Classical Greece', in W. J. Slater, Jr, ed., *Dining in a Classical Context*, Ann Arbor, Michigan, 1991
Roediger, D., *The Wages of Whiteness*, New York, Verso, 1991
Rogan, J., *Starmakers and Svengalis: the History of British Pop Management*, Futura Publications, 1988
'Rolling Stone', *The Complete Covers 1967–1997*, Harry Abrams, Inc., New York, 1997
Rubin, W., ed., *Primitivism in Twentieth-Century Art: Affinity of the Tribal and the Modern*, 2 vols., New York, Museum of Modern Art, 1984
Said, E., *Orientalism* (1978), Penguin, 1991
Sandford, C., *Sting: Demolition Man*, London, 1998
Savage, J., *England's Dreaming: Sex Pistols and Punk Rock*, Faber, 1991
Sawyer, C., *The Arrival of B. B. King: The Authorized Biography*, Da Capo, New York, 1982
Shaar Murray, C., *Crosstown Traffic: Jimi Hendrix and Post-War Pop*, Faber, 1989
Shapiro, H., *Waiting for the Man*, New York, 1988
Shay, J., *Achilles in Vietnam: Combat Trauma and the Undoing of Character*, Simon and Schuster, New York, 1994
Sheehan, N., *A Bright Shining Lie: John Paul Vann and America in Vietnam*, Johns Hopkins Press, Baltimore, 1979
Silverman, K., *The Acoustic Mirror*, Bloomington & Indiana, 1988
Solie, R., 'Whose Life'? The Gendered Self in Schumann's *Frauenliebe* Songs', in S. P. Scher, ed., *Music and Text: Critical Inquiries*, CUP, 1992, pp. 219–40.
Sontag, S., 'Notes on Camp' (1964), in *Against Interpretation*, 1978
Spitz, B., *Dylan: A Biography*, Michael Joseph, 1989
Stearns, M. W., *The Story of Jazz*, Oxford, 1956
Steiner, G., *The Death of Tragedy*, London, 1961
– *Antigones*, Clarendon Press, Oxford, 1984
Stewart-Baxter, D., *Ma Rainey and the Classic Blues Singers*, Studio Vista Books, 1970
Strauss, R., *The Correspondence Between Richard Strauss and Hugo von Hofmannsthal*, trans. H. Hammelmann and E. Osers, Collins, 1952
Thornton, L., *Women as Portrayed in Orientalist Painting*, Poche Couleur, ACR Edition, Paris, 1994

Turner, S., *Trouble Man: The Life and Death of Marvin Gaye*, London, 1998
Ventura, M., *Shadow-Dancing in the USA*, St Martin's Press, New York, 1985
Vermorel, F. and J., *Starlust: The Secret Fantasies of Fans*, London, W. H. Allen, 1985
Wagner, R., *Opera and Drama (Richard Wagner's Prose Works*, trans. W. Ashton Ellis, 1893, repr. St Clair Shores, Michigan, Scholarly Press, 1972
Walton, O., *Music: Black, White, and Blue*, New York, 1972
Ward, B., *Just My Soul Responding: Rhythm and Blues, Black Consciousness and Race Relations*, UCL Press, 1998
Warner, M., *Monuments and Maidens*, London, 1985
Whitcomb, I., *After the Ball: Pop Music from Rag to Rock*, Simon and Schuster, New York, 1972
White, C., *The Life of Little Richard*, New York, 1984
Whitely, S., ed., *Sexing the Groove: Popular Music and Gender*, Routledge, London and New York, 1997
Wilson, J., *The Earth Shall Weep: A History of Native America*, Picador, 1998
Winkler, J. and Zeitlin, F., *Nothing to Do With Dionysos?*, Princeton University Press, 1990
Yorke, R., *Led Zeppelin: From Early Days to Page and Plant*, Virgin, London (1974), revised ed. 1999
Young, J., *Nico: Songs they Never Play on the Radio*, Arrow, 1994
Zeitlin, F., *Playing the Other*, Chicago Press, 1996

Index

Abrokwa, Nana Kwame, 211–12, 227
AC/DC, 12, 216, 245, 287, 288
Achilles, 59, 60, 113, 187, 233, 326
Adès, Thomas, 97, 146, 193
Advert, Gaye, 269, 270, 319, 322, 341
Adverts, 269
Aegisthus, 235
Aeneas, 55, 58, 84, 90, 187
Aerosmith, 65, 160, 175, 279, 281, 295, 307
Aeschylus
   Lycurgeia, 229
   The Persians, 325
   Suppliant Women, 329
Africa, African, 3, 11, 27, 67, 137, 139, 141, 142, 145, 190
African music, 164, 171, 306
African-American writing, 45
Afrika Baambata, 165–6, 337
Agamemnon, 187, 234, 235
aggression, 2, 12, 14, 60, 193, 286, 357
   the guitar hero, 79
   and guitar-playing, 251, 320
   impersonating, 123
   male, 15, 23, 27
   male blues, 194
   military, 63
   rock, 16, 44, 205, 228, 246, 252
   smashing guitars, 213–14
agrarian rap, 167
Aids, 199
Aithra, 101
Ajax, 23, 229, 234, 236, 241, 244
Aldon Music, 302
Alice Cooper, 326
All My Loving (film), 251
Almodovar, Pedro, 59, 60

Altamount, 220–22, 232, 235, 246, 253, 269
AMC, 60
America, impersonating, 245–6
American Bandstand, 36, 47
American Top Fifty, 168
American Top Forty, 39
American Top Twenty, 159
American Youth for Democracy, 43
Amis, Martin, 73
Amos, Tori, 5, 14, 62, 194
amplification, amps, 40, 80, 81–2, 206, 215, 242, 264, 322, 335
anarchy, 44, 258, 261, 285–6
Andersen, Hans: *The Little Mermaid*, 100, 103
Anderson, Orlando, 210
androgyny, 328, 329
Andromeda, 92
anger, 7, 9, 54, 187, 189, 197, 198, 199, 232, 242, 258, 264, 266, 267, 284, 304, 354
Anglin, Jack, 78
The Animals, 118, 158, 159, 238, 263
Anka, Paul, 114
Anne, HRH The Princess Royal, 164
Anthrax, 160, 216
anthropology, 141, 276
anti-parent, 4, 34–5, 44, 45, 85, 120, 203–4, 252, 258, 263, 266–7, 352, 353
Antigone, 325
anxiety, 12, 14, 27, 60, 284, 340, 349
apartheid, 281
Aphrodite *see* Venus
Apocalypse Now (film), 256
Apollo, 24, 25, 188

Apollo Theatre, New York, 159
Ares, 179
Argonauts, 84, 113
aria, 95, 109–10, 247, 332, 334
Ariadne, 87, 90, 91, 96, 98, 100, 103, 136, 282, 348
Aristophanes, 92, 137, 234
  Lysistrata, 286
Aristotle, 136
Arkansas, 40, 41
armour, 11, 54, 58–61, 64–5, 108, 194, 288, 289, 326
army, 92, 114, 223–4
Aronowitz, Al, 303
Arrested Development, 167
arrows, 61, 62, 63, 100, 109
Artaud, Antonin: 'Manifestos', 230
Arthur, King, 233
artificiality, 345
  and electricity, 39, 335
  female, 104, 110, 330, 334
  male, 12
  music, 6
  pop, 3, 181
  punk, 341
  rock, 303, 325
ASCAP (American Society of Composers, Authors and Publishers), 176
Atkins, Chet, 79, 123
Atkins, Susan, 253–4
Atlanta, Georgia, 250–51, 287
Atlantic Monthly, 207
ATV, 319
Auden, W. H., 189
audience, 18–19, 101, 115, 240, 337, 341
  antagonism towards, 270, 271
  black, 161, 165, 177, 180, 181
  black radio shows, 34, 35
  death at Altamount, 220–22
  female, 294, 295
  feminist, 313
  folk, 9, 263, 265
  gangsta rap, 213
  heavy metal, 213
  male, 14, 315, 322, 323, 347
  and new technology, 38–9

'overhearing' scenes, 95
pop, 6
punk, 342
radio, 271
response to black music, 139
rock, 4
and the rock hero, 242
segregation, 138
size, 51
teenage, 48, 127, 214, 268
and the tragic hero, 241
white, 8, 181, 209
see also crowd
authenticity, 5, 6, 9, 170, 209, 337
  black, 39
  blues, 8, 12
  and counter culture, 272
  erotic, 192
  folk, 8, 263, 265
  maleness, 14
  rock, 3, 7, 10, 11, 14, 156, 223, 324
  and working-class, 7
Avalon, Frankie, 114
Ayers, Kevin, 179

Babes in Toyland, 321
baby, 34, 63, 109, 190, 275–8, 288
Baby Spice (Emma Bunton), 23
Bachelard, Gaston, 108
Back to the Future I (film), 37
backing tapes, 270
Bad Company, 216
Baerwald, David, 334
Baez, Joan, 253
Bailey, Joanna, 78
Baker, Josephine, 139
Baker, Nicholson, 73
Balanchine, George, 332
Baldwin, James, 174–5
Balin, Marty, 220
The Ballad of Andy Crocker (film), 199
ballads, 264, 306
The Band, 114, 262
Bangs, Lester, 314
banjo, 40, 147, 148
Banshees, 217
barbaroi (non-Greek speakers), 136

INDEX

Barry, Jeff, 302
Barstow, Josephine, 333
Barth, Paul, 40
Batten, Jennifer, 317
battle, 85, 89, 233
Baudelaire, Charles, 30, 109
Bay Area Angels, 220
Bay City Rollers, 351
Beach Boys, 253
Beastie Boys, 39–40, 143, 167, 178, 238
beat, 5, 11, 37, 143, 148, 149, 154, 163, 337
beat generation, 11, 143, 150
beat poets, 301
The Beatles, 3, 4, 48, 72, 114, 116, 117, 150, 156, 160, 170, 179, 190, 194, 199, 215, 238, 245, 254–5, 256, 268, 281, 297, 301, 303, 339, 340
Beatty, Warren, 98
Beauchamp, George, 40
Bee Gees, 328
Beethoven, Ludwig van: *Fidelio*, 192, 205, 329, 348
Bell, Alexander, 94
Bellerophon, 83, 112
Belly, 320
Benjamin, Bunny, 163
Beowulf, 233
Berkeley University ('Vietnam Day Committee'), 253
Berry, Chuck, 16, 37, 39, 42, 44, 47, 51, 74, 75, 154, 157, 159, 161, 165, 261, 279, 302
bestiality, 136
Bikini Kill, 321
Billboard magazine, 35
Birmingham, Alabama, 138, 159
The Birth of a Nation (film), 147
bisexuality, 110
Bizet, Georges: 'Habanera' (*Carmen*), 62, 86
Bjelland, Kat, 86, 93
Bjork, 56, 273
Black Flag, 203, 232, 235, 245, 250, 252, 254, 255, 266, 270–71, 308
black hero, 197, 207
black jackets, 8, 264

black magic, 216, 245
black music, 15, 34, 35–6, 43, 44, 45, 129, 134, 138, 139, 140, 143–6, 151, 152, 154, 158, 159, 161, 162, 176, 181, 199, 219, 246
black nationalism, 167
Black Power, 252–3
Black Sabbath, 216, 219, 232, 320
black styles, 154, 155, 158, 159, 160, 163, 167, 176
The Black and White Minstrel Show, 137
The Blackboard Jungle (film), 159
blacking up, 181, 258
blackness, 8, 15, 43, 138, 141, 148, 155, 182, 187, 189, 207, 218–19, 227, 232–3, 258, 354
Blair, Tony, 15, 288
Blake, William: *Songs of Experience*, 232
blindness, 107, 187, 194, 236, 240
blood, 185, 188
Bloomfield, Mike, 264
blow jobs, 15, 307, 310, 312
'blue beat', 163
Blue Beat label, 163
'blue note', 146
bluegrass, 264
bluegrass violin, 335
blues, 28, 38, 66, 81, 153, 189, 197, 246, 261, 302, 306
  acoustic Delta, 114
  Chicago, 114, 159, 205
  city, 150
  country, 74, 165, 208
  and country music, 44, 75, 78, 206
  Delta, 9, 192, 199
  electric, 74, 120, 208, 263
  first recorded, 34, 73–4, 142, 157–8
  and folk, 8–9
  idealization of, 8
  male, 42, 72, 73, 74, 79, 193, 198, 208
  and maleness, 16
  misogyny, 278, 280
  renaissance, 199, 213
  and rock, 114, 129, 279
  rolling-stone image, 124

384

and the slave narrative, 45
sorrow empowers, 97
urban, 67, 74
violence, 212
'white', 143
women's, 14
blues-folk, 159
blues-rock, 153, 291
Blur, 226
boat, 87, 88
body, the, 6, 9, 15, 25, 28, 41, 49, 51, 52, 60, 81, 93, 94, 115, 174, 236, 242, 253, 297, 332, 335
Bolan, Marc, 237, 343
Bon Jovi, Jon, 64
Bonham, John, 237
boogie woogie, 37, 153
Booker T, 207
Boomtown Rats, 126
Boone, Pat, 114, 159
Botticelli, Sandro, 53
Bowie, Angie, 240
Bowie, David, 17, 115, 117, 126, 149, 202, 238–9, 241, 245, 313, 341, 344, 357
Aladdin Sane tour, 239
Boy George, 247, 326, 344
boys
fantasy, 295
identification, 117
impersonating men, 202, 324
men impersonating, 288
and rock, 9–12
voice, 98
'boysy', 284, 288, 312, 316
Boyzone, 5, 244, 277, 292, 340
bra, 106, 108, 111, 309
Brady, Paul, 95
Brahms, Johannes, 17
The Breeders, 320
Breedlove, Lynn, 315, 320–1, 343
Brenston, Jackie, 159
Brill Building, Broadway, 302, 303
Brit Awards, 10, 270
British Fascism, 219
'British invasion', 114
British Top Thirty, 166
British Top Twenty, 287

Broadcast Music Incorporated, 176
Broonzy, Big Bill, 34, 74, 198
Bros, 312
The Brothers baseball team, 242
Brown, Clarence 'Gatemouth', 40
Brown, James, 55, 151, 163, 165, 166, 181, 201, 309
Brown, Roy, 134, 156
Brown, Willie, 68
Browne, Jackson, 199
Bruce, Jack, 115
Bryant, Jimmy, 40
Buckingham, James Silk, 135
Bugliosi, Vincent, 254
bull, 136
Bunton, Emma (Baby Spice), 23
Burchill, Julie, 322
Burden, Eric, 118, 158
Burnel, Jean-Jacques, 285
Burning Spear, 151
Burton, James, 80
Bush, Kate, 194
Buster, Prince, 164
Bute, 18
Butterfield, Paul, 264
The Buzzcocks, 319
The Byrds, 263
Byron, George Gordon, Lord: *Don Juan*, 125

cabbalistic symbols, 26
Cale, John, 310
Calhoun, Charlie, 177
California, 252, 253, 254, 256, 266, 308
California Committee on Un-American Activities, 43
Callas, Maria, 350
Calloway, Cab, 140
Calypso, 85, 86, 99, 103, 105, 282
calypso (music), 164
Campbell, Joseph, 240
Campbell, Sterling, 1
Can, 101
Capote, Truman, 307
Carew, Roy, 213
Carlisle Grammar School, 17
Carnegie Hall, 35, 43

INDEX

Carpenter, Karen, 87, 91, 122, 237
Carpenter, Richard, 91, 122
Carpenters, 87
Carr, Bob, 250
Carter, A. P., 75, 77, 154
The Carter Family, 77
'Carter lick', 77
Carter, Maybelle, 77
Carter, Sara, 77
Cash, Johnny, 75, 76–7, 154, 158, 278, 300, 302
Cass, Mama, 237
castrati, 331–2
castration, 53, 58, 83, 194, 284
catharsis, 97
Cavafy, Constantine P., 85
Cave, Nick, 123, 188, 215–16, 277–8, 279
censorship, 29, 59, 177
Central America, 199
Chalpin, Ed, 168
chamber music, 17
chaos, 26, 52, 53
character, 330
Charlatans, 4, 5, 112, 343
Charles, Ray, 156, 177
Charleston, 138, 139
chart pop, 4, 11
charts, 39, 47
   black, 36
   pop, 35, 162
   R&B, 161, 162, 183
   white, 161
Charybdis, 86, 103, 282
Chaucer, Geoffrey, 240
Cheltenham Literary Festival ('Rock 'n' Roll Day'), 314
Cher, 256
Cherry, Naomi, 319
Chess label, 159
Chicago, 40–41, 42, 46, 68, 74, 78, 116, 150, 153, 160, 212, 267
Chickasaw tribe, 246
Chimaera, 83
choirs, 18
Chordettes, 296
chords, 36, 76, 80, 153, 154, 278, 318, 324

power, 251, 306
Chotaw tribe, 246
Christian, Charlie, 40
Christie, Linford, 175
Church fathers, 85
Circe, 85, 86, 93, 99
civilization, 57
Clapton, Eric, 10, 39, 68, 69, 79, 114, 115, 118, 170, 172, 193, 205, 241, 251, 295, 317
Clark, Dick, 36
Clarke, Ossie, 214–15, 223, 270
The Clash, 81, 318
class, 252
   and rock authenticity, 7
   see also middle-class; working-class
classical music, 35, 43, 271, 290
   guitarists, 317
   and rock, 49, 303
   twentieth-century, 144
Clemons, Clarence, 170
Cleveland, 313
Cliff, Jimmy, 164
Clinton, Bill, 15, 126, 249
Clinton, George, 181, 182
Clytemnestra, 23, 235, 275, 325
The Coasters, 302
Cobain, Kurt, 9–10, 196, 237, 239, 240, 242, 346–7
Cochran, Eddie, 302
cock, 92, 206, 219, 282, 298
   artificial, 14, 123, 321–2
   baring onstage, 111, 326
   black stereotyping, 137, 174–5, 177
   cock-pride, 289, 296, 297
   and the drum, 151
   Heaven's severed, 53
   Hermes, 124
   an imaginary, 11
   inflatable, 167, 178
Cocteau, Jean, 96
codes
   courtly, 196
   cultural, 155
   for living, 265
   rock, 14
Cohen, Leonard, 101, 103
Cold War, 49

Cole, Nat King, 138
collectivity, 151, 152
Collins, Rob, 4, 5, 6, 112
Colorado *see* Columbine High School
Coltrane, John, 154
Columbine High School, Littleton, Denver, Colorado, 222, 235, 249, 250, 251, 254, 325
Colvin, Claudette, 44
Combs, Sean 'Puff Daddy', 169
Comets, 114
communication, 34, 45, 46, 62, 63
Communism, 42, 43, 134
community, 24, 25, 31, 39, 45, 46, 75, 115, 133, 147, 148, 151, 336
Como, Perry, 44, 47
composer, 302, 332
conductor, 294
conflict, 54
  sexual, 57
Connor, Charles, 176–7
Conrad, Joseph: *Heart of Darkness*, 141
Cooder, Ry, 171
Cooke, Sam, 47, 350
Cooper, Carol, 315
Cooper, Dennis: *Guide*, 226
Cornerhouse, 355
Cornwell, Hugh, 285
Cosmopolitan, 25
Costello, Elvis, 153, 165
Cotton Club, New York, 140, 180, 189
counter-culture, 252, 261, 271–2
'country and western', 337
country music, 7, 37, 38, 150, 166, 255, 302, 306
  and blues, 44, 75, 78, 206
  female, 77–8
  and folk, 303
  harmony, 291
  a hybrid, 75
  life as a struggle, 76
  male, 77, 78
  mysogyny, 278
  and rock, 49, 154
  women's, 14

Coverdale, David, 280
'covers', 36, 39, 153, 324
Coward, Noël: *Private Lives*, 29
cowboy films *see* Westerns
Cox, Ida, 74
Cranach, Lucas
  Venus and Amor, 106, 107
  Venus in a Landscape, 106–7
Craven, Beverley, 62
Crawford, Cindy, 328
Cream, 114, 115
creativity, 2, 7, 24, 27, 39, 56, 58, 63, 64, 116, 117, 133, 153, 160, 188, 205, 229, 272, 281, 292, 293, 294, 301–4, 311, 331, 354
Creech, Papa John, 170
Creek tribe, 246
Creon, 236
Crete, 18, 46, 83, 87, 88, 92, 133
Crew Cuts, 36, 39
Crickets, The, 39, 114
Crockett, Davy, 228
Crosby, Bing, 8, 138
Crosby, John, 138
cross-dressing, 239, 325–7, 329, 334, 338, 348, 349
cross-over, 182–4
Crow, Sheryl, 84, 334
crowd, 31, 186, 270, 346
  ecstasy, 185, 231
  see also audience
crowd-surfing, 2, 271, 341
Crowley, Aleister, 26, 216
Crudup, Arthur 'Big Boy', 34, 38, 158
Crusaders, 112, 113, 134
The Crystals, 194, 332
Cuba, 171
culture
  black, 15, 133, 139, 142, 151, 157, 184, 276
  counter-, 252, 261, 271–2
  Gothic, 217
  Greek, 23, 24, 52, 53, 59, 185–6, 188
  homosexual, 110
  mother-, 285
  parent, 206
  pop, 6, 264, 341
  popular, 3, 15, 26, 27, 155, 185, 186

INDEX

rave, 268
rock, 2, 6, 12, 50, 52, 142, 190, 272, 273, 274, 289, 290, 291, 314, 354
Western, 2, 24, 53
white, 145, 151, 152, 155, 184, 276
youth, 46, 47, 190, 268, 314
Cupid *see* Eros
Cyclops, 86, 233
Cyprus, 53

Da Capo Companion to Popular Music, 126–7
Dahmer, Jeffrey, 250
Daily Mail, 48
Daltrey, Roger, 214
Damon, Matt, 355
Danae, 90
dance, 18, 24, 33, 49, 145, 328
  black, 148, 149
  soul with, 163
  Western, 149
  white, 148
  wild, 185, 186
Dancing Rabbit Creek, Treaty of, 246
Dancing in the Street (television history of rock), 237
darkness, 185, 187–8, 189, 207, 218, 219, 239, 241, 242, 247, 252, 256, 258, 275, 348, 354, 358
Darwin, Charles, 190
Davis, Ray, 245
De La Soul, 166
de-melanization, 182
Dead Kennedys, 270
Dean, James, 243
death, 23, 25, 29, 30, 31, 67, 70, 215, 219, 229, 231, 232, 237, 238, 243, 248, 278
  see also murder; suicide
Death Row Records, 210
Death in Venice, 62
Decca, 223
Dee, Donna, 313
defiance, 14, 44, 45, 64, 193, 194, 198, 204, 235, 239, 258, 272
Dekker, Desmond (and The Aces), 164
Delaney, Matt, 74

Delphi, 188
delusion, 269
Demeter, 348
democracy, 136
Denny, Sandy, 102
Depression, 74, 75, 199
desegregation, 138
Desire, 350, 351, 353, 3, 9, 55, 57, 64, 261, 353
  conflicting desires, 23
  doubleness of, 106–10, 284, 350
  Eros as, 52
  faked, 284
  female, 13, 16, 23, 32, 63, 67, 110–11, 193, 258, 293, 294, 333, 353
  for girls, 281
  homosexual, 109
  and love, 61
  male, 2, 104, 110, 294
  in opera, 62
  punishment through, 57–8
  punk and, 320
  for the rock god, 179
  rock music's big theme, 30
  in songs, 13
  teenage, 49, 64
  unrequited, 63
despair, 47, 48, 63, 76, 101, 109
destruction/destructiveness, 58, 59, 241, 242, 244
Detroit Lions, 147
Detroit Spinners, 350
DiCaprio, Leonardo, 355
Diddley, Bo, 122, 123, 151, 161, 198, 202
Didion, Joan, 222, 253, 314
Dido, Queen of Carthage, 55, 90
Dietrich, Marlene, 89, 90, 105
Diomedes, 242
Dion and the Belmonts, 162
Dionysus, 25, 27, 84, 136, 185, 186, 221, 229–32, 234–7, 241, 295, 329–30, 334, 348
dirt, 134
disco, 162, 267, 268
disguise, 36
Disney, Walt, 26, 95, 122

388

INDEX

distortion, 40, 122, 336
diva, 294, 331
Dixon, Thomas: *The Clansman*, 140, 147
Dixon, Willie, 159, 198, 202, 296, 300
DJs (disc jockeys), 313–14
Dodd, Coxsone, 163
Dodds, E. R.: *The Greeks and the Irrational*, 185, 186
Domingo, Placido, 293
Domino, Fats, 159
Donelly, Tanya, 318, 320–21
Donovan, 7
doo wop, 164, 181, 302
The Doors, 159, 215
Doors, 159
Dorsey Brothers, 47
doubleness
   of desire, 106–10, 284
   women's, 104–5, 284
Dowland, John, 196
Doyle, Roddy: *The Commitments*, 148, 151–2, 174, 201–2
drag, 327, 328
drama
   Greek, 13
   male, 95
Dre, Dr, 168
The Drifters, 176
drowning, 16, 31, 86, 87, 93
drugs, 117, 129, 148, 167, 182, 188, 189, 203, 213, 222, 223, 231, 232, 235, 237, 238, 241, 252–3, 256–7, 265, 286, 303, 336
drum dances, 150–51
drum machine, 167, 336
drum 'n' bass, 4
drums, 149–51, 246, 265, 285, 322, 332, 336, 337
duet, 109, 110
Dukowski, Charles (Chuck), 254, 271
Duran Duran, 343
Durcan, Paul: 'The Death by Heroin of Sid Vicious', 30
Dylan, Bob, 4, 7–8, 12, 29, 48, 64, 66, 72, 73, 104, 110, 114, 116, 121, 199, 206, 208, 219, 262–5, 267,
292–3, 300–305, 314, 330, 335, 337–8, 345, 356

Earth, 52, 53, 187, 188
Earth (planet), 56, 109, 283
East 17, 312
Easton, Sheena, 328
Echo, 16, 31, 32, 93, 96, 127, 258, 293, 294, 295, 300, 312, 329, 331, 333, 334, 347, 352
echo-cardiogram, 95
economics, 118, 206, 272
Eddy, Duane, 79
education, 258
   musical, 24
Edward the Black Prince, 50
Edwards, Richey, 10, 112, 237, 324, 345
Elastica, 318
electricity, 2, 7, 34, 35, 40, 41, 42, 45–6, 56, 81, 148, 263, 265, 335–8
electro, 162, 165
Eliot, T. S.: *East Coker*, 144, 145
Ellington, Duke, 36, 43, 131, 139, 146, 153, 179–81, 294, 307, 333
   Black Brown and Beige, 35, 43
   A Drum is a Lady, 150
Eminem, 168–9, 304
Empedocles, 58–9
English Disco, Los Angeles, 308
entrails, 187
erection, 71, 72, 175, 178, 179, 299
Eros, 31, 32, 52, 53, 55, 58, 61–4, 66, 100, 104, 106–10, 179, 228, 288, 348–53
Erotokritos (Cretan epic romance), 18, 348
Estefan, Gloria, 90
'ethnic' music, 190
Euripides, 92–8, 229, 235, 243, 263, 324
   Bacchae, 235, 275, 329–30
   Hippolytus, 94, 275
   Medea, 89, 90, 92
Europa, 23, 88, 89, 90
Eurydice, 30, 31, 32, 84, 315, 352

INDEX

Evans, Nicholas
  The Horse Whisperer, 248
  The Loop, 248
Eve, 274, 279
evil, 256, 274, 278, 279
evolution, 190
exclusion, 312
exclusivity, 11
exoticism, 134, 139, 207
experimenting, 263

Factory Records, 217
Faithfull, Marianne, 113, 127, 219, 292–5, 298, 301, 307, 328, 330
faking, 104, 111, 283, 284, 330, 334, 336, 337, 338, 340
Fame (film), 46
family, 23, 77, 78, 243, 251, 254, 266, 276, 357
fans, 3, 7, 9, 80, 117, 127, 161, 177, 202, 223, 232, 241, 242, 269, 341, 351
  the commercial fan base, 269–70
  heavy metal, 231, 287
  quest for identity, 351, 352
  rock, 246, 268
  the star-fan bond, 343–7
  stars' need, 353
  street violence, 219
fantasy, 9, 15, 29, 64, 133, 136, 138, 179, 180, 181, 193, 294, 339
  fans', 343, 344, 345, 347, 353
  male, 2, 11, 32, 86, 135, 175, 194, 279, 283, 284, 286, 295, 328, 331, 334
  misogynist, 305
  of omnipotence, 194, 354
  of rape, 285
  sexist, 289
  sexual, 137, 311, 324–5
  teenage, 280, 289, 305
  white, 219, 227, 257, 305, 324
Farrakhan, Louis, 167
fascism, 222
Fates, 187
father
  and anti-parent rock, 266–7

father-son conflict, 16, 53, 203–4, 266–7, 347
  power of, 64
  sexuality, 53
father-figure, 93, 100
Faulkner, William: *Old Man*, 195
FBI, 43
feedback, 122, 336
Feelgood, Dr, 215
Feline, Emma, 313
femaleness, 281, 338
femininity, 3, 127, 183, 283, 325
feminism, 285, 297–8, 306, 320
Fender, Leo, 40, 185
field songs, 74
Financial Times, 90
fire, 52, 54, 55, 56, 57, 63, 153, 160, 194
Flash, Grandmaster, 165, 170
Fleetwood Mac, 28, 198
Flex, Funkmaster, 169, 211
Flyte, Keith, 226
folk movement, 301
folk music, 7, 17, 89, 116, 146
  authenticity, 8, 263, 265
  and blues, 8–9
  and country, 303
  protest songs, 262
folk-rock, 263, 265, 337–8
Four Tops, 162
Fowley, Kim, 247
Fox Theatre, Detroit, 181
foxtrot, 139
fragging, 224
fragmentation, 31
Frampton, Peter, 26, 31
Franco, General Francisco, 29
Franklin, Aretha, 151–2, 350
Franklin, Benjamin, 335
Frazer, Sir James: *The Golden Bough*, 141
Freberg, Stan, 36
Free, 216
Freed, Alan, 35–6, 39, 44, 158, 169, 185
freedom, 31, 34, 35, 44, 49, 120, 127, 147, 198, 250, 253, 258, 261, 272, 299

390

emotional, 296
girls', 297
male, 282
of rock 'n' roll, 296
sexual, 299
and sexuality, 296
teenage, 258, 262
The French Lieutenant's Woman
 (film), 87
Freud, Sigmund, 31, 50, 133, 141, 189, 190
Friday, Nancy: *Men in Love*, 175
Frith, Simon, 179, 272, 273
frustration, 47, 48, 71, 169, 194, 195, 202, 204, 345, 353
Fuller, Simon, 312
funk, 134, 162, 163, 169, 181
Funk Brothers, 163
Funkadelic, 181
Fuqua, Harvey, 36
Furies, 53, 186, 187, 188, 232, 236, 274, 275
Fury, Billy, 51, 54
fusion, 35, 39

Galileo Galilei, 283
Gallagher, Noel, 112
gangs, 117, 118
gangsta rap, 167, 184, 210, 226, 248, 286, 356
garage, 4, 11, 320
Garbage, 315
Garfunkel, Art, 190
'Gas Chamber' Nancy, 308
Gately, Steve, 340
Gaye, Frankie, 199
Gaye, Marvin, 23, 85, 121, 147, 149, 151, 156, 159, 161, 163, 170, 177–8, 199, 200, 237, 239, 241
Geffin, David, 196
gender bending, 327, 338
George, Nelson: *Hip Hop America*, 169
Georgia, 246, 250
Germany, rap in, 211–12
Gershwin, George, 86, 87, 196, 333
Gettysburg, 113
G.I. Blues (film), 64, 212

Gilmore, James, 248
Ginn, Greg, 254
Ginn, Raymond, 254
Ginsberg, Allen, 330
girl power, 11
girls
 desire for, 281
 stereotyping, 175
 worship of groups, 117
glam rock, 181, 267–8, 326, 327, 334–5, 338, 340–1
Glastonbury Festival, 226
Glitter, Gary, 352
Gluck, Christoph Wilibald, 30
go-go, 165
Godin, Dave, 170
Godin Acousticaster, 318
Goethe, Johann Wolfgang von, 331
Goffin, Gerry, 302
Golden Fleece, 84, 87, 89
Goldenberg, Billy, 212
Good Vibrations store, San Francisco, 321
Gordon, Kim, 319, 320
Gordy, Berry, 200, 332
Gore, Lesley, 299–300
Gorgons, 83
gospel, 74, 146, 147, 163, 164
Goth music, 232
'Goths', 217, 218–19
Grail, the quest for the, 113
Grant, Eddy, 280
Grant, Marshall, 302
The Grateful Dead, 220, 253, 256, 299
Graves, Robert: *The White Goddess*, 292
Great White, 285, 286, 298
Greece/Greeks, ancient, 1, 12, 14, 15, 26, 58, 135–7, 185, 189, 190, 191, 232, 358–9
 literature, 257
 theatre, 229, 231
 tragedy, 91, 229, 235–6, 237, 243, 248, 275, 329, 330
Green, Al, 200
Green (Gartside), 350
Green, Peter, 79, 123, 198–9, 241
Greenwich, Eddie, 302

INDEX

Gregory, Enoch, 151
Grossman, Albert, 264
Groupie (Fabian), 298, 299, 307, 311, 312
groupies, 2, 51, 64, 149, 285, 297, 306–12, 340
Grundy, Bill, 237
grunge, 268, 272, 320
Grunte, Captain Obadiah, 336
Guess Who, 280
guilt, 236
guitar, 206
   acoustic, 41, 74, 78, 263, 265
   air, 15, 73, 117, 356
   blues, 66–72, 77, 195
   cock, 215
   destruction, 80–81, 213–14, 215, 227, 241, 242
   electric, 8, 40–42, 45, 46, 74, 79, 80, 264, 273, 318, 336
   equated with maleness, 73, 75
   Fender, 40–41, 185
   a fetishized instrument, 2
   Gibson, 40, 216
   history, 66
   hollow-body, 40
   male, 75, 82
   pop, 79
   rock, 66, 72, 73, 81
   solid-body, 40
   Stratocaster, 15
   symbolism, 66, 73, 80, 127, 317
   technique, 68, 69, 70, 76, 79, 80, 81, 123, 318
   women guitarists, 317–18
Guitar magazine, 317
guitar hero, 79, 81, 340
Guitar School, 317
gun-laws, 2, 249–50
guns, 30, 59–60, 167, 206, 246–51, 253, 288, 325
Guns 'N' Roses, 255
Guthrie, Woody, 8, 208, 263
Guyville, 52–3, 58

Hades, 84, 188, 283
Haggard, Rider, 149
Haight-Ashbury, San Francisco, 222, 252–3, 299
hair-style, 116, 182, 296, 309, 324, 327
Haley, Bill, 114, 159, 177, 279
Hall, Darryl, 163
Hammerstein, Oscar, II, 89
Hampton, Lionel, 153
Handel, George Friederic: *Messiah*, 18
Handke, Peter: *Offending the Audience*, 342
Hardy, Thomas: *Far from the Madding Crowd*, 94
Harlem, New York, 139, 155, 161, 209
Harlem Renaissance, 140, 180
harmony, 3, 6, 11, 25, 28–9, 43, 62, 66, 75, 78, 144–7, 151, 154, 162, 306, 333
   of misogyny, 290–91
Harrison, George, 48, 190, 281
Harrison, Jane, 141
Hart, Lorenz, 87, 94, 196
Harvey, P. J., 5, 14, 88, 315
Hayes, Isaac, 200
Hays Code, 59
Heaney, Seamus, 293
Heaven, 52, 53, 56, 83, 87, 347
heavy metal, 9, 12, 64, 120, 166, 167, 175, 195, 215–19, 227, 231, 232, 243, 245, 251, 256, 279, 280, 288, 289, 295, 326
Hecate, 232
Hecuba, 236, 275
Hegamin, Lucille, 74
Helen, 59, 88, 97, 101, 104
Helena, 41, 68
Hell, Richard, 258
Hell's Angels, 220, 221–2, 232, 246, 253
helplessness, 89
Helstrom, Echo, 301
Henderson, Rose, 74
Hendrix, Jimi, 3, 23, 26, 27, 31, 80–81, 85, 100, 101–2, 117, 128, 142, 153–4, 161, 164, 168, 172–3, 175, 177, 178, 180, 181, 183, 199, 213, 215, 218, 225–6, 237, 241, 242,

243, 263, 265, 266, 268, 291, 297,
    298–9, 301, 317
Hephaestus *see* Vulcan
Heraklion, Crete, 17
Heraklion Town Choir, 18
Hercules, 83, 84, 108, 112, 124, 205,
    229, 235–6, 238, 241, 326
Hercules (film), 26
Hermes, 124
hero/heroism, 12, 16, 23, 29, 32, 60,
    81, 83–4, 87, 98, 99, 100, 112,
    187, 195, 203, 228, 243, 252, 357
  adventure hero, 233–4
  battle hero, 233
  black hero, 197, 207
  epic heroes, 233–4, 236
  rock hero, 142, 197–8, 215, 233,
    234, 241, 242
  and rock misogyny, 290–91
  tragic heroes, 234–8, 240, 241, 244
  see also guitar hero
Herodotus, 88
Hersh, Kristin, 5, 48, 102, 319, 320
Hestia, 124
Heston, Charlton, 249, 250
hiddenness, 61, 67
High School Confidential (film), 261
Hill, Rose Lee, 74
'hill-billy', 337
hip hop, 40, 45, 143, 165, 166–7, 169,
    170, 209, 211, 336
Hippolytus, 229, 235
history, 6, 47, 188, 354
  blues, 323
  Greece, 136
  invention of, 88
  living, 9
  music, 303
  pop, 302
  of rock, 2
  Western, 12
Hitler, Adolf, 25, 217
Hizbollah movement, 108
Hofmannsthal, Hugo von, 101
Hole, 319
Holiday, Billie, 13, 35, 55, 86, 87, 96,
    97, 98, 159, 181, 192, 330, 332
Holland, Eddie, 96–7

Holly, Buddy, 39, 114, 302
Hollywood Democratic Committee,
    43
Homer, 29, 234
  The Iliad, 59, 60, 106, 113, 123, 187,
    207, 233
  The Odyssey, 25–6, 85, 113, 123,
    207
homogenization, 44
Hood, Robin, 112
Hooker, John Lee, 165, 202
Hope, 57
Hornby, Nick: *High Fidelity*, 12,
    47–8, 62, 64, 81, 119, 289, 348,
    353
The Horse Whisperer (film), 248
House of Pain, 304
House, Son, 68, 192–3
Howlin' Wolf, 42, 68, 79, 114, 160,
    202, 208
Hucknall, Mick, 160
human condition, the, 96, 241, 242
humour, 45, 176, 177, 184, 354
Hutchence, Michael, 23, 237, 238, 239
Hydra, 83, 115
Hynde, Chrissie, 250, 309, 311, 316,
    317, 318, 339, 353, 357

I Was Born A Slave (Library of Black
    America), 45
identity, 27, 32, 49, 87, 114, 137, 153,
    257, 324, 327, 344
  quest for, 351, 352
  racial, 182
The Idler magazine, 226
illusion, 16, 104, 111, 326, 338
imitation, 69, 133, 143, 162, 336–7
imperialism, 137, 149
impersonation, 39, 133, 134, 139, 143,
    194, 227, 233, 324–38, 358
  boys impersonating men, 202, 324
  impersonating America, 245–6
  men impersonating boys, 288
  rock's conspiracy of, 341
impotence, 71–2, 194, 200, 319
The Impressions, 200
inauthenticity, 5, 263, 340
incest, 127, 136

393

INDEX

Indeep, 313
India, 137
Indians (Native Americans), 149–50, 246–7, 249, 250, 251
Indigo Prime, 255
individuality, 50, 115, 148, 149
infantilism, 27, 275, 277, 278
Ingres, Jean-Auguste-Dominique
    La Grande Odalisque, 135
    Odalisque and Slave, 135
innovation, 45, 301, 337
Ino, 99, 103, 105
Iommi, Tommy, 216
irony, 288
Islam, 108
Island Records, 210
isolation, 93, 115

Jackson, Michael, 182, 183, 184, 317, 326
Jackson Five, 182
Jagger, Mick, 64, 69, 73, 111, 113, 115, 117, 123, 126, 127, 149, 157, 164, 170, 175, 194, 201, 204, 214–15, 216, 219, 220–1, 223, 231, 241, 258, 265, 268, 270, 295, 297, 298, 300, 306–9, 326, 327, 328, 334–5, 335, 339, 340, 342–3, 353
Jamaica, 163, 164, 246
Jamerson, James, 163
James, Alex, 226
James, Elmore, 68, 202
James, Rick, 183
Jamiroquai, 166
Jarboe, 286–7, 288, 311
Jason, 55, 84, 87, 89, 91, 100, 104, 112
Jay Kay, 166
Jay-Z, 209–10, 227
jazz, 8, 35, 38, 40, 43, 81, 134, 138, 139, 140, 146, 153, 154, 155, 189
    avant-garde, 336
    guitarists, 317
    radio audiences, 271
    trad, 116
    white, 246
    women's, 14, 74
jazz-blues, 192

Jefferson, Blind Lemon, 67, 71, 213, 227, 278
Jefferson Airplane, 170, 203, 220, 252
Jethro Tull, 142
Jett, Joan, 320
Jocasta, 235
Joel, Billy, 156, 165, 173
John, Elton, 154
Johnny B, 212
John's Children, 281
Johnson, Lonnie, 8–9, 67, 278
Johnson, Robert, 28, 67–70, 72, 78, 117, 120, 157, 192, 193, 200, 201, 213, 237, 278–9, 302, 303, 327
Johnson, Tommy, 213
Johnson, Wilko, 215
Joint Anti-Fascist Refugee Committee, 43
Jones, Brian, 23, 64, 68, 80, 114, 157, 202, 214, 219–20, 237, 239, 241
Jones, George, 77
Jones, Steve, 237
Jonson, Mick, 239
Joplin, Janis, 26, 31, 97, 237, 299–300
journalism, 290, 310–11, 314–16
journey, 113, 118, 121, 124, 189
joy, 63, 134, 237
Joy Division, 217
Joyce, James, 85
    Ulysses, 110
Judas Priest, 287, 288
juke boxes, 8, 34
juke-house, 122, 123, 213
Jung, Carl Gustav, 101, 141
Juno, 54, 106
Jupiter, 54, 88

Karajan, Herbert von, 290
katabasis (descent to the underworld), 187
Keane, Dolores, 95
Keats, John, 303
Keeting, Ronan, 292
Keisker, Marion, 37–8
Kemp, Lindsay, 240
Kennedy, Jimmy, 9
Kenyatta, Jomo, 151
Kern, Jerome, 89

Kerouac, Jack: *On the Road*, 120, 123
KFFA radio, 34
King, Carole, 90, 302
King, Martin Luther, 8, 43, 252, 262
King, Stephen: *The Stand*, 216
The King and I (film), 144
King Biscuit Time (radio show), 34
Kings, 81
Kingston, Jamaica, 164
Kinks, 245
Kirshner, Don, 302
Kiss, 239, 287, 327
Kiss Me magazine, 355
KLF, 270
KMFDM, 217, 222, 232
Knebworth, 112
Knights of the Round Table, 112
Knossos, Crete, 18
Knupfer (artist), 107
Konietsko, Sascha, 222
Korean War, 228, 251
Kraftwerk, 154, 166, 336
Kronfield, Eric, 210
Kronos, 53, 83, 347
Krush Groove (film), 167
Ku Klux Klan, 147

L7, 321
LA Guns, 51, 309
LaBianca, Mr and Mrs, 253
laddishness, 285, 286, 288
Lady and the Tramp (animated film), 122
Ladysmith Black Mambazo, 170, 171
Laing, R.D., 186
Lamacq, Steve, 10
Lambert, Kit, 213–14
Lammas, 41
land, 246, 247
lang, k.d., 5, 329
Last Action Hero (film), 216
Latifah, Queen, 168
Lauper, Cyndi, 328
Lawrence, D. H., 141, 189
Leadbelly, 8, 196, 208–9, 225, 248, 263, 264
Leaving Las Vegas (film), 334
Led Zeppelin, 26, 65, 71, 81, 212, 215, 216, 237, 279–80, 295, 296, 309, 320
Lee, Peggy, 35, 98, 122
Leiber, Jerry, 157, 302
Lenin Stadium, Moscow, 64
Lennon, John, 31, 34, 64, 116, 122, 143, 150, 237, 281, 297, 303, 353
Lennox, Annie, 312, 328, 329, 334
Lerner, Sammy, 89, 90
Lewin, Miss (piano teacher), 17
Lewinsky, Monica, 126, 312
Lewis, Furry, 213
Lewis, Jerry Lee, 156, 158, 261
Lewis, Percy Wyndham: *Paleface*, 141–2
Library of Black America, 45
Life Magazine, 209
Lightning, Lori, 308
Little Richard, 16, 44, 48, 51, 89, 114, 149, 156, 159, 176, 177, 182, 212, 279, 307, 326
Little Rock, Arkansas, 138
Littleton massacre *see* Columbine High School
Live Aid, 149
Live Flesh (film), 59
Living Colour, 172
Lloyd-Webber, Andrew, 229, 244
Lockwood, Robert, Jr, 40
Lohan, Sinead, 318
Lomax, Alan, 7, 8, 49, 71, 73, 75, 78, 150, 208, 264
  Negro Folk Songs as Sung by Leadbelly, 208
Lomax, John, 8, 208
London, Jack: *The Call of the Wild*, 246
London's Most Wanted, 313
loneliness, 63, 67, 91, 96, 97, 115, 205, 240, 241, 304
Lorca, Federico García, 29
Los Angeles, 252, 254, 256, 308, 320
  'Whiskey a Go Go Bar', 175
Los Angeles Times, 266
Louisiana Purchase, 246
Love, Courtney, 97, 320
lovesong, 55, 57, 91, 196, 333
Lunch, Lydia, 254

INDEX

The Lustful Turk, 135
lute, 66
Lydon, John *see* Rotten, Johnny
Lymon, Frankie, 36
Lynott, Phil, 237

M People, 84
McCarthy, Joseph, 43–4, 49
McCartney, Paul, 64, 116, 122, 150, 156, 297, 340
McCoy, Ethel, 74
McDaniels, Gene, 159
McDowell, Fred, 118
McGahern, John: *The Pornographer*, 103
McLaren, Malcolm, 44, 171, 268, 285, 319, 345, 346
MacNeice, Louis, 270
McPhatter, Clyde, 176
McTell, Blind Willie, 72
Madison Square Garden, New York, 295, 305
madness, 185, 186–7, 189, 230, 231, 232, 239
Madonna, 154, 328, 329, 334
Madonna, the, 53
The Magnificent Seven (film), 112
Mailer, Norman, 46
 'The White Negro', 246
Malcolm X (Malcolm Little), 43
male bonding, 113, 117
male-female antagonism, 53
maleness, 1, 7, 11, 15, 23, 32, 227, 291, 297, 357
 authentic, 14
 black, 153, 258, 324
 creative, 304
 the 'dark embryo' of civilization, 189
 of early blues, 67
 equating the guitar with, 73
 female hymns to, 332
 glamorous images of, 118
 heroic, 205, 311
 infant, 61
 the laddish form of, 288
 and male Western song, 258
 and marriage, 281

mask of, 155
myths and, 12, 112, 246
 in relation to sex, 53
rock, 13, 15, 239, 245, 274
spoof, 12
staging, 292–6
'teen gurl' ideal of, 355
Man-Sized Action, 179
managers, management, 128, 213–14, 267, 290, 302, 309–10, 312–13
Mandelstam, Osip, 30
manhood, 189, 202, 266, 267, 294
 Hollywood, 248
 rock, 226
Manic Street Preachers, 10, 112, 237, 266
Manilow, Barry, 343
The Manish Boys, 202
Manson, Charles, 217, 222, 232, 235, 250, 253–6, 345
Manson, Marilyn, 232, 254, 255
 The Long Road Out of Hell, 217
Manson, Shirley, 5, 270, 309, 315, 317, 319, 340, 356–7
mantinadas (improvised rapping couplets), 18
Mapplethorpe, Robert, 328
'March on Washington' rally (1963), 262
Marcus, Greil, 143, 156, 182, 314
Mariana, 97
Maritain, 189
Marley, Bob, 164, 165, 171, 237
marriage, 281
Mars, 58, 59, 61–4, 107, 228, 288–9
Marsyas, 25
Martha and the Vandellas, 149
Martin Luther King Foundation, 161
Martin-Smith, Nigel, 312
mascara, 104, 283, 327, 330, 331
masculinity, 3, 12, 67, 134, 304, 327, 357
 American, 247, 248, 249, 251
 as armour, 59
 black, 15
 and country music, 154
 in crisis, 286
 and the gun, 247

396

INDEX

'natural', 195
primitive, 358
and rock, 14, 227
suffering, 193
white, 15, 247
mask, 104, 133, 155, 180, 231, 258, 324, 325, 329
masquerade, 105, 324, 331
Massive Attack, 355, 356
masturbation, 73, 118, 127, 228, 251, 319, 320
Matheson, Hans, 178
Mayfield, Curtis, 200
mbaqanga, 170
MC5, 215
MCA, 204, 266
MCs (mike controllers), 4, 117, 313, 355
Meat Puppets, 48
Medea, 55, 87–91, 100, 104, 188, 229, 275, 325
Medusa, the Gorgon, 83, 84, 92, 115
melancholy cult, 196
melisma, 145–6, 155
melody, 18, 28–9, 66, 77, 145–6, 148, 154, 291, 333
Melody Maker, 165
Memphis, Tennessee, 12, 34, 40, 41, 245
Memphis Minnie, 74–5, 300
Memphis Recording Studio, 37
men
  black, 258, 304
  power, 16, 58, 64, 66, 194, 274, 280
  roving, 27, 120–24, 281
  white, 258
Men Are From Mars Women Are From Venus (Gray), 102
mento, 164
Mercury *see* Hermes
Mercury, Freddie, 178, 237, 326, 347
Merimée, Prosper, 331
mermaids, 100, 102, 283
Metallica, 216
microphone, 124, 206
Middle Ages, 207
middle-class, 116, 258
Miller, Mitch, 114

millionaires, teenage, 50
Mime Troupe, 240
Minos, King, 88, 136
Minotaur, 83, 87, 100, 136
Mintz, Leo, 35
Miracles, 332
mirror, 124, 128, 258, 268, 282, 283, 293, 341
Mirror, 340
misogyny, 12, 16, 58, 72, 100, 209, 217, 274, 301, 354
  blues, 278, 280
  collective, 328
  the harmony of, 290–91
  heavy metal, 284–9
  Lonnie and Robert Johnson, 278–9
  male need for, 297
  in myth, 274–5
  and punk, 320
  rap, 304–5
  rock, 304
  in the rock industry, 289–90
  and sexiness, 306–12
  theatre of, 284–9
  and women guitarists, 322–3
Mississippi Delta, 9, 34, 40, 41, 67, 114, 124, 171, 197, 205
Mississippi Hills, 150
Mitchell, Joni, 123, 194
mixing desk, 82
mixing 'n' scratching, 4, 117, 165, 313
mobility, 55, 123
modernism, 15, 139, 141, 184, 185
mojo, 66–7, 71, 72
Mojo (film), 178
Mojo magazine, 4, 72, 314, 356
monody, 92, 93
Monroe, Bill, 75, 154
Monroe, Marilyn, 217, 334
Monster Magnet, 285
Monterey festival, 80, 161, 172, 177, 242
Monteverdi, Claudio
  Ariadne Abandoned, 91
  The Coronation of Poppea, 110
Montgomery, Alabama, 44
Moog synthesizer, 336
Moon, Keith, 214, 237

397

INDEX

Moonglows, 350
Moore, Christy, 18, 103
Moore, Gary, 171, 172
Moore, Scotty, 38, 79
Morissette, Alanis, 204
Morrison, Jim, 23, 26, 31, 55, 85, 111, 159, 177, 178, 215, 216, 219, 231, 232, 237, 239, 241, 244, 268, 271, 324, 341, 348, 353, 355
Morrison, Van, 328
mothers, 203
   power, 274–5, 280, 288
Mothers of Invention, 266
Motorhead, 216
Motown, 36, 162, 163, 200, 303, 332
Motown Appreciation Society, 170
Mott the Hoople, 1
Mozart, Wolfgang Amadeus, 96, 110, 332
   Escape from the Seraglio, 135
   The Magic Flute, 143
   Marriage of Figaro, 89, 94–5, 105
Mugger, 308
Murcia, Billy, 237
murder, 29, 30, 93, 210, 213, 215, 216, 221, 222, 231, 237, 238, 247, 250, 319
Murray, Charles Shaar, 172
Murray, Gilbert, 141
Muse, the, 292, 294, 331
Museum of Modern Art (MOMA), New York, 142
Museum of Scotland, 15
music
   black *see* black music
   defined, 24
   powers, 24, 25, 29, 30, 31
   white, 129
'Music of Black Origin' prizegiving, 160
Music Journal, 138
mutuality, 28
My Generation (Farrell, Guinness and Lloyd), 16, 303–4
My Lai massacre, Vietnam, 235, 256
myth(s), 9
   Christian, 54
   defined, 24

of desire, 136
of difference, 4
of Dionysus, 229, 230
of discovering fire, 56–7
the founding myth of rock 'n' roll, 37
frontier, 251
Greek, 1, 4, 16, 23, 27, 30–32, 52, 53, 57, 58, 87, 88, 101, 104, 109, 115, 153, 179, 205, 231, 257, 274, 275, 293–4, 324, 349, 353
heroic, 243
history of, 6–7
male, 89, 90, 103, 104, 105, 284
and maleness, 12, 112
of Orpheus, 25, 29, 31
popular, 190
primitive, 141
recycled, 30–31
and rock music, 15, 64, 353
sacred, 33
sung, 26–9
Western, 2, 87, 228
white, 150

Naked Nashville (TV documentary), 78
Napier-Bell, Simon, 29
narcissism, 31, 124–9, 194, 218, 273, 293, 299, 321, 354
Narcissus, 23, 28, 31, 32, 93, 112, 124, 126, 258, 282, 293, 295, 300, 312, 333, 341, 347, 352
Nash, Johnny, 350
Nation of Islam, 167
National Gallery, London, 24
National Rifle Association, 249, 250
National Top Forty, 183
nature, natural, 1, 6, 9, 121, 125, 185, 207, 227, 248, 249, 257, 275
Naxos, 90, 91
need, 14, 16, 60, 63, 64, 99, 152, 194, 195, 278, 279, 280, 284, 291, 292, 297, 304
Nefertiti, 26
Nelson, Ricky, 80
Neptune, 85, 100
Nero, 110

Neuwirth, Bobby, 7
New Musical Express, 10, 118, 226
New York, 139, 140
New York City Ballet, 332
New York Dolls, 237, 239, 326
The New York Herald Tribune, 35
New York Times, 183
Newman, Randy, 119
Newport Folk Festival, 264, 337
Newsweek, 138
Nicholson, Geoff: *Flesh Guitar*, 237, 242
Nico, 50, 256, 257
Niggaz With Attitude, 167, 168, 209, 227
Night, 187, 188
Nighthawk, Robert, 68
Nirvana, 196
Noriega, General, 208, 216
North Alabama White Citizens Council, 39, 155
Notorious B.I.G. (Christopher Wallace), 209
Notting Hill (film), 292
Nugent, Ted, 286

Oasis, 112, 312, 355
Oates, John, 163
O'Brien, John: *Leaving Las Vegas*, 334
Ocean, 53, 54
O'Connor, Sinead, 5, 194, 327
Odysseus, 26, 85, 99, 234
  see also Ulysses
Oedipus, 23, 26, 229, 231, 235, 236, 238, 241, 244
Oenone, 97
Oklahoma, 246, 247, 249
Oklahoma! (musical), 246, 247, 248
Ol' Dirty Bastard, 210
Oldham, Andrew, 214
Olivier, Laurence, 238
Olympic Games (1968), 253
Ono, Yoko, 34, 102, 275, 281
'open road', 27, 111, 124, 125, 299, 347–8
opera, 13, 14, 62, 89, 91–7, 110, 143, 192, 196, 229, 275, 294, 330

oppression, 147, 198, 203–6, 266
The Oprah Winfrey Show (television programme), 97
oral sex, 127, 184
Orbison, Roy, 16, 79–80, 158
orchestra, 96, 149
Orestes, 229, 236
orientalism, 134–5, 136, 143, 154, 257
Orpheus, 24–32, 45, 76, 84, 112, 138, 155, 230, 347, 352
otherism, 134–5, 137, 257, 261, 267
Ottoman Empire, 134
outlaw status, 253
Ovid, 89, 90
Owens, Buck, 75
Owsley, Stanley, 253

PA crews, 82, 322
Page, Jimmy, 81, 216, 280
Palmer, Robert, 80, 149, 185, 231, 232, 235
  Dancing in the Street, 238
  History of Rock, 202
Palmer, Tony, 251
Pan, 93, 232
Pandora, 57, 100, 274, 279
Paramount Catalogue (1924), 74
parents *see* anti-parent; father; mother
Parents' Music Resource Centre, 266
Parfitt, Andy, 211
Paris, France, 139, 230
Paris is Burning (film), 328
Paris of Troy, 87–8, 97, 107
Parker, Alan, 46
Parks, Rosa, 44
Parliament, 181
Parmenides, 187
Parnes, Larry, 54
parody, 92, 182, 218, 239, 254, 258, 285, 286, 295, 328
Pasiphae, wife of King Minos, 136
paternalism, 75, 78
Paterson, Don, 41
pathos, 91–2
Patroclus, 113
Patton, Charlie, 68, 195, 213
Penelope, 348
Penguin Song Book, 17

INDEX

penis *see* cock
Pentheus, 229, 235, 236, 329–30
The People, 146
Perkins, Carl, 158
Perkins, Luther, 302
Perry, Joe, 282
Perry, Lee 'Scratel', 163
Perseus, 83, 84, 92, 115
Persians, 139
persona, 329, 356
Pet Shop Boys, 312
Peter Paul and Mary, 262
Phaedra, 94, 136, 326
Phair, Liz, 5, 13, 52–3, 58, 102, 321
Philippe, Louis, 36, 302, 303
Phillips, Esther, 351
Phillips, Sam, 37, 38, 39, 52, 150, 158, 337
Phiri, Ray, 170
Piaf, Edith, 13
Picasso, Pablo, 139, 141, 142
Piccadilly Circus, London, 52
Pickett, Wilson, 156
Pill, the, 307
Pink Floyd, 33, 336
Pirner, Dave, 1, 12–13, 25
Pitt, Brad, 355
Pixies, 319
Plant, Robert, 215, 296
Plaster Casters, 178, 299
Plato, 56, 63, 186, 188, 348–9
   Charmides, 55
The Platters, 162
Poe, Edgar Allan, 278
poetry, 29–30, 31, 55, 96, 186, 188, 233, 270, 292–3
Polanski, Roman, 253
Police, 113, 165
politics, 8, 29, 39, 42, 44, 88, 167, 170, 192, 199, 243, 252, 266, 286
   sexual, 291, 312
   the sexualization of, 200
Pollock, Jackson, 142
Polygram, 210
polyrhythms, 145
pop
   chart, 4, 11
   compared with rock, 3–4
   rock as a subset of, 4
Pop, Iggy, 60–61, 111, 178, 215, 265–6, 271, 326, 341, 348
pop psychology, 102
Pope, Alexander, 135
   The Rape of the Lock, 88
Popplewell, Mr, 175
'popular music', 4, 35, 49, 275
potency, 72, 135, 349
pottery, 56
Poulenc, Francis: *La Voix Humaine*, 96
power
   bluesmen's, 73
   creative, 194
   electricity, 46, 81
   father's, 64
   female, 97, 275, 276
   girl, 11
   loss of, 64
   magic marine, 103
   male, 16, 58, 64, 66, 194, 274, 280, 295, 313
   and misogyny, 100, 274, 275
   mother's, 274–5, 280, 288
   of music, 24, 25, 29, 30, 31
   of poetry, 30
   rock, 15, 118, 275, 324
   of rock 'n' roll, 34
   suffering as, 192–8
   technological, 64
   teenage, 45, 50, 308
   of the tragic hero, 238
   white, 184
'power chords', 251, 306
power-struggle, 53–4
Powers, Bill, 250
Presley, Elvis, 34, 37–8, 39, 44, 46, 47, 48, 50, 51, 64, 79, 113–14, 116, 120, 126, 127, 128, 134, 138, 143, 150, 154, 156–8, 165, 177, 202, 205, 212, 227, 228, 237, 258, 279, 296, 302, 326, 337, 354
primitivism, 15, 38, 139–42, 207
primitivity, 9
Prince, 126, 127, 180–84, 239, 248, 273, 326–7, 338, 345
Procrustes, 83

The Prodigy, 12, 50, 112, 168, 226, 243, 285, 288, 304, 356
production, 272–3, 290, 302, 332
prohibition, repeal of, 8
Prometheus, 55–8, 160, 161, 162, 167, 169, 243, 244
protest movement, 264
protest songs, 261, 262, 264
psyche, 49, 53, 58, 189, 236, 240, 243, 264, 297
   male, 112, 297
   rock, 155
   the teenage, 290
   white American, 246
Psyche, 31–2, 348–52
psychedelia, 222, 252, 253
Psycho (film), 297
psychoanalysis, 134, 257
Public Enemy, 160, 166, 167–8
Puccini, Giacomo, *La Bohème*, 196
Puff Daddy, 169
punk, 7, 14, 44, 71, 164, 166, 167, 181, 219, 232, 243, 245, 246, 268, 270, 272, 285, 319–21, 334, 340, 341–3, 356
Purcell, Henry: *Dido and Aeneas*, 192

Q Magazine, 55, 59
Queen, 178, 239, 326
quest, 328–9, 347–8, 349, 351, 352, 358

race relations, 2, 35
Racine, Jean, 96, 236
racism, 137, 141, 158, 174, 175, 176, 184, 207, 250, 298
radio, 29, 34–5, 40, 41, 43–6, 68, 77, 101, 177, 244
Radio 1 (BBC), 210
Radio Information Centre, 271
rage, 47, 72, 193, 195, 200, 204, 258, 353
   jealous, 70–71
   sexual, 70
ragtime, 153, 155
Raincoats, 319
Rainey, Ma, 73–4, 93, 158
Rammstein, 217, 222, 232, 269
Ramones, 2, 47, 261, 318

rap, 15, 18, 147, 154, 155, 162, 166–9, 209–12, 232, 257, 288, 355
   agrarian, 167
   gangsta, 167, 184, 210, 226, 248, 286, 356
   misogyny, 304–5
Rap Show (BBC Radio 1), 210, 211
rape, 88, 147, 194, 215, 223, 231, 248, 280, 285, 288, 295, 296, 305
rave culture, 268
Ray, Johnnie, 176
Razaf, Andy, 13
Reagan, Ronald, 184
rebellion, 4, 45, 49, 54, 85, 206, 244, 261, 268, 279, 289
record companies, 36, 40, 42, 47, 50, 267, 272, 302
record industry, 74
recordings, 26, 34, 45, 269, 335, 336
   and artifice, 336
   the first blues, 34, 73–4, 142, 157–8
   the first country music, 75
   first recording of an electric guitar, 40
   the first rock 'n' roll, 36
   the first rock 'n' roll hit, 36, 37
   Muddy Waters, 78
   pop, 270
   Presley, 37–8
   Robeson banned, 43
   women pop singers, 96
Red Hot Chilli Peppers, 111, 179
Redding, Otis, 156, 158
Reed, Lou, 79–80, 144, 159
reggae, 151, 154, 164–5, 246
Reid, Vernon, 172, 173, 201
Reinhardt, Django, 79
relationships, 3, 13, 24, 27, 28, 53, 57, 67, 101, 113, 115, 126, 147, 202, 215, 236, 243, 268, 269, 270, 343–7, 349, 357, 358
Renaissance, 88, 107, 207, 232, 349
repression, 45, 49, 133, 138, 265, 281, 297
resentment, 53, 104, 195, 200, 202, 203, 204, 278, 280, 284, 343, 345, 353, 354
Reservoir Dogs (film), 112

INDEX

Revue des Nègres, 139
Reznor, Trent, 219
Rhea, 26
Rhodes, Nick, 343
rhythm, 3, 9, 11, 27, 40, 44, 66, 77, 79, 143–50, 152, 154, 159, 176, 291, 323
rhythm and blues (R & B), 42, 72, 150, 153, 154, 161, 164–3, 166, 271, 302
Richard, Cliff, 114, 272
Richards, Keith, 10, 39, 64, 68–9, 79, 113, 114, 117, 120, 157, 164, 170, 193, 194, 201, 205, 215, 221, 223, 251, 328, 340
Rickenbacker company, 40
Riddle (a black musician), 77
riffs, 6, 37, 39, 41, 69, 73, 80, 81, 115, 123, 143, 251, 285, 337, 355
Right Said Fred, 127
Righteous Brothers, 159, 162, 350
rights
  black, 43
  civil, 7, 43, 44, 199
  human, 262, 265
  workers', 42
Rilke, Rainer Maria, 29
Rimbaud, Arthur, 328
Riot Grrrl consciousness, 320
Roberts, Monty, 248
Robertson, Robbie, 48, 262
Robeson, Paul, 42–3
rock god, 51, 54, 64, 111, 127, 179, 285, 311, 334, 353
rock hero, 142, 197–8, 215, 233, 234, 241, 242
rock music
  about male rule, 65
  aggression, 16, 205, 228, 246, 252
  artificiality, 303, 325
  authenticity, 3, 7, 10, 11, 14, 156, 223, 324
  and blues, 114, 129, 279
  boys and, 9–12
  and classical music, 49
  cock, 71, 72, 122, 123, 179, 194, 321, 322
  'commercial', 3, 265
  compared with pop, 3–4
  and country music, 49, 154
  critics, 128
  deepest role, 353
  and desire, 30
  development, 70–71
  and disco, 267
  glam, 181, 268, 326, 327, 338, 340–41
  heavy, 321
  male, 111, 126, 186, 317
  the male group as the key unit, 116–18
  masculinity, 14
  misogyny, 304
  origins of, 4, 190
  phallus-worship, 178–9, 191
  political, 262
  power, 15, 118, 275, 324
  progressive, 3
  protest strain, 265–6
  psychedelic, 222
  radio audiences, 271
  theatricality, 235
  traditional ways of seeing women, 14
  and tragedy, 235
  violence, 213, 227–8, 235, 251–2, 258
  white, 71, 159, 162, 218, 286
  women's, 14, 27, 102, 315–16, 356
rock 'n' roll
  aggression, 44
  'anarchy', 44
  anti-history, 47
  freedom of, 296
  origin, 35, 38, 40, 189
  sexuality of, 296
  teenage music, 45, 46, 49, 50
  and theft, 39
  white, 155
Rock 'n' Roll Hall of Fame, 156, 182
Rock 'n' Roll High School (film), 261
rock stars, 2, 64, 178, 235, 237, 238, 241, 268, 272, 301, 305, 314–15, 326
  female, 309, 312
rockabilly, 114, 302

INDEX

Rodgers, Jimmie, 75, 77, 143, 154
Rodgers, Paul, 216
Rodgers, Richard, 94
Rodney, Winston, 151
Rogers, Jimmy, 42
Rolling Stone, 1, 10, 13, 169, 170, 183, 210, 220, 222, 253, 342–3, 345
Rolling Stones, 3, 41, 64, 72, 111, 114–18, 143, 159–60, 164, 165, 177, 178, 190, 193, 199, 200, 203, 212, 214, 215, 219–23, 226, 238, 243, 245, 250, 265, 268, 269, 272, 289, 294–5, 297, 298, 301, 303, 304, 306, 327, 343, 356
Rollins, Henry, 203, 235, 240, 255, 256, 266, 271, 341
romanticism, 4, 9, 15, 29, 124–5, 126, 141, 220, 253
Ronettes, 332
Rose, Billy, 176
Roth, David Lee, 177, 295, 310, 311, 325, 339
Rotten, Johnny (John Lydon), 164, 186, 237, 268, 342–3, 345, 346, 351, 352
Rousseau, Jean-Jacques, 8
Royal Albert Hall, London, 264
Royal Court Theatre, London, 342
Rubin, Rick, 167
Rushdie, Salman, 354
  The Ground Beneath Her Feet, 31
Russell, Marcus, 312
Russia, Robeson's visit, 42
Russian Symbolism, 88
Russian War Relief Fund, 43

sacrifice, 241–4
Sade, Marquis de, 333
St Eustache choir, Paris, 18
Salt 'n' Pepa, 168
sampling, 166, 278, 336, 337, 355
San Francisco, 222, 252, 253, 299
San Francisco General Hospital, 252
Santana, Carlos, 253
Sappho, 55
Sargent, Sir Malcolm, 159, 189
Satan, Satanism, 54, 68, 70, 214–17, 219, 245, 257, 274

Savage Garden, 294
Savery, Roelandt, 24
Schola Cantorum, 18
'School for non-violence' (Baez), 253
schools, 39, 279, 295, 297, 353, 357
Schubert, Franz, 3
Schwarzenegger, Arnold, 216
Scritti Politti, 350
Scylla, 86, 103, 113
sea, 85–8, 90, 99–105, 282, 283
Sedaka, Neil, 302
seduction, 89
Seeger, Pete, 7, 264
segregation, 35, 36, 39, 40, 43, 44, 138, 161–2
self, 31, 134, 135, 257, 258, 261, 358
self-image, 15, 23, 32, 53, 67, 81, 120, 122, 124, 126, 189, 205, 206, 258, 293–4
Seminole tribe, 246
Semonides, 274
sex, 117, 148, 222
  and creativity, 56, 58
  fire and, 56
  the goddess of *see* Venus
  and guns, 247
  the key to performance and sound, 42
  maleness in relation to, 53
  the origin of, 53
  and politics, 88
  rock, 203
  sado-masochistic, 257
  and soul music, 174
  spiritual, 163
  and violence, 228–9, 251
  and war, 59
Sex Pistols, 44, 164, 214, 219, 232, 237, 268, 272, 318, 341, 342, 343, 345, 346, 351, 352–4
sexism, 284, 288, 297, 306, 311, 313, 314, 322
sexuality, 18, 42, 49, 63, 351, 358
  black, 40, 133, 137, 176, 197
  black music, 146
  blues, 49
  conventional, 319
  'deviant', 182

of Elvis, 44
a father's, 53
female, 103
and freedom, 296
gay, 267
Hendrix, 81
and individuality, 50
male, 11, 14, 15, 51, 60, 88, 123, 128, 197, 216, 249, 280, 291, 300
rock, 119, 245
and the rock hero, 242
of rock 'n' roll, 296
stereotyping, 207
teenage, 45, 49
and a woman alone, 93
Shadows, 114, 238
Shakespeare in Love (film), 325
Shakespeare, William, 96, 236, 243
All's Well That Ends Well, 325, 329, 348
King Lear, 86, 279
Measure for Measure, 97
The Merchant of Venice, 348
Richard III, 238
Twelfth Night, 94, 328
Shakur, Tupac, 9–10, 26, 210
shamans, 31, 84
Shangri Las, 302
Shirelles, 296, 297
Showboat (film), 42
Shrimpton, Chrissie, 298
Sidney, Philip: *Asphodel and Stella*, 274
sign language, 94
Simon, Carly, 97–8, 333
Simon, Paul, 5, 28, 170, 170–71, 173, 190, 251, 305
Simply Red, 160
Sinatra, Frank, 9, 12, 49, 179, 196, 307
Sing Out magazine, 262
Sioux, Siouxsie, 218, 319
Sirens, 25, 85, 86, 103, 283
SIW (Security of the First World), 168
ska, 163–4, 246
slavery, 45, 131, 135, 136–8, 146, 151, 161, 168, 207, 250, 251, 261, 280, 298
Sledge, Percy, 162

Sleeping Beauty (animated film), 95
Slick, Grace, 252, 299
Slim, Guitar, 40
Slits, 319
Smith, Bessie, 13, 73, 88, 142, 158, 331
Smith, Chris, 303
Smith, Mamie, 73
Smith, Mary Louise, 44
Smith, Patti, 11, 102, 142, 199, 250, 318, 328
Smith, TV, 272, 319, 322
Smothers Brothers, 252
Snoop Doggy Dog, 248, 304, 306
Snow, Mat, 4, 50, 273, 289, 354–5
society, 297
adult, 45, 258
blackness in, 354
divine, 52
and femaleness, 281
Greek, 24
parent, 289
white, 45, 258
Socrates, 55
Soft Machine, 102
Solaar, M.C., 167
soliloquy, 95, 97
solitude, 93, 96, 118
solo, 79, 80, 81, 148
son *see* father–son conflict
songwriting, 116–17, 303, 316, 321
Sonic Youth, 255, 319
Sophocles, 243
Antigone, 236
Oedipus at Colonus, 238
Women of Trachis, 238
soprano, 91, 96, 109–10, 294, 334, 351
Soul, 350, 351, 353, 47, 81, 147, 148, 151–2, 154, 162–3, 164, 166, 169, 174, 201, 350
Soul Asylum, 1
soul, the, 6, 25, 30, 33, 189, 190, 349
American, 248
the Christian, 85
the male, 10, 101, 354
see also psyche/Psyche
soul-funk, 165
The Sound of Music (film), 104, 145
South Africa, 170, 171

INDEX

South Bank Show (television programme), 171
'spanking the plank', 41
sparagmos see Dionysus
Spector, Phil, 162, 194, 303, 332
Spice Girls, 168, 273, 312, 334
Spin, 226
Spinal Tap, 309
spirituals, 264
spitting, 75, 270, 271, 287, 291, 355
Springfield, Dusty, 29, 156
Springsteen, Bruce, 5, 7, 32, 55, 84, 86, 105, 149, 156, 170, 171, 173, 266–7, 273, 281, 282, 345
SST (record company), 255, 256
stadium rock, 287, 340, 343
Stalin, Joseph, 43
Stanford University, 253
Star Trek television and film series, 238
Starr, Ringo, 150
Starr, Sable, 308
Stax label, 207
Steele, Tommy, 54
Steely Dan, 166
Steinbeck, John: *The Grapes of Wrath*, 75–6
stereotypes, 3, 15, 137, 161, 174, 175, 179, 180, 184, 189–90, 197, 207, 299, 319, 322, 334
Sternberg, Josef von, 105
Stewart, Rod, 101
Sting, 5, 59, 64, 113, 165, 237, 278
Stock Aitken Waterman, 355
Stockhausen, Karl-Heinz, 336
Stoller, Mike, 157, 302
Stone, Sly, 181, 200
Stooges, 60, 215, 266
Stoppard, Tom: *The Real Thing*, 350
Storace, Nancy, 105
Stormtroopers of Death, 216
STP (scientifically treated petroleum; hallucinogenic drugs), 252
Stranglers, 285, 314, 320
Strauss, Richard, 104, 229
  Ariadne on Naxos, 93, 96
  Helen in Egypt, 101

Stravinsky, Igor: *The Rite of Spring*, 139, 324
Streep, Meryl, 87
street, 339
Stroppy Cow label, 321
Styrene, Poly, 319, 334, 341
suffering, 235, 350
  as power, 192–8
suicide, 9, 10–11, 199, 217, 237–42, 250, 256, 287, 325, 346
Sun label, 37, 150, 337
Sunset Sound Studio, Los Angeles, 300
suprematism, 355
  aggression, 194
  Dylan and, 301, 304
  fanning flames of, 300
  and groupies, 312
  and male freedom, 299
  and misogyny, 284
  in the musical texture and shape, 306
  white, 147
Supremes, 96
Sutherland, Gavin, 101
Swans, 287
swastika, 245, 255
Swift, A. K., 212
sword-dance, 18
symbolism, symbols, 2, 15, 26, 28, 29, 66, 73, 80, 81, 122, 133, 135, 140, 155, 187, 207, 215, 218, 227, 232, 251
synthesizers, 5, 269, 278, 336

Take That, 312, 340
Tampax incident, 320, 342
tape loops, 336, 337
Tate, Sharon, 222, 253–4
Tchaikovsky, Pyotr Ilyich, 95
  Eugene Onegin, 94
team spirit, 112–15, 117
technique, 6, 68, 69, 70, 76, 77, 79, 80, 81, 123, 265, 318
techno, 336
technology, 6, 34, 38–9, 57, 60, 82, 87, 264, 269, 270, 322, 336, 337
teenagers, 2, 4, 12, 15, 16, 27, 28, 34–5,

405

40, 44–51, 72, 73, 134, 145, 148, 156, 189, 198, 263, 266
American, 248
bedroom, 118–19, 251, 305
freedom, 258, 262
identity, 257
mass market, 49
opposition, 265, 267
and politicians, 265
power, 45, 50, 308
protest, 203–5
psyche, 290
sexual individuality, 149
the teenage anthem, 125
see also anti-parent
telephone, 2, 28, 94, 96
television, 35, 36, 43, 44, 47, 250
Tennessee Two, 302
Tennyson, Alfred, Lord, 112
   Idylls of The King, 99
   'The Lady of Shalott', 97
   Locksley Hall, 135
Texas swing, 38
Tharpe, Sister Rosetta, 74
theatre
   of cruelty, 230
   interactive, 343
   and rock violence, 227–8, 229–32
theatricality, 2, 13, 111, 235, 240, 258, 270, 334, 340, 343
theft, 39, 56, 57, 58, 134, 152, 153–60, 162
Theseus, 83, 84, 87, 90, 91, 100, 112, 124, 136, 205, 234, 236, 348
Thompson, Hank, 77
Thompson, Hunter S., 314
   Hell's Angels, 253
Thornton, Big Mama, 157, 158
Three Musketeers, 112
Thrill Kill Kult, 217
Throbbing Gristle, 179
Throwing Muses, 318, 319
Time Out magazine, 237
Tin Pan Alley, 8, 263
Titanic (film), 141
toasting, 165
tonality, 154, 291

Top of the Pops (television programme), 321
torchsong, 13, 55, 57, 89, 192
Tosh, Peter, 164, 182
Townshend, Irving, 150
Townshend, Pete, 172, 173, 213–14, 270
trad jazz, 116
tragedy, 91, 92, 94, 95, 96, 136, 185, 186, 229, 230, 234–7, 240, 243, 248, 275, 329, 330
transformation, 33–4
transistor, 40
transvestitism, 239, 257
Trenchcoat Mafia, 217–18, 249, 257, 269
tribal art, 139
Tribe 8, 320, 323
Tricky, 166, 210
Trojan War, 88, 106, 112
troubadour songs, 18, 196
Troy, 88, 112, 327
Trynka, Paul, 4, 41–2, 46, 150, 160, 166, 171–2, 202–3, 218, 317–18, 319
tunings, 68, 80
Turks, 134, 137
Turner, Big Joe, 177
Turner, Ike, 182
Turner, Tina, 160, 182
The Turtles, 166
Twitty, Conway, 158
2 Live Crew, 304
Tyler, Bonnie, 100
Tyler, Steve, 279–80, 281–2, 295–6, 305

UK Top Ten, 168
UK Top Thirty, 166
Ulysses, 27, 84–7, 93, 99, 105, 112, 113, 187, 233, 282, 326, 348
   see also Odysseus
underwear, 2, 106, 108
underworld, 30, 31, 55, 56, 84, 115, 187, 188, 274
United Nations, 170
United States see America
Upsetters, 114, 326

'urban jungle', 140
urine, 287, 305

values
  aesthetic, 2
  black, 184
  cultural, 249
  ethical, 2
  male, 23–4
  musical, 301
Van Dyke, Earl, 163
Van Halen, 149, 177, 287, 295, 310–11, 339
Van Halen, Alex, 310, 311
Van Halen, Eddie, 287
Vanilla Ice, 168, 169
Vanity Fair magazine, 328
Variety, 176
vaudeville, 74, 238
Vee, Bobby, 114
veil, 105, 106, 107–9, 111, 283, 330, 334
Velvet Underground, 159, 235, 256–7, 310, 336
ventriloquism, 92, 143, 193, 330
Ventures, 212
Venus, 52–6, 58, 59, 61, 63, 99, 100, 106–10, 153, 228, 282, 283, 284, 330, 349, 350, 352
Verdi, Giuseppe, 18, 96, 332, 333
  Rigoletto, 95
  La Traviata, 96
Viagra, 110, 284
Vicious, Sid, 47, 214, 232, 237, 238, 239, 243, 285, 341, 346
Vick, Graham, 333
victim, 89
Victims Anonymous, 194
Victoria, Queen, 18
videos, violent, 47
Vietnam war, 2, 199–200, 214, 218, 219, 223–6, 251, 252, 256, 265, 280
Vikings, 113
Vincent, Gene, 203
Vinton, Bobbie, 302
violence, 12, 14, 16, 25, 26, 27, 29, 30, 31, 36, 59, 64, 67, 70, 72, 75, 76, 77, 124, 167, 169, 182, 185, 186, 241, 354, 358
  against Indians (Native Americans), 251
  American male, 247
  black, 258
  development of rock violence, 213, 227–8, 235, 251–2
  empowering, 207–26
  of the family, 243
  glamorous in America, 246
  sex and, 228–9, 251
  the Sex Pistols' image, 345, 346
  and theatre, 227–8, 229–32
  videos, 47
  white, 233
  to women, 277, 285–8, 298, 305, 311
Virgil, 55
Virgin Megastore, 271
Virgin Records, 313, 355
Virginia, 246
virility, 60, 67, 70, 199, 247, 248, 249, 251
virtuosity, 70, 79, 268
Visconti, Tony, 327
Voice, 315
voices, 5, 6, 62, 93–4
  castrato, 330–31
  male, 97
  women's, 95–7, 122–3, 330–34
voodoo, 215
Vox magazine, 218
Vox Pop, 319
voyeurism, 141
Vulcan, 54–8, 60, 62, 63, 102, 105, 153, 160, 162, 167, 169
vulnerability, 27, 54, 58, 59, 60, 63, 64, 97, 99, 108, 142, 194, 197, 228, 277, 288, 353

WABC, 36
Wadham College, Oxford, 18
Wagner, Richard
  Opera and Drama, 332
  Tristan and Isolde, 62
wah-wah pedal, 336
The Wailers, 164, 182
Walker, Alice, 157, 158

INDEX

Walker, T-Bone, 37, 40, 74, 208, 317
war, 2, 52, 57, 58, 59, 61, 62, 64, 88, 113, 149, 207, 223–6, 228, 288, 291
   nuclear, 245
War (group), 161
Warhol, Andy, 177
Warren G, 304
water, 101
Waters, Muddy, 8, 41, 42, 49, 66, 67, 68, 72, 74, 78, 79, 114, 117, 158, 160, 165, 183, 198, 202, 263, 265, 296, 297, 300
Watkins, Tom, 312
Watson, Tex, 253
Watteau, Jean Antoine
   Cupid Disarmed by Venus, 107
   Judgement of Paris, 107
Wayne, John, 247–8
Weil, Simone, 233
Weizman, Danny, 204
Wells, Kitty, 78
Wends, 17
West Side Story (Bernstein), 95, 115
Westerns, 246, 251, 253
Westminster Abbey, 17
Westwood, Tim, 169, 210–11
What's Love Got to Do with It? (film), 182
Wheatstraw, Peetie, 213
When Harry Met Sally (film), 284
Whitcombe, Ian, 178
White, Booker Washington, 213
White, Robert, 163
white music, 129
white samite, 330
white samite syndrome, 100–101
Whitesnake, 71, 178, 280, 286
Whitman, Walt, 124, 128, 141, 220, 293
   Collected Works, 126
   Song of Myself, 125–6
   Song of the Open Road, 125
The Who, 47, 117, 149, 213–14, 215, 231
Wilde, Marty, 54

Williams, Hank, 75, 76, 77, 154
Williams, Robbie, 353
Williams, Tennessee
   Battle of Angels, 195–6, 229
   Orpheus Descending, 29, 196, 229
Williamson, Sonny Boy, 34, 41, 213
Williamson, Sonny Boy, II, 68
Wills, Bob, 75
Wilson, Dennis, 253
Wilson, Morris, 180, 183
Wilson, Woodrow, 139
WINS radio station, 35
Wired magazine, 46
Wolfe, Tom, 266, 314
Womack, Bobby, 161
womb, 102, 188
women
   abandoned, 90–93, 97, 98, 99, 193, 258
   artificiality, 104, 110, 330, 334
   black, 304
   dead, 278
   desire, 13, 16, 23, 32, 63, 67, 110–11, 193, 258, 293, 294, 333, 353
   doubleness, 104–5, 284
   as emblem of imprisoning society, 282–3
   as engulfment, 282
   and Greek heroes, 23
   guitarists, 317–18
   identified as anti-freedom, 280–81
   power, 97, 275, 276
   rock's traditional ways of seeing, 14
   violence to, 277, 285–8, 298, 305, 311
   a woman's power in opera, 97
   women's bands, 319–23
   women's rock, 14, 27, 102, 315–16, 356
Wonder, Stevie, 166
Woodstock Festival, 225
Wordsworth, William, 293
working-class, 116, 137
   and authenticity, 7
   and disco, 267
   faked, 339
worksongs, 264
Wright, Betty, 164

408

Wright, Johnny, 77–8
WSM, 150
Wu Tang Clan, 210
Wyatt, Robert, 102
Wycherley, Ronnie *see* Fury, Billy
Wyman, Bill, 214
Wyndorf, Dave, 285

X-Ray Spex, 319

The Yardbirds, 159, 202

Yeats, W. B.: 'On Women', 86
Young, Angus, 287
Young, James, 50
Young, Lester, 96
Young, Neil, 97
Young, Paul, 85, 121

Zappa, Frank, 266
Zeus, 23
Zinnerman, Ilke, 68
Zulu, 149